# Bergen County New Jersey Deed Records

## 1689-1801

Compiled by
John David Davis

HERITAGE BOOKS
2010

# HERITAGE BOOKS
*AN IMPRINT OF HERITAGE BOOKS, INC.*

**Books, CDs, and more—Worldwide**

For our listing of thousands of titles see our website at
www.HeritageBooks.com

Published 2010 by
HERITAGE BOOKS, INC.
Publishing Division
100 Railroad Ave. #104
Westminster, Maryland 21157

Copyright © 1995 John David Davis

Other books by the author:
*Bucks County, Pennsylvania Deed Records, 1684-1763*
*Frederick County, Virginia Minutes of Court Records, 1743-1745*
*West Jersey, New Jersey Deed Records, 1676-1721*

All rights reserved. No part of this book may be reproduced or transmitted in any form or by any means, electronic or mechanical, including photocopying, recording or by any information storage and retrieval system without written permission from the author, except for the inclusion of brief quotations in a review.

International Standard Book Numbers
Paperbound: 978-0-7884-0311-8
Clothbound: 978-0-7884-8467-4

DEDICATED

to my mother

BETH

## TABLE OF CONTENTS

| | |
|---|---|
| Preface | vii |
| Bergen Co., New Jersey Deed Book A | 1 |
| Bergen Co., New Jersey Deed Book B | 18 |
| Bergen Co., New Jersey Deed Book C | 38 |
| Bergen Co., New Jersey Deed Book D | 64 |
| Bergen Co., New Jersey Deed Book E | 95 |
| Bergen Co., New Jersey Deed Book F | 118 |
| Bergen Co., New Jersey Deed Book G | 144 |
| Bergen Co., New Jersey Deed Book H | 162 |
| Bergen Co., New Jersey Deed Book K | 182 |
| Bergen Co., New Jersey Deed Book L | 208 |
| Bergen Co., New Jersey Deed Book M | 234 |
| Bergen Co., New Jersey Deed Book N | 261 |
| Bergen Co., New Jersey 1793 Tax List | 285 |
| Index | 307 |

# PREFACE

Abstracted from Microfilm Copies
Available through the
Genealogical Library,
Salt Lake City, Utah

In 1674, New Jersey, (originally named "Nova Caesaria"), was split into East Jersey and West Jersey, by a boundary line extending straight north through the country from Little Egg Harbor (near Tuckerton) to the "utmost branch of the Delaware River". By an Act of the Assembly of East Jersey in 1682, the province was divided into the four counties of Bergen, Essex, Middlesex and Monmouth. Bergen County was just the narrow strip between the Hudson and Hackensack Rivers, until it was enlarged in 1709 to include New Barbadoes Township. The area, comprised all the land between the Hudson and the Passacic Rivers as far as the junction of the Pompton River, and above the Pompton and Wanaque rivers. The county seat was established at the village of Hackensack, which was not in Hackensack Township, but across the river in New Barbadoes Township. Recording of deeds, at the county seat, began in 1715 and included deeds from as early as 1689. Of particular interest to the genealogist, is that these deed books have suffered extensive damage, including the loss of the index of names and may represent a new source of information.

Although a hand written deed can run several pages in a deed book, the bulk of the information is largely repetitive and can be reduced to just a few lines of interest to genealogists. The format followed in the abstraction of the deeds of Bergen County, New Jersey is:

[Date of transaction], [Name of grantor(s) (the "&" between a male and female given name means husband and wife)], [Place of residence of grantor(s)], [Name of grantee(s)], [Place of residence of grantee(s)], [Sales price], [Area of land involved], [Location of land], [Neighbors], [Chain of deed], [Other landmarks], [Signature of grantor(s)(an (X) between the given name and the surname, means that person could not write], [Signature of witnesses], [Signature of others]

If it is not in the abstract, it can be assumed that it was not in the deed. Genealogists can draw their own conclusions from the information available. For example, a large amount of land sold for a very low price to a grantee with a surname different than that of the grantor, may be an in-law, however, if this was not stated in the deed, and the genealogist must confirm this possibility with other available sources.

The deeds were recorded by the county clerk, a man of learning, but in many cases, they did not deal well with the spelling of some of the names of that era. In many cases, they make a very creative phonetic attempt to spell the names of people and places. In addition, they vary the spelling of long standing residents of the area from transaction to transaction, (and many times, within the same deed). This in combination of the very poor condition of the deed books, has led to the most "used" spelling of the name being utilized for all occurrences of that name. In all other cases, each name of a person, place or thing is presented as it has been deciphered, with no attempt to change spelling to conform with today's accepted interpretation. The genealogist is invited to check all possible spellings of a name of interest and may even want to personally review the deed record.

# Chapter 1

## Volume A

**Bergen County Courthouse Deed Records**

**Recorded in 1715-1728**

15 Apr 1714, Ryon & Rebecca **Ryerson**, of Hackensack, Essex Co., Nova Caesaria to Jurian **Westervelt**, of same £46 originally granted to Martin **Camble** who sold to Blonina **Bogart**, merchant of New York City...Peter **Bogart**, of New York City, New York sold tract, 11 Nov 1700 to George **Ryerson**, of Poynton, and to Ryon **Ryerson** and Francis **Ryerson**, both of New York City.

1714, Jacob & Margaret van **Winkle**, of Bergen, Bergen Co., New Jersey to Able **Ridonzase**... line of Elizabeth **Patterson**. Signed Jacob (x) van **Winkle** and Margaret (x) van **Winkle**. Wit: Edmund **Kingsland** and George **Ryerson**.

20 Aug 1714, Gysbert & Loria van **Blerkum**, of Bergen Co., New Jersey to Martin **Wenman**, of same, £430...between Wendel **Diedericks** and Catharine **Mativeson**. Wit: Robert **Sickels**, George **Ryerson** and John **Berry**.

27 Feb 1707, Bartholomew & Magdalena **Feurt** of New York City to John **Stagg**, of Bergen Co., New Jersey, £5...Bonny Creek...line of Elias **Boudinot**. Wit: Edward **Earle** Jr., John **Concklin**, David **Provoost** and George **Ryerson**.

16 Jan 1704, Maj. John **Berry** of Bergen Co., New Jersey to Juriaen **Westervelt**, £30, 234 acres, between Hackensack River and Saddle River ...bounded by Clyde Johnston **Cooper** and Albert **Albertson**. Wit: William **Laroe**, Edward **Earle**, George **Ryerson** and Capt. Thomas **Lawrence**.

7 Dec 1709, Sarah **Sandford**, widow of William **Sandford**, late of New Barbadoes to Catharine van **Emburgh**, wife of Johann van **Emburgh**, she being the daughter of William **Sandford**, of same, 150 acres... Frank Creek. Wit: Joannis **Davis**, William **Pinhorne** and Edward **Earle**.

31 May 1708, John **Berry**, Gentleman, of New

Barbadoes, Essex Co, Nova Caesaria to Walling Jacob van Winkle, Yeoman, of same, £75.6, 108 acres... corner to John Stagg.

17 Feb 1709, John Berry, of Bergen Co., New Jersey to Walling Jacob van Winkle, £140, 500 acres, between said John Berry and Nathaniel Kingsland, now owned by Isaac Kingsland. Wit: David Provoost and Thomas van Boskerk.

8 Jun 1712, Jacob Zabriskie, yeoman, of New Barbadoes, Bergen Co., Nova Caesaria, manager of the estate of the late Albert Zabriskie to John Zabriskie, £300, area of town of Hackensack... Hackensack River ...line of Peter Vander Linde and Boren Epkese Banta. Signed Meihoth (x) Zabriskie, widow of Albert Zabriskie. Wit: Andreas van Orden, Potter Durie, John Conrad Codweis Cornelius Christian, Wert Epkese Banta and David Provoost.

17 Apr 1716, Johannes Bosh, blacksmith, of Orange Co., New York to John Wright, blacksmith, of Bergen Co., New Jersey, £7, lot of land by Hackensack Church... Lactors Creek. Signed Johannes Bosh. Wit: Robert Love, Paulus vander Beck and Cornelius Bryant.

2 Sep 1707, Ludwig Ackerman to Johannis Boss £3.75, church lot in Hackensack. Wit: Edward Earle.

4 Sep 1708, Hendrick Jorisen Brinkerhof yeoman, of Hackensack, Bergen Co., Nova Caesaria to Carl Jorten Brinkerhof, yeoman, of same, adjoining Luke Hartmann...line of Clas Petterson.

1708, Clasoh Jorisen Brinkerhof, wife of Hendrick Jorisen Brinkerhof, gives her permission to sell to Cornelius Jorten Brinkerhof. Signed Clasoh Jorisen (x) Brinkerhof. Wit: John van Horne and Roelif Bogart.

22 Jan 1710, Loverance & Catharine van Gallen, of Bergen Co., Nova Caesaria to Cornelius

Brinkerhof, yeoman, of same, £70, adjoining Janito Mackelson Vreeland. Signed Loverance van Gallen and Catharine van Gallen. Wit:Cornelius Garrabrants, John Thomas and Roger Mompeson.

1716, Loverance & Catharine Van Gallen, yeoman, of Bergen Co., New Jersey to Cornelius Brinkerhof, £146. Signed Loverance van Gallen. Wit: Rutgert van Horne and David Provoost.

20 May 1711, Henry Johnson van Oostrum, of Ulster Co., New York to Johannes Sip, of Bergen Co., New Jersey, line of Garret Corteen and Nicholas. Signed Henry Johnson (x) van Oostrum. Wit: George Ryerson and Thomas van Boskerk.

28 May 1716, Loverance van Boskerk, yeoman, of Hackensack, Bergen Co., New Jersey to Lutheran Church of Hackensack, line of Nicholas Lozier. Signed Loverance van Boskerk. Wit: Joost (x) Zabriskie and Derick (x) Wammamaker.

24 Dec 1710, Enoch & Mary Vreeland, merchant, of New York City to Rutgert van Horne, of Prembrebegh, Bergen Co., Nova Caesaria, £45. Signed Enoch (x) Vreeland and Mary (x) Vreeland. Wit: Enoch Mackelsen and Andres van Boskerk.

1 Apr 1701, Michael van Bechteen, of Rasston, Somerset Co., Nova Caesaria to Rutgert van Horne, of Bergen Co., Nova Caesaria, £200 ... line of Enoch Mackelsen... Vitio Hartmann in her will to her children, Elias and Enoch Hartmann, Johann Cornelius and Janmetre Mackelsen, wife of Derick van Bechteen and mother of Michael van Bechteen. Signed Michael (x) van Bechteen. Wit: Cornelius and Christoff Breste, John Conrad Codweis and David Provoost.

18 May 1702, Poulus Donewise, yeoman, of New Jersey to Rutgert van Horne, of same, along Hudson River...land of Cornelius Vreeland. Signed Poulus (x) Donewise. Wit: Cornelius Christoff Bockenhoven and David Provoost.

2 Mar 1701, Bartell & Elenor Jacobus, of Bergen

Co., New Jersey to Rutgert van Horne, of same, £412, patented 12 May 1668. Signed Bartell (x) Jacobus and Elenor (x) Jacobus. Wit: Andreas Loverence, Rettman van Loverence and David Provoost.

4 Mar 1710, Loverance & Catriantia van Gallen, of New Jersey to Rutgert van Horne, of same, £225. Signed Loverance (x) van Gallen and Catriantia (x) van Gallen. Wit: L. & Catharine Slator and Roger Mompeson.

23 Mar 1710, Loverance & Catriantia van Gallen, of New Jersey to Rutgert van Horne, of Bergen Co., New Jersey, £0.25, west of Johannis Mackelson...Great Creek...between Enoch Mackelson and Elias Mackelson. Signed Loverance (x) van Gallen and Catriantia (x) van Gallen. Wit: L. & Catharine Stator.

5 Nov 1716, Garret Garretson of Bergen Co., New Jersey to Warner Burger, of same. Signed Garret Garretson. Wit: David Provoost and Jacob Juriansen.

6 Jun 1702, Thomas & Susanna Brucker, of Essex Co., New Jersey to John Daviss, of same, £6, NE side of Garret Lydecker land...Hackensack River. Signed Thomas (x) Brucker and Susanna (x) Brucker.

5 Jul, 1702, John Daviss, of Essex Co., New Jersey to Johannes van Emburgh. Signed John (x) Daviss.

19 Apr 1707, Charles & Catharine Mackelson, of Hackensack, Bergen Co., Nova Caesaria to Mathias DeMott, blacksmith, of Bergen Co., Nova Caesaria, £120, in and about town of Bergen... between Dofew Harmansen and Hendrick D. Backer ...between Fredrick Phillips and Dowg Harmansen ...between Derick Tunison and Garret Corteen... part of land patented by Caspar Steinmott, 5 May 1668, who sold to Charles Mackelson on 6 Apr 1693. Signed Charles (x) Mackelson and Catharine (x) Mackelson. Wit: Jan Varick, John Conrad

Codweis and David Provoost.

23 Apr 1715, Clase & Carhina Romine, yeoman, of Bergen Co., New Jersey to John Romine, of same, £400, west side of Hackensack River and next to Saddle River...line of Isaac van Giesen and Jurion Westervelt...paid to heirs of John Berry ...indenture made 15 Jul 1696 between John Berry and Clase Romine, father to the said John Romine. Signed Clase Romine and Carhina (x) Romine. Wit: David Ackerman, John Bardan, Thomas van Boskerk and George Ryerson.

16 Jan 1715, William & Elenor Stagg, of Bergen Co., New Jersey to Jacob van Norshandt, blacksmith, of same, £246, by Danioll Rutan... line between Breishetome Feurt and Elias Boudinot...Persaik River...Berrys Creek... purchased by John Stagg and Abraham Rutan of Hans Balho Feurt. William (x) Stagg and Elenor (x) Stagg. Wit: Thomas van Boskerk and George Ryerson.

1 Sep 1716, Edward & Elisabeth Earle, of Secaukus Island, Bergen Co., New Jersey to Henry Mayer, of New Barbadoes Creek, Bergen Co., New Jersey, on Hackensack River...purchased by Edward Earle Sr., deceased who sold to his son the said Edward Earle in 1710... between line of Maj. Nathaniel Kingsland and Bartholomew LaFeurt of New York and land of Hendrick Juriansen, Nicholas Kip and Thomas Francis...was purchased of Maj. John Berry of New York City... 2nd tract purchased by Edward Earle Sr. in 1704...Kothawak River.

17 Jan 1717, Elenor Mollemott, (who before her late marriage was the widow of John Christian, deceased of Bergen Co., New Jersey, will dated 20 Feb 1705), of Bergen Co., New Jersey to John Wright, blacksmith, of same, £100, New Barbadoes Creek and Hackensack River... bounded on north by land formerly belonging to Herman Brass, deceased and on the west by Henry Meyer. Signed Elenor (x) Mollemott.

1 Mar 1717, Gilbert & Elenor van Blerkum, of Bergen Co., Nova Caesaria to Henry Mayer, of Noch Co., Nova Caesaria, £19, 40 acres, New Barbadoes Creek, north side of Hackensack River...known by name of Quacksack. Signed Gilbert (x) van Blerkum and Elenor (x) van Blerkum. Wit: Johannis van Emburgh and Garret (x) van Dien.

3 Jun 1708, Henry Epkon Banta, yeoman, of Hackensack, Bergen Co., Nova Caesaria to Jacob Henrichson Banta, of same, Hackensack River ...bounded on north by Henry Joseph Brinkerhof and on south by Rudolfus Bogart... line of Anton Brinkerhof...Overpeck Creek... bounded on east by Hudson River. Signed Henry (x) Epkon Banta. Wit: Jacob Varick, John Conrad Codweis and David Provoost.

3 Jan 1717, Thomas Francis, Derick Brinkerhof, Jacob Brinkerhof and Antiea van Giesen, all of Bergen Co., New Jersey, £100, an agreement... road to John Berry. Signed Thomas (x) Francis, Derick (x) Brinkerhof, Jacob (x) Brinkerhof and Antiea (x) van Giesen. Wit: Paulus vander Beck, Isaac (x) van Giesen, Thomas Laroe and Thomas van Boskerk.

John Berry, of Bergen Co., New Jersey to Hendrick Hopper, of Essex Co., New Jersey, £40, 190 acres, between Hackensack and Saddle Rivers...against Hendrick Juriansen and Lubbert Lubbertson...bounds of Johann Christian. Signed John Berry and Hendrick (x) Hopen. Wit: Albert Terhune, Albert Stevenson and William Pinhorne.

9 Mar 1718, William van Schyve, of Bergen Co., New Jersey to Wooten Williamson van Schyve, late of same, 80 acres, between Hackensack and Saddle Rivers...formerly purchased of Jacob Morris 23 Mar 1697. Signed William (x) van Schyve. Wit: Thomas van Boskerk and George Ryerson.

18 Feb 1720, Andris Lovervance, of New Hackensack, Bergen Co., New Jersey to his brother, Peter Loverance, of same, £172,

Hackensack River. Signed Andris Lovervance. Wit: Joan Los Marsl Jandos Marosl DeYoung, David Provoost and John Demarest.

1714, Albourt Bogart, yeoman, of Hackensack, Bergen Co., New Jersey to Jacob Banta. Signed Albourt (x) Bogart.

17 Dec 1710, Anthony Brackholst, of Essex Co., New Jersey, Arent Schuyler, of same, Nicholas & Judith Bayard, of New York to George Ryerson, John Moott, Samuel Berry, David Mandeville and Hendrick Mandeville, 4000 acres, Hackensack River, and 1250 acres and 2750 acres. Signed Anthony (x) Brackholst. Arent (x) Schuyler, Nicholas (x) Bayard and Judith (x) Bayard. Wit: William Sandford.

16 Apr 1694, Magdalina Hans vander Bilt, widow of Hendrick Janson Spear and with the consent of her husband Jan Aronlson vander Bilt, of Bergen Co., New Jersey at a place called Mingague Harness to Garret Ivers Garretson, of same, land of former husband, with consent of Aronlson vander Bilt...adjoining Bartole Claesen. Wit: Jan Aronlson vander Belt, Hendrich van (x) Spear, Hans Hendrich (x) Spear, Banent Hendrick (x) Spear, Brefant Androsen Lovers, Gilbert Bogart, William Douglas and David Provoost.

20 Oct 1719, David & Ann Danielsen, of Bergen Co., New Jersey to Potter Garretson yeoman, of same, £5, from Corsack River to Saddle River...land of Johannes Garretson. Signed David (x) Danielsen. Wit: Adam King, Mary King, Thomas van Boskerk and George Ryerson.

12 Oct 1719, Garret & Nise Garretson, of Prombrepough, Bergen Co., New Jersey to David Daniolsen, of Bergen Co., New Jersey, £5, Saddle River, between lands of Garret Juriansen on south and Bovert Bovertson van Horne on the north. Signed Garret (x) Garretson. Wit: Adam Kings, Mary Kings, Thomas van Boskerk and George Ryerson.

12 Oct 1719, David & Ann Daniolsen, of Saddle River, Bergen Co., New Jersey to Garret Garretson Jr., of Bergen Co., New Jersey, £105, corner to Daniole Hennion...to Johannis Hennion land... sold to David Daniolsen by Joseph Veale, Mary Bently and Richard Ashietas 30 Aug 1717. Signed David (x) Daniolsen. Wit: Adam Kings, Mary Kings, Thomas van Boskerk and George Ryerson.

26 Oct 1717, Joannis Bollen, of Chester Co., Pennsylvania to Samuel Demarest and David Demarest, of Hackensack, Bergen Co., New Jersey, Between Hackensack River and Overpeck Creek...patent granted from Philip Charrett, governor of New York in 1674 to Joannis Bollen Sr. late father of said Joannis Bollen. Signed Joannis (x) Bollen. Wit: Lucas van Horne and David Provoost.

1 Apr 1716, David Daniolson & Annetyo Hennion, yeoman, of Saddle River, Bergen Co., Nova Caesaria to Jurion Westervelt, of New Barbadoes, Bergen Co., Nova Caesaria, £125, land of Garret Garretson. Signed David (x) Daniolson Hennion and Annetyo (x) Daniolson Hennion. Wit: John Arnold, John Conrad Codweis, Thomas Laroe and John Bardan.

5 Nov 1705, Albertus & Marikotois Zabriskie, of Hackensack, Bergen Co., Nova Caesaria to John Cornelis Bogart of same, £100, 300 acres, Hackensack Twp., Saddle River. Signed Albertus (x) Zabriskie. Wit: Thomas Laroe, Rudolphus vander Linde, John Conrad Codweis and David Provoost.

15 Jan 1704, Henry Harding, of Barbados Island to Alexander O'Hare, merchant, of New York City, Eson Co., neck of land lying between Hackensack River and Borsack River called by name "New Barbadoes"...heretofor did belong to Maj. Nathaniel Kingsland who was the grandfather of said Henry Harding...which tract was taken in joint tendency with Col. Henry & Hoesba Applewhite, Mary Walley, widow, John & Carolina

Barrow and Nathaniel Kingsland, all of the Island of Barbadoes and Edmund Kingsland, of New Barbadoes, Bergen Co., New Jersey. Signed Henry (x) Harding. Wit: Elias Boudinot, merchant and attorney of New York City, James Emott, Zukano Harris, of New Jersey and William Pinhorne.

2 Feb 1719, Roelif & Elisabeth Bogart, yeoman, of Hackensack, Bergen Co., Nova Caesaria to Albourt Bogart, of same. Signed Roelif (x) Bogart and Elisabeth (x) Bogart. Wit: Jacob Bogart, David Demarest Jr. and David Provoost.

21 Nov 1696, Hendrick Epkoy, Cornelius Epkoy John Cornelius, Martin Paulisen, Hendrick Juriansen, Roelif Westervelt and John Lott, all of Hackensack, Bergen Co., East Jersey to Rollos vander Linde, Albert Zabriskie, Derick Epkoy Loverence, Lovorane Cornelius Christian and Garret Mandeville, £50 from Derick Epkoy, £15 from Rollos vander Linde, £12.5 from Albert Zabriskie, £7.5 from Garret Mandeville, and £5 from Cornelius Christian, Hackensack River ...Overpeck Creek...line of Elias Mackelson. Signed Hendrick (x) Epkoy, Cornelius (x) Epkoy, John (x) Cornelius, Martin (x) Poulusen, Hendrick (x) Juriansen, Roelif (x) Westervelt and John (x) Lott. Wit: William Laroe, Loverence Loverencesen, Anche (x) Terhune, Joannis (x) Laroe and George Ryerson.

20 Sep 1720, Jury & Charity Bower, of Hackensack, Bergen Co., New Jersey to William Bower, of same, £50, Hackensack Twp., formerly purchased of John Lott, John Cornelius, Hendrick Juriansen, Cornelius Epkoy, Hendrick Epkoy, Roelif Westervelt...bounded by Cornelius Christian and Derick Epkoy, deceased. Signed Jury (x) Bower and Charity (x) Bower. Wit: Stephen Bourdett, Hannah Bourdett, Thomas Lawrence and Jan Bardan.

William Bowers, yeoman of Lolloh Town, Middlesex Co., Massachusetts to Incroape Bowers, of Hackensack, Bergen Co., New Jersey, £50, in town of Hackensack. Signed William (x) Bowers. Wit:

Johann van Emburgh and William Sandford.

5 May 1715, Elias & Cornelia Smith, of Horback, Essex Co., Nova Caesaria and Mickole & Chattrian vander Cook, of same to Thomas Juriansen, of same, £200, 2740 acres, patented 11 Nov 1695, east side of Boguanock River...line of Nicholas Bogart and Anthony Brackholst...surveyed by Potter Corteen 1 Dec 1707.. granted by Arent & Sevantio Schuyler 1 May 1707 to Powlus & Chatrian vander Beck who sold 5 May 1712 to Elias Smith and Mickole vander Cook. Signed Elias Smith, Cornelia (x) Smith, Mickole vander Cook and Chattrian (x) vander Cook,(in pencil is Sarah vander Cook). Wit: John Arnold, John Conrad Codweis, Simon van Ness, Thomas Laroe and Thomas van Boskerk.

1720, Joshua Bosh, blacksmith, of Saddle River, Bergen Co., New Jersey to Thomas Juriansen, farmer, of Aquakinana, Essex Co., New Jersey, £84, 84 acres, on Saddle River, east side of Passaic River... sold to said Bosh 1716 by John Corteen. Signed Joshua (x) Bosh. Wit: Hermanus (x) Grant, John (x) Smith.

30 Apr 1720, Samuel & Mary Demarest Sr., weaver, of Hackensack, Bergen Co., New Jersey to John Zabriskie, of same, £107, 215 acres, east side of Hackensack River...corner to John Durie... line of Martin Ryerson...patented by Peter Simmons, who sold to William Docary, of London, who gave to his daughter, who sold to William Mackelson of Long Island, who sold to Andrew Mackelson, who sold to said Samuel Demarest. Signed Samuel Demarest and Mary (x) Demarest. Wit: David Demarest, Simon Demarest, and George Ryerson.

22 Oct 1720, Johann & Catharine van Emburgh, of Bergen Co., New Jersey to their daughter, Rachel King, wife of John King, £0.25, 2.5 acres, on New Barbadoes Creek, on Copack River...line of Jan Schuyler. Signed Johann (x) van Emburgh and Catharine (x) van Emburgh. Wit: Capt. Thomas van Boskerk and George Ryerson.

3 Dec 1707, Daniel Cromline and Elias & Mary Boudinot, of New York City to Edmond Kingsland, of Essex Co., New Jersey, 2/3 part of their 1/6 part of land belonging mostly to Nathaniel Kingsland, of Barbodos, Hackensack River. Signed Daniel Cromline, Elias Boudinot and Mary Boudinot. Wit: William Chambers and Roger Mompeson.

5 Jun 1714, Johann & Mary Thompson, of Borgois Bergen Co., New Jersey to Mathias DeMott, blacksmith, of same, £200, 9.5 acres ... line of Paulus Potter...land late of Thomas Fredericksen ...13 acres, bounded on south by Hendrick Bartrim...1.5 acres...line of Herman Edwards, Hendrick van Orstrant and Arian Potter...and 40 acres...between Garret Corteen and John Arents Toers. Signed Johann Thompson and Mary (x) Thompson. Wit: Samuel Bayard, Johann Garretson and David Jansen.

1706, William & Ann Day, of Bergen Co., New Jersey to Mathias DeMott, blacksmith, of same, £67. Signed William (x) Day. Wit: Robert Sickels, John Pinhorne and David Provoost.

31 Oct 1705, Tunis Dowson & Bregho Talman, of Orange Co., New Jersey to Matthias DeMott, blacksmith, of Bergen, New Jersey, £2.5, near Bergen behind Christian Patterson...between Garret Corteen and Caspar Slynmott...between Adrian Post and Derick Tunison Jr., patented 12 May 1668 by Dow Harmansen. Signed Tunis Dowson (x) Talman and Bregho Dowson (x) Talman. Wit: Casparus Danole van Boskerk and William Huddolstow and David Provoost.

5 May 1711, Tunis & Bregho Dowson Talman, yeoman, Abraham & Doruko Haring, yeoman, and Dow Talman, bachelor, all of Orange Co., New Jersey bound to Matthias DeMott, yeoman, of Bergen Co., New Jersey for £1000, for land sold 31 Oct 1703. Tunis (x) Talman, Bregho (x) Talman, Abraham (x) Haring, Doruko (x) Haring and Dow (x) Talman. Wit: Albert Corteen and Abraham Blaslin, David Provoost and William (x)

Huddolstow.

13 Sep 1705, Mary Holdipp, widow of Hillcord Holdipp, gentleman, late of Barbadoes to Daniole Cromline and Elias Boudinot, merchants, of New York City, £100, patented by John Lord Barclay and George Carott Knight, who sold to Nathaniel & Mary Kingsland and William Sandford...said Barclay and Knight with Potter Watson and Ralso Wyatt sold again to said Kingsland and Sandford neck of land known as New Barbadoes...Nathaniel Kingsland willed to his nephew Isaac Kingsland, to his son John Kingsland, his son Nathaniel Kingsland Jr., his daughter Isabella Harding wife of Henry Harding, his daughter Carolina Berry, wife of John Berry Jr. and to his daughter Mary Holdipp, wife of said William Holdipp, also to daughter Hoster Applewhite, wife of Thomas Applewhite...Mary Holdipp sells her one sixth part of land. Signed Mary Holdipp. Wit: Robert Daykins, Charles Cromline, of New Jersey and William Sandford.

15 Feb 1706, Bartholomew & Magdalena Feurt, of New York City to Edmund Kingsland, of New Barbadoes, New Jersey, £100, formerly owned by Maj. Nathaniel Kingsland, late of Island of Barbadoes, who sold to William Sandford. Signed Bartholomew Feurt and Magdalena Feurt. Wit: Davis William Chambers, of New York and Roger Mompeson.

15 Dec 1720, Johannis Stynmott, of Bergen Co., New Jersey to his wife Ann Stynmott, for love and affection, all his estate and chattel goods...after her decease to his sister Hannah Pryor's children, ie. Caspar, Jacob, Loohyle, Johannis and Joan Pryor. Signed Johannis (x) Stynmott. Wit: Abraham Masaer, William (x) Day, John Conrad Codweis and David Provoost.

6 Feb 1720, Johannis & Janotne Meyer, blacksmith, of Bergen Co., New Jersey to William Provoost, of New York City, £150, west side of Hackensack River bounded on the south by the Dutch Church...between land formerly owned by

Nicholas Laroe and Hendrick van Giesen, which now belongs to Abraham Ackerman. Signed Johannis Myor and Janotne (x) Myor. Wit: Paulus vander Beck, John Wright, of Bergen Co., New Jersey, and David Provoost.

5 Aug 1720, William & Elenor Stagg, of Bergen Co., New Jersey to John Stagg, of same, £100, corner to Garret van Vorst...line of John Norg, deceased. Signed William (x) Stagg and Elenor (x) Stagg. Wit: Henry Brackholst and Edmund Kingsland, of Bergen Co., New Jersey, and George Ryerson.

6 Feb 1720, David & Ann Danielsen, of Saddle River, Bergen Co., New Jersey to Garret Garretson, of same, £5, bounded on north by Johannis Neafie. Signed David Danielsen. Wit: Edmund Kingsland, Martin Paulisen and George Ryerson.

4 Jun 1720, Garret & Nise Garretson, of Dombropough, Bergen Co., New Jersey to their son Garret Garretson Jr., yeoman, of same, £5, between Hackensack and Saddle River...bounded on the north by Johannis Garretson. Signed Garret Garretson and Nise (x) Garretson. Wit: Edmund Kingsland, Jacobus Garretson, of Bergen Co., New Jersey and George Ryerson.

6 Jun 1720, Garret & Nise Garretson, of Bergen Co., New Jersey to their daughter Elisabeth Barentsen, wife of Derick Barentsen, of same, for love and affection, on Passaic River... between Garret Garretson Jr. and David Danielsen. Signed Garret Garretson and Nise (x) Garretson. Wit: Edmund Kingsland, Jacobus Garretson, of Bergen Co., New Jersey and George Ryerson.

6 Jun 1720, Garret & Nise Garretson, of Bergen Co., New Jersey to their daughter, Ann Neafie, wife of Johannis Neafie, £5, Saddle River. Signed Garret Garretson and Nise (x) Garretson. Wit: Edmund Kingsland, Jacobus Garretson, of Bergen Co., New Jersey and George Ryerson.

10 Jun 1720, Garret & Nise Garretson, of Bergen Co., New Jersey to their son Abraham Garretson, of same, £5, Saddle River... bounded on north by Potter Garretson. Signed Garret Garretson and Nise (x) Garretson. Wit: Edmund Kingsland, Jacobus Garretson, of Bergen Co., New Jersey and George Ryerson.

4 Mar 1694, John Berry, of Bergen Co., New Jersey to Holkosh Hanson, of Essex Co., New Jersey, £64, Hackensack River between Jurrianse Linbe on the north and Charles Houseman on the south. Signed John Berry. Wit: William Lawrence, Thomas Lawrence, John Edsall and George Ryerson.

12 Mar 1718, Andreas van Boskerk, yeoman, of Bergen Co., New Jersey to Nickole Anderson, of New York City £120...line of Garret Garretson. Signed Andreas van Boskerk. Wit: Enoch Mackelson, Harman Van Reypen and David Provoost.

25 Mar 1721, John Barberie, Andrew Fresnean and Potter Fauconnier, gentleman, of New York City to Garret van Dien, of Bergen Co., New Jersey, £260, 425 acres, Saddle River...corner to land sold in 1712 by the late Theodore Fauconnier to Pitt Jan van Blerkum. Signed John Barberie, Andrew Fresnean and Potter Fauconnier. Wit: David Provoost and Potter Barberie.

27 Mar 1708, Alexander & Joane Allaies, of New York City to Edmund Kingsland, of Essex Co., New Jersey, £0.25, New Barbadoes...corner to Maj. John Berry...line of Jacob Sandford. Signed Alexander Allaies. Wit: John Barberie, John Pinhorne and David Provoost.

25 Feb 1708, Articles of agreement between, Garott Stynmott and Johannis Stynmott to purchase a certain farm in Bergen Co., New Jersey patented 1685. Signed Garott Stynmott. Wit: Abraham Masaer, William (x) Dayling, John Conrad Codweis and David Provoost.

18 Aug 1721, Potter Demarest and Abraham Brower, executors of the estate of John Demarest, of

Bergen Co., New Jersey to Eldrick Brower ,weaver, of Bergen, Bergen Co., New Jersey, £200, gist mill and 6 acres, east side of Hackensack River...bounded on south side by Ryon Ryerson and on the north by Cornelius Cooper... branch running into Saddle River. Signed Potter Demarest and Abraham Brower. Wit: Edmund Kingsland, Mary Kingsland, Thomas van Boskerk and George Ryerson.

4 Mar 1689, John Berry, of Bergen Co., New Jersey to Lawrence Ackerman, of Essex Co., New Jersey, £75, 295 acres, between Hackensack River and Saddle River...line of Garret van Dien and David Provoost. Signed John Berry. Wit: John Edsall, Isaac Lawrence and David Provoost.

18 Jan 1721, Garret & Vroutine van Dien, yeoman, of Bergen Co., New Jersey to John Wright, of same, £73, New Barbadoes...corner to John Volk, Hackensack River...line of Maj. Edward Raling, Poulus vander Beck and Andrew van Boskerk, son of Thomas van Boskerk Signed Garret van Dien and Vroutine (x) van Dien. Wit: Paulus van Boskerk, Abraham Volk and David Provoost.

5 Jun 1720, Garret & Nise Garretson, of Bergen Co., New Jersey to their son, Johannis Garretson, of same, £5, Portanko River... between Garret Garretson on south and Potter Garretson on north... Abraham Garretson on the east. Signed Garret Garretson and Nise (x) Garretson. Wit: Thomas van Boskerk, Edward Kingsland, Jacob Garretson and George Ryerson.

16 Oct 1722, Hannah Earle, widow, of Leiscow, power of attorney to her grandson, Edward Earle, of same. Signed Hannah (x) Earle. Wit: William Anderson.

2 Aug 1722, John & Aertine Wright, blacksmith, of Bergen Co., New Jersey to William Provoost, of New York, £280, both sides of the Hackensack River... sold to Ludwig Ackerman, 2 Sep 1701 and he sold to Johannes Bosh, 8 Mar 1716, who sold to Garret van Dien, 12 Sep 1716. Signed John

Wright and Aertine Wright. Wit: Paulus vander Beck and David Provoost.

Maryon Camble, widow of John Camble, gentleman, late of Perth Amboy, Middlesex Co., New Jersey to Blandance Bayard, of New York City, £60, land in Essex Co., New Jersey. Signed Maryon Camble. Wit: Thomas van Boskerk.

20 Jan 1715, Claes Romine, yeoman, of Bergen Co., New Jersey to Paulus vander Beck, yeoman, of same, £90, 60 acres, west side of Hackensack River, joining John Bardan and David Ackerman... line of Poulus vander Beck and Isaac van Giesen. Signed Claes Romine. Wit: Jan Bardan, Jan (x) Verway and Jorst Ryerse.

1722, Garret & Viont van Dien, yeoman, of Bergen Co., New Jersey to Hendrick Beer, of same, £70 ...corner to John Varick...line of Johannis van Emburgh...line of Johannis Wright. Signed Garott van Dien and Viont (x) van Dien. Wit: Paulus van Boskerk, David Provoost and Thomas van Boskerk.

30 Jun 1703, John Berry, of New York City to John Christeen, of Essex Co., New Jersey, £150, 300 acres...in Essex Co., New Jersey, Saddle River... line of Charles Maclesand. Signed John Berry and John Christeen. Wit: Abraham Gouverneur, Jan Harris, Edward Moore, Maj. John Berry and James Smith.

1 Mar 1722, Adolf Brower, of Hackensack, Bergen Co., New Jersey to Cornelius Haring and Barent Nagel, both of Orange Co., New York, executors of the estate of Johannis Haring, late of Hackensack, £81.4, 150 acres ... Schraelingburg Twp., bounded on north by Carrol Debane... road to Schssebrook. Signed Adolf Brower. Wit: David Demarest, Jacob Demarest and Thomas van Boskerk.

26 Mar 1724, Garret Stoothof, gentleman, of Flatland, Kings Co., New York to Hendrick vander Linde, yeoman, of Bergen Co., New Jersey, £15, 40 acres, Saddle River, between John Cortlandt and Helmegh Roeliffe...purchased of Garret

Stoothof. Signed Garret Stoothof. Wit: Hendrick Wickoff, Daniel Stillwell and James Alexander.

1717, Andris Fredericksen and Thomas Fredericksen both of Bergen Co., New Jersey to David Lawrence Ackerman, yeoman, of same, £10, east side of Passiac River...west side of Saddle River ... line of Joserva Bos, blacksmith, Warner Burger and Jacob Demarest. Signed Andris (x) Fredericksen and Thomas (x) Fredericksen. Wit: Warner Burger, Poutus vander Beck and Thomas van Boskerk.

16 Dec 1724, Warner & Margaretha Burger, miller, of Hackensack, Bergen Co., New Jersey to Abraham Varick, of same, of New Barbadoes, Bergen Co., New Jersey, east side of Passiac River and west side of Saddle River...line of Andris and Thomas Fredericksen... on south by Lawrence Toor, ...on east by Jacob Morris. Signed Warner Burger and Margaretha (x) Burger. Wit: Herman Shinnsman, Richard Pollet and Thomas van Boskerk.

Chapter 2

Bergen County
Courthouse
Deed Records
Volume B

Recorded
in
1728-1736

11 Jan 1726, John & Aertje Wright, of New Barbadoes, Bergen Co., New Jersey to Abraham Varick, of same, £80, joining Jacob Brinkerhof ...on north by Henry Brass... on southwest by Henry Major. Signed John Wright and Aertje Wright. Wit: Thomas van Boskerk.

20 Aug 1720, David Lawrence Ackerman, of Saddle River, Bergen Co., New Jersey to Derick van Seil, of same, £14, 8 acres...line of Warner Burger and Jacob Marinus. Signed David Lowrents Ackerman. Wit: Herman Garretson, George Vreeland and Thomas van Boskerk.

23 Sep 1728, Richard Backer, of Bergen Co., New Jersey to James Duncan, of same, £72.9, 106 acres... bounded by the Kings Road and said Duncan... line of George Willock Signed Richard Backer. Wit: Md Carle, Thomas Smith and Thomas van Boskerk.

17 May 1727, George Willock, formerly of Perth Amboy, New Jersey, but now of Philadelphia, Pennsylvania, Andrew & Katherin Johnston, of Perth Amboy, New Jersey to Johannes Lawrence Ackerman and Jacobus Lawrence Ackerman, of Hackensack, Bergen Co., New Jersey, £247.5, lot #2 on map made by Alexander McDowell...line of Jacobus Kip... adjoining John Romine. Signed George Witlocks, Andrew Johnston and Katherin Johnston. Wit: Ryer Ryerson, Thomas van Boskerk and Peter Stoutenburgh.

18

15 Jun 1699, David Danielsen, yeoman, of Bergan Co., New Jersey to Garret van Dien, of Essex Co., New Jersey, Hackensack Twp., bounded on south by land Maj. John Berry sold to said van Dien 26 May 1693. Signed David Danielsen. Wit: Edward Earle Jr., Johannes van Emburgh and Thomas van Boskerk.

15 Jun 1699, Thomas & Susanna Bricker, of New Barbadoes, Essex Co., New Jersey to Gorrot Lydecker, 1 acre, by church on Hackensack River. Signed Thomas (x) Bricker and Susanna Bricker. Wit: Dr.Johannes van Emburgh, Jan Romine and Thomas van Boskerk.

14 May 1716, Ryck Lydecker and his mother Neeltie Lydecker, of Hackensack, Bergen Co., New Jersey to Abraham Varick, £48, 2 acres, Hackensack River. Signed Ryck Lydecker and Neeltie Lydecker. Wit: Richard (x) Edsall and Thomas van Boskerk.

18 Mar 1726, Hendrick Hopper, of New Barbadoes, Bergen Co., New Jersey to Garret Hopper, of same, £150, line of Hendrick vander Linde... Saddle River ...line of Abraham Ackerman and Hendrick Brass ...sold by Maj. John Berry 17 May 1694. Signed Hendrick (x) Hopper. Wit: Johannis Ackerman, Poulus vander Beck and Thomas van Boskerk.

2 Nov 1725, David Ackerman, of New Barbadoes, Bergen Co., New Jersey to Hendrick Beer, of same, £5, line of Johannes van Emburgh and Egbert Ackerman...bounded on southwest by Hendrick Kuyper...purchased of said Egbert Ackerman 18 Apr 1724. Signed David Ackerman. Wit: Poulus vander Beck, Jacobus Ackerman and Thomas van Boskerk.

25 May 1695, John Berry, of Bergen Co., New Jersey to Garott Lydecker, of Essex Co., New Jersey, £65, 220 acres, on New Barbadoes neck in Essex Co., New Jersey, adjoining Henrick Kip. Signed John Berry and Garott Lydecker. Wit: Thomas Noell, Thomas Lawrence, Richard Berry,

William Sandford, Tunis (x) Johnson and Thomas van Boskerk.

1 May 1705, Gerard & Neeltie Lydecker, yeoman, of Essex Co., New Jersey to Nicholas Kip, yeoman, £115, 220 acres, New Barbadoes neck...east to land of Hendrick Kip...Saddle River...purchased of John Berry 23 May 1695. Signed Garret Lydecker, Neeltie Lydecker and Nicasius Kip. Wit: Thomas (x) Francis, John Conrad Codweis and Thomas van Boskerk.

13 Dec 1724, Derick & Catharina van Seil, yeoman, of Saddle River, Bergen Co., New Jersey to Abraham Varick, gentleman, of New Barbadoes, Bergen Co., New Jersey, £24, 8 acres, east side of Passaic River...formerly sold to Andrew and Thomas Fredericksen who sold in 1717 to David Lawrence Ackerman who sold to said van Soil... line of Thomas Juriansen and Warner Burger. Signed Derick (x) van Seil and Catharina (x) van Seil. Wit: David Provoost, Herman Shinnsman and Thomas van Boskerk.

24 Apr 1724, John Barberie, Peter Fauconnier and Andrew Fresnean, all of New York City to John Verway, of Bergen Co., New Jersey, £100, 200 acres, formerly owned by Jacob Haily...west side of Saddle River...line of Garret Ackerman and Thomas van Boskerk. Signed John Barberie, Peter Fauconnier and Androw Fresneau. Wit: Ralleau Andre Desbrosses, David Provoost, Poulus vander Beck and Thomas van Boskerk.

30 Apr 1720, Samuel & Mary Demarest Sr., weaver, of Hackensack, Bergen Co., New Jersey to John Durie, smith, of same, £118, 234 acres, east side of Hackensack River... bounded on west by Cornelius Haring... on south by John Zabriskie ... patented by Peter Sonmans who sold to William Degraw, of London who gave to his daughter who sold to William Mackelson who sold to Andrew Mackelson who sold to said Demarest. Signed Samuel Demarest and Mary (x) Demarest. Wit: David Demarest, Simon Demarest, Pieter (x) Westervelt, Thomas Lawrence and John Bardan.

11 Apr 1721, Juris & Fraina Morris, yeoman, of Hackensack, Bergen Co., New Jersey to John Durie, smith, of same, £100, 107 acres, patented 16 Aug 1686 by Gawin Lowry, and his heirs Mille & Rebeca Forster, Mary Haigs and Obadiah Haigs who sold to Mathias Francis, of Hackensack, New Jersey on 10 Aug 1696 sold to said Morris 3 May 1704 ...bounded on south by Carrol Debane. Signed Juris (x) Morris and Fraina (x) Morris. Wit: David Demarest, Nicolas (x) Parcel and Thomas van Boskerk.

19 Mar 1717, Juris & Fraina Morris, brewer, of Hackensack, Bergen Co., New Jersey to Carrol Debane, yeoman, of same, £100, 113 acres, patented 17 Aug 1686 by Gawin Lowry, and his heirs Mille & Rebeca Forster, Mary Haigs and Obadiah Haigs sold to Rouluf vander Linde on 10 Aug 1696, who in his will gave to his son Hendrick vander Linde who sold to said Morris, Johanis Hartwick and John van Schiven... Hackensack Twp...corner to John van Schiven. Signed Juris (x) Morris and Fraina (x) Morris. Wit: David Demarst, Robert Livesey and Thomas van Boskerk.

20 Mar 1717, John & Geerchen van Schiven, of Hackensack, Bergen Co., New Jersey to Carrol Debane, yeoman, of same, £47, 56 acres, kings road...bounded on south by Johanes Harty. Signed John (x) van Schiven and Geerchen (x) van Schiven. Wit: Richard Edsall, Juris (x) Morris and Thomas van Boskerk.

12 Dec 1728, John & Abigil Earle, of Bergen Co., New Jersey to Abraham Varick, of same, £53, 36 acres, Quacksack...line of Jacobus Brinkerhof and Jacob Banta. Signed John Earle and Abigil Earle. Wit: Richard Edsall, Stephen Bourdett and Thomas van Boskerk.

27 Sep 1729, William Provoost, merchant, of Hackensack, Bergen Co., New Jersey to Abraham Varick, of same, £0.25, east side of church lot being opposite of Johannis van Emburgh... purchased of Thomas Bricker and thereafter by a

writing of Ryck Lydecker and Neeltie Lydecker.
Signed William Provoost. Wit: Henry Brass, Peter
Stoutenburgh and Thomas van Boskerk.

19 May 1710, Isaac van Giesen, yeoman, of New
Barbadoes, Bergen Co., New Jersey to the heirs
of Henry Joris Brinkerhof, late of Hackensack,
Bergen Co., New Jersey, £150, 200 acres,
adjoining land formerly sold to Garret Lydecker
...purchased by said van Giesen from John Berry
4 Dec 1697. Signed Isaac van Giesen. Wit: John
Conrad Codweis, Martin Paulisen and Thomas van
Boskerk.

20 Apr 1696, John Berry to people of Hackensack,
Bergen Co., New Jersey, land for a church.
Signed John Berry. Wit: William Lawrence, Thomas
Lawrence, Albert Terhune and Thomas van Boskerk.

23 Mar 1712, John Berry, gentleman, of
Hackensack, Bergen Co., New Jersey to people of
Hackensack, Bergen Co., New Jersey, for good
will, 2.75 acres, formerly owned by Anthony
Anthoneson... line of Johannes Meyer and Dr.
Johannes van Burgh. Signed John Berry. Wit:
Richard Edsall, Thomas Lawrence and Thomas van
Boskerk.

7 May 1698, Maj. John Berry, of Bergen Co., New
Jersey to Rutt van Horne, of same, Nikasie Kip
and Thomas Francis, both of Essex Co., New
Jersey, £200, between the said Berry and
Nathaniel Kingsland, of Barbadoes, deceased...
bounded by Mathias Hopper...except that part
sold by said Berry to Garret Lydecker...land
sold by Mathias Hopper to Pieter Cornelis
Bryant. Signed John Berry. Wit: William
Lawrence, Edward Earle Jr. and Thomas Lawrence.

2 Jan 1729, Abraham & Hendrikjo Ackerman Jr.,
blacksmith, of Bergen Co., New Jersey to Peter
Houtenburgh, schoolmaster, of New Barbadoes,
Bergen Co., New Jersey, £60, west side of kings
highway...line of John Christeen and Peter
Stoutenburgh. Signed Abraham Ackerman and
Hendrikjo (x) Ackerman. Wit: John Hunt, Hendrick

Labagh, George Ryerson, Isaac van Giesen and Peter Houtenburgh.

30 Dec 1729, Abraham & Hendrikjo Ackerman Jr., blacksmith, of Bergen Co., New Jersey to John Christeen, gentleman, of New Barbadoes, Bergen Co., New Jersey, £60, line of William Provoost ...certain post where some smiths sinders is now buried in the presence of Hendrick Labagh and John Bardan. Signed Abraham Ackerman and Hendrikjo (x) Ackerman. Wit: Peter Stoutenburgh, Isaac van Giesen, Hendrick Labagh and George Ryerson.

2 Jan 1729, Abraham & Hendrikjo Ackerman Jr., blacksmith, of Bergen Co., New Jersey to John Hunt, saddler, of New Barbadoes, Bergen Co., New Jersey, £60, line of John Christeen and William Provoost. Signed Abraham Ackerman and Hendrikjo (x) Ackerman. Wit: Peter Stoutenburgh, Isaac van Giesen, Hendrick Labagh and George Ryerson.

31 Mar 1729, Mamerise, Manes, Wachtauj and Phillip, Towiskbeing and Kahawan, Indians to James Johnson, yeoman and Edward Jaroleman, yeoman, of Bergen Co., New Jersey, three half vats beer and four gallons of rum. All made their mark. Wit: Peter Stoutenburgh and Thomas van Boskerk.

12 Jan 1729, Peter Sonmans, of Perth Amboy, Middlesex Co., New Jersey to William Sandford van Emburgh, doctor, of New Barbadoes, Bergen Co., New Jersey, £0.25, 120 acres, surveyed 12 Jan 1729 by Richard Edsall. Signed Peter Sonmans. Wit: Abraham Gouverneur, Johann Minfarl, Robert Lettice Hooper and Peter Stoutenburgh.

4 May 1723, Jacobus van Cortlandt an accounting of estate, £288.95 and £213.7, Nicholas Demoresque in his will did name his four children, Sarah, Nicholas, Jacob and John Demoresque and Sarah Demoresque married Theophilus Elsworth, of New York City and now John Demoresque is the youngest and only

survivor of the four children who by his last will named Nicholas Elsworth, son of said Theophilus & Sarah Elsworth. Signed Jacobus van Cortlandt. Wit: Ronsolacer Nicoll and J. Chambers.

10 Jul 1723, Theophilus Elsworth, to Samuel Moore, £270, one half of land accounted for by Jacobus van Cortlandt. Signed Theophilus Elsworth. Wit: Sarah Elsworth, John Le Roux, John Chambers and Robert Lettice Hooper.

4 Apr 1726, William & Elizabeth Patterson, inn holder, James & Ann Martin, cordwiner, all of Elizabeth Town, Essex Co., New Jersey to John Stevens, of Perth Amboy, New Jersey and William Williamson, merchant, of Elizabeth Town, Essex Co., New Jersey, £140, one half of 1500 acres, land of George Duncan, deceased...patented granted from Phillip Cartwright, governor of New Jersey, 10 Jun 1669 to Capt. John Berry, gentleman, of New Barbadoes, New Jersey... between Hudson River and Overpeck Creek... bounded by Capt. Nicholas Varlott and Samuel Edsall...sold, 5 May 1699 to Thomas Nowell, gentleman, of New York, who in his will granted after his wife's decease to his son Monseth Nowell and to his wife's son, Richard Hall...the said Elizabeth Patterson and Ann Martin being heirs to their fathers, Moutoth Nowell and Richard Hall, respectively. Signed William Patterson, Elizabeth Patterson, James Martin and Ann Martin. Wit: John Harriman, Richard Edsall, Michael Kearney, George James Duncan and Thomas Lawrence. John Stevens signs a note for £80 to Samuel Moore. William & Elizabeth Patterson sign a note for £80 to Samuel Moore.

27 Apr 1700, John Edsall, son and heir of Samuel Edsall quit claim to John Smith, son and heir of Michael Smith, said Michael Smith, in 1671, for £20, purchased from Samuel Edsall land in Borghon Co., New Jersey, bounded by John Berry and John Edsall...surveyed by John Reid... bounded by David Danielsen...Francina Lawrence, widow of Michael Smith, her dower of one third

part of the aforesaid promised during her
natural life. Signed John Edsall. Wit: Edward
Earle Jr., Samuel Moore and John (x) Day

1 Feb 1724, Louis Carre, Peter Fauconnier and
Thomas Bayeux, merchants, all of New York City,
and the major part of the executors of the will
of Elias Boudinot, merchant, late of New York
City to Jan Juriansen, yeoman, of Bergen Co.,
New Jersey, £1, 333 acres, sold to said Elias
Boudinot by Maj. Nathaniel Kingsland 6 Jan
1702...corner to John Stagg who purchased of
Bartholomew Feurt... line of Daniel Rutan and
Harport Garrabrants...also 15 acres on line of
Jacob van Norstrandt and 15 acres on west side
of Berry's Creek...also 95 acres surveyed by
Abraham van Wyck and 87.5 acres. Signed Louis
Carre, Peter Fauconnier and Thomas Bayeux. Wit:
Edmond Kingsland, Abraham Gouverneur and William
Provoost.

2 Feb 1724, Louis Carre, Peter Fauconnier and
Thomas Bayeux, merchants, all of New York City,
and the major part of the executors of the will
of Elias Boudinot, merchant, late of New York
City to Jan Juriansen, yeoman, of Bergen Co.,
New Jersey, £642, 333 acres, purchased of
Nathaniel Kingsland 6 jan 1702, by said Elias
Boudinot, who wrote his will 16 Aug
1719...corner to John Stagg's land purchased of
Bartholomew Feurt ...line of Daniel Rutan and
Jacob van Norstrandt ...line of Harport
Gerbrantse ...also 15 acres on line of van
Norstrandt and 15 acres on west side of Berry's
Creek...also 95 acres surveyed by Abraham van
Wyck and 87.5 acres. Signed Louis Carre, Peter
Fauconnier and Thomas Bayeux. Wit: Edmond
Kingsland, Abraham Gouverneur and William
Provoost.

15 Dec 1730, Peter Sonmans power of attorney to
Hans Spear, said Peter Sonmans, of Perth Amboy,
Middlesex Co., New Jersey bound himself to Hans
Spear, of Newark, New Jersey, for £300, and said
Spear came to an agreement with Arent Schuyler
for the £300 with interest of £8 per annum.

Signed Peter Sonmans. Wit: David Rouset, Robert Crannell Jr. and William Provoost.

26 Dec 1709, Edward Earle, yeoman, of Bergen Co., New Jersey to his son Edward Earle Jr., of same, patented by Nicholas Varlott and Nicholas Bayard, from Phillip Cartwright and John Lord Barclay, who sold to said Earle. Signed Edward Earle. Wit: John Gardner, Robert Love and William Provoost.

19 May 1724, George Willock, gentleman, late of Perth Amboy, New Jersey, now of Philadelphia, Pennsylvania to Andrew Johnston, merchant of Perth Amboy, New Jersey and John Romine, yeoman, of Hackensack, Bergen Co., New Jersey, £228, 681 acres, Christian's Pond...seven parts of swamp land. Signed George Willock and Andrew Johnston. Wit: John Barclay, Lewis Johnston, George Leslie and William Provoost.

29 Aug 1721, Claes & Sarah Andries, yeoman, of Goinoenepa, Bergen Co., New Jersey to Rutgert van Horne, of same, £225, road to Bergen, also lot of land bounded by Cornelius Michiels... a stone laid by said Andries and Cornelius Hindriksen Brinkerhof. Signed Claes Andries and Sarah (x) Andries. Wit: Johann Jansen, L. Johnson and David Provoost.

12 Jun 1731, Aghtie Vreeland, widow of Enoch Vreeland, of Bergen Co., New Jersey to her children Jacob Vreeland and George Vreeland, both of same, love and affection, bounded on southwest by Andres van Boskerk...Hudson River. Signed Echtie (x) Vreeland. Wit: John Cavelier, Michael (x) Vreeland and William Provoost.

16 Aug 1731, Aghtie Vreeland, widow of Enoch Vreeland, of Bergen Co., New Jersey to her children Elias Vreeland and Benjamin Vreeland, love and affection, 120 acres, sold to said Vreeland by Rut van Horne. Signed Echtie (x) Vreeland. Wit: John Cavelier, Michael (x) Vreeland, Adolph Brass and William Provoost.

4 Dec 1697, John Berry, of Bergen Co., New Jersey to Isaac van Giesen, of same, £70, 200 acres plus extra for £10 more, formerly contracted for by Johannes Johnson ... bounded by Garret Lydecker. Signed John Berry and Isaac van Giesen. Wit: Thomas Lawrence, Richard Edsall and Peter Stoutenburgh.

3 Jun 1731, Abraham & Garrabrant Houseman, weaver, of New Barbadoes, Bergen Co., New Jersey to Hendrick van Giesen and Reynier van Giesen and Joris van Giesen, all of same, 200 acres, west side of Hackensack River...northwest by Albert Terhune...corner to Isaac van Giesen, which he purchased of Jacob Zabriskie...sold to Isaac & Cornelia van Giesen by Abraham & Garrabrant Houseman 27 May 1730...in exchange for land, 200 acres, contracted for by Johannes Johnson bounded by Hendrick Kip and Gysbert van Blerkum...sold to Isaac van Giesen by John Berry 4 Dec 1697. Signed Abraham Houseman and Garrabrant (x) Houseman. Wit: Mergreta Stoutenburgh and Peter Stoutenburgh.

14 Dec 1730, Col. Edmund Kingsland, of New Barbadoes, Bergen Co., New Jersey, Timothy & Elizabeth Bagley gentleman, of New York City and Richard & Martha Warman, of Bergen Co., New Jersey (late Martha Mompeson, which said Elizabeth Bagley and Martha Warman were two of the children of William Pinhorne, late of Mount Pinhorne, of Bergen Co., New Jersey) of the first part, Mary Pinhorne, widow of William Pinhorne, deceased, of the second part and Thomas Alsop, of New Town, Long Island, New York, of the third part. For £0.25 paid by Thomas Alsop to those of the first part grant land in Bergen Co., New Jersey...Bergen side of Hackensack River...Cromkill Creek...line of Edward Earle...Elsworths Creek. Signed Edmond Kingsland, Timothy Bagley, Elizabeth Bagley, Richard Warman and Martha Warman. Wit: William Kingsland, Ann Mompeson and William Provoost.

9 Aug 1715, Barent & Margarita Cooly, gentleman, of New York City to Thomas van Boskerk, of

Hackensack, Bergen Co., New Jersey, John Bardan, of New Barbadoes, Bergen Co., New Jersey and Paulus vander Beck, of New Barbadoes, Bergen Co., New Jersey, £140, 2 acres with house, purchased by said Cooly 23 Nov 1706 from John & Sarah Varick...line of Dr. Johannes van Emburgh and David Provoost...also house and lot purchased of David & Catherine Provoost Sr., 10 Jun 1709... bounded by John Wright, said Cooly and Johannes van Inburgh. Signed Barent Cooly and Margarita (x) Cooly. Wit: Cornelius (x) Epken Banta, Warner Burger, John Conrad Codweis and David Provoost.

22 Nov 1731, William Provoost, Paulus vander Beck and Richard Edsall, all of Bergen Co., New Jersey to Hendrick Brass, of same, £150, courthouse. Signed William Provoost, Paulus vander Beck and Richard Edsall. Wit: Harmon Lutkins, Peter Stoutenburgh and William Provoost.

15 Dec 1730, Col. Edmund Kingsland, of New Barbadoes neck, Bergen Co., New Jersey, Timothy & Elizabeth Bagley, of New York City and Richard & Martha Warman, of Bergen Co., New Jersey (late Martha Mompeson, which said Elizabeth Bagley and Martha Warman were two of the children of William Pinhorne, late of Mount Pinhorne, of Bergen Co., New Jersey) of the first part, Mary Pinhorne, widow of William Pinhorne, deceased, of the second part and Thomas Alsop, of New Town, Long Island, New York, of the third part, said William Pinhorne wrote his will 10 May 1719 and his wife Mary Pinhorne should enjoy all his land during her natural life and after her decease it should be divided into four equal parts...one part to his grandson, John Pinhorne and a one fourth part to Edmund Kingsland, Elizabeth Bagley and Martha Warman...Mary Pinhorne is executor of estate and desires to pay outstanding bills...£1680, all land said Alsop now on...Bergen side of Hackensack River...Cromkill Creek...line of Edward Earle...Elpworths Creek. Signed Edmond Kingsland, Timothy Bagley, Elizabeth Bagley,

Richard Warman and Martha Warman. Wit: William Kingsland, Ann Mompeson and William Provoost.

13 May 1731, Hans Spear, yeoman, of Newark, Essex Co., New Jersey, attorney for Peter Sonmans to Jacob Zabriskie, £60, 1067 acres, south side of Saddle River...corner to John Berry. Signed Hans (x) Spear. Wit: Nicholas Hardwick, Henry vander Linde and William Provoost.

19 Jun 1731, Peter Sonmans, of Perth Amboy, Middlesex Co., New Jersey and Hans Spear, of Newark, Essex Co., New Jersey to Jacob Zabriskie, of Wieramins, Bergen Co., New Jersey, £100, 260 acres, Dupe Valletie Brook ...Klyne Paseack Brook. Signed Peter Sonmans and Hans (x) Spear. Wit: Adam King, John Nevill, William North and William Provoost.

12 Jan 1729, Peter Sonmans, of Perth Amboy, Middlesex Co., New Jersey to John Guest, of New Barbadoes, Bergen Co., New Jersey, £0.25, 120 acres, corner to William Sandford van Emburgh, surveyed by Richard Edsall. Signed Peter Sonmans. Wit: Abraham Gouverneur and Robert Lettice Hooper.

22 Mar 1731, David L. Ackerman, farmer, of New Barbadoes, Bergen Co., New Jersey to Elias Williams, yeoman, of same, £5, corner to Warner Burger and Abraham Ackerman Jr. Signed David Ackerman. Wit: Hendrick Bohr, Peter Stoutenburgh and William Provoost.

26 Jun 1731, Garret & Vroutie van Dien, yeoman, of New Barbadoes, Bergen Co., New Jersey to Coeuradus Bos, weaver, of same, £13, corner to Abraham Ackerman Jr....line of William Provoost and Juryan Westervelt. Signed Garret van Dien and Vroutie (x) van Dien. Wit: Hendrick (x) Kip, Peter Stoutenburg and William Provoost.

17 Aug seventh year of the reign of Queen Ann, Maj. John Berry, late of New York City, but now in Bergen Co., New Jersey to Isack Vreeland,

yeoman, of Essex Co., New Jersey, £160, 242 acres, land of Tadoas Michiels...formerly sold to said Berry by John Christeen, deceased. Signed John Berry and Isaac (x) Vreeland. Wit: Hendrick vander Heul, Thomas Norton, James Wright and James Alexander.

17 Dec 1730, Hartman Claesen, of Essex Co., New Jersey to Peter van Boskerk, yeoman, of same, £500, 500 acres, Samuel Edsall, late of Queens Co., New York on 20 Feb 1695 sold to Hans Harmansen, Constable Hook containing 500 acres, and said Harmansen, in his will gave to his daughter Tryntie, now wife of said Peter van Boskerk and to his grandson, the said Hartman Claesen, son of another daughter called Annetje, who died before her father. Signed Hartman (x) Claesen. Wit: Joseph Ogden, Lawrence van Boskerk and William Provoost.

3 Jun 1731, Hendrick van Giesen, Joris van Giesen and Reynier van Giesen, all yeoman of New Barbadoes, Bergen Co., New Jersey and Klaefye van Giesen, spinster, of New Barbadoes, Bergen Co., New Jersey to Abraham Houseman, 200 acres, of same, formerly owned by Johannes Johnson...adjoining Hendrick Kip and Gysbert van Blerkum...purchased by Isaac van Giesen from Maj. John Berry 4 Dec 1697...adjoining Albert Terhune and lot Isaac van Giesen purchased of Jacob Zabriskie. Signed Hendrick (x) van Giesen, Joris van Giesen, Reynier van Giesen and Klaefye (x) van Giesen. Wit: Margrieta Houtenburgh, Peter Stoutenburgh John Parker and Isaac van Giesen.

30 Mar 1730, Lucas & Jannottye Kiersted, yeoman, of Bergen Co., New Jersey to Evert van Zile, blacksmith, of same, £100.4, 200 acres, corner to William Stagg. Signed Lucas Kiersted and Jannottye (x) Kiersted. Wit: Davyed L. Ackerman, Peter Stoutenburgh, Wilyam (x) Remsy, Jan (x) Varick and William Provoost.

1 Aug 1729, Eriens Christians Hoyer, merchant, of Hackensack, Bergen Co., New Jersey to David

Demarest, of same, £24, Hackensack Twp., house of John Banta on line of Simon Demarest. Signed Eriens Christians Hoyer. Wit: Joost van Boskerk, Cattrine Hoyer, Treyutie (x) van Boskerk and Thomas van Boskerk.

16 Nov 1728, James & Ann Martin, cordwinder, of Essex Co., New Jersey to Samuel Moore, yeoman, of Bergen Co., New Jersey, £160, one fourth tract of Thomas Nowell...within patent of Maj. John Berry. James Martin and Ann Martin. Wit: Thomas Lawrence, Richard Edsall and William Provoost.

15 Feb 1732, Elenor Mollemott, widow, of Bergen Co., New Jersey to her son John Christeen, yeoman, of same, for love and affection, 300 acres, bounded on north by Gisbert van Blerkum and on south by Isaac Vreeland. Signed Elenor (x) Mollemott. Wit: Thomas van Boskerk, Poulus vander Beck and William Provoost.

6 Oct 1728, Henry & Elsie Mayer, gentleman, of New Barbadoes, Bergen Co., New Jersey to Enoch Earle, of same, £200...purchased by Edward Earle Jr., deceased from Maj. John Berry, who sold to said Mayer. Signed Henry Mayer and Elsie Mayer. Wit: John Earle, Philip Earle and William Provoost.

8 Feb 1732, Enoch & Hannah Earle, of Beaukus, Bergen Co., New Jersey to Gerard Comfort, cooper, of New York City, £110, purchased by Edward Earle from Maj. John Berry. Signed Enoch Earle and Hannah Earle. Wit: Henry Mayer, Edward Earle, John Neilson and William Provoost.

8 Aug 1727, Marmaduke & Rebecca Earle, of Bergen Co., New Jersey to Stephen Bourdett, goldsmith, of New York City, £130, 60 acres, place called Quaksack, adjoining William Earle...bounded by Thomas Franks...adjoining Silvester Earle. Signed Marmaduke Earle and Rebecca Earle. Wit: Enoch Earle, Abraham (x) Jonsen and Thomas van Boskerk.

3 Jun 1731, Johannis & Catharine van Emburgh, doctor, of Bergen Co., New Jersey to his son William Sandford van Emburgh, doctor, of same, for love and affection, line of Lawrence Ackerman. Signed Johannis van Emburgh and Catharine van Emburgh. Wit: Richard Warman, Wyntie (x) Westervelt, Peter Stoutenburgh and William Provoost.

16 May 1734, Cornelius & Marytie Drake, (late Marytie Lawrence Toers), of Bergen Co., New Jersey to Jacob vander Beck, of same, £140, Saddle River, sold to Lawrence Arent Toers by William Nicoll 24 Aug 1695...corner to Johannis Neafie...line of Garret Stoothof. Signed Cornelius Drake and Marytie (x) Drake. Wit: William Provoost.

2 Dec 1728, Peter Sonmans, gentleman, of Perth Amboy, New Jersey to Cornelius Banta, son and heir of Epka Banta, deceased, yeoman, of Hackensack, Bergen Co., New Jersey, £0.25, 240 acres...Gawin Lowry, yeoman, of Bergen Co., New Jersey with good liking of Peter Sonmans 13 Aug 1686 sold to Richard Pope, 240 acres, who by power of attorney to Leonard Huygode Alyee, who sold 27 May 1695 to Cornelius Epka Banta, who by his will 3 Dec 1703 conveyed to his son Epka Banta...said Richard Pope with Gawin Lowry, because said Pope was 13 Aug 1686 under 21. Signed Peter Sonmans. Wit: Johannis van Emburgh and William Provoost.

28 May 1704, James Alexander to John Jaroleman. £1.5. Signed James Alexander. Wit: Lewis Morris.

1734, Hessel Peterson, yeoman, of Essex Co., New Jersey to Claas Vreeland, Cornelius Dooremus, Aldrih Brower, of same, Thomas Outwater, of Monache, Bergen Co., New Jersey and Roelif van Houten, yeoman, of Orange Co., New York, north side of Garret Newkerk. Signed Hefsel Pieterse. Wit: Derick (x) Vreeland, Isaack Kip Jr. and William Provoost.

31 Oct 1716, John Demarest Sr., of Hackensack,

Bergen Co., New Jersey and John Demarest Jr., yeoman, of New Castle Co. to Cornelius Claesen, yeoman, of Orange Co., New York, 256 acres, patented 9 Aug 1686 to Gouverneur, who sold to said John Demarest Sr., who sold to said John Demarest Jr., 20 Mar 1695. Signed John Demarest and John Demarest. Wit: Joost DeBaun, Jan Alyee, David Demarest and William Provoost.

18 Mar 1712, John Barberie, Peter Fauconnier and Andrew Fresnean, all of New York City to Johannis van Blerkum, alias Capt. Bergie, £30, 105 acres, between Pequaneck River and Saddle River... purchased of Indians 18 Nov 1709 ...corner to Daniel Rutan's 450 acres and Johannis van Seil land of 157 acres. Signed John Barbarie, Peter Fauconnier and Andrew Fresnean. Wit: Peter Barberie, John Moore Jr. and William Provoost.

30 Sep 1728, Johannis Lawrence Ackerman, weaver, of Saddle River, Bergen Co., New Jersey to Jacob Lawrence Ackerman, yeoman, of same, one half of 440 acres, corner to Jacobus Kip...line of John Berry... purchased of George Willock and Andrew & Catharine Johnston 19 May 1727. Signed Johannis Lawrence (x) Ackerman. Wit: Paulus vander Beck, Jacobus vander Beck and William Provoost.

13 Sep 1728, Jacobus Lawrence Ackerman, yeoman, of Saddle River, Bergen Co., New Jersey to Johannis Lawrence Ackerman, weaver, of same, one half part of 440 acres just described. Signed Jacobus Lawrence (x) Ackerman. Wit: Paulus vander Beck, Jacobus vander Beck and William Provoost.

27 Oct 1705, Barent Christian Bekenne Zabriskie, yeoman, of Bergen Co., New Jersey to Jacob Zabriskie, £1000, line of Christian Claas Lozier, Lawrence van Boskerk and Jan Bogart formerly owned by Albert Zabriskie, deceased, who sold 500 acres. Signed Christian (x) Zabriskie. Wit: David Provoost, John Peers and William Provoost.

10 Dec 1734, Jacob Zabriskie, yeoman, of Bergen Co., New Jersey to Christyne Zabriskie, yeoman, of same, £60, 1067 acres, south side of Saddle River... corner to John Berry. Signed Jacob Zabriskie. Wit: David Provoost, John Peers and William Provoost.

16 Jan 1730, John Hunt, saddler, of Bergen Co., New Jersey to Abraham Ackerman Jr., of same, £60. Signed John Hunt. Wit: Johannis David Ackerman, Peter Stoutenburgh and William Provoost.

2 Apr 1735, Elenor Mollemott, widow of John Christeen, of Bergen Co., New Jersey to her son John Christeen, yeoman, of same, now that he is over 21, his two thirds part and continued maintenance of his said Elenor Mollenot... bounded on north by Gisbert van Blerkum and on south by Isaac Vreeland. Signed Elenor (x) Mollemott and John Christeen. Wit: Par Parmylor, Abraham Lodge and William Provoost.

8 Jul 1730, Stephen & Hannah Bourdett, goldsmith, of New York City to James Lee, carpenter, of same, £200, 60 acres, west side of Hackensack River place called Quacksack...line of William Earle, Silvester Earle and Thomas Francis. Signed Stephen Bourdett and Hannah Bourdett. Wit: John vander Nan, H. Demeyer and William Provoost.

28 Apr 1732, Cornelius Mattyse, of Hackensack, Bergen Co., New Jersey to John Durie, blacksmith, of same, £60, his land except 25 acres he sold to Jacobus Varick. Signed Cornelius (x) Mattyse. Wit: David Demarest, Andris van Boskerk and William Provoost.

20 May 1730, Peter Sonmans, of Perth Amboy, Middlesex Co., New Jersey to Cornelius Mattyse, yeoman, of Bergen Co., New Jersey, £10, 120 acres, formerly granted to Claas Janse Roney, Jacob Zabriskie and Peter Sonmans by Indians. Signed Peter Sonmans. Wit: David Demarest, Jan Durie and William Provoost.

4 Aug 1730, John & Samotie Romine, of New Barbadoes, Bergen Co., New Jersey to Richard Warman, of Hackensack Twp., Bergen Co., New Jersey, £100, line of Jurie Westervelt. Signed John Romine and Samotie Romine. Wit: Jurie Westervelt, James Duncan and William Provoost.

7 Jun 1735, John & Naomi Christeen, yeoman, of Bergen Co., New Jersey to Thomas DeKey, of Orange Co., New York and Elenor Morris, widow, of Bergen Co., New Jersey, both executors of will of Joseph Morris, deceased, of Bergen Co., New Jersey, £700, bounded by Mathew Benson, (formerly William Lawrence) and Michael Smith Jr. of Michael Smith Sr., deceased...contains one half part of land granted by Samuel Edsall by gift to his son-in-law Benjamin Blagge and William Lawrence...sold to David Danielsen by Edward Blagge 19 May 1703. Signed John Christeen and Neomi Christeen. Wit: Richard Edsall, David Provoost and William Provoost.

2 Jul 1717, Johannis & Catharine van Emburgh, of New Barbadoes, Bergen Co., New Jersey to Gilbert van Emburgh, £200, line formerly marked by John Houseman...corner to James Davis and Arent Schuyler. Signed Johannis van Emburgh and Catharin van Emburgh. Wit: Edmond Kingsland, Mary Kingsland and William Provoost.

10 Sep 1734, John Bardan Jr., Cornelius Kip and Thomas Dooremus to Abraham Brooks, of Bergen Co., New Jersey, £20, 10 acres, George Dooremus in his will 25 Mar 1733 named said Bardan and Dooremus his executors, bounded by Cornelius Kip and Derick Day. Signed John Bardan, Cornelius Kip and Thomas Dooremus. Wit: David Provoost, Francis Hendrix and William Provoost.

28 Feb 1707, Bartholomew & Magdalena Feurt, of New York City to Jacob Wallings van Winkle, of Essex Co., New Jersey, £5, 110 acres, between Maj. John Berry and Maj. Nathaniel Kingsland. Signed Bartholomew Feurt and Magdalena Feurt. Wit: Gustavus Kingsland Jr., John Pinhorne and William Provoost.

2 Sep 1735, Abraham Folch to David Jones, the promise to never again lie about the wife of said Jones. Wit: John Berry, Garret van Vorst, Edward Wessels, Cornelius Stagg, Daniel Mackleen, William Anns, Benjamin Codweis and John Stagg.

28 Oct 1727, James Johnston, of New Jersey to Hendrick Sieberie Banta Jr., of Hackensack, Bergen Co., New Jersey, £100, 200 acres, corner to Andrew van Boskerk Jr. Signed James Johnston. Wit: Edmond Kingsland, David Provoost and Thomas van Boskerk.

4 Apr 1736, Hendrick Sieberie & Annetie Banta, of Bergen Co., New Jersey to Johannes Stagg, of same, £280, 200 acres, corner to Andrew van Boskerk Jr. Signed Hendrick Sieberie (x) Banta and Annetie (x) Banta. Wit: David Provoost, Francis Hendrix and William Provoost.

5 Nov 1735, Hendrick Brass, cordwinder, of New Barbadoes, Bergen Co., New Jersey to Jacobus van Voorhees, yeoman, of Kings Co., New York, £120. Signed Henry Brass. Wit: Paulus vander Beck, Andrew van Boskerk and William Provoost.

1 May 1712, John Barberie, Elias Boudinot, Andrew Fresnean and Peter Fauconnier, all merchants, of New York City and Lucas Kiersted, yeoman, of Bergen Co., New Jersey to Garret Ackerman, yeoman, of Bergen Co., New Jersey, £130, 478 acres, land purchased of Indians 14 Sep 1711...west side of Saddle River...corner to Andrie Hopper and David Ackerman. Signed John Barberie, Elias Boudinot, Andrew Fresnean and Peter Fauconnier. Wit: Andrew Marschalik, John White, Poulus (x) Yorks and William Provoost.

8 Apr 1736, Martha Warman, widow, of New Barbadoes, Bergen Co., New Jersey to David Provoost, merchant, of same, £0.25, 4.25 acres, corner to Juris Westervelt. Signed Martha Warman. Wit: Mary Ludlow, Abraham Lodge and William Provoost.

9 Apr 1736, Martha Warman, widow of Richard Warman, of New Barbadoes, Bergen Co., New Jersey to David Provoost, merchant, of same, 4.25 acres, corner to Juris Westervelt. Signed Martha Warman. Wit: Mary Ludlow, Abraham Lodge and William Provoost.

10 Apr 1736, Martha Warman, widow of Richard Warman, of New Barbadoes, Bergen Co., New Jersey to David Provoost, merchant, of same, £450. Signed Martha Warman. Wit: Mary Ludlow, Abraham Lodge and William Provoost.

## Chapter 3

## Bergen County Courthouse Deed Records Volume C

### Recorded in 1736-1771

3 May 1737, James Lee, carpenter, of Bergen Co., New Jersey to Abraham Lodge, £80, Quacksack, bounded on east by Hackensack River...bounded by William Earle and Abraham Ackerman...purchased of Stephen & Hannah Bourdett. Signed James Lee. Wit: Catharine (x) Lee, David Provoost and William Provoost.

23 Jul 1735, Jacob Arents, doctor, of Newark Essex Co., New Jersey to Jacobus and Cornelius Brinkerhof, brothers, one of Hackensack and the other of Bergen, Bergen Co., New Jersey, £50, 200 acres, works of Phillip Schuyler. Signed Jacob Arents. Wit: David Lawrence Ackerman, Francis Hendrix and William Provoost.

13 Feb 1725, John Sip, Wander Diedericks and Johannis Garretson, JP's, Bergen Co., New Jersey to Clasen Matty DeMott, for defense. Signed John (x) Sip, Wander (x) Diedericks and Johannis Garretson. Wit: Peter Marselius and William Provoost.

18 Mar 1712, John Barberie, Elias Boudinot, Andrew Fresnean and Peter Fauconnier, all merchants, of New York City to Johannis van Seil, of Bergen Co., New Jersey, £45, 157.5 acres, purchased of Indians 18 Nov 1695 under seal of Peter Sonmans...corner to Johannis van Blerkum. Signed John Barberie, Elias Boudinot, Andrew Fresnean and Peter Fauconnier. Wit: Peter Valleau, Richard Moore, John Christeen and

William Provoost.

27 Apr 1733, Warner & Mary Richards, of Bergen Co., New Jersey to John Richards, of same, £100, 100 acres, bounded on east by Harp Garrabrants, deceased, on west by Hendrick Folch and William Ernis. Signed Warner Richards and Mary Richards. Wit: Samuel Richards, George Smith and William Provoost.

4 Nov 1737, Hendrick Spear, of Salem, Essex Co., New Jersey an agreement to build a mill with John Jaroleman, of Essex Co., New Jersey. Signed Hendrick Spear and John Joreleman. Wit: Jonathan Sargent, Johann Caspar Cogh and William Provoost.

29 Oct 1714, Wiert & Mary Banta, of Hackensack, Bergen Co., New Jersey to Hendrick Banta Jr., of same, £60, bounded by Roelif Westervelt, Hackensack van Cortlandt, Andreas van Norden and Samuel Demarest Sr. Signed Wiert (x) Banta and Mary (x) Banta. Wit: Richard (x) Edsall, Abraham Cample, David Mandeville and William Provoost.

24 Apr 1728, Ruth van Horne, of Gemoneya, Bergen Co., New Jersey to Aefie Vreeland, of same, £325.4, 320 acres...two tracts, patented by Thomas Rudyard, deceased... line of Joseph Read, heirs of David CoSaart and Johannis Sebring. Signed Ruth van Horne. Wit: John (x) Paulisen, John van Horne and William Provoost.

1 May 1719, Lawrence Williamson, of Pishadawa, Middlesex Co., New Jersey to Enoch Vreeland, farmer, of Pemberypogh, Bergen Co., New Jersey, 346 acres, 13 Sep 1715 said Williamson purchased of Peter Nevins, who purchased of Octavo Caenroot, of New York City, who sold by power of attorney for Jacob van Storlant and John Heyser Marsh of London...corner to George Researrick ...line of Abraham Bohe...Langevelt's land and Elisabeth Tysen. Signed Lawrence Williamson. Wit: Jan DeWitte, Abraham Gouverneur and Thomas Farmer.

6 Apr 1738, Warner & Mary Richards, of Bergen Co., New Jersey to his son John Richards, of same, £25, 18 acres, line of William Ernis. Signed Warner Richards and Mary Richards. Wit: Henry Harris and William Provoost.

6 May 1720, Martin Ranger, of Hackensack, Bergen Co., New Jersey bound to John Durie, of same, £80, debt to church...to Peter Haring. Signed Martin (x) Ranger. Wit: David Demarest, Simon David Demarest, Andris van Orden and William Provoost.

20 Apr 1738, Agreement between David Demarest, Simon Demarest, Peter Demarest Lukus van Horne, David Samuel Demarest and David Samuel Demarest Jr., all yeoman of Hackensack, Bergen Co., New Jersey and Aria Demarest, yeoman, of same, line of Joost Zabriskie, re-aline divisions between their properties...heirs of Samuel Demarest Jr., deceased. Signed Peter Demarest, David Demarest Sr., David Samuel (x) Demarest, David Demarest Jr., Aria (x) Demarest, Lukus van Horne. Wit: Martin Wynkoop, Cort Corsen and William Provoost.

13 May 1738, Lukus & Aeltie van Horne, yeoman, of Hackensack, Bergen Co., New Jersey to David Demarest, carpenter, of same, £80, 1.2 acres. Signed Lukus van Horne and Aeltie (x) van Horne. Wit: Simon Demarest, Cornelius (x) van Horne and William Provoost.

6 Nov 1713, Cornelius & Fryntie van Brunt, Joost & Aeltie van Brunt and Claas & Maria van Brunt, all yeoman of Kings Co., New York to Garret Garretson, of Bergen Co., New Jersey, patented 20 Mar 1687 by Richard Townly, Elbert Elbertse, Jaque Cortlandt, Richard Stillwell, William Nicoll, Catharine Houghland, Peter Jacobs Marinus, Rut Joosten and Hendrick Mattysien... left to survivor Rut Joosten, who willed to his heirs said van Brunts. Signed Cornelius van Brunt, Joost van Brunt, Nicholas van Brunt and Maria van Brunt. Wit: Jacob van Lieton, John Sperling and David Provoost.

3 May 1736, Richard Ashfield, merchant, of New York City to Peter Post, yeoman, of Bergen Co., New Jersey, £0.5, 428 acres...corner of Cornelius Brinkerhof. Signed Richard Ashfield. Wit: Clasparius Schuyler, Daniel Harsmander and William Provoost.

14 May 1736, Richard Ashfield, merchant, of New York City to Peter Post, yeoman, of Bergen Co., New Jersey, £3, 428 acres, corner Cornelius Brinkerhof and Jacobus Brinkerhof. Signed Richard Ashfield. Wit: Clasparius Schuyler, Daniel Harsmander and William Provoost.

14 Feb 1735, John & Vroutie Bardan, yeoman, of Hackensack, Bergen Co., New Jersey to Abraham Garretson, yeoman, of same, for exchange of 580 acres this 280 acres, purchased by said Bardan, Gisbert van Blerkum and John Bogart 22 Aug 1732, from Andrew Johnston, Edward Vaugham, William Skinner and George Leslie, of Perth Amboy, New Jersey...map by Alexander McDowell...parties divided land 24 Jul 1733. Signed John Bardan and Vroutie (x) Bardan. Wit: Jacob Outwater, David Demarest and William Provoost.

10 Feb 35, Jacob & Martyntie Outwater yeoman of Bergen Co., New Jersey to Abraham Garretson, yeoman, of same, exchange of 130 acres, this 204 acres, purchased by said Outwater, 19 May 1727, from John Stone, of Bergen Co., New Jersey...between Peter Garretson and Johann Neafie. Signed Jacob Outwater. Wit: Jan Bardan, David Demarest and William Provoost.

11 Dec 1710, Garret Garretson, late of Bergen Co., New Jersey, deceased to his son John Garretson, yeoman, of same, £200, 17 acres, will wrote 13 Oct 1688...between Samuel Edsall and Adrian Post, also lot between Geurt Carter and Arnet Lawrence ...bounded on south by Dauwe Harmansen and east by Derick Tunison...formerly belonged to Adrian Post who purchased from Cornelius Steinway. Signed Garret Garretson. Wit: Robert Sickels, Martin Winne, John Conrad Codweis and David Provoost.

2 May 1696, Maj. John Berry, of Bergen Co., New Jersey to Nicholas Devaux, of Essex Co., New Jersey, £40, 215 acres, between Hackensack and Saddle River ...line of Charles Houseman. Signed John Berry. Wit: Thomas Lawrence and Edward Earle Jr.

28 Jan 1739, Francytie Earle, the wife of Nathaniel Earle, blacksmith, of StiemRapie, Bergen Co., New Jersey to Henry Mayer, yeoman, of Quacksack, Bergen Co., New Jersey, £200, 127 acres, half of 254 acres descending jointly to Janitie and said Francytie by...bounded on south by John Banta and on north by Jacobus van Voorhees. Signed Francytie (x) Earle. Wit: Edward Earle Sr., John Genst Jr., Alice Earle and William Provoost.

29 Jan 1739, Henry Meyer, yeoman, of Quacksack, Bergen Co., New Jersey to his son-in-law, Nathaniel Earle, love and affection, 127 acres, just described. Signed Henry Meyer. Wit: Edward Earle, John Genst Jr., Alice Earle and William Provoost.

5 Apr 1739, Thomas Applewhite, of St. Thomas Parish, Ireland power of attorney to Robert Watch March, to sell his land. Signed Thomas Applewhaite. Wit: Theophilis Morris, William Dever and John Hamilton, all of New Jersey. Recorded at the request of George L. Carting.

24 Jul 1733, Whereas Gisbert van Blerkum, John Bogart and John Bardan, all of Bergen Co., New Jersey purchased of Andrew Johnston and William Skinner, both of Perth Amboy, Middlesex Co., New Jersey and Edward Vaugham, of Elisabeth Town, Essex Co., New Jersey, executors of will of George Willock and with consent of George Leslie, lots in Pomptan, Bergen Co., New Jersey... surveyed by Alexander McDowell. Signed Jan Bardan, Gisbert van Blerkum and John (x) Bogart. Wit: Joseph Bartrim and William Provoost.

17 Sep 1737, Gisbert van Blerkum, of New

Barbadoes, Bergen Co., New Jersey to Cornelius cor van Houten, yeoman, of Essex Co., New Jersey, £200, all his rights in land released to him by John Bardan and Jacobus Bogart. Signed Gisbert van Blerkum. Wit: John van Blerkum, Paulus vander Beck and William Provoost.

2 Aug 1740, Garret van Ale, of Saddle River, Bergen Co., New Jersey to Roelif cor van Houten, miller, of same, £65, land purchased by Gisbert van Blerkum, John Bogart and John Bardan, all of Bergen Co., New Jersey from Andrew Johnston and William Skinner, both of Perth Amboy, Middlesex Co., New Jersey...said John Bogart being introduced by his two brothers Steven and Isaac Bogart...said Isaac Bogart exchanged with Peter van Ale who sold to Henry van Ale and the said Garret van Ale. Signed Garret (x) van Ale. Wit: Isaac vander Beck, Paulus vander Beck and William Provoost.

1 Sep 1740, John Christeen, yeoman, of New Barbadoes, Bergen Co., New Jersey to Edward Kingsland, of same, £5, 8 acres, on bank of Saddle River, line of Arya van Winkle. Signed John Christeen. Wit: Herman Shinnsman, Paulis vander Beck and William Provoost. Recorded at the request of Isaac Kingsland.

5 Aug 1740, John Romine, yeoman, of Bergen Co., New Jersey to John Romine Jr., yeoman, of same, £125, 203 acres, purchased from George Willock and Andrew Johnston...division to said John Romine Jr. and Roelif Romine. Signed John Romine. Wit: John Burger, David Provoost and William Provoost.

5 Aug 1740, John Romine, yeoman, of Bergen Co., New Jersey to Roelif Romine, yeoman, of same, £125, purchased from George Willock and Andrew Johnston. Signed John Romine. Wit: John Burger, David Provoost and William Provoost.

12 Apr 1740, Jacobus & Angenietie Brinkerhof, yeoman, of Hackensack, Bergen Co., New Jersey to Johannis van Wagener, yeoman, of same, £275, 625

acres, corner to Richard Ashfield...purchased of Joseph Kerbride. Signed Jacobus Brinkerhof and Agenietie (x) Brinkerhof. Wit: Robert Livesey, Johannis vander Hoof and William Provoost.

9 Apr 1740, John & Sametie Romine, yeoman, of Hackensack, Bergen Co., New Jersey to Claas Romine, yeoman, of Essex Co., New Jersey, £580, bounded by Isaac van Giesen and Juris Westervelt. Signed John Romine and Sametie Romine. Wit: John Roosevelt, David Provoost and William Provoost.

12 May 1741, Richard Ashfield, of New York City, the only grandson and heir, of Patience Ashfield, who was the only sister and heir of Thomas Hartone to Anthony Beam, Abraham Sip and Caenraot Sip, all of Wynachte, Saddle River Twp., Bergen Co., New Jersey, £195.25, 683 acres, line of Joseph Kerbride. Signed Richard Ashfield. Wit: Jacob Abrahamse, S. Johnston and James Alexander.

1732, James & Elisabeth Duncan, gentleman, of Bergen Co., New Jersey to Johannis Benson, yeoman, of same, £100, 41 acres, Overpeck Creek. Signed James Duncan and Elisabeth Duncan. Wit: Jacob Day, Ryck Lydecker and William Provoost.

4 Mar 1729, James & Elisabeth Duncan, yeoman, of Bergen Co., New Jersey to Jacob Day, of same, £30, 12 acres, line of Samuel Moore. Signed James Duncan and Elisabeth Duncan. Wit: Richard Edsall, Philip Edsall and William Provoost.

26 May 1741, James & Elisabeth Duncan, of Bergen Co., New Jersey to Michael Vreeland, of Stony Point, Bergen Twp., Bergen Co., New Jersey, £65, 12 acres, line of Samuel Moore and John Berry...line of John Roma, Richard Baker and Henry Banta. Signed James Duncan and Elisabeth Duncan. Wit: Martha Warman, Henry (x) Day, James McKinley and William Provoost.

27 May 1735, Richard & Hila Edsall, (said Richard is oldest son and heir of Ruth Edsall,

deceased), yeoman, of Bergen Co., New Jersey to Michael Vreeland, yeoman, of same, £625. patented by Samuel Edsall and Nicholas Varlott ... also land from Jacob Milbourne...line of Mary Edsall...bounded by John Day and heirs of Siebese Banta. Signed Richard Edsall and Hila Edsall. Wit: Abraham Lodge and William Provoost.

29 Nov 1723, Lawrence & Freytie van Boskerk, yeoman, of Bergen Co., New Jersey, Reynier & Mettie van Giesen, yeoman, of Essex Co., New Jersey and Roelif van Houten, yeoman, of Bergen Co., New Jersey on behalf of his children from his wife Achie, daughter of Cornelius Machielle Vreeland, deceased to Michael Vreeland and Daniel van Winkle, both yeoman, of Bergen Co., New Jersey, £4000, between John Aevtle vander Bilt and Paul Dawesa...willed by said Cornelius Vreeland 6 Sep 1712. Signed Lawrence van Boskerk, Freytie van Boskerk, Reynier van Giesen, Mettie (x) van Giesen and Roelif van Houten. Wit: Herman Shinnsman, David Provoost, John (x) Sip and Johannis Philip van Lambecker.

29 Nov 1723, Lawrence & Freytie van Boskerk, yeoman, of Bergen Co., New Jersey, Reynier & Mettie van Giesen, yeoman, of Essex Co., New Jersey and Roelif van Houten, yeoman, of Bergen Co., New Jersey on behalf of his children from his wife Achie, daughter of Cornelius Machielle Vreeland, deceased to Michael Vreeland and Daniel van Winkle, both yeoman, of Bergen Co., New Jersey, £140, willed by said Cornelius Vreeland. Signed Lawrence van Boskerk, Freytie van Boskerk, Reynier van Giesen, Mettie (x) van Giesen and Roelif van Houten. Wit: Herman Shinnsman, David Provoost, John (x) Sip and Johannis Philip Lambecker.

7 Oct 1724, Michael Duncan, of New York City to James Duncan, lands, slaves and livestock received from his father, George Duncan, deceased, whose will 16 Jan 1715 gave to his children, James Duncan and said Michael Duncan, executors of will were Adolph Phillip Edsall, Jacobus van Cortlandt and Petter Barbarsen

March. Signed Michael Duncan. Wit: Thomas Wenman.

2 Jul 1741, Gabiel & Francis Ludlow, merchant, William & Mary Ludlow, merchant, George & Martha Duncan, merchant, Thomas & Mary Duncan, merchant, all of New York City, Thomas & Christian Dekey, gentleman, of Orange Co., New York, (which said Francis Ludlow, Mary Ludlow, George Duncan, Thomas Duncan and Christian Dekey, are children of George Duncan, deceased, late of Hackensack, Bergen Co., New Jersey) to James Duncan, £0.5, estate rights. Signed Gabiel Duncan, Francis Ludlow, William Ludlow, Mary Ludlow, George Duncan, Martha Duncan, Thomas Duncan, Mary Duncan, Thomas Dekey and Christian Dekey. Wit: Rhoda Morland, Abraham Lodge and James Alexander.

12 Apr 1740, Cornelius Brinkerhof, yeoman, of Bergen Co., New Jersey to Heliningar van Wagener yeoman, of same, £200, 625 acres, Pahaques River... above Indian Buryan place... corner to Richard Ashfield. Signed Cornelius Brinkerhof. Wit: Robert Livesey, Johannis vander Hoof and William Provoost.

29 Oct 1735, Cornelius Arsmitt yeoman, of Albany, New York to Rutgert van Horne, of yeoman, Bergen Co., New Jersey, £308, patented by Wessel Weggersen 13 Mar 1675, who sold 16 Sep 1696 to Douwse Aukins, who sold 18 Mar 1728 to said Arsmitt...bounded by Cornelius Abrahamse and Joas vander Linde. Signed Cornelius Arsmitt. Wit: Lawrence van Boskerk, Abraham Gouverneur and James Alexander.

17 Nov 1740, Rutgert van Horne, yeoman, of Gemonapa, Bergen Co., New Jersey to Dedrick Cadmus, of Pemnepo, Bergen Co., New Jersey, £308, land just described...bounded by Jacob Berentse van Horne. Signed Ruth van Horne. Wit: Michael Andries, John Cavelier and William Provoost.

12 Dec 1730, Hendrick Laroe, Samuel Laroe,

yeoman, both of Rampogh, Bergen Co., New Jersey and Wybregh Laroe, their mother and widow, of Hackensack, Bergen Co., New Jersey to Abraham Laroe, yeoman, of Hackensack, Bergen Co., New Jersey, £18, 60 acres...James Laroe and John Alyee, both deceased, purchased of Indians...formerly bounded by Gawen Lauries, but now by Peter Fauconnier...sold in presence of Peter Sonmans to said James Laroe, Nicholas Lozier and Peter Alyee, son of said John Alyee...said James Laroe in his will, 14 Nov 1728, gave to wife Wybregh Laroe and sons, Hendrick Laroe, Samuel Laroe and Abraham Laroe. Signed Hendrick (x) Laroe, Samuel (x) Laroe and Wybregh (x) Laroe. Wit: Jonathan Traphagen, William (x) Alex, Abraham (x) van Gelder, Jan (x) Banta, Wybregh (x) van Bussen and John Christeen.

26 Jun 1735, Thomas Dekey, innholder, of Orange Co., New York and Elenor Morris, widow of Joseph Morris, of Bergen Co., New Jersey to John Christeen, yeoman, of Bergen Co., New Jersey, £700, Overpeck Creek...bounded on sourtwest by Mathew Benson, formerly belonging to William Lawrence...southwest of house of Michael Smith ...sold by Samuel Edsall to his son-in-law Benjamin Blagge and William Lawrence...part sold to David Danielsen by Edward Blagge, son and heir of said Benjamin Blagge, 19 May 1703. Signed Thomas Dekey and Elenor Morris. Wit: Richard Edsall, David Provoost and William Provoost.

14 May 1742, Johannis & Hendrickie Stagg, Jacob & Antie Stagg, yeoman, all of Bergen Co., New Jersey, Abraham & Marritie Stagg, mason, of Orange Co., New York to Elias E. Vreeland and George E. Vreeland, both yeoman, of Bergen Co., New Jersey, £618, 216 acres, purchased by Margarite Stagg, 1703 from John Berry, who sold to her two sons the said John Stagg and William Stagg 12 Nov 1712 ...said William Stagg sold 5 Dec 1720 to said John Stagg who willed 27 Dec 1738 to his sons, the said Jacob Stagg and Abraham Stagg and George Stagg...the said George

Stagg sold 15 Feb 1739 to the said Johannis Stagg...Walling Jacobus line...bounded on northwest by Richard Berry...southwest by Hannah Hall. Signed Johannis (x) Stagg, Abraham Stagg, Hendrickie (x) Stagg, Antie (x) Stagg, Marretie (x) Stagg. Wit: John Berry, George Vreeland and William Provoost.

8 jun 1743, William McDowell, executor of estate of Dr. John McDowell, deceased and Andrew McDowell, of Bergen Co., New Jersey to Paulus Loots, yeoman, of same, £50, negro Jo, age about 19. Signed William McDowell and Andrew McDowell. Wit: David Provoost and William Provoost.

22 Mar 1727, Marmaduke & Rebecca Earle, yeoman, of Hackensack, Bergen Co., New Jersey to Jacobus Brinkerhof, yeoman, of Bergen Co., New Jersey, £50, 63, acres, corner to lot of 40 acres Henry Mayer purchased of Gisbert van Blerkum...on west by Hendrick vander Linde... on south by Moenaghe...other half sold to Jacob Banta. Signed M. D. Earle and Rebekah Earle. Wit: Roelif Bogart, Elisabeth (x) Bogart and David Demarest.

6 Jul 1742, Thomas Dekey, innholder, of Orange Co., New York and Elenor Morris, widow of Joseph Morris, of Bergen Co., New Jersey to John Christeen, yeoman, of Bergen Co., New Jersey, £700, Overpeck Creek and on southwest by Cornelius Brinkerhof, formerly by William Lawrence. Signed Thomas Dekey and Elenor Morris. Wit: Samuel Morris Jr., Samuel Edsall, Jacob DeBane and Joseph Bonnel

14 Jun 1748, Samuel Edsall, Isaac Kingsland and Abraham Laroe, all of Bergen Co., New Jersey bound to King, £800, said Samuel Edsall to be sheriff. Signed Samuel Edsall, Isaac Kingsland and Abraham Laroe. Wit: George Bogart.

9 Oct 1717, Joseph Healy, distiller, of Stain, Middlesex Co., New Jersey, Mercy Benthall, of Greece Church Stocel London, widow and Richard Ashfield, grandson and heir of Patience Ashfield

to Derick Day, yeoman, of Bergen Co., New
Jersey, £120, 600 acres, Thomas Hart in his will
19 Dec 1704 gave to his sister Patience and the
said Mercy Benthall, land and named said Joseph
Healy, executor...corner to Johannis Deriemer
and Kip van Dam. Signed Joseph Healy, Mercy
Benthall and Richard Ashfield. Wit: Kip van Dam,
William Bicklay, John Chambers and David
Provoost.

9 Apr 1730, Peter Sonmans, of Perth Amboy,
Middlesex Co., New Jersey to Derick Day, yeoman,
of Pachgannick, Bergen Co., New Jersey, £50, 200
acres, line of Richard Ashietas (Ashfield).
Signed Peter Sonmans. Wit: Richard Edsall, H.
Demeyer and Robert Lettice Hooper.

13 Dec 1748, David & Jannetie Brower, boatman,
of New York City to David Demarest Jr., Carrol
Debane, Jacobus Peck, Cornelius Lydecker, elders
and Abraham Lydecker, Quilliam Bogart, Aury
Banta and David Christie, deacons of the church
of Schraelingburg, Bergen Co., New Jersey, £100,
17 acres, John Demarest willed 29 Mar 1714 to
his daughter Lea Brower, wife of Abraham Brower
for their life, then to their eldest son Petrus
Brower who with his wife Dina Brower sold to his
brother said David Brower...line of Cucas van
Horne and Jacobus van Boskerk. Signed David
Brower and Jannetie (x) Brower. Wit: Benjamin
Demarest, David Demarest and Derick Kuyper.

13 Oct 1750, Garret Hawlenbeck, Reynier van
Giesen and Jacob Titsort bound to King for £800,
said Garret Hawlenbeck to be sheriff. Signed
Garret Hawlenbeck, Reynier van Giesen and Jacob
Titsort. Wit: Thomas Watson and Abraham
Gouverneur and Derick Kuyper.

24 Apr 1750, Hendrick & Ariaentie vander Linde
yeoman, of Hackensack, Bergen Co., New Jersey to
John Durie, yeoman, of Schralenburg, Bergen Co.,
New Jersey, £100, 150 acres, line John
Zabriskie. Signed Henry vander Linde and
Ariaentie vander Linde. Wit: Roelif vander
Linde, Samuel Verbrick and Derick Kuyper.

Apr 1751, Judge George Ryerson in court where Helena Macphidvis sued Derick van Horne, of Hackensack, Bergen Co., New Jersey, for £139.1, through her attorney Abraham Lodge, for deal made 18 Mar 1839 at New Barbadoes. Wit: David Provoost and Reynier van Giesen.

Oct 1750, repeat of suit.

Jan 1751, Judge George Ryerson in court where Simon Johnson sued Derick van Horne, of Hackensack, Bergen Co., New Jersey, for £128.4, through his attorney Abraham Lodge, for deal made 26 Sep 1746. Wit: David Provoost and Reynier van Giesen.

25 Apr 1751, Samuel Moore Jr., of Hackensack, Bergen Co., New Jersey to Michael Vreeland, of Hony Point, Bergen Co., New Jersey, £180, 300 acres, Overpeck Creek...line of Michael Moore. Signed Samuel Moore. Wit: James McKinley, Hendrick (x) Day and David Kuyper.

25 Jul 1753, Theodorus Valleau, Hendrick vander Linde and Peter Valleau bound to King for £800, said Theodorus Valleau to be sheriff. Signed Theodorus Valleau, Henry vander Linde and Peter Valleau. Wit: Johannis Bogart, Hendrick Claes van Giesen and Jacobus Peck.

23 May 1753, Magdelen Valleau, widow, of Bergen Co., New Jersey to Dederick Tise and Johannis Tise, both farmers, of Bergen Co., New Jersey, £115, 200 acres, purchased in consideration of Peter Fauconnier corner to Isaac Bogart. Signed Magdelen Valleau. Wit: Cornelius Kuyper, Theodore Valleau and Jacobus Peck.

14 Nov 1753, Hendrick Banta and Aury Degroot, Peter Degroot, Michael Vreeland, William Day John Day, Mary Edsall (alias Banks), John Christeen and John Edsall, all of Bergen Co., New Jersey deed from Mary Gouverneur, widow, of New York City, Jacoba Gouverneur, spinster, Jasper & Maria Farmar, merchant and Nicholas Gouverneur, gentleman, line of John Smith and

Adrian Houghland. Signed Ary Degroot, John Christeen, John Edsall, Mary (x) Edsall, John (x) Day, William Day, Michael (x) Vreeland, Peter Degroot and Hendrick (x) Banta. Wit: Abraham Gouverneur, Isaac Day, George Tearman, James McKinley and Reynier van Giesen.

15 Aug 1753, Hendrick & Ariaentie vander Linde, yeoman, of New Barbadoes, Bergen Co., New Jersey to Jan Durie Sr. and Daniel Herrnig, both yeoman, of Sebralenburgh, Bergen Co., New Jersey, £425, 489 acres, corner to Jacob Demarest. Signed Henry vander Linde and Ariaentie vander Linde. Wit: Isaac DeBane, Robert Livesey and Jacobus Peck.

23 May 1753, Magdelen Valleau, widow, of Bergen Co., New Jersey to Johannis Pulisfelt, of same, £120, 200 acres, purchased in consideration of Peter Fauconnier corner to Isaac Bogart. Signed Magdaline Valleau. Wit: Theodore Valleau, David van Orden and Jacobus Peck.

9 Dec 1737, Mathew & Johanna Benson, of Bergen Co., New Jersey to Cornelius Brinkerhof, of Gemoeupagh, Bergen Co., New Jersey, £550, 500 acres, formerly sold to Samuel Edsall and William Lawrence...corner to John Edsall. Signed Mathew Benson and Johanna (x) Benson. Wit: Abraham Lodge, John van Horne and George Ryerse.

7 Nov 1737, Thomas & Francis Lawrence to Mathew Benson, of Harlem, New York City, £600, 550 acres, Samuel Edsall, in his will, 12 Jul 1676, gave to his two sons-in-law, Benjamin Stagg and William Lawrence...Overpeck Creek... said William Lawrence sold 12 Oct 1709 to Thomas Lawrence. Signed Thomas Lawrence and Francis Lawrence. Wit: Thomas Dekey, Joseph Morris and William Provoost.

2 May 1745, Roelif & Marretie van Houten, of Tappan, Orange Co., New York to Cornelius Brinkerhof, of Bergen Co., New Jersey, £50, 9.25 acres, corner to Hendrick vander Hoof and Zacharias Sickels. Signed Roelif van Houten and

Marretie (x) van Houten. Wit: Paulus vander
Vorst, Johannis Ferdon and George Ryerse.

30 Jun 1740, Michael Andries, farmer, of
Gemoinepa, Bergen Co., New Jersey to his friend
Cornelius Brinkerhof, for love and affection,
division line of Jacob Garret van Wagener and
Lawrence van Boskerk. Signed Michael Andries.
Wit: Cornelius (x) Garrabrants, Garrabrant
Garrabrants, Zacharias Sickels and Reynier van
Giesen.

1 May 1730, Michael Andries, farmer, of
Gemoinepa, Bergen Co., New Jersey to Cornelius
Brinkerhof, yeoman, of Bergen Co., New Jersey,
£120, division line of Jacob Garret van Wagener
and Lawrence van Boskerk. Signed Michael
Andries. Wit: Johannis Schuyler, Zacharias
Sickels and Reynier van Giesen.

21 Jul 1753, Jacoba Gouverneur, spinster, Jasper
& Maria Farmar, (late Maria Gouverneur),
merchant and Nicholas Gouverneur, gentleman, all
of New York City to Arya Degroot, Hendrick
Siebesse Banta, Peter Degroot, Michael Vreeland,
William Day John Day, Mary Edsall (alias Banks),
John Christeen and John Edsall, all of Bergen
Co., New Jersey, £1200, 800 acres, Samuel
Edsall, gentleman, late of Bergen Co., New
Jersey sold to Jacob Milbourne, who died
intestate and land went to his eldest brother
William Milbourne, of Boston, Massachusetts
...said William Milbourne also died intestate
and land went to his eldest son William
Milbourne, baker, of Boston, Massachusetts, who
sold 24 May 1715 to Abraham & Maria Gouverneur,
gentleman, of New York City, after the death of
Abraham Gouverneur, his wife Maria Gourverneur
named as executors of her will daughters the
said Jacoba Gourverneur, Elizabeth Gourverneur,
now deceased, the said Maria Gourverneur, wife
of Jasper Farmar, a nephew Nicholas Gourverneur
and a friend Paul Richards ...bounded by Hudson
River. Signed Jacoba Gouverneur, Jasper Farmar,
Maria Farmar and Nicholas Gouverneur. Wit:
Abraham Lodge, James Duane, Abraham N.

Gouverneur, Adolph Waldron and James Alexander.

26 Dec 1754, David & Antie van Orden, mason, of Hackensack, Bergen Co., New Jersey to David Demarest, of Old Bridge, Bergen Co., New Jersey, exchange of land south of Abraham Mourison, 19 acres. Signed David van Orden and Antie (x) van Orden. Wit: Theodore Valleau, David van Boskerk and Samuel Moore.

4 Jan 1755, Johannis Derick Banta and Derick Johannis Banta, both yeoman, of Bergen Co., New Jersey to John Roelif Bogart, yeoman, of same, £60, line of Jacob Banta, Hellabrant Lozier and Johannis Westervelt...except part sold to Benjamin Johannis Westervelt. Johannis Derick (x) Banta and Derick Johannis (x) Banta. Wit: Abraham Gouverneur, Joost Zabriskie and Reynier van Giesen.

29 Apr 1755, Jonathan Belcher power of attorney to Isaac Kingsland. Signed Jonathan Belcher.

1 Apr 1754, Abel Smith, gentleman, of Ceaeoeus, Bergen Co., New Jersey to his sons, Job and Daniel Smith, of same, £1000, by William Pinhorne, deceased and Edward Earle. Signed Abel (x) Smith. Wit: David Taylor, James Edsall and Reynier van Giesen.

Apr 1756, court orders appointment of Isaac Concklin as corner. J. Belcher.

24 Jul 1756, Isaac Kingsland, William Kingsland and Jacob Titsort £800 to King. Isaac Kingsland to be sheriff. Signed Isaac Kingsland, William Kingsland and Jacob Titsort. Wit: Abraham Gouverneur, Abraham Ackerman and Lowiers L. van Boskerk.

29 Jun 1754, David Davidie Ackerman, yeoman, of Sebratenburgh, Bergen Co., New Jersey to Isaac Concklin, carpenter, of Hackensack, Bergen Co., New Jersey, £463, corner to Abraham Ackerman... line of Johannis Demarest, Peter vander Burgh and Dr. John Patterson...land purchased from

Jacob Titsort. Signed David Ackerman. Wit: David L. Ackerman, James van Bueren and Jacobus Peck.

5 Aug 1754, Abel Smith, gentleman, of Ceaeoeus, Bergen Co., New Jersey to his son, Philip Smith, of same, £600, line of Martha Warman and William Earle...by land sold to other sons, Job and Daniel Smith. Signed Abel (x) Smith. Wit: Daniel Smith and Job Smith.

24 Mar 1752, Lucas Kiersted, of Dormuns, Bergen Co., New Jersey to Jacobus Peck, £50, bond to free the negro slave Hannebal. Signed Lucas Kiersted. Wit: Thomas Cartwright, James Cochran, Abraham van Boskerk, John (x) van Saen and F. Hackert.

25 Feb 1744, Jacobus Peck, shoemaker, of Schralenburg, Bergen Co., New Jersey to John Durie and Daniel Herrnig, both of Sobrisho, Bergen Co., New Jersey, £40, 0.5 acres, from Adolph Brower, deceased. Signed Jacobus Peck. Wit: David Demarest, Cornelius Wynkoop and Lawrence van Boskerk.

20 Sep 1755, Abraham Garretson, blacksmith, of Bergen Co., New Jersey to Hendrick van Allen £100, 50 acres... line of Arent Schuyler. Signed Abraham Garretson. Wit: George Ryerson Money paid to Henry & Mary Brackholst.

13 May 1760, Isaac Concklin, of New Barbadoes, Bergen Co., New Jersey to Gedion van Emburgh, of same, £146, corner to Abraham Ackerman and Johannis Demarest...line of George Tearman and Silvester Earle. Signed Isaac (x) Concklin. Wit: Guilliam Bertholf, Jacob Titsort and Lawrence L. van Boskerk.

1 May 1761, Luke Ryerson Jr., merchant, of Bergen Co., New Jersey to Jacob Mead, of same, £80, indentured for voyage. Signed Luke Ryerson Jr. Wit: David Brown, John Wright and Samuel Nowell.

22 May 1750, John Christeen, gentleman, of Bergen Co., New Jersey to his son-in-law, Abraham Montanye, as dowry for his daughter Sarah Christeen, 200 acres, patented 20 Feb 1668, between Hudson River and Overpeck Creek. Signed John Christeen. Wit: Samuel Moore.

10 Jan 1760, John Christeen, gentleman, of Bergen Co., New Jersey to his son-in-law, John Day, as dowry for his daughter Naomi, 250 acres, line of Peter Degroot and Smith. Signed John Christeen. Wit: Abraham Montanye, Jacob Banta and Samuel Moore.

24 Mar 1761, Samuel & Sarah Moore, of Hackensack, Bergen Co., New Jersey to Thomas Moore, of same, £50, 100 acres. Signed Samuel Moore and Sarah (x) Moore. Wit: James Moore and Samuel Moore.

28 Apr 1761, Samuel & Sarah Moore, of Hackensack, Bergen Co., New Jersey to Thomas Moore, of same, £130. Signed Samuel Moore Sr. and Sarah (x) Moore. Wit: John Moore, Derick (x) Vreeland and Samuel Moore.

19 Aug 1762, Abraham & Helena Avia Ackerman, of Orange Co., New York to John DeNoyillas, merchant, of same, £251.6, 80 acres, except lot sold to Jacob Banta...formerly in possession of Joseph Veale and William Earle ...line of John vander Hoof and Jacob Bogart. Signed Abraham Ackerman and Helena (x) Ackerman.

3 Oct 1762, George & Annake Tearman, shopkeeper, of Saddle River, Bergen Co., New Jersey to David Simmons, of Bergen Co., New Jersey, £100, house and lot, corner to Abraham Ackerman Jr., line of William Provoost...line of Cornelius and Hendrick van Dien. Signed George Tearman and Nancy Tearman. Wit: Jacob Titsort and William Earle Jr.

10 Sep 1762, Joseph & Mary Fitch, merchant, of Sebratenburgh, Bergen Co., New Jersey to Jacobus Peck, of same, £600, 220 acres, bounded by Peter

Sonmans...bought of Hendrick Hopper, who bought of Jesias Valleau who bought of John Burnet, William Burnet and Cortland Steinway. Signed Joseph Fitch and Mary (x) Fitch. Wit: Jacob Peck, David Peck, Michael Sously and Lawrence L. van Boskerk.

20 May 1764, Joseph & Mary Fitch, merchant, of Sebratenburgh, Bergen Co., New Jersey to Hayman Levy, merchant, of New York City, £1100, 220 acres...corner to Peter Dubois. Signed Joseph Fitch and Mary (x) Fitch. Wit: Jacob Titsort, Benjamin Holmes, John DeCrimsheir, Solomon McCohen and Isaac Moses.

5 Feb 1764, Peter & Susanna van Blerkum, yeoman, of Bergen Co., New Jersey to Garret van Dien, of same, £76, 25 acres. Signed Peter van Blerkum and Susanna (x) van Blerkum. Wit: William Wright and Fredmanus van Blerkum.

21 Apr 1750, Philip Earle, of Bergen Co., New Jersey to Uriah Hill, of Westchester Co., New York, £70, 42 acres, between the two orchards of Gynbert van Blerkum and Henry Major. Signed Philip Earle. Wit: Jacob Titsort, Anthony Hill and Joseph (x) Veal.

30 May 1764, Uriah Hill, of White Plains, Westchester Co., New York to William Hill, £600, furs, action of sheriff Hendrick van Seoik, of Albany, New York for £171 owed and £131.55 owed Thomas Shipboy, of same...his two brothers, William and Andrew Hill will pay two debts. Signed Uriah Hill. Wit: William Hooker Smith and William Buirtis.

8 Jul 1850, David John Ackerman, farmer, of Bergen Co., New Jersey to Stephen Baldwin, carpenter, of same, livestock. Signed David Ackerman. Wit: John Westervelt, Abram Westervelt and Roelif Westervelt.

1 Dec 1762, Claes Romine, yeoman, of Hackensack, Bergen Co., New Jersey to John Claes Romine, goldsmith, of same, £700, 40 acres...line of

Derrick Terhune and David Provoost...second parcel of 20 acres...line of Abraham Westervelt, Abram Westervelt, Niasey Kip and Jores van Giesen. Signed Claes Romine. Wit: John Day Jr., Jacob Titsort and Thubias Rickman.

2 Sep 1765, Johannes Demarest, Ruloph Westervelt appointed by Samuel Provoost, George Tearman, Peter van Orden and John J. Banta to receive and dispose of estates. Signed Johannis Demarest and Roelif Westervelt. Wit: Hendrick Kuyper and John Berry. Recorded at the request of Johannis Demeray.

22 May 1764, Ebenezer Foster and Catharine Loofbourrow, of Woodbridge, Middlesex Co., New Jersey to Cornelius Brinkerhof, of same, £50.1, bounded by John Van Horne and Michael Cornelius Vreeland. Signed Ebenezer Foster and Catharine Loofbourrow. Wit: Thomas Juglis, William Pike and Thomas Gach. Recorded at the request of Hartman Brinkerhof.

1 May 1759, Antelbee and Elizabeth Earle, of Bergen Co., New Jersey to Hendrick Cornelius Brinkerhof, of same, £120, 26.25 acres, adjoining Daniel Smith, Job Smith and Philip Earle. Signed Antelbee Earle and Eliza Earle. Wit: John Edsall, James McKinley and Reynier N. Giese.

2 Sep 1765, William Kingsland, John Schuyler and William Provoost bound to king for £800. William Kingsland to be sheriff. Signed William Kingsland, John Schuyler and William Provoost. Wit: Isaac Brown and Reynier van Giesen.

2 Apr 1764, Walter Parcel, yeoman, of Hackensack, Bergen Co., New Jersey to Carrol Debane, of same, £60, 30 acres, line of Jacob Demarest. Signed Walter (x) Parcel. Wit: Laurens L. van Boskerk, Pieter Y. Demarest and Johannis Demarest.

7 Mar 1757, Johannis van Horne, yeoman, of Stotterdam, Bergen Co., New Jersey to Cornelius

van Emburgh, of same, £5, bounded by Garret Garretson van Wagener. Signed Johannis (x) van Horne. Wit: Marrilys (x) van Horne, Lybetje (x) van Horne, Lybetje (x) Lutkins and Reynier van Giesen.

6 Jun 1764, Derick van Horne, yeoman, of Bergen Co., New Jersey to Jacobus Brinkerhof, yeoman, of same, £35, line of Silvester Earle, David Banta and Hendrick Banta. Signed Derick van Horne. Wit: Guilliam Bertholf and Reynier van Giesen.

5 Jun 1759, Johannes Garretson, yeoman, of Staten Island, New York to Andres Hennion, carpenter, of Bergen Co., New Jersey, £200, 100 acres, purchased by Abraham Garretson, (son of said Johannes Garretson) from George Dooremus, of Bergen Co., New Jersey 27 Jun 1753...line of Benjamin Spear. Signed Johannes (x) Garretson. Wit: Isaac Kingsland, Johannis Cadmus and Reynier N. Giese.

5 Oct 1762, Hartman Cadmus, Isaac Cadmus and Abraham Cadmus, (the present heirs of Thomas F. Cadmus, late of Bergen Co., New Jersey) of Bergen Co., New Jersey to Johannis Cadmus, (present heir of Anderies F. Cadmus, late of same), of same, £0.25, purchased by Thomas F. Cadmus and Anderies F. Cadmus from Richard Townly. Signed Hartman Cadmus, Isaac (x) Cadmus and Abram (x) Cadmus. Wit: George Vreeland, Helmegh I. van Houten and Reynier N. Giese.

5 Jun 1752, Stephen Bourdett Sr., goldsmith, of New York, now in Bergen Co., New Jersey to Abraham Valleau and Stephen Bourdett Jr., of Bergen Co., New Jersey, £500, land in Orange Co., New York...bounded by Johannes Minaer, Herman Dowsen and Tunis Dowsen...to include that not sold by Capt. John Hutchins Signed Stephen Bourdett. Wit: Theodore Hallen, Jonathan Rose and Lourens L. van Boskerk.

9 Jul 1765, Samuel Moore, yeoman, of New Barbadoes, Bergen Co., New Jersey to David

Demarest, of same, £590, 11.75 acres, bounded by Thomas Moore...second parcel of 3.75 acres...line of John Moore...third parcel of 3 acres...fourth parcel of 19.25 acres bounded by Lawrence van Horne and Michael Vreeland. Signed Samuel (x) Moore. Wit: Thomas Moore, John Day and Lourens L. van Boskerk.

3 Sep 1764, Lambert & Elizabeth Laroe, of Bergen Co., New Jersey to Thomas Boggs, of same, £530, 100 acres, purchased by said Laroe from William & Jane van Allen and David & Catharine Hennion 30 Sep 1758...corner to Adolpus Shaorts. Signed Lambert (x) Laroe and Elizabeth (x) Laroe. Wit: Joseph Watson, Johannes Ester(lin) and George Ryerse.

18 Jul 1763, Peter Garretse van Wagener, yeoman, of Shotterdam, Bergen Co., New Jersey to his son Johannis van Wagener, love and affection, three parcels. Signed Peter Garretse (x) van Wagener. Wit: John Bardan, John D. Bardan and Reynier N. Giese.

18 Jul 1763, Peter Garretse van Wagener, yeoman, of Shotterdam, Bergen Co., New Jersey to his son Garret van Wagener, love and affection, three parcels...corner to Daniel Romine...line of Reynier Bardan. Signed Peter Garretse (x) van Wagener. Wit: John Bardan, John D. Bardan and Reynier N. Giese.

21 Mar 1767, Samuel Benson & Catharine Lydecker, merchant, of Hackensack, Bergen Co., New Jersey to John Benson, farmer, of Bergen Co., New Jersey, £1080, 125 acres, line of Samuel Edsall, Jacob Covashausen and Garret Lydecker, the elder...second parcel of 15 acres, bounded by Garret Lydecker, the younger...line of Samuel Moore and Michael Vreeland. Signed Samuel B. Lydecker and Catharine Lydecker. Wit: Jacob Titsort, Joost Earle and Glybert Ackerman.

13 Oct 1765, Isaac & Johanna Kingsland, of Bergen Co., New Jersey to Daniel Isaac Brown, of same, £400, corner to Evert Ryckman. Signed

Isaac Kingsland and Johanna Kingsland. Wit: William Provoost and Effe Provoost.

1 Jun 1763, Tennes Hennion, yeoman, of Saddle River, Bergen Co., New Jersey to Edo Marselius, yeoman, of same, 19.35 acres, adjoining John Bardan and John Hennion. Signed Tunis (x) Hennion. Wit: David Hennion and Johannis Hennion.

Dec 1764, Helmegh & Janetye Vreeland to Edo Marselius.

Page 464...has name Alexander May.

Page 465...Lorinese & Hannah Winner to Edo Marvelses...conveyed by George Hilcocks and Andrew & Catharine Johnston to Jacob & Helena Sip 16 Mar 1735.

2 Mar 1769, John Bardan, of Bergen Co., New Jersey, (eldest heir at law to Albert Bardan to Edo Marvelses, £650, 176 acres, whereas John Bardan, father of Albert Bardan and grandfather of said John Bardan ...John Bardan and Jacob Bardan, sons of Albert Bardan... second parcel of 211 acres...third parcel of 4.18 acres...fourth parcel of 15 acres. Signed John Bardan. Wit: Timothy Lewis, Elee van Cobleiune and George Ryerse.

9 Apr 1728, Peter Fauconnier, of Bergen Co., New Jersey to Peter Johnse van Blerkum, of same, £60, 315 acres, part of 395 acres...granted Garret van Dun...John van Emburgh. Signed Peter Fauconnier. Wit: James David, John (x) Thompson, John Tearman, John van Emburgh and John Fell.

19 Dec 1769, John van Blerkum, yeoman, of Bergen Co., New Jersey to Harremanus van Blerkum and Peter van Blerkum, £500, concerning estate of Peter Jan van Blerkum, deceased. Signed Jan (x) van Blerkum. Wit: Roelif Westervelt, Albert (x) Zabriskie and John Fell.

Peter & Ann van Blerkum, yeoman, of Bergen Co.,

New Jersey to Haramanus van Blerkum. Signed Peter (x) van Blerkum and Ann van Blerkum. Wit: Johannes D. Ackerman and Hub. Cairns.

Jan Dooremus to Samuel van Saen. Signed Cornelius Dooremus. Wit: David Hennion, Hendrick Dooremus and George Ryerse.

20 Sep 1766, Cornelius Dooremus, of Bergen Co., New Jersey to David Hennion, of same, £115.85.

20 Aug 1768, Michael Vreeland, of Bergen Co., New Jersey to Johanna van Winkle, (daughter of Cornelius Michaelse Vreeland, division of land... between John Antje vander Bilt and Paul Dowese...purchased by said Cornelius Michaelse Vreeland 17 Mar 1696 from William Douglas...agreed upon Robert Ogden, Ephriam Tenill and Jonathan Hampton, of Elizabethtown to decide between them. Signed Johanna (x) van Winkle and Michael (x) Vreeland. Wit: Jonathan Hampton and Ephraim Tenill.

26 May 1748, Johannis Stagg, yeoman, of Saddle River, Bergen Co., New Jersey to Peter van Zile, of same, £61, line of Abraham Vreeland. Signed Johannis (x) Stagg. Wit: Abraham Vreeland and Theodore Valleau.

175x, George Ryerse, of Bergen Co., New Jersey to Peter van Lite, of same, adjoining Robert Hunter. Signed George Ryerse. Wit: Robert Romine, John Bardan and Peter Zabriskie.

23 Jan 1720, Catharine Macklane and her first and third sons, William and Solomon Macklane, all of New Barbadoes, Bergen Co., New Jersey to Gisbert van Blerkum, of same, £140, 200 acres, adjoining Johannis Johnston. Signed Catharine (x) Macklane, William Macklane and Solomon (x) Macklane. Wit: Henry Mayer, Paulus vander Beck and Peter van Winkle.

5 Nov 1733, George Leslie, gentleman, of Perth Amboy, Middlesex Co., New Jersey to Matire Demott, blacksmith, of Bergen Co., New Jersey,

£250, 330 acres, patented 10 Dec 1702 by Michael Hawden, of New York City, who sold 17 Jul 1706 to John Johnston and George Willock, both of New Jersey, deceased and John Johnston sold his interest to George Willock on 6 Apr 1707 ...adjoining Maj. John Berry and James Duncan. Signed George Leslie. Wit: William Kingsland, Isaac Kingsland and William Provoost.

21 May 1746, Johannis Waldron, of Hackensack, Bergen Co., New Jersey to Mattis Demoot, of Bergen, Bergen Co., New Jersey, £180, adjoining Maj. John Berry, Hendrick Banta Jr., (who purchased of Walter Briggs) and James Duncan. Signed Johannes Waldron. Wit: Samuel Moore, Jacob (x) Brower and Garret Hawlenbeck.

3 Mar 1770, Peter Post, miller, of Pumpton, Bergen Co., New Jersey to Gorlyme Dooremus, yeoman, of Paquanack, Bergen Co., New Jersey, £100, 20 acres, Saddle River Twp. Signed Peter Post. Wit: John Thomas, Philip Price and George Ryerse.

7 May 1770, Abraham & Polly Lozier, gentleman, Hackensack, of Bergen Co., New Jersey to Jacob Lozier, of same, £103, 26.92 acres, corner to Johannes Bogart...second parcel of 2 acres... corner to Guoline Bogart. Signed Abram Lozier and Mary Lozier. Wit: Jacobus van Boskerk, Par. Parmylor and Lawrence L. van Boskerk.

11 Jun 1770, John F. Ryerson, of Saddle River, Bergen Co., New Jersey to Garrabrant Garretson, Garret Garretson, Jury Westervelt and John Westervelt, all of same, an agreement on the division line between their lands. Wit: Reynier N. Giese.

8 Dec 1769, Michael Moore, John Moore and Thomas Moore, farmers of Bergen Co., New Jersey to Cristopher Benson, of New York City, £0.25, 110 acres. Signed Michael Moore, John Moore and Thomas Moore. Wit: Abraham Montanye, Abraham Ferdon and John Stevens.

1 May 1769, Robert & Mary Earle, of the english neighborhood, Hackensack, Bergen Co., New Jersey to Garret Hawlenbeck, of same, £500, 76 acres...line of John Day. Signed Robert Earle and Mary Earle. Wit: Robert Hill, John Day and Peter Zabriskie.

10 Apr 1756, Johannes Pulisfelt, of Campgaw, Bergen Co., New Jersey to his sons Jacobus Pulisfelt and Christian Pulisfelt, £120, 200 acres, purchased from Magdalena Valleau. Signed Johannes Pulisfelt. Wit: Jacob (x) Storm and John Fell..

18 Sep 1770, John van Blerkum, of Acquacknonk, Bergen Co., New Jersey to Michael Vreeland, of Bergen Twp., Bergen Co., New Jersey, £70, Hackensack River and Bergen Twp. Signed John (x) van Blerkum. Wit: Reynier van Giesen, Guilliam Bertholf and Henry Godwin.

4 Jan 1771, Catherine Fisher, (widow of Peter Fisher, yeoman, deceased), of Bergen Co., New Jersey power of attorney to her brother-in-law, Weynett van Gelder, of Orange Co., New York. Signed Catherine (x) Fisher. Wit: John Griffith, James van Gelder and John Fell.

1 Jun 1770, David & Elizabeth Simmons, of New Barbadoes, Bergen Co., New Jersey to Peter van Zile, of Saddle River, Bergen Co., New Jersey, £80, 25 acres. Signed David Simmons and Elizabeth Simmons. Wit: Peter Zabriskie and Abraham Ackerman.

Chapter 4

Bergen County
Courthouse
Deed Records
Volume D

Recorded
in
1771-1787

30 Jul 1765, Jacob & Elizabeth Roome, gentleman, of New Barbadoes, Bergen Co., New Jersey to Daniel Isaac Brown, of same, £314, 12 acres, corner to John Bardan and William Provoost... second parcel...corner to David Bardan. Signed Jacob Roome and Elizabeth Roome. Wit: Abraham van Boskerk, Rowland Hill and Lawrence van Boskerk.

4 Aug 1770, Jacob & Elizabeth Roome, gentleman, of New Barbadoes, Bergen Co., New Jersey to Daniel Isaac Brown, of same, £76.5, 5 acres. Signed Jacob Roome and Elizabeth Roome. Wit: Rowland Hill, Htye van Boskerk and Lawrence van Boskerk.

20 Apr 1771, Garret & Hannah Hawlenbeck, of Hackensack, Bergen Co., New Jersey to Roelif Benjamin Westervelt, of same, £450, 63 acres, bounded by Jacobus Cornelius Bogart, John Day and Robert Earle. Signed Garret Hawlenbeck and Hannah Hawlenbeck. Wit: Mary Earle, Guilliam Bertholf and Reynier van Giesen.

18 Jun 1771, Christoyaum Pulisfelt and Jacobus Pulisfelt, of Bergen Co., New Jersey, make division of land willed to them by their father Joannis Pulisfelt 16 May 1754 100 acres...line of Isaac Bogart, Harmana Nix and Barent van Horne. Signed Christian Pulisfelt and Jacobus Pulisfelt. Wit: Isaac Bogart, Guilliam Bertholf

and Reynier van Giesen.

1 Jul 1771, Johannis Vreeland, of Chamumapow, Bergen Co., New Jersey to Michael Vreeland, of Stoney Point, Bergen Co., New Jersey, land trade, formerly belonging to Derick Claesen, deceased...also lot deeded 26 Jun 1701 Michael Vreeland to Johannis Vreeland. Signed Johannis Vreeland. Wit: David Day, John Day and Reynier van Giesen.

1 Jul 1771, Michael Vreeland, of Stoney Point, Bergen Co., New Jersey to Johannis Vreeland, of Chamumapow, Bergen Co., New Jersey, land trade. Signed Michael (x) Vreeland. Wit: David Day, John Day and Reynier van Giesen.

2 Jul 1771, Johannis Vreeland, of Chamumapow, Bergen Co., New Jersey to John Vreeland, of Stoney Point, Bergen Co., New Jersey, £30, 5 acres, bounded by Claes Vreeland, George Vreeland, John van Horne and App Post. Signed Johannis Vreeland. Wit: David Day, John Day and Reynier van Giesen.

21 Mar 1750, Rev. William Skinner, (executor of last will of George Willock), George Leslie and Andrew Johnston to Roeloff Romine, son of John Romine, yeoman, of Bergen Co., New Jersey, £190, 217 acres... map drawn by Alexander McDowell ...corner to lot formerly owned by Johannis and Jacobus Ackerman. Signed William Skinner, George Leslie and Andrew Johnston.

Nov 17xx, Jacobus Post and Garret Garretson, of Saddle River, Bergen Co., New Jersey £800 bond, said Jacobus Post to be sheriff. Signed Jacobus Post and Garret Garretson. Wit: James van Bueren, Henry Godwin and Peter Zabriskie.

2 May 1770, Abraham & Polly Lozier to Abraham Maby, carpenter, of Orange Co., New York, £61, purchased of Lucas Lozier... corner to Cornelius van Aerlandt. Signed Abraham Lozier. Wit: Cornelius van Aerlandt and Reynier van Giesen.

31 Dec 1770, Jacobus Brinkerhof, Hendrick Brinkerhof, Seba Brinkerhof, Hendrick George Brinkerhof, Margritye Brinkerhof, Jacob Outwater, Abraham Allen, Enoch & Catharine Vreeland, George & Ann Campbell and John Richards, all of Bergen Co., New Jersey and John Morin Scott, attorney of New York City to Hendrick Kip, Peter Kip, Isaac Kip, Peter Zabriskie, Hendrick van Voorhees, Isaac van Voorhees, Nicouse van Voorhees, Jacob van Voorhees, Antie Brinkerhof, wife of Jacob Brinkerhof, Sarah Demarest, wife of David Demarest, Elizabeth Kip, wife of John Kip, Margretye Cooper, wife of Hendrick Cooper, Catharine Brinkerhof, wife of Jacobus Brinkerhof, Albert Terhune, Necaus Terhune, Jacob Terhune, Johannis Terhune, Ann Zabriskie, wife of Joost Zabriskie, Wyntie Westervelt, wife of Casparus Westervelt, Elizabeth van Reypen, wife of Daniel van Reypen, Gerettie Parrlesse, wife of John Parrlesse, Lawrence Ackerman, Jacobus H. Brinkerhof, Nicholas H. Brinkerhof, George H. Brinkerhof, Hendrick H. Brinkerhof, of Antie H. Brinkerhof, all of Bergen Co., New Jersey, £5, 5.5 acres, 30 acres, 34 acres, and 8.75 acres. Signed Jacobus (x) Brinkerhof, Hendrick (x) Brinkerhof, Seba Brinkerhof, Hannah Campbell, Margrityе (x) Brinkerhof, George Campbell, Abraham Allen, Enoch Vreeland, Catharine (x) Vreeland, John Morin Scott, John Richard and Jacob (x) Outwater. Wit: Gill Burgan, William Sarrell and Reynier van Giesen.

8 Jan 1772, George & Anna Vreeland, gentleman, of Bergen Precinct Bergen Co., New Jersey to Edo Marselius, of Saddle River, Bergen Co., New Jersey, £700, 127 acres. Signed George Vreeland and Anna (x) Vreeland. Wit: Guilliam Bertholf, Jacob (x) van Wagener and Peter Zabriskie.

21 May 1771, Jacob Vreeland, of North River, Bergen Co., New Jersey to Derick Vreeland, of english neighborhood, of Bergen Co., New Jersey, £300, 50 acres. Signed Jacob (x) Vreeland. Wit: Naomi Day, John Day and Peter Zabriskie.

27 Feb 1771, John W. Day, of North River, Bergen Co., New Jersey to Jacob Vreeland, of same, £140, patent of Samuel Edsall...line of William W. Day. Signed John W. Day. Wit: David Day, John Day and Peter Zabriskie.

2 Jan 1772, William W. Day, cooper, of New York City to Jacob Vreeland, of North River, Bergen Co., New Jersey, £282, 47 acres...line of John W. Day. Signed William Ancha (x) Day. Wit: Mary Demarest, John Day and Peter Zabriskie.

1 Oct 1772, William & Mary Lee, carpenter, of Hackensack, Bergen Co., New Jersey to William Beckman, of New York City, £212, 28 acres, corner to Cornelius van Vorst. Signed William Lee and Mary Lee. Wit: Samuel Moore, John W. Day and Lawrence van Boskerk.

4 Mar 1765, Robert Finn, of Gofin, Orange Co., New York to Elizabeth Finn, widow of Soloman Finn, of Bergen Co., New Jersey, £0.25, held by said Soloman Finn, by deeds from Stephen Camp, 14 Jun 1762 and from Ezekiel Harris, 15 Aug 1764. Signed Robert Finn. Wit: Anthony Brodrick, John Bardan and George Ryerson.

16 Nov 1772, Stephen & Nelly Bourdett, of Hackensach, Bergen Co., New Jersey to Jacob Quackinbush, of same, £125, 8 acres, line of Abraham Lydecker and the widow Lea Demarest. Signed Stephen Bourdett and Elenor Bourdett.

18 Nov 1720, Joseph Healy, of Middlesex Co., New Jersey, Mercy Benthall, widow, of Greece Church, London, England and Richard Ashfield, grandson and heir of Patience Ashfield to John Bardan, of Hackensack, Bergen Co., New Jersey, £72.5, 362 acres...Thomas Hart in his will 19 Dec 1704 gave to his sister Patience and the said Mercy Benthall, land and named said Joseph Healy, executor...appointed power of attorney to Rip van Dam, merchant, of New York City and John Rodman, gentleman, of Long Island...corner to David Hennion. Signed Joseph Healy, Mercy Benthall and Richard Ashfield. Wit: Tennes van

Woerdt, John Smith, John Chambers and David Provoost.

11 May 1738, John Bardan, of Hackensack, Bergen Co., New Jersey to his son, Albert Bardan, £200. Signed Jan Bardan. Wit: Jacobus Bertholf and Daniel Demarest.

10 Sep 1756, Aaeto Degroot, of Hackensack, Bergen Co., New Jersey to Jacob Demott, of same, £7.6, 2 acres, sold by Samuel Moore to Joseph Forbie, 1 Sep 1752 who sold 2 Mar 1754 to Degroot heirs... said Aates Degroot now sells. Signed Aaeto Degroot. Wit: Theodore Valleau, Stephen Bourdett and Samuel Moore.

29 Jul 1755, Samuel Moore Sr., Michael Moore and John Moore, all of Bergen Co., New Jersey to Mathias Demott, of Bergen, Bergen Co., New Jersey, £36, 10 acres, corner to Maj. John Berry, Michael Moore and Abraham Day. Signed Samuel Moore, Michael Moore and John Moore. Wit: Samuel Moore and Isack Delemater.

20 Apr 1756, Michael Demott, Hendrick Demott and Jorie Demott, executors of will of Mathias Demott, all of Bergen Co., New Jersey to Jacob Demott, £0.25. Signed Michael Demott, Hendrick Demott and Jorie Demott. Wit: Abraham Sickels, Joseph van Winkle and Peter Zabriskie.

22 Jun 1763, Samuel Moore Sr. and John Moore, both yeoman, of Hackensack, Bergen Co., New Jersey to Jacob Demott, of same, £27, 5.5 acres. Signed Samuel Moore and John Moore. Wit: Thomas Moore, John (x) Oster, Samuel Moore, John Moore and Peter Zabriskie.

9 May 1772, John & Maricha Bardan and Hendrick Bardan, of New Barbadoes, Bergen Co., New Jersey to Cornelius Cooper, of same, £380, line of Paulus vander Beck and Isaac vander Beck...one third of land of said John Bardan. Signed John Bardan, Maricha (x) Bardan and Hendrick Bardan. Wit: Isaac vander Beck, William Sarrell and Peter Zabriskie.

3 Sep 1772, Jacob & Elizabeth Roome, of Bergen Co., New Jersey to Hendrick Redner, of Paramus, Bergen Co., New Jersey, £1, 2.5 acres...corner to John Fisher and Cornelius Lozier. Signed Jacob Roome and Elizabeth Roome. Wit: Willimina Maria Wels, Elizabeth (x) Demsey and Lawrens van Boskerk.

2 Apr 1756, Peter Zabriskie, merchant, of New Barbadoes, Bergen Co., New Jersey to John Chapple, of same, £34, corner to William Earle. Signed Peter Zabriskie. Wit: John (x) Bardan, Guilliam Bertholf and Jacob Titsort.

20 Apr 1772, William & Annice Ryerse, Poequanack, Saddle River, Bergen Co., New Jersey to Martin Ryerse, of Waggan, Saddle River, Bergen Co., New Jersey, £80, 40 acres...between Garrabrant van Houten and Jacobus Jacobusse. Signed William (x) Ryerse and Annice (x) Ryerse. Wit: Anna Ryerse, Martin Ryerse Jr. and George Ryerse.

12 May 1772, Cornelius & Jane Lozier, of Franklin Precinct, Bergen Co., New Jersey to John Bardan, of New Barbadoes Precinct, Bergen Co., New Jersey, £550, 137 acres, purchased by John van Voorhees and William van Voorhees, deceased from John Hamilton, Andrew Johnston and John Burnet, 2 Apr 1745...willed, 1 Jan 1757, by said John van Voorhees together with the wives of the said Garret Ackerman, Peter Post, John Laroe and David Ackerman to his son Albe van Voorhees. Signed Cornelius Lozier and Jannetie (x) Lozier. Wit: Cornelius Cooper, William Sarrell and Peter Zabriskie.

12 Jun 1774, Nehemiah Howell, of Hunterdon Co., New Jersey to Mary Shaw, of New York City, £86, purchased 25 Apr 1765 from Peter Zabriskie... corner to Hendrick Bush. Signed Nehemiah Howell. Wit: Henry Godwin and Peter Zabriskie.

14 Jan 1773, David & Catharine vander Pool, of Newark, Essex Co., New Jersey to James van Emburgh, of New Barbadoes, Bergen Co., New

Jersey, £25.2, 8 acres...line of Samuel Davis. Signed David vander Pool and Catharine (x) vander Pool. Wit: James Murphy, Gideon Stevens and Reynier van Giesen.

27 Jun 1772, Jacob & Johanna Billue, of Franklin Twp., Bergen Co., New Jersey to Abraham van Gelder, of same, £185.5, 92.75 acres...corner to William Stagg. Signed Jacob Billue and Johanna (x) Billue. Wit: James Christie, John van Saen and John Fell.

1 Nov 1773, Jacobus & Hannah Laroe, of Yapock, Pancklen Twp., Bergen Co., New Jersey to Lambertas Jenkins, of same, £303, 101.5 acres ...corner to Samuel Bertholf. Signed Jacobus S. Laroe and Hannah (x) Laroe. Wit: Jacobus Kock, Samuel Carols and Peter Zabriskie.

10 Nov 1774, John Outwater, William Provoost and Derick Lozier post £800 bond. John Outwater to be sheriff. Signed William Provoost and Derick Lozier. Wit: Peter Earle, Jacob vander Beck and Peter Zabriskie.

12 Dec 1774, Guilliam & Susannah Demarest, yeoman Saddle River Precinct, Bergen Co., New Jersey to John Springer, yeoman, of same, £300, 26 acres...corner of large tract conveyed to John Barberie, Peter Fauconnier and Andrew Fresnean. Signed Guilliam Demarest and Susannah (x) Demarest. Wit: William Provoost, Isaac Concklin and John Fell.

15 Nov 1752, Daniel Haring, yeoman, of Schralenburgh, Bergen Co., New Jersey to John Durie, yeoman, of same, his share in joint purchase from Andrew Earle, 489 acres, 15 Aug 1753...line of Peter Zabriskie. Signed Daniel Haring. Wit: Robert Livesey, Rachel (x) Livesay and Lourens L. van Boskerk.

1 May 1773, John & Martiye Spear, shoemaker, of Bergen Co., New Jersey to Joost Demarest, corrier, of same, £68, 15 acres...east side of Hackensack River...line of John J. van Boskerk.

Signed John Spear and Maria (x) Spear. Wit:
Johanny Demarest, Maryrite (x) Kip and Lourens
L. van Boskerk.

14 Jun 1775, Jacob Roome, of New Barbadoes,
Bergen Co., New Jersey to John Terhune and
Gabriel van Norden, both of same, £5, 24 acres,
by road running from New Barbadoes to Orange
Town... line of William Provoost, Joost
Zabriskie and David Bardan...van Emburgh's lot.
Signed Jacob Roome. Wit: William Provoost,
Rowland Hill and Peter Zabriskie.

31 Jan 1776, John Terhune and Gabriel van
Norden, both of New Barbadoes, Bergen Co., New
Jersey to Nicholas Bogart, merchant, of New York
City, £643, 24 acres...purchased of Jacob Roome,
14 Jun 1775. Signed John Terhune and Gabriel van
Norden. Wit: Archibald Campbell, Jacob vander
Beck and Peter Zabriskie.

5 Feb 1776, William Sandford van Emburgh, of New
Barbadoes, Bergen Co., New Jersey to Nicholas
Bogart, merchant, of New York City, £70, corner
to Rowland Hill...purchased of Jacob Roome.
Signed William S. van Emburgh. Wit: S. Heyden,
Gilbert van Emburgh and Peter Zabriskie.

4 Mar 1776, James M. & Eva Collogh, of weaver,
of New Barbadoes Precinct, Bergen Co., New
Jersey to Nicholas Bogart, merchant, of New York
City, £90, corner to Dr. William Sandford van
Emburgh and Daniel Jessup. Signed James M.
Collogh and Eva Collogh. Wit: Gilbert van
Emburgh, Alexander Crookshank and Peter
Zabriskie.

24 Nov 1776, John Bardan, of Wekeke, Bergen Co.,
New Jersey, oldest son and heir of Albert
Bardan, deceased to Jacob Bardan, of same,
brother of said John Bardan, land trade, 362
acres ...corner to David Hennion. Signed John
Bardan. Wit: Ryer Ryerson, Casparus Schuyler and
George Ryerse.

10 Jun 1779, Henderius Kuyper, James Bourd and

Garnet Lydecker, commissioners, of Bergen Co., New Jersey to Isaac Nicoll, yeoman, of Orange Co., New York, £4734, whereas Albert Zabriskie joined the British Army 7 Dec 1776, his land was taken and sold to highest bidder...line of Joost Zabriskie. Signed Henderius Kuyper, James Bourd and Garnet Lydecker. Wit: Hendrick Bardan, James van Houten and Petrus Haring.

18 Jan 1780, Jacob van Winkle, of Bergen Precinct, Bergen Co., New Jersey to Margaret van Winkle, daughter of Abraham van Winkle, son of said Jacob van Winkle and Catharine Baldwin, £0.5 and love and affection...line of George Demott, Garret van Reypen and Daniel van Winkle. Signed Jacob van Winkle. Wit: Isaac van Giesen, Peter Wilson and Joost Beam.

15 Jan 1781, Andrew W. & Mary Hopper, yeoman, of Ramapo, Bergen Co., New Jersey to Garret W. Hopper, yeoman, of same, £200, 139 acres...line of Jacobus Bogart...one fourth of tract formerly belonging to Hendrick Laroe, deceased...except land sold by Johannes Laroe to Isaac Bogart who sold to John van Allen 8 Dec 1769...agreement 14 Jan 1781 between Andrew Hopper and Garret W. Hopper. Signed Andrew W. Hopper and Mary (x) Hopper. Wit: Henry Wammamaker, Abraham Westervelt and Roelif Westervelt.

25 Jul 1773, Mary Lien, John Lien, (executor of estate of Abraham Lien, deceased) and Daniel Lien, ( executor of estate of Conrad Lien, deceased), all of Wamayack, Bergen Co., New Jersey to Anthony Beam, of same, surveyed for Joseph Kerbride...mistake in purchase of 639 acres by Richard Ashfield, deceased, of New York City. Signed Mary (x) Lien, John Lien and Daniel (x) Lien. Wit: John Meyer, Thomas Briggs and George Ryerse.

5 May 1773, Wilhelm Ferdon, farmer, of Orange Co., New York to John Nagel, of same, £28, 5 acres. Signed Wilhelm Ferdon. Wit: Roelif (x) van Houten, John Haring and John Perry.

21 Nov 1757, Turnis & Annetye van Houten, of
Orange Town Twp., Orange Co., New York to John
Nagel, of same, £125, 70 acres...line of Abraham
Abr. Haring. Signed Turnis van Houten and
Annetye (x) van Houten. Wit: Anna (x) Nagel and
Abraham Haring of Orange Co., New York.

29 Oct 1765, William Nagel, yeoman, of Orange
Town Twp., Orange Co., New York to John Nagel,
of same, said William and John were willed by
their father Barent Nagel...to be divided after
decease of their mother Sarah Nagel...line of
Henry Ludlow, Resolurt Nagel, William Ferdon and
John Ferdon. Signed William Nagel. Wit: Abraham
Haring.

17 Jun 1767, Conrad & Maritye Wammamaker,
yeoman, of Bergen Co., New Jersey to Peter
Wammamaker, of same, £225, 78 acres...corner to
Christian Wammamaker. Signed Conrad (x)
Wammamaker and Maritye (x) Wammamaker. Wit:
William Isaac, Thomas Boggs, Dederick
Wammamaker, Peddter Wammamaker and Lawrence L.
van Boskerk.

26 Feb 1753, Conrad Wammamaker, yeoman, of
Bergen Co., New Jersey to Peter Wammamaker,
yeoman, of same, line of Ludwig Wammamaker.
Signed Conrad (x) Wammamaker. Wit: Jonathan
Rose, Timothy Rose and Lawrence L. van Boskerk.

9 Apr 1784, Daniel Kenney, of Bergen Co., New
Jersey to Jacob Bamper, of New York City, £1000,
line of Peter Lutkins, John Bardan and John van
Giesen. Signed Daniel Kenny. Wit: John Johnston
and John Fleming.

12 Feb 1782, Moses & Hannah Carpenter, yeoman,
of Bergen Co., New Jersey to Henry Allison, of
Orange Co., New York, £650, 25 and 30 acres.
Signed Moses Carpenter and Hannah (x) Carpenter.
Wit: Peter Haring.

8 Apr 1779, Henderius Kuyper and James Bourd,
commissioners, of Bergen Co., New Jersey to John
W. Hopper, £2120.6, lands of Christian

Zabriskie, who joined the army of the King...
bounded by Thomas Boggs, Conrad Laroe and
William ???. Signed Henderius Kuyper and James
Bourd. Wit: Peter van Allen.

27 Apr 1781, John W. Hopper, of Bergen Co., New
Jersey to John Rutan, £315. Signed John W.
Hopper. Wit: John Cleves Seymmes.

1 Apr 1781, Hendrick & Maria Zabriskie, yeoman,
of New Barbadoes Precinit, Bergen Co., New
Jersey to Andries Zabriskie, yeoman, of same,
£12, line of David Terhune. Signed Hendrick
Zabriskie and Maria (x) Zabriskie. Wit: David
Terhune, Christian Zabriskie and Roelif
Westervelt.

1 May 1784, John Romine, of Franklin, Bergen
Co., New Jersey to Francis Romine, of same, £28,
101 acres. Signed Jan Romine. Wit: Albert van
Zile, Rachel van Zile and Theodore van Kalle.

3 Jun 1777, Isaac van Giesen, of New Barbadoes
Precinct, Bergen Co., New Jersey to Rev. Derick
Romine, of same, £500, 33 acres...corner to the
widow Baldwin and John Outwater. Signed Isaac
van Giesen. Wit: James Chapple, Peter Wilson and
John Benson.

Oct 1784, Sheriff of Bergen Co., New Jersey to
seize goods of William Dobbs, deceased to pay
John Ackerman.

Oct 1784, Sheriff of Bergen Co., New Jersey to
seize goods of Nicholas Lozier to pay Ann
Baldwin.

3 Jun 1774, Anthony Hill, of Fredericksburgh,
Dutchess Co. New York, heir of Uriah Hill owes
Stephen Case, £300. Signed Anthony Hill. Wit:
Aybijah Lutkins, Zephaniah Waolsey, of New York,
Gilbert Livingston and Benjanin Eley.

22 Nov 1774, Edmund William & Mary Kingsland, of
Bergen Co., New Jersey to William Richards, of
Burlington Co., New Jersey, £1458.7, 27 acres...

corner to John Richards, deceased, William Ernis and Thomas Applewhite...division made 9 Dec 1762 by Azariah Dunham and Josiah Hornblower...line of John M. Scott. Signed Edmund William Kingsland and Mary Kingsland. Wit: John Jaroleman, Henry Kingsland and Petrus Haring.

31 Jan 1785, Simon & Elizabeth van Winkle, John Degraw and Richard Degraw, £62.8, Lundert Degraw, deceased willed to his daughter Elizabeth Degraw (van Winkle) and son John Degraw... bounded by Abraham Houseman and Nicholas Terhune. Signed Simon van Winkle and Elizabeth (x) van Winkle. Wit: Abraham Ackerman and Abraham van Houten.

14 Feb 1777, Jacobus S. Laroe agreement with Lambertes Jenkins, 100 acres. Signed Jacobus S. Laroe. Wit: Jacobus Cough, Mary (x) Cough and Joost Beam.

2 Dec 1784, Cornelius Haring, of Bergen Co., New Jersey to Albert Wilson, £74, former property of Lewis Millinberry, who joined the army of the King. Signed Cornelius Haring. Wit: Samuel Bertholf, Crynase Bertholf and Roelif Westervelt.

28 Jan 1785, Sheriff of Bergen Co., New Jersey to collect £19, from Abraham Allen for Christopher van Orstrant.

29 Jan 1785, Sheriff of Bergen Co., New Jersey to collect £50, from John Post for Francis Baird.

Jan 1785, Sheriff of Bergen Co., New Jersey to collect £5, from David Demarest for Abraham Beaiver.

25 Jan 1785, Sheriff of Bergen Co., New Jersey to collect £127, from Henry Ellison for Robert Johnson, deceased.

Jan 1785, Sheriff of Bergen Co., New Jersey to collect £3, from James & Mary Jaroleman for John

Hunman.

25 Mar 1785, Sheriff of Bergen Co., New Jersey to collect £21.35 from Peter Hurley for Abraham Manning.

13 Apr 1767, John Hn. Banta, of Bergen Co., New Jersey to Daniel Cammazaar, of same, £60, 7 acres, bounded by John Westervelt, Martin Rulisson and John Cornelius's Creek. Signed John (x) Hn. Banta. Wit: Robert Livesey, John Day and Reynier van Giesen.

27 Mar 1783, Daniel Kamaka, of Clarks, Bergen Co., New Jersey to his grandson Daniel Eckerson, of same, good will and affection, all his estate. Daniel (x) Kamaka. Wit: James Kip and Henry Day.

4 Apr 1770, George & Margritye Brinkerhof, of Clarks, Bergen Co., New Jersey to John Ackerson, Daniel Cammazaar & Jasie Cammazaar, of same, £875, bounded by the widow Chambers, Christian and John Zabriskie...line of Hendrick Kip, now in possession of Nicaway Kip. Signed George Brinkerhof and Margritye (x) Brinkerhof. Wit: Jacobus Brinkerhof, John Benson and Abraham Westervelt.

2 Mar 1785, Sheriff of Bergen Co., New Jersey to collect £0.25, form John Lozier for John & Ann Harris.

2 Mar 1785, Sheriff of Bergen Co., New Jersey to collect £42, from Daniel Christie for William & Ann Grant, heirs of Stephen Baldwin, deceased.

2 Mar 1785, Sheriff of Bergen Co., New Jersey to collect £50, from Abraham Allen, son and heir of Abraham Allen, deceased for Janet Hopper.

2 Mar 1785, Sheriff of Bergen Co., New Jersey to collect £63, from Simon and Joost van Winkle for Peter Zabriskie.

3 May 1785, Peter P. van Blerkum, yeoman, of

Franklin Twp., Bergen Co., New Jersey to
Johannes van Emburgh, of same, line of Major
Kingsland, deceased, and Cornelius van Dien and
Cornelius Haring. Signed Peter P. van Blerkum.
1785, Bm. vander Linde, Allebert Terhune, Barent
Terhune, Garret Hopper, Eldert Jacobus Rutan,
Peter Hopper, Harman van Reypen and John J.
Zabriskie make agreement with Robert Law. Wit:
Christeen Blauvelt and Abraham Westervelt.

26 Mar 1785, Sheriff of Bergen Co., New Jersey
to collect £25 from James Outwater for John
Terhune.

26 Mar 1785, Sheriff of Bergen Co., New Jersey
to collect £30 from John Terrill for John Moore.

10 May 1785, John J. Rutan, of Franklin Twp.,
Bergen Co., New Jersey to Garret H. Blauvelt, of
same, £407, 137 acres, formerly in possession of
John van Voorhees who purchased of William van
Voorhees, deceased, who purchased from John
Hamilton, Jan Anderso Jansen and John Bennett 2
Apr 1745. Signed John J. (X) Rutan. Wit: Garret
Hopper, Hester Hopper and Abraham Westervelt.

5 Feb 1783, John & Mary Benson, Abraham
Vervalen, Elizabeth Vervalen, Barney Nagel, Mary
Nagel, William Lozier, Caty Benson, (now Harris,
wife of John Harris) and Jan Lozier, of Bergen
Co., New Jersey to John Ackerman, of same,
£1400, line of Andreas Zabriskie, deceased, and
Samuel Campbell...line of Lawrence van Horne and
Galem Bogart, deceased. Signed John Benson, Mary
(x) Benson, Abraham Vervalen, Elizabeth
Vervalen, Barney Nagel, Mary Nagel, William
Lozier, Jan Lozier, John Harris and Caty (x)
Harris. Wit: David Jacobus Demarest, Peter Cole,
Jacob Smith, Abraham Smith and Jacob vander
Beck.

9 Jan 1785, Luke van Winkle, of Bergen Co., New
Jersey to John T. van Iderstine, of same. Signed
Luke van Winkle. Wit: Jannes J. van Iderstine,
Charles Slade and Joost Beam.

7 Jun 1785, John van Allen, yeoman, of Bergen Co., New Jersey to John J. Ryenon, of same, £90, 18 acres...line of widow Linah Ryenon. Signed John (x) van Allen. Wit: Samuel Bush, Jacob Ackerman and Petrus Haring.

8 Jan 1767, Peter & Marytie Wammamaker, of Ramapugh, Bergen Co., New Jersey to Christian Wammamaker, of £93.75, 35 acres. Signed Peidder Wammamaker and Marytie (x) Wammamaker. Wit: William Grant, Thomas Boggs and Lauren L. van Boskerk.

10 May 1783, Adolpus Wammamaker, of Orange Co., New York to Derik C. Wammamaker, of Bergen Co., New Jersey, 113 acres...bounded by Christian Wammamaker. Signed Adolpus Wammamaker. Wit: Nicholas (x) Thurman and Abraham Westervelt.

17 May 1783, Garret W. & Margaret Hopper, yeoman, of Franklin Twp., Bergen Co., New Jersey to Derik C. Wammamaker, of same, line of Peter Wammamaker. Signed Garret W. Hopper and Margaret Hopper. Wit: Nicholas (x) Thurman and Abraham Westervelt.

2 Oct 1781, Isaac van Giesen, of New Barbadoes, Bergen Co., New Jersey to John van Giesen, £50, 50 acres and 2 acres. Signed Isaac van Giesen. Wit: John Outwater, Stephen (x) Terhune and Abraham Westervelt.

28 Jul 1774, Jacobus Paulus & Lectye Pulisfelt, of Franklin Precinct, Bergen Co., New Jersey to Garret H. Blauvelt, of same, £165, 50 acres, corner to Isaac Bogart. Signed Jacob (x) Pulisfelt and Lectye (x) Pulisfelt. Wit: Abraham Blauvelt and Potten (x) Smith.

7 Jul 1785, Daniel & Vannetye Durie, yeoman, of Harrington Twp., Bergen Co., New Jersey to Albert Alyee, of same, £1200, 154 acres and 17 acres, sold to said Daniel Durie by Samuel & Weyntye Durie 6 Jun 1767...line of late David van Boskerk and Jacob van Wagener...line of Simon Demarest, deceased and Cornelius

Kuyper...conveyed by Elizabeth Valleau to said
Durie 6 May 1773 ...corner to Stephen Bourdett.
Signed Daniel Durie and Vannetye (x) Durie.
16 Feb 1785, Sheriff of Bergen Co., New Jersey
to collect £15.8, from John Neafie for Joost
Beam.

16 Feb 1785, Sheriff of Bergen Co., New Jersey
to collect £35, from John Willis for Abraham
Allen.

17 Jun 1785, Sheriff of Bergen Co., New Jersey
to collect from John Terrill for John Moore.

8 Apr 1785, Aaron Kingsland, of New York City to
Joseph Kingsland, merchant, of same, £73, 31
acres...late occupied by Isaac Kingsland, now by
Abraham Kingsland. Signed Aaron Kingsland. Wit:
John Harris and Joseph Harris.

15 Jun 1785, Sheriff of Bergen Co., New Jersey
to collect £100, from John Vreeland for Michael
van Winkle.

13 May 1785, Harman & Rachel van Huysen, of New
York City to Robert Nice, of same, £125, 36.5
acres and 52 acres. Signed Harmanus van Huysen
and Rachel (x) van Huysen. Wit: Henry van Dalson
and John van Emburgh.

1 Aug 1785, John van Allen and Hessel Dooremus,
of Bergen Co., New Jersey to Cornelius vander
Hoof, yeoman, of same, £860, 221 acres... corner
to Garret van Allen and John van Allen. Signed
John (x) van Allen and Hessel Dooremus. Wit:
Abraham Manning and Abraham Westervelt.

2 Aug 1783, John H. van Allen, Garret van Allen
and Hepel van Allen, (heirs of Doctor Andreas
van Allen), all of Bergen Co., New Jersey to
Cornelius vander Hoof, of same, £860, 221 acres,
Rundrick van Allen, deceased, in his will, gave
his land to John van Allen, Garret van Allen,
Hepel van Allen, Cornelius & Elizabeth vander
Hoof and Doctor Andreas van Allen. Signed John
van Allen, Garret van Allen and Hepel (x) van

Allen.

7 Feb 1785, Antilby & Elizabeth Earle, of Bergen Co., New Jersey to Hendrick C. Brinkerhof and Hartman Brinkerhof of same, £120, 76 acres ...adjoining Daniel Smith and Philip Earle. Signed Antilby Earle. Wit: John van Houten and Daniel van Reypen.

20 Aug 1785, Philip & Veautye Earle, of Bergen, Bergen Co., New Jersey to Hendrick Berry, of same, £50, 10 acres. Signed Philip (x) Earle and Veautye (x) Earle. Wit: John van Giesen, John Vreeland and Abraham Vreeland.

13 Oct 1785, Sheriff of Bergen Co., New Jersey to collect £16.65 from Garret Ackerman and Roelif van Houten for Abraham Manning.

25 Oct 1785, Sheriff of Bergen Co., New Jersey to collect £15.6 from Michael Cook for Abraham Gould.

25 Oct 1785, Sheriff of Bergen Co., New Jersey to collect £25 from Johann Bush for Abraham Manning.

Oct 1785, Sheriff of Bergen Co., New Jersey to collect £20 from Henry Allison for Abraham Manning.

8 Feb 1775, Elias Baudinot, of Elisabeth, Essex Co., New Jersey to James Bourd, of Bergen Co., New Jersey, £25, 0.76 acres. Signed Elias Baudinot. Wit: Elisha Baudinot, John Ogden and Mary (x) Corsen.

8 Feb 1775, Elias Baudinot, of Elisabeth, Essex Co., New Jersey to James Bourd, of Bergen Co., New Jersey, £37, 30 acres. Signed Elias Baudinot. Wit: Elisha Baudinot, John Ogden and Mary (x) Carson.

8 Feb 1775, Elias Baudinot, of Elisabeth, Essex Co., New Jersey to James Bourd, of Bergen Co., New Jersey, £9, 16 acres, 18 acres and 12 acres

...possession of David Bourd...sold to Cornelius Bourd, 28 Feb 1739. Signed Elias Baudinot. Wit: Elisha Baudinot, John Ogden and Mary (x) Carson.

1762, John van Zile, of Saddle River, Bergen Co., New Jersey to Hendrick Messeher, of Essex Co., New Jersey, £128, 50 acres. Signed John (x) van Zile. Wit: Peter (x) van Zile and Isaac Concklin.

25 Oct 1785, Sheriff of Bergen Co., New Jersey to collect £30 from Isaac Bogart, deceased, (Jacob Bogart) for William Kingsland, deceased, (Henry Kingsland).

25 Oct 1785, Sheriff of Bergen Co., New Jersey to collect £70, from Garret Garretson of Abraham Garretson for Lawrence Law.

27 Dec 1785, Henry & Hannah Allison, yeoman, of Bergen Co., New Jersey to Simon Durie, of same, £616, 25 acres...Harrington Twp...bounded by Garret Ackers. Signed Henry Allison and Hannah Allison. Wit: Garret Lehrman, Jonathan Loverence Jr. and Peter T. Schink.

28 Oct 1785, Sheriff of Bergen Co., New Jersey to collect £100 from John Vreeland for Michael van Winkle.

25 May 1785, Benjamin P. Demarest, weaver, Peter P. Demarest, mason, David P. Demarest, farmer, John P. Demarest, carpenter and Jacob P. Demarest, all of Hackensack, Bergen Co., New Jersey to David P. Demarest, of same, £0.25, 69 acres...Sohealinburgh in Hackensack Precinct. Signed Benjamin P. Demarest, Peter P. Demarest, David P. Demarest, John P. Demarest and Jacob P. Demarest. Wit: David Haring, John Manntius Quackenhus and Peter Haring.

1 Feb 1777, Peter DeVime, of Bergen Co., New Jersey to Ann DeVime, of same, £150, 35 acres... line of Henry Hopper. Signed Peter DeVime. Wit: Jacobus van Zandt, John W. Watkins and John Cleves Seymmes.

11 Jan 1786, Walter Rutherford, James Parker and John Stevens, all three general proprietors of New Jersey to Albert H. Zabriskie and Jacob H. Zabriskie, £400, 90 acres, Ramopack Tract. Signed Walter Rutherford, James Parker and John Stevens. Wit: Edmund Harwell and John Thompson.

27 Jan 1786, Sheriff of Bergen Co., New Jersey to collect £94 from Ann Lozier and John Lozier for Joost Zabriskie.

27 Jan 1786, Sheriff of Bergen Co., New Jersey to collect £20 from John Lozier, deceased for John Zabriskie.

20 Nov 1779, John & Mary Bardan, yeoman, of Bergen Co., New Jersey to Daniel Kenney, of Morristown, Morris Co., New York, £575, 12 acres... former property of Henry Lutkins, who joined the army of the King...bounded by Peter Lutkins and Herman Lutkins. Signed John Bardan. Wit: James Fleming and George Ryerson.

2 Feb 1780, Robert Bell and John Lozier, of Bergen Co., New Jersey to Daniel Kenny and John van Giesen, of same, £100, land purchased of John Bardan 22 Jan 1700. Wit: Roelif Westervelt.

15 Oct 1785, Cornelius Haring, agent for Bergen Co., New Jersey to Jacobus Paulisen, £30, Isaac Blanch and Cornelius Haring before Isaac Blanch 30 Oct 1736.

20 Oct 1786, Albert C. Zabriskie and John C. Zabriskie, of Hackensack Precinct, Bergen Co., New Jersey to John Smith, of same, £25, 73.5 acres...line of Jacob Demoot and John Moore, deceased. Signed Albert C. Zabriskie and John C. Zabriskie. Wit: Roelif Westervelt, Benjamin Westervelt and Peter Haring.

13 Nov 1782, Nicholas & Alida Bogart, of New Barbadoes Precinct, Bergen Co., New Jersey to John Cassady, of Bergen Co., New Jersey, £100, house and lot in Hackensack...bounded by Doctor William Sandford van Emburgh ...former property

of Adam Boyd. Signed Nicholas Bogart and Alida
Bogart. Wit: Abraham Varick and Wessel T.
Wessels.

31 Mar 1786, Sheriff of Bergen Co., New Jersey
to collect £137 from Richard Deylog for John
vander Beck.

31 Mar 1786, Sheriff of Bergen Co., New Jersey
to collect £164, from Hezekial Thompson for
Elias Dayton.

13 Dec 1784, Cornelius Bogart, miller, of Bergen
Co., New Jersey to Richard Degraw, merchant, of
same, £60, New Barbadoes Precinct...bounded by
William Provoost. Signed Cornelius Bogart. Wit:
John van Blerkum and John Bardan.

17 Apr 1785, Cornelius Bogart, miller, of Bergen
Co., New Jersey to Richard Degraw, merchant, of
same, £30. Signed Cornelius Bogart. Wit: Conrad
(x) Staker.

30 Jun 1760, Hendrick vander Linde, of New
Barbadoes Precinct, Bergen Co., New Jersey to
Roelif vander Linde, Dominic Benjamin vander
Linde, of Bergen Co., New Jersey and Samuel ver
Bruyck, (says Dominic ver Bruyck in rest of
deed), of Tappen, Orange Co., New York, £400,
part of Samuel Beyerd patent. Signed Hendrick
vander Linde. Wit: Isack Huysman, Roelif
Westervelt and John Coe, of Orange Co., New
York.

20 Feb 1786, Catrientye van Houten, widow of
Helmegh van Houten, deceased, Yammetye van
Houten, Pruntie van Houten, Fehr van Houten and
Mathew & Gentry Cronkhite, all of Saddle River
Twp., Bergen Co., New Jersey to Samuel van Saen,
of same, 3 acres. Signed Catrientye (x) van
Houten, Yammetye (x) van Houten, Pruntie (x) van
Houten, Fehr (x) van Houten, Mathew (x)
Cronkhite and Gentry (x) Cronkhite. Wit: John
Day and Lucas van Saen.

2 May 1785, dispute between Daniel Haring and

Albert Bogart, over lands in Harrington Twp., Bergen Co., New Jersey...posted £200 to await judgement of Peter Haring, Cornelius Haring, of Bergen Co., New Jersey and John Haring, of Orange Co., New York. Signed Peter Haring, Cornelius Haring and John Haring. Wit: John Benson.

15 Jun 1786, Sheriff of Bergen Co., New Jersey to collect £200 from Hermanus van Huysen for John J. Westervelt.

15 Jun 1786, Sheriff of Bergen Co., New Jersey to collect £17.4 from Solomon vander Beck for Samuel Reading.

15 Jun 1786, Sheriff of Bergen Co., New Jersey to collect £13 from Lambertus Terhune for Jacobus Laroe.

15 Jun 1786, Sheriff of Bergen Co., New Jersey to collect £67.55 from Bernard van Bryck for Isaac Bardan.

9 Oct 1784, Hendrick & Annatye Brinkerhof, of Hackensack Precinct, Bergen Co., New Jersey to Peter Wilson, of New Barbadoes Precinct, Bergen Co., New Jersey, £133, 19 acres...adjoining Joris Brinkerhof...line of Richard Day, Nicose Brinkerhof and heirs of Jacob Brinkerhof. Signed Hendrick Brinkerhof and Johannah (x) Brinkerhof. Wit: Joris Brinkerhof and Henry Banta.

9 Apr 1785, Jacobus & Abby Brinkerhof, Hendrick & Johannah Brinkerhof and Nicolic & Elizabeth Brinkerhof, all of Hackensack Precinct, Bergen Co., New Jersey and Joris & Lena Brinkerhof, of New Barbadoes Precinct, Bergen Co., New Jersey to Peter Wilson, of New Barbadoes Precinct, Bergen Co., New Jersey, £52.5, 5 acres...line of Seba Brinkerhof and heirs of Jacob Brinkerhof. Signed Joris Brinkerhof, Mardalena Brinkerhof, Nicose Brinkerhof, Elizabeth (x) Brinkerhof, Jacobus Brinkerhof, Abby (x) Brinkerhof, Henry Brinkerhof, Johannah (x) Brinkerhof. Wit: Adam

Boyd, Hendrick van Giesen, Albert C. Zabriskie and John C. Zabriskie.

3 Nov 1775, Henderius Kuyper and James Bourd, commissioners, of Bergen Co., New Jersey to Peter Wilson, of New Barbadoes Precinct, Bergen Co., New Jersey, £3367, 1000 acres...land seized from John Marselius, late, of Hackensack Twp., Bergen Co., New Jersey. Signed Henderius Kuyper and James Bourd. Wit: D. Romine and Garret Lydecker.

3 Jun 1779, Isaac van Giesen, of New Barbadoes Precinct, Bergen Co., New Jersey to Peter Wilson, of same, £500, 33 acres...corner of widow Baldwin and John Outwater. Signed Isaac van Giesen. Wit: Hendrick van Giesen and James Chapple.

19 Mar 1783, Archibald & Catharine Campbell, of New Barbadoes Precinct, Bergen Co., New Jersey to Peter Wilson, of same, £160, 10 acres...corner to Hendrick Bosch...line of Peter Zabriskie. Signed Archibald Campbell and Catharine Campbell. Wit: Isaac van Giesen and Hannah Campbell.

16 May 1778, Hendrick & Annetye Bosch, of New Barbadoes Precinct, Bergen Co., New Jersey to Archibald Campbell, of same, £100, 10 acres. Signed Hendrick Bosch and Annetye (x) Bosch. Wit: Peter Wilson and Quilliam Bertholf.

29 Mar 1784, Archibald Campbell, of New Barbadoes Precinct, Bergen Co., New Jersey to Evert Ryckman, of same, £70, bounded by Simon Simmons. Signed Archibald Campbell. Wit: Peter Zabriskie and Abraham Allen.

4 Apr 1785, Henry & Mary Denny, of New Barbadoes Precinct, Bergen Co., New Jersey to John Romine, of same, £175, corner to John Cassady. Signed Henry Denny and Mary Denny. Wit: Robert McCullen and Peter Wilson.

4 Jun 1785, John & Julia Romine, of New Barbadoes Precinct, Bergen Co., New Jersey to Martha Duzan, £175. Signed John Romine. Wit: Robert McCullen and Peter Wilson.

14 May 1768, Peter Zabriskie, of New Barbadoes Precinct, Bergen Co., New Jersey to Hendrick Burk, blacksmith, of same, £0.25, line of Lucas Brass. Signed Peter Zabriskie. Wit: Albert van Voorhees and William Sarrell.

10 Jun 1784, John J. Westervelt, off Hackensack Precinct, Bergen Co., New Jersey and Annatye Burk, of New Barbadoes Precinct, Bergen Co., New Jersey (executor of the last will of Hendrick Burk) to Peter Wilson, of New Barbadoes Precinct, Bergen Co., New Jersey, £150, LawWater Marsh...line of Guilliam Bertholf...purchased by Hendrick Burk from Henry Brass, Abraham Ackerman and Lucas Brass 17 Sep 1737. Signed John J. Westervelt and Annatye (x) Burk. Wit: Jacob Bennett and John Dunlap.

30 Mar 1784, Evert & Sarah Ryckman, of New Barbadoes Precinct, Bergen Co., New Jersey to Peter Wilson, of same, £355. corner to Simon Simmons...line of Jacob Quackinbush and William van Emburgh. Signed Evert Ryckman and Sarah (x) Ryckman. Wit: John Dunlap and John Romine.

6 Sep 1780, Henderius Kuyper and James Bourd, commissioners, of Bergen Co., New Jersey to Peter Wilson, of New Barbadoes Precinct, Bergen Co., New Jersey, £204.8, 8.75 acres...seized of Daniel J. Brawn, late of Hackensack, Bergen Co., New Jersey, for offending against persons of this state...corner to David Bardan and William Provoost. Signed Henderius Kuyper and James Bourd. Wit: Garret Lydecker and David Bourd.

3 Jun 1779, Henderius Kuyper, Garret Lydecker and James Bourd, commissioners, of Bergen Co., New Jersey to Isaac van Giesen, yeoman, of Bergen Co., New Jersey, £975.5, 33.5 acres... seized of John Meyer, late of Hackensack, Bergen Co., New Jersey for joining the army of the

King...bounded by widow of William Baldwin and John Outwater. Signed Henderius Kuyper, Garret Lydecker and James Bourd. Wit: Durie D. Romine.

18 Sep 1771, John van Boskerk, sheriff of Bergen Co., New Jersey to Quilliam Bertholf, of New Barbadoes, Bergen Co., New Jersey, £170, William Kingsland won suit for £200 against Isaac Kingsland 1768...land of said Isaac sold to pay debt...line of Evert Ryckman. Signed John van Boskerk. Wit: Evert Ryckman and Abraham J. van Boskerk.

Quilliam & Nrose Bertholf, of New Barbadoes, Bergen Co., New Jersey, to Evert Ryckman, £170. Signed Quilliam Bertholf. Wit: Archibald Campbell and William van Emburgh.

15 Jun 1786, Sheriff of Bergen Co., New Jersey to collect £30.7 from William Clark for Richard Phillips.

15 Jun 1786, Sheriff of Bergen Co., New Jersey to collect £17.4 from John M. Quackenhus for John van Boskerk.

15 Jun 1786, Sheriff of Bergen Co., New Jersey to collect £34.35 from Martin Scholtzen for John Jacob Fuerk.

23 Jan 1772, Abraham & Phebe Godwin, of Bergen Co., New Jersey to Martin Ryenon, of same, £190, 4.9 acres...between said Godwin and Garrabrant van Houten. Signed Abraham Godwin and Phebe Godwin. Wit: George Ryenon and Garrebrant van Houten.

19 Mar 1785, Abraham vander Beck and Paulus vander Beck, both yeoman, of Franklin Twp., Bergen Co., New Jersey to Peter van Blerkum, of same, £24, line of Albert Hopper. Signed Abraham vander Beck and Paulus vander Beck. Wit: Jan vander Beck and John van Emburgh.

15 Jun 1786, Sheriff of Bergen Co., New Jersey to collect £100 from Paulus Banta for Wiert

Banta.

24 Jul 1786, Beatus & Catharine Quackenhus, of Franklin Twp., Bergen Co., New Jersey to Abraham Ackerman, of same, £37, 15 acres...line of John Romine. Signed Beatus Quackenhus and Catharine (x) Quackenhus. Wit: Conrad (x) Staker and Rozel Abraham Westervelt.

15 Jun 1786, Sheriff of Bergen Co., New Jersey to collect £274 from Jacob Bamper for Joseph Griswold.

26 Apr 1774, Douglas & Gesse Cairns farmer, of Paramus, Bergen Co., New Jersey to John Benson Albert Benson, Genet Benson, Jacob Benson, Elizabeth Benson and Cornelius Benson, of Bergen Co., New Jersey, £50, 32.6 acres...patented 29 Mar 1753...corner to Derick Wammamaker. Signed Douglas Cairns. Wit: Will Cairns and John Cairns.

2 Apr 1786, Oliver Benson, Genet Benson, Jacob Benson and Elizabeth Benson, of Bay of Quinche, Canada power of attorney to Mathew Benson, of same. Signed Albert Benson, Genet (x) Benson, Jacob (x) Benson and Elizabeth (x) Benson. Wit: Paul Hulf and Peter van Aertene.

29 Sep 1786, Mathew Benson, blacksmith, of Bay of Quinche, Canada to Coomack Fox, farmer, of Bergen Co., New Jersey, £75, line of Derick Wammamaker. Signed Mathew Benson. Wit: James Christie and Peter (x) Meysinger.

15 Jun 1786, Sheriff of Bergen Co., New Jersey to collect £164 from Hezekial Thompson for Elias Dayton.

10 Oct 1786, Cornelius Provoost, of Harrington Precinct, Bergen Co., New Jersey to Daniel D. Haring, of same, £179.35, 34 acres... line of Capt. James Christie. Signed Cornelius Provoost. Wit: Isaac Vreoll and Isaac Blanch.

4 Nov 1779, Henderius Kuyper and Garret

Lydecker, commissioners, of Bergen Co., New
Jersey to Beckman van Bueren, £1125, 25 acres...
seized from Daniel S. Demarest, late of
Hackensack Twp., Bergen Co., New Jersey. Signed
Henderius Kuyper and Garret Lydecker. Wit: James
Bourd and Adam Boyd.

4 Nov 1779, Henderius Kuyper and James Bourd,
commissioners, of Bergen Co., New Jersey to
Wiert Banta and John Christie, £2128, seized
from Aaron Demarest. Signed Henderius Kuyper and
James Bourd. Wit: John Day and John A. Hopper.

25 Aug 1784, Cornelius Haring, of Bergen Co.,
New Jersey to Beckman van Bueren, £170, 12.75
acres...seized of John Spear and Jacob Demarest
for joining the army of the King...line of Peter
Wilson. Signed Cornelius Haring. Wit: John
Neafie and Peter Haring.

27 Oct 1786, Sheriff of Bergen Co., New Jersey
to collect £112 and £120 from Richard Wammamaker
for Anne Tuers.

27 Oct 1786, Sheriff of Bergen Co., New Jersey
to collect £41.5 from William Hammel for John
Rozell.

27 Mar 1781, Jonathan Ferd, of Morris Co., New
Jersey to William Leonard, of Bergen Co., New
Jersey, £2500, 52 acres...Saddle River
Precinct...line of George Ryerson. Signed
Jonathan Ferd. Wit: David Leonard and Catel
Russell.

20 Jan 1783, William Leonard, yeoman, of Bergen
Co., New Jersey to Genioh Gardner, yeoman, of
same, £0.25, 34 acres. Signed William Leonard.
Wit: William Hulms and Henry (x) Hulms.

27 Oct 1786, Sheriff of Bergen Co., New Jersey
to collect £10.5 from Sarah Quillem, widow of
James M. Quillem for ??? Zabriskie.

17 May 1786, Margaret Meysinger, administrator
of the estate of Conrad Meysinger, Nicholas

Meysinger and Susanna Meysinger, all of Franklin Twp., Bergen Co., New Jersey to James Christie, of same, £58, 11.5 acres...bounded by heirs of Cornelius Meysinger. Signed Margried Meysinger, Nicholas (x) Meysinger and Susanna (x) Meysinger. Wit: Joseph Johnson and Peter (x) Meysinger.

4 Nov 1779, James Bourd and Garret Lydecker, commissioners of Bergen Co., New Jersey to Beckman van Bueren, £369, 22 acres...seized of Henry Marsh, late of Hackensack, Bergen Co., New Jersey... corner to John J. Demarest. Signed James Bourd and Garret Lydecker. Wit: Jacob Terhune and Abraham Westervelt.

17 Mar 1778, Garret van Allen, of Franklin, Bergen Co., New Jersey to Frederik Storm, of same, £59, 14 acres...part of lot formerly belonging to Peter van Ale and Hendrik van Ale...line of Cornelius Bogart. Signed Garret van Allen. Wit: Jacobus S. Bogart and Roelif Westervelt.

16 Jan 1770, John van Allen, yeoman, of Ramapugh, Bergen Co., New Jersey to Frederik Storm, of same, £168, 13 acres...Saddle River Precinct...corner to Luches Bogart. Signed John (x) van Allen. Wit: Nathan Smith and George Ryerson.

21 May 1779, Hendrick van Allen, of Franklin, Bergen Co., New Jersey to Frederik Storm, of same, £180, 20 acres...part of lot formerly belonging to Peter van Ale and Hendrik van Ale. Signed Hendrick (x) van Allen. Wit: Abraham Mammen and Roelif Westervelt.

24 Sep 1783, John Manntius & Lryntye Quackenhus, yeoman, of Hackensack Precinct, Bergen Co., New Jersey to Beckman van Bueren, of same, £353, 78.5 acres...corner to David S. Demarest and David D. Demarest ...corner to Richard Cooper and William D. Demarest. Signed John Manntius Quackenhus and Lryntye Quackenhus. Wit: David Haring and John Banta.

1787, Casparus Schuyler to his son-in-law William Colfax, for love and affection, 130 acres...tract of land known by name Michael Heart's land... bounded by Derick van Reypen. Signed Caspar Schuyler. Wit: John Outwater and John Benson.

15 Jul 1785, Thomas & Anna Harris, of Hackensack Precinct, Bergen Co., New Jersey to John Ja Westervelt, of same, £165, 17 acres...west branch of Overpeck Creek...line of said John and Darvis Westervelt and Peter Lozier and Hilbrant. Signed Thomas Harris and Anny Harris. Wit: John Benson and Elias Day.

5 Nov 1779, Henderius Kuyper and James Bourd, commissioners, of Bergen Co., New Jersey to John van Allen, £9775.8, 262 acres...seized of John L. Ryerson, late of Saddle River Precinct, Bergen Co., New Jersey...line of Cornelius Westervelt...bounded by widow Ryerson. Signed Henderius Kuyper and James Bourd. Wit: Garret Lydecker and Peter van Allen.

5 Nov 1779, Henderius Kuyper and Garret Lydecker, commissioners, of Bergen Co., New Jersey to John van Allen, £1875, seized of John L. Ryerson. Signed Henderius Kuyper and Garret Lydecker. Wit: James Bourd and Peter van Allen.

8 Sep 1760, Steven Bogart, Paramus, Bergen Co., New Jersey to Abraham Rutan, of same, £7, 2 acres...part of Ramapag Patent...west side of Saddle River. Signed Steven Bogart. Wit: Roelif Westervelt and Stephen Baldwin.

21 Mar 1780, John G. Ackerman, of Harrington Precinct, Bergen Co., New Jersey to Abraham W. Rutan, of Franklin Precinct, Bergen Co., New Jersey, £60, 3 acres...line of Abraham Terhune. Signed John G. Ackerman. Wit: Abraham van Boskerk and Garret J. Hopper.

8 Sep 1764, Garret D. Ackerman, of Bergen Co., New Jersey to Abraham Rutan, of same, £60, 20 acres...corner to William Carnes and P. Carnes.

Signed Garret D. (x) **Ackerman**. Wit: Roelif
**Westervelt** and Stephen **Baldwin**.

4 Nov 1799, James **Bourd** and Garret **Lydecker**,
commissioners, of Bergen Co., New Jersey to
Cornelius van **Horne**, £1407, 56 acres, seized
from John J. **Ackerman**, late of Franklin Twp.,
Bergen Co., New Jersey...line of Peter van
**Blerkum** and Thomas van **Dien**. Signed James **Bourd**
and Garret **Lydecker**. Wit: Henderius **Kuyper** and
Adam **Boyd**.

12 Apr 1784, Cornelius van **Horne**, of Franklin
Twp., Bergen Co., New Jersey to Abraham
**Westervelt**, of same, £350, 56 acres...line of
John A. **Ackerman**, blacksmith and Peter P. van
**Blerkum** ...line of Thomas van **Dien** and Andrew
van **Dien** and heirs of Jacobus van **Voorhees**,
deceased. Signed Cornelius (x) van **Horne**. Wit:
Cornelius (x) van **Horne** Jr. and John **Benson**.

4 Jan 1787, Garret **Bertholf**, of Pomtokin, Saddle
River Precinct, Bergen Co., New Jersey to Geiles
**Bertholf**, of same, £100, 105 acres. Signed
Garret **Bertholf**. Wit: Archibald **Campbell** and
John P. **Post**.

25 Jun 1784, Archibald **Campbell**, innkeeper, of
New Barbadoes Precinct, Bergen Co., New Jersey
to Thomas **Chapple**, of same, £45, line of William
van **Emburgh**. Signed Archibald **Campbell**. Wit:
John **Cassady** and Peter **Wilson**.

23 Oct 1785, Capt. Jonas & Chloe **Ward**, of
Hanover, Morris Co. to Robert **Hill**, merchant, of
New York City, £272, 25 acres...lot No. 12
Bergen Twp. Signed Jonas **Ward**. Wit: Nathan
**Squire** and Mathias van **Reypen**

11 May 1785, Jacobus J. **Bogart**, yeoman, of
Bergen Twp., Bergen Co., New Jersey to Cornelius
**Haring**, of Franklin Precinct, Bergen Co., New
Jersey, £800, 138 acres...in Ramapagn
Precinct...corner to Garret **Hopper** and Jacobus
**Bertholf**. Signed Jacobus J. **Bogart**. Wit: John
**Benson** and Henderius **Kuyper**.

3 Nov 1779, Henderius Kuyper and Garret Lydecker, commissioners, of Bergen Co., New Jersey to Adam Boyd, £250, line of Peter Zabriskie, John Bond and Jacobus Bogart...seized from James van Bueren. Signed Henderius Kuyper and Garret Lydecker. Wit: James Bourd and Peter van Allen.

4 Nov 1799, James Bourd and Garret Lydecker, commissioners, of Bergen Co., New Jersey to Adam Boyd, £720.5, seized from John Lutkins, late of Saddle River Precinct, Bergen Co., New Jersey. Signed James Bourd and Garret Lydecker.

3 Jun 1779, Henderius Kuyper, James Bourd and Garret Lydecker, commissioners, of Bergen Co., New Jersey to Adam Boyd, yeoman, same, £234.35, ...seized of Daniel Jessup, late of Hackensack, Bergen Co., New Jersey for joining the army of the King. Signed Henderius Kuyper, James Bourd and Garret Lydecker. Wit: Harmonus van Huysen and Henry Wammamaker.

Jul 1784, Cornelius Haring, commissioner, of Bergen Co., New Jersey to John Stevens Jr., of New York City, £18360, in Bergen Twp. seized of William Bogart. Signed Cornelius Haring. Wit: Petrus Haring and John Benson.

20 Aug 1784, Cornelius Haring, commissioner, of Bergen Co., New Jersey to John Stevens Jr., of New York City, £5357, bounded by William Jackson, Peter Marselius and Jacobus Bogart... seized of William Bogart. Signed Cornelius Haring. Wit: Petrus Haring and John Benson.

28 Jun 1757, Guilliam & Leah Bertholf to Derick van Dien, 90 acres. Signed Guilliam Bertholf. Wit: Hendrick (c) van Dien.

1 Jul 1784, Jacobus & Annatye Brinkerhof, Nieucoe & Elizabeth Brinkerhof, George & Sarah Brinkerhof and Henry & Mardalena Brinkerhof, all of Bergen Co., New Jersey to Henry Denny £150, 30 acres... corner to Abraham Ackerman. Signed Jacobus Brinkerhof, Annatye (x) Brinkerhof,

Nicose Brinkerhof, Elizabeth (x) Brinkerhof,
Henry Brinkerhof and Mardalena Brinkerhof. Wit:
Simon Simmons and John Romine.

Chapter 5

Bergen County
Courthouse
Deed Records
Volume E

Recorded
in
1787-1789

3 Nov 1779, Henderius Kuyper and James Bourd, commissioners, of Bergen Co., New Jersey to Henry Denny, £131.25, bounded by said Denny... seized from Derick Ackerman. Signed Henderius Kuyper and James Bourd. Wit: Henry van Winkle and Garret Lydecker.

2 Apr 1731, John alias Hans Spear, yeoman, of Newark, Essex Co., New Jersey, (attorney for Peter Sonmans, of Perth Amboy, Middlesex Co., New Jersey) to Henry vander Linde, yeoman, of Hackensack, Bergen Co., New Jersey, £80, 205 acres...corner to John van Orden...line of Abraham Le Roux and Jacob Zabriskie...corner to John Bogart, John Bernard van Dussen and John Durie. Signed Hans (x) Spear. Wit: Nicholas Hardwick and John Hernt.

Jan 1787, Sheriff of Bergen Co., New Jersey to collect £30.75 from William Colfax, Anthony Mandeville, Garret Vreeland and Isaac Ledsend for Yellis Bertholf.

Jan 1787, Sheriff of Bergen Co., New Jersey to collect £49.3 from William Colfax for Gillis Bertholf.

Jan 1787, Sheriff of Bergen Co., New Jersey to collect £16.1 from John Genchen for Henry Mead.

25 Jan 1787, Sheriff of Bergen Co., New Jersey

to collect £46.6 from Lawrence Toers and Jacob Toers, (heirs of Lawrence Toers, deceased) for Thomas van Reypen.

16 Jan 1787, Peter Ward, sheriff of Bergen Co., New Jersey to Peter Hageman, of New York City, £95.55, 71 acres...corner to John Campbell, Dawer Westervelt, John Westervelt, Simson Demarest and Albert C. Zabriskie... property of Paulus Banta Wert Banta sued Paulus Banta. Signed Peter Ward. Wit: John Neafie and Nicholas Derpey.

Jan 1786, Sheriff of Bergen Co., New Jersey to collect £60 from William Hammel for Johannes G. Bogart.

3 Nov 1779, Garret Lydecker and James Bourd, commissioners, of Bergen Co., New Jersey to Samuel Sayre, £1320.65, 30 acres & 12.5 acres, corner Henry Volk...line of Cornelius van Horne ...seized of Abraham A. Quackinbush, late of Hackensack Twp., Bergen Co., New Jersey. Signed Garret Lydecker and James Bourd. Wit: John Hopper and Albert Zabriskie.

22 Jul 1768, Johannes & Ante Vreeland, of Gemonipand, Bergen Co., New Jersey to Egbert Post, of Bergen, Bergen Co., New Jersey, £30, 1 acre...bounded by Claes Vreeland and John van Horne. Signed John Vreeland and Ante (x) Vreeland. Wit: Johannes Diedericks and Mathius Newkerk.

16 Jan 1785, Cornelius Haring, commissioner, of Bergen Co., New Jersey to Benjamin Shotwell, £600, 60 acres...part of 131 acres, purchased by John Frane Ryenon and Derick Ryenon seized of John F. Ryenon, late of Saddle River Precinct, Bergen Co., New Jersey, for joining the army of the King. Signed Cornelius Haring. Wit: John Haring and John Benson.

24 Feb 1786, Cornelius Haring, commissioner, of Bergen Co., New Jersey to Benjamin Statwell, of Middlesex Co., £726, 93 acres...corner to

Nicholas Meysinger and Peter Wammamaker...seized of Derick A. Wammamaker, late of Franklin Twp, Bergen Co., New Jersey for joining the army of the King. Signed Cornelius Haring. Wit: John Haring and John Benson.

Mar 1787, Sheriff of Bergen Co., New Jersey to collect £116.8 from Thumis Hennion for Isaac vander Beck.

Mar 1787, Sheriff of Bergen Co., New Jersey to collect £141 from Cornelius Roelif van Houten for Isaac vander Beck.

8 Jul 1786, Joseph & Sarah Griswold, distiller, of Queen Co., Long Island to Peter D. Demarest, of Harrington Twp., Bergen Co., New Jersey, £490, 84 acres...corner of late, George Cadmus, Samuel Durie. Signed Joseph Griswold and Sarah Griswold. Wit: William Dyckman, William van Dalson and Henry van Dalson.

1 May 1787, John Stevens, James Parker and Walter Rutherford, general proprietors of New Jersey to Albert A. Terhune, of Bergen Co., New Jersey, £353, 156 acres. Signed John Stevens, James Parker and Walter Rutherford. Wit: Cornelius van Boskerk and Gilbert Sherer.

1 May 1784, Jacob & Maria Cough, of Franklin Precinct, Bergen Co., New Jersey to Crynase Bertholf, of same, £350, 38.5 acres...bounded by Andres Hopper, Samuel Bertholf and John W. Hopper. Signed Jacob Cough and Maria (x) Cough. Wit: Cornelius Haring and John Neafie.

6 Apr 1785, Nicholas & Neome Lozier, of Hackensack Precinct, Bergen Co., New Jersey to David Lozier, of Franklin Twp., Bergen Co., New Jersey,, £540, 8 acres & 4 acres & 2 acres...line of Abraham Lydecker, Steven Bourdett and widow Lea Demarest...line of Benjamin Westervelt. Signed Nicholas Lozier and Neome (x) Lozier. Wit: John van Wagener and John Benson.

4 May 1787, Michael H. & Genetye Vreeland of Wood, Essex Co., New Jersey and Cornelius H. & Elizabeth Vreeland, of Gemanapa, Bergen Co., New Jersey (grandsons of Michael Hartman Vreeland, deceased and sons of Hartman M. Vreeland, deceased) to Claes Vreeland, farmer, of Gemanapa, Bergen Co., New Jersey, £0.25, Michael Hartmanse Vreeland, deceased, late of Gemanapa, Bergen Co., New Jersey in his will dated 18 Mar 1783 devised to his son the named Claes Vreeland... said Claes to pay his brothers and sister £350 and if the grandson, (son of said Claes) Michael Vreeland should survive his father and live to 21, then he would receive...if said grandson died then sons Randy Hartman and Garret Vreeland to receive. Signed Michael H. Vreeland, Genetye (x) Vreeland, Cornelius H. Vreeland and Elizabeth Vreeland. Wit: Benjamin Helm and Abraham Willis.

1 May 1787, Benjamin Shotwell, of Woodbridge, Middlesex Co., New Jersey to Henry Wammamaker, of Franklin Twp., Bergen Co., New Jersey, £195.85, 93 acres...corner to Nicholas Meysinger and Peter Wammamaker...purchased from Cornelius Haring 24 Feb 1787. Signed Benjamin Shotwell. Wit: James Bonney and Abraham Westervelt.

7 Feb 1787, Andreas J. Zabriskie and John J. Zabriskie, farmers, of New Barbadoes Precinct, Bergen Co., New Jersey to Albert J. Zabriskie, blacksmith, of Harrington Twp., Bergen Co., New Jersey, their one fourth share of 40 acres... John Zabriskie, deceased, of New Barbadoes Precinct, Bergen Co., New Jersey, in his will 11 Jun 1783, devised to his four sons: Jacob, Andreas, Albert and John Zabriskie. Signed Andreas Zabriskie and John J. Zabriskie. Wit: Cornelius Rome and Abraham Westervelt.

13 apr 1886, Albert & Maria Alyee, yeoman, of Harrington Twp., Bergen Co., New Jersey to Richard Kuyper, yeoman, of New Barbadoes, Bergen Co., New Jersey, £1050, 124 acres & 9 acres & 16 acres...corner to Cornelius Kuyper and Jacob van Wagener...line of Jacob van Boskerk...corner

Stephen Bourdett. Signed Albert (x) Alyee and Maria (x) Alyee. Wit: John Westervelt and John van Wagener

20 May 1774, Adrian & Adriana Brinkerhof to Benjamin & Elizabeth vander Linde, (parents of said Adriana) promissory on chattel goods. Signed Adrian Brinkerhof and Adiana Binkerhof. Wit: Roelif Westervelt and John Westervelt.

Jun 1887, Sheriff of Bergen Co., New Jersey to collect £15 from George Leslie for John Ryerson.

30 Jun 1787, Dutch Reformed Church, of Hackensack, Bergen Co., New Jersey names trustee: Hartman Brinkerhof, Roelif Terhune Nicamic Terhune, George van Giesen and Hendrick Berry. Signed Edmond William Kingsland. Wit: John Terhune, Nicholas Kip, Philip Berry, Casparus Westervelt and Jan Romine.

3 Jul 1787, Trustees of Dutch Reformed Church, of Hackensack, Bergen Co., New Jersey adopt law of New Jersey. Signed Nichase Terhune, George van Giesen, Hendrick Berry, Hartman Brinkerhof and Roelif Terhune.

Jun 1887, Sheriff of Bergen Co., New Jersey to collect £637 from Richard Day for Isaac vander Beck.

Jun 1887, Sheriff of Bergen Co., New Jersey to collect £15.2 from Richard Day for Elijah Squire.

29 Oct 1784, Peter Zabriskie, of New Barbadoes, Bergen Co., New Jersey to Board of Justice, Bergen Co., New Jersey, £0.25, town of New Barbadoes. Signed Peter Zabriskie. Wit: Richard Day and Adam Boyd.

18 May 1785, Peter Zabriskie, of New Barbadoes Precinct, Bergen Co., New Jersey to Board of Justice, Bergen Co., New Jersey, £18, corner to Adam Boyd. Signed Peter Zabriskie. Wit: Peter Wilson and Isaac Stymott.

13 Apr 1787, Daniel D. & Angenike Haring, tailor, of Harrington Twp., Bergen Co., New Jersey to Abraham Demarest, merchant, of same, £90.25, 10 acres...line of Cornelius van Horne ... corner of patent formerly of Samuel Demarest, deceased... corner to land conveyed to Jacob Haring by said Daniel D. Haring. Signed Daniel D. Haring and Angenike Haring. Wit: Christain van Horne and Daniel Christie.

14 Aug 1787, Dutch Reformed Church of Scralinburgh, Bergen Co., New Jersey names trustee. Signed Morta Roeliffe, Richard Heathen, Abraham Demarest, Albert Bogart and John Demott.

13 Jun 1787, Sheriff of Bergen Co., New Jersey to collect £43.5 from Garret Bertholf for Martin Ryenon.

12 Feb 1787, Abraham Allen and Peter Allen, sons of Abraham Allen, deceased and Sarah Allen, widow of Abraham Allen, deceased, all of New Barbadoes Precinct, Bergen Co., New Jersey to Thomas Chapple, of same, £51.25, 10.25 acres... Bayling Spring ...line of John Chapple and Sike Brinkerhof. Signed Abraham Allen, Peter Allen and Sarah (x) Allen. Wit: Nicholas Roosevelt and Gilian Outwater.

1 Feb 1787, John & Mary Banta, anner, of New Barbadoes Precinct, Bergen Co., New Jersey to Thomas Chapple, carpenter, of same, £21, 3 acres ...corner between John Banta and John Chapple. Signed John Banta and Mary (x) Banta. Wit: James Chapple and Elias Provoost.

1 Dec 1773, Peter Kip, of Bergen Co., New Jersey to Hendrick Kip, of same, £10 and love and affection, line of Maj. John Berry and Maj. Nathaniel Kingsland...2nd tract of 50 acres... line Elias Baudinot...Jane Tongretaw sold to John Stagg 9 Aug 1727, who sold to said Peter Kip, 21 Mar 1741...except 2 acres sold to Johannes Tea... beginning in line of John Juriansen. Signed Peter (x) Kip. Wit: Cornelius van Vorst and Maling (x) van Vorst.

12 Jun 1787, Sheriff of Bergen Co., New Jersey to collect £52.9 from Abraham Manning for John Carl.

8 Apr 1786, John & Nancy Dooremus, of Preakness, Bergen Co., New Jersey to Henry Kip, of same, £80, 6 acres. Signed John Dooremus and Nancy (x) Dooremus. Wit: John Hennion and Jacob Dooremus.

15 May 1787, John J. & Margaret Mead, of New York to John Hopper, of Bergen Co., New Jersey, £700, 176 acres...Saddle River Twp. lying between Garret van Reypen and James Jacobusse. Signed John Mead and Margaret (x) Mead. Wit: Henry Mead and Mary Mead.

3 Oct 1787, Peter & Fenety Leishear, of Ramapo, Bergen Co., New Jersey to Area Westervelt, of Teanafly, Bergen Co., New Jersey, £139, 9 acres...line of said Area Westervelt, John Westervelt and Dawer Westervelt. Signed Peter (x) Lozier and Arene (x) Lozier. Wit: John Benson Jr. and John Hopper.

1 Oct 1787, Hellabrant Leishear, of Teanafly, Bergen Co., New Jersey and Peter Leishear, of Ramapo, Bergen Co., New Jersey (grandsons of Hellabrant Leishear, deceased of Teanafly, Bergen Co., New Jersey) to said Peter Leishear, 9 acres & 8 acres... line of Dawer Westervelt and John Westervelt ...line of Area Westervelt, Benjamin Westervelt and Anne Harris. Signed Hellabrant Lozier and Peter (x) Lozier. Wit: John Benson Jr. and Aury Westervelt.

27 Nov 1784, Cornelius Haring, agent for confiscated property of Bergen Co., New Jersey collected £14.35 from Joseph Johnson for a bond due from John Zabriskie, a fugitive. Signed Cornelius Haring.

14 May 1786, received from Joseph Johnston, £26.65...payment for bond of John Zabriskie. Signed Cornelius Haring.

25 Oct 1787, Sheriff of Bergen Co., New Jersey

to collect £50 from Richard Ryerson for John J. Ryerson.

25 Oct 1787, Sheriff of Bergen Co., New Jersey to collect £32.35 from John van Houten for George Ryerson.

25 Oct 1787, Sheriff of Bergen Co., New Jersey to collect £100 from John Jacobus Ackerman for Thomas van Reypen.

25 Oct 1787, Sheriff of Bergen Co., New Jersey to collect £50 from John Hopper for Henry Mead.

25 Oct 1787, Sheriff of Bergen Co., New Jersey to collect £12.5, from Peter Fisher, deceased, (property in hands of James Bourd, David Bourd and Philip Schuyler) for Amfrid Davenport.

25 Oct 1787, Sheriff of Bergen Co., New Jersey to collect £18 from Simon van Winkle for Albert A. Terhune.

25 Oct 1787, Sheriff of Bergen Co., New Jersey to collect £22.05 from Samuel Sayre for Christian Campbell.

15 Sep 1787, Cornelius Haring, commissioner, of Bergen Co., New Jersey to Isaac Nicoll, of Hackensack Precinct, Bergen Co., New Jersey, £169, 52 acres...Franklin Twp., seized of John L. Ryerson, late of Saddle River Twp., Bergen Co., New Jersey, for joining the army of the King. Signed Cornelius Haring. Wit: Petrus Haring and Abraham Haring.

29 Jan 1788, received from Meseslies Marselius £94.9 for bond on Peter Demarest. Abraham Westervelt.

4 Feb 1788, heard last will of Gabriel Ogden, of Pompten, Bergen Co., New Jersey. That brother Charles Ogden, pay debts. To Nelly Lasy and four children, the one half of property the other half to his four brothers. To his mother all his part of the arc furnace in Newark and after her

death to his brothers. To Nelly Lasy, the negro winch Fellis...to daughter Elizabeth Ogden,the negro child Dinah...to son Gabriel Ogden and old clothes to servant Dick. Signed Garret Hawlenbeck, John Willing and Dominic Demisten.

13 Jul 1785, Lewis & Cuphemia Forman, of Mammoth Co., New Jersey to Hermanes Spear, of Essex Co., New Jersey, £31.5, 7.66 acres... Franks Creek... corner to John van Emburgh. Signed Lewis Forman and Affey Forman. Wit: Hendrick Hendricksen and P. Schenck.

6 Feb 1756, Johannes vander Hoof, weaver, of Bergen Co., New Jersey to his brother, Jacob vander Hoof, of New York City, love and affection, between Jacob Outwater and said Johannes. Signed Johannes vander Hoof. Wit: Egbert vander Hoof and Roelif vander Linde.

24 Jan 1763, Jacob Outwater, of Monachkey, New Barbadoes Precinct, Bergen Co., New Jersey to his son-in-law, Jacob van Norstrandt, of same, £5, line of Richard Edsall Sr. Signed Jacob Outwater. Wit: John Outwater and Thomas Outwater.

Abraham & Annaetye Banta to John H. Banta. Signed Abraham (x) Banta and Annaetye (x) Banta. Wit: Cornelius Haring and Jacobus (x) Terhune. Peter Haring witnessed signature of Jannetie Banta.

25 Mar 1765, Mary Laroe, (widow of Hendrick Laroe, deceased), of Ramapo, Saddle River Precinct, Bergen Co., New Jersey to Isaac Bogart, yeoman, of Campeau, of Saddle River Precinct, Bergen Co., New Jersey...bounded by Jacobus C. Bertholf and John Laroe...one fourth of land in will of Hendrick Laroe, 16 Jun 1753 ...surveyed by George Ryerson. Wit: Johannes Laroe and Henry van Gelder.

19 Nov 1762, Johannes & Margaret Laroe, of yeoman, of Bergen Co., New Jersey to Jacobus Bogart, of Ramapo, Bergen Co., New Jersey,

£64.6, 11.75 acres...line of Isaac Bogart.
Signed Johannes Laroe and Margaret (x) Laroe.
Wit: Andrus Hopper and John Haring.

25 Mar 1765, Jacobus & Rebecca Laroe, yeoman, of
Ramapo, Bergen Co., New Jersey to Isaac Bogart,
of same,£550, Saddle River Precinct...bounded by
Jacobus C. Bertholf and John Laroe...being
fourth part of land in will of Hendrick Laroe.
Signed Jacobus (x) Laroe and Rebecca (x) Laroe.
Wit: Abraham (x) van Gelder and Guilliam
Bertholf.

13 Dec 1762, Claes Romine, yeoman, of New
Barbadoes, Bergen Co., New Jersey to Cornelius
Bogart, merchant, of Paramus, of New Barbadoes
Precinct, Bergen Co., New Jersey, £700, 10 acres
& 16 acres & 76.5 acres...line of David M.
Provoost and Abraham Westervelt...line of Derick
Terhune and Richard Kip. Signed Claes Romine.
Wit: Nicholas (x) Kip and Quilliam Bertholf.

17 Apr 1772, Lawrence van Boskerk and Abraham
van Boskerk, both of Werimus, New Barbadoes
Precinct, Bergen Co., New Jersey to Cornelius J.
Bogart, of Paramis, New Barbadoes Precinct,
Bergen Co., New Jersey, £512, 128 acres...
corner to Albert Terhune. Signed Laurins van
Boskerk and Abraham van Boskerk. Wit: Cornelius
van Boskerk and Hendrick (x) Hopper.

1 May 1786, Cornelius Haring, John Haring and
John Neafie, all of Franklin Twp., Bergen Co.,
New Jersey to Frederick Crins, of Harrington
Twp., Bergen Co., New Jersey, £118.9, 118 acres
...Harrington Twp...bounded by George Hackinback
and Thomas van Boskerk. Signed Cornelius Haring,
John Haring and John Neafie. Wit: Peter Ward and
John Hopper.

3 Jan 1788, Isaac & Rachel vander Beck Jr., of
Hobekem, Bergen Co., New Jersey to Thomas
Gardner, of New York City, £575, 1.75 acres...
New Barbadoes Precinct...corner to John Carl.
Signed Isaac vander Beck and Rachel vander Beck.
Wit: Abraham vander Beck and Robert Campbell.

Mar 1788, Sheriff of Bergen Co., New Jersey to collect £9 from Andrus Meyer and John Meyer for Nathan Smith.

Mar 1788, Sheriff of Bergen Co., New Jersey to collect £10 from Peter Hennion for Nathan Smith.

Mar 1788, Sheriff of Bergen Co., New Jersey to collect £60 from Robert Neil for John Varick.

6 Oct 1787, William Parcel, laborer, of Harrington, Bergen Co., New Jersey to James Christie, carpenter, of Hackensack Precinct, Bergen Co., New Jersey, £5, 120 acres...line of Johannes Peck Daniel Haring, Cornelius vander Vorst and Daniel D. Demarest...line of Peter J. Demarest, Hendrick Demarest and Roelif Demarest. Signed William (x) Parcel. Wit: Benjamin Blacklidge and Benjamin Blacklidge.

1 Dec 1784, Cornelius Haring, commissioner, of Bergen Co., New Jersey to Daniel Baldwin, of New York City, £800, 69 acres...corner to James Bogart...seized of William Bayard, late of Bergen Twp., Bergen Co., New Jersey for joining the army of the King. Signed Cornelius Haring. Wit: Peter (x) Lozier and Sayer Crane.

28 Mar 1788, Daniel & Phebe Baldwin, of Bergen Precinct, Bergen Co., New Jersey to Daniel Smith, of same, £630, former land of William Bayard. Signed Daniel Baldwin and Phebe Baldwin. Wit: John Outwater and John Smith.

11 Mar 1788, John Durie, gentleman, of Bergen Co., New Jersey to John Banta, carpenter, of same, £100, New Barbadoes Precinct...line of Daniel Haring. Signed Jan Dierei. Wit: Samuel Beckman and Jacobus van Boskerk.

9 Nov 1784, Peter & Cathalintye Westervelt, yeoman, of Harrington Twp., Bergen Co., New Jersey to John Banta, yeoman of same, 14 acres ...part of land sold by Cornelius Haring to said Peter Westervelt. Signed Peter (x) Westervelt and Cathalintye (x) Westervelt. Wit: Cornelius

Haring and Garret Durie.

23 Jul 1773, John Durie, David Durie and Peter Demarest, (executors of the will of John Durie Sr., dated 16 Feb 1773, late of Hackensack Precinct, Bergen Co., New Jersey) to John Banta, yeoman, of New Barbadoes Precinct, Bergen Co., New Jersey, £65. Signed Jan Durie, David Durie and Pieter Demarest. Wit: Benjamin Westervelt and John P. Durie.

23 Apr 1788, Cornelius & Jane Lozier, miller, of Franklin Twp., Bergen Co., New Jersey to Hendrick Fredericksen Jr., of same, £70, 60 acres ...bounded by Abraham Spear and Benjamin Spear...sold to said Lozier by John van Boskerk, late sheriff, of Bergen Co., New Jersey for wit directed against Amos Spear, administrator of Barent Spear, deceased 28 Feb 1771. Signed Cornelius Lozier and Jane (x) Lozier. Wit: Cornelius Haring and Albert van Voorhees.

11 May 1784, Cornelius Haring, commissioner, of Bergen Co., New Jersey to Jacobus J. Bogart, of Franklin Twp., Bergen Co., New Jersey, £4545, 104 acres...seized of William Bayard, late of Bergen Twp., Bergen Co., New Jersey for joining the army of the King. Signed Cornelius Haring. Wit: Peter J. Demarest and Benjamin Blacklidge.

12 May 1762, map drawn by George Ryerse shows John Bertholf, 87 acres; Jacob Cough, 10 acres; Jacobus Laroe, 78 acres; Jacob Cough, 67 acres; Jacobus Laroe, 10 acres and John Bertholf, 30 acres.

27 Mar 1788, Sheriff of Bergen Co., New Jersey to collect £28 from Abraham Ackerman for Jacobus Bertholf, administrator of Guilliam Bertholf, deceased.

1 May 1788, John & Catharine Neafie, of Franklin Twp., Bergen Co., New Jersey to Jacobus Bogart, of Bergen Twp., Bergen Co., New Jersey, £1375, 99 acres....corner Peter Ward and Derick Tise. Signed John Neafie and Catharine (x) Neafie.

Wit: John Benson Jr. and Abraham Westervelt.

17 Apr 1788, James & Leah Bertholf, of Franklin Precinct, Bergen Co., New Jersey, Benjamin & Maritye Bertholf, Andrew & Hendrickie Stimson, John Bertholf and Nesultye Bertholf, (widow of Guilliam Bertholf, deceased), all of New Barbadoes Precinct, Bergen Co., New Jersey to John Cassady, of New Barbadoes Precinct, Bergen Co., New Jersey, £300, 15 acres...corner to widow Hughes, late deceased and Lawrence A. Ackerman...line of John Varick. Signed James Bertholf, Benjamin Bertholf, Andrew Stimson, Hendrickie Stimson, John Bertholf and Nesultye (x) Bertholf. Wit: Peter Wilson and Patrick Dillon.

7 Apr 1784, Sampson & Rebecca Dyckman, yeoman, of West Chester Co., New York to Wert Banta, yeoman, of Bergen Co., New Jersey, £700, 120 acres...bounded by David van Norder, David Anderson, John Bogart, William Verbergh and Jacob van Zane. Signed Sampson Dyckman and Rebecca Dyckman. wit: James Tuttle and Elisha Hammond.

7 May 1788, John & Rebecke Benson, of Franklin Twp, Bergen Co., New Jersey to Cornelius L. Bogart, of same, £445, 38 acres...bounded by Andrew Hopper, Samuel Bertholf and John W. Hopper. Signed John Benson and Rebeke (x) Benson. Wit: John van Winkle and Cornelius van Houten.

20 Jun 1787, Cornelius Haring, commissioner, of Bergen Co., New Jersey to Andrew van Seil and George Douglas, both of New York City, £750, 20 acres...line of Abraham van Seil...seized of Michael van Seil, late of Bergen Twp., Bergen Co., New Jersey, for joining the army of the King. Signed Cornelius Haring. Wit: Adam Boyd and John Benson.

Mar 1788, Sheriff of Bergen Co., New Jersey to collect £937.5 from Abraham for Richard Day.

16 Jan 1786, James L. & Elizabeth Bogart, of New York City to Cornelius L. Bogart, of Franklin Twp., Bergen Co., New Jersey, £530, 90 acres... willed to said James L. Bogart by Lucas Bogart ...bounded by Stephen Bertholf. Signed James L. Bogart and Elizabeth Bogart. Wit: Abraham Rutan and Henry Lines.

27 Jun 1768, Guilliam & Rachel Bertholf, yeoman, of Saddle River Precinct, Bergen Co., New Jersey to Luke Bertholf, mason, of New Barbadoes, Bergen Co., New Jersey, £625, 150 acres...corner to Hendrick van Allen. Signed Guilliam (x) Bertholf and Ragel (x) Bertholf. Wit: Christian Zabriskie, Cornelius L. Bogart and Peter J. van Allen.

20 Aug 1784, Abraham Ackerman, of Franklin Twp., Bergen Co., New Jersey to Lawrence J. Ackerman, of same, 250 acres of which 228 acres was willed to said Abraham Ackerman and Lawrence Ackerman by their father Jacobus Ackerman, deceased and remaining 20 acres was purchased by said Abraham and Lawrence from Johannes Tuers. Signed Abraham Ackerman. Wit: Abraham van Houten and Abraham Westervelt.

28 Apr 1787, John & Jane van Giesen, of New Barbadoes Precinct, Bergen Co., New Jersey to Garret Oldis, of same, £185.4, 12 acres... corner to Harmon Lutkins, Albert van Voorhees and Peter Lutkins. Signed John van Giesen. Wit: Jacob Zabriskie and John van Sice.

20 Jul 1754, Henry & Mary Brackholst, of Pompton, Bergen Co., New Jersey, (heir of Anthony Brackholst, deceased) to David Marinus, £200, 100 acre... corner to Bartham van Giesen. Signed Henry Brackholst and Mary Brackholst. Wit: Phillip Schuyler and Peter Schuyler.

2 Dec 1760,, David & Anna Marinus, minister, of Essex Co., New Jersey to Garret van Houten, of Stollerdam, Bergen Co., New Jersey, £400, 100 acres...corner to Bashan van Giesen. Signed David Marinus and Anna Marinus. Wit: Johannes

Paulisen and Petrus Paulisen.

3 Apr 1772, Jacob van Norstrandt, blacksmith, of Bergen Co., New Jersey to Garret van Houten, yeoman, of same, 10 acres...line of Jacob Mallings van Winkle and Peter Kip. Signed Jacob van Norstrandt. Wit: Henry Palmer and Jacob van Norstrandt Jr.

15 Apr 1769, Peter van Houten, (oldest son and heir of the late Adriaen van Houten, of Pompton, Bergen Co., New Jersey), Hendrick van Houten, of Stotterdam, Bergen Co., New Jersey, Hendrick & Catharine Hopper and Johannis van Houten, of Pompton, Bergen Co., New Jersey, (all children of the late Peter van Houten, of Stotterdam, Bergen Co., New Jersey) to Garret van Houten, of Totawa, Bergen Co., New Jersey, £0.25, fourth part of large tract conveyed to Helmegh Roeliffe 2 Nov 1696 who sold to Peter Helmegh van Houten 27 Oct 1711...bounded by Thomas Fredericksen, Helmegh van Houten and Johannes van Houten. Signed Peter (x) van Houten, Johannis van Hauten, Helmich van Houten, Hendrick Hopper. Wit: David Marinus and Johannis (x) van Houten.

2 Nov 1763, Abraham Godwin, innkeeper, of Totawa, Bergen Co., New Jersey to Garret van Houten, yeoman, of same, £60, 46.5 acres... sold to said Godwin 19 Jun 1760 by Martin Ryerson and in part by deed from George Ryerse for 102 acres on 1 Oct 1761...corner to Richard Ashfield, deceased. Signed Abraham Godwin. Wit: Johannes A. van Houten and Mary Ryerse.

10 Jun 1787, John & Elizabeth Ackerman, of Franklin Twp., Bergen Co., New Jersey to Albert Wilson, of same, £270, 3 acres...corner to Cornelius Bogart and David Ackerman. Signed John G. Ackerman and Elizabeth (x) Ackerman. Wit: John Garretson and John van Houten.

9 Oct 1750, Peter & Susannah Vergeseau, goldsmith, of New York City to Mary Catharine Baudinot, widow, of Elizabeth Town, Essex Co., New Jersey, Elias Baudinot, goldsmith, of

Philadelphia, Pennsylvania and John & Mary
Emott, mariner, of Elizabeth Town, Essex Co.,
Nwe Jersey, £33, their share...Elias Baudinot,
late of New York City, in his will dated 16 Aug
1719, gave to said Mary Catharine Baudinot one
third of his real estate and the other two
thirds to his five children, Elias, John, David,
Mary and Susannah Baudinot and said children
John and David died before age 21...sold to
Elias Baudinot and Bartholomew Feurt by
Nathaniel Kingsland. Signed Peter Vergeseau and
Susannah Vergeseau. Wit: Ahasucrus Elsworth,
George Elsworth and Francis Troy.

4 Oct 1750, Mary Catharine Baudinot, (widow of
Elias Baudinot, merchant, of New York City,
deceased), of Elizabeth Town, Essex Co., New
Jersey, Elias Baudinot, goldsmith, of
Philadelphia, Pennsylvania and John & Mary
Emott, mariner, of Elizabeth Town, Essex Co.,
New Jersey to John Juriansen, yeoman, of New
Barbadoes Neck, Bergen Co., New Jersey, £100, 30
acres. Signed Maria Catherine Baudinot, Elias
Baudinot, John Emott and Mary Emott. Wit: John
Ross and George Motter.

Jun 1788, Sheriff of Bergen Co., New Jersey to
collect £200 from Jacob Ackerman for Catharine
Goelet, executor of will of Mary Goelet

29 Sep 1711, Elias & Mary Catharine Baudinot to
John Juriansen, of Ackquackenung, Bergen Co.,
New Jersey, 15 acres...line of Bartholomew Feurt
and Nathaniel...purchased in 1707 by John vander
Vope. Signed Elias Baudinot and Mary Catharine
Baudinot. Wit: Garret Juriansen, Jacobus Bogart
and John Conrad Sodwill.

Jun 1788, Sheriff of Bergen Co., New Jersey to
collect £30.9 from Robert Nice for William
Willock.

1 Apr 1784, Jacobus & Ann Alyee, yeoman, of
Bergen Co., New Jersey to Peter van Boskerk,
yeoman, of same, £550, 20 acres & 100 acres
...bounded by Jacob Debane, Peter Debane and

Abraham Hopper, deceased. Signed Jacobus (x)
Alyee and Ann (x) Alyee. Wit: John van Boskerk
and Abraham van Boskerk.

3 Jun 1779, Henderius Kuyper, Garret Lydecker
and James Bourd, commissioners, of Bergen Co.,
New Jersey to Henry Folks, yeoman, of Bergen
Co., New Jersey, £1921.5, 122.5 acres...bounded
by Abraham Quackinbush and Abraham Demarest...
seized of David Peck, late of Seralinburgh,
Hackensack Twp., Bergen Co., New Jersey, for
joining the army of the King. Signed Henderius
Kuyper, Garret Lydecker and James Bourd. Wit:
John Day and Philip Bourd.

Jun 1788, Sheriff of Bergen Co., New Jersey to
collect £72 from John Post for Frederick Storm.

3 Nov 1787, William Sackett, of New York City to
Enoch Smith, of Island of Seacauces, Bergen Co.,
New Jersey, £155, 18.75 acres...adjoining James
Sackett, deceased. Signed William Sackett. Wit:
Henry Earle and John Day.

11 Apr 1788, Job & Phebe Hedden, of Bergen Twp.,
Bergen Co., New Jersey to Enoch Smith, of same,
£187, 31 acres...corner to Samuel Sackett...
line of Nicholas (Firk) Fish...bounded by John
Kingsland. Signed Job Hedden and Phebe (x)
Hedden. Wit: John Hendricksen, Rodman Field, Job
Smith and Jonathan Baker.

Oct 1788, Sheriff of Bergen Co., New Jersey to
collect £200 from John J. van Horne for
Cornelius Westervelt.

6 Dec 1786, Cornelius Haring, commissioner, of
Bergen Co., New Jersey to James Thompson, of
Philadelphia, Pennsylvania, £1100, 18 acres &
100 acres...sold by Warner & Mary Richards to
John Richards, 26 Apr 1738 & 27 Apr 1733...
corner William Ernis...line of Harps Garrabrants
and Hendrick Volk...seized from John Richards,
late of New Barbadoes Precinct, Bergen Co., New
Jersey, for joining the army of the King. Signed
Cornelius Haring. Wit: Isaac Blanch Jr. and

Richard J. Blanch.

Oct 1788, Sheriff of Bergen Co., New Jersey to collect £37.05 from Elephalet Richards for Abraham Manning.

31 May 1788, Johannes & Ann Banta, yeoman, of Hackensack Precinct, Bergen Co., New Jersey to Joost Zabriskie, yeoman, of same, £550, 58 acres ...corner of land late of Derick Banta. Signed John J. Banta and Anne Banta. Wit: Roelif Bogart and David Haring.

31 May 1788, Douwe & Rebecca Westervelt, of Tunefly, Bergen Co., New Jersey and John & Elizabeth Westervelt, of Cordwaenin, Bergen Co., New Jersey to Joost Zabriskie, yeoman, of Hackensack Precinct, Bergen Co., New Jersey, £155, 31 acres...line of Cornelius Demarest, John Bogart and Rebecca Bogart, deceased...line of Johannis Lotes, deceased and Peter Demarest. Signed Dower Westervelt, Rebecca Westervelt, John Westervelt and Elizabeth (x) Westervelt. Wit: Roelif Bogart and David Haring.

2 May 1781, John Mead, yeoman, of Pecquanck, Bergen Co., New Jersey to Henry Mead, £0.25, his half...corner to George Ryerse and Jacob van Houten said John Mead and his brother, Henry Mead willed 52 acres from their father 24 Jul 1774 Jacob Mead, deceased. Signed John Mead. Wit: Garret Jacobusse and Abraham Ryerse.

19 Sep 1781, John Mead, yeoman, of Pecquanck, Bergen Co., New Jersey to Henry Mead, £35 plus young negro man, 40 acres...in Saddle River Twp...between George Ryerse and Jacob Jacobusse. Signed John Mead. Wit: Abraham Ryerse and David Brawn.

24 Feb 1768, Jacobus Jacobusse, yeoman, of Pecquanck, Bergen Co., New Jersey to Jacob Mead, of same, £25, line of Tunis Ryerse...willed to said Jacobus Jacobusse by his father Garret Jacobusse. Signed Jacobus (x) Jacobusse. Wit: John Mead and Anne Ryerse.

14 Mar 1769, John van Houten Jr., weaver, of Bergen, Bergen Co., New Jersey to Henry J. Mead, cordwinder, of same, £147, 51 acres...corner to Jacob Jacobusse and Jacob Mead. Signed Johannis J. van Houten. Wit: Jacob Hawlenbeck, Richard Stanton and Jacob Ackerman.

18 Jul 1788, Ichabod Grumman, innholder, of Bergen Co., New Jersey to Moses van Ame, of Richmond Co., New York, £0.25, 6.8 acres... corner to Cornelius van Vorst. Signed Ichabod Grumman. Wit: Abraham Spear.

19 Jul 1788, Ichabod & Hannah Grumman, innholder, of Bergen Co., New Jersey to Moses van Ame, of Richmond Co., New York, £280, 6.8 acres...lot 17, butting on Newark Bay. Signed Ichabod Grumman and Hannah Grumman. Wit: Abraham Spear.

5 May 1785, Gabriel H. Ludlow, (executor of the will of Henry Ludlow, late of New York City), of New York City to Wilhelm Ferdon, farmer, of Harrington, Bergen Co., New Jersey, £1215, 243 acres...in Harrington Twp...corner to Johannis H. Blauvelt, Roelif van Houten, Derick Vervalen, deceased... Henry Ludlow in his will dated 8 Jan 1780 named as executors: Gabriel H. Ludlow, William H. Ludlow, Richard Morris and Charles Shaw. Signed Gabriel H. Ludlow. Wit: Johannis H. Blauvelt and David Haring.

21 Apr 1784, James Bertholf, Hendrick Bertholf, Benjamin Bertholf and John Bertholf, (heirs of Guilliam Bertholf, deceased, of Bergen Co., New Jersey), all of Bergen Co., New Jersey to Simon Simmons Jr., coppersmith, of same, £50, 0.5 acres...corner to Henry Bear. Signed James Bertholf, Hendrick Bertholf, Benjamin Bertholf and John Bertholf. Wit: John Outwater and Selvester Marinus.

4 Mar 1768, Simon & Rachel van Emburgh, yeoman, of New Barbadoes Neck, Bergen Co., New Jersey to John Schuyler, of same, £25, 1 acre...corner to Abraham van Emburgh. Signed Simon van Emburgh

and Rachel van Emburgh. Wit: James Shepherd and
Charles Osborne.

3 Mar 1768, William van Emburgh, of New
Barbadoes, Bergen Co., New Jersey to Simon van
Emburgh, of same, £0.25, 8 acres...bounded by
Abraham van Emburgh, Gilbert van Emburgh,
Jacobus van Emburgh and John Schuyler. Signed
William van Emburgh. Wit: John Schuyler and
Peter Schuyler.

17 May 1788, Arent J. Schuyler, of New Barbadoes
Neck, Bergen Co., New Jersey to Joseph Field, of
same, £0.25, 1 acres...Simon & Rachel van
Emburgh sold 4 Mar 1768 to Col. John Schuyler
and said Arent J. Schuyler is son and heir of
Col. John Schuyler. Signed Arent J. Schuyler.
Wit: Philip A. Schuyler and John J. Roosevelt.

15 Apr 1760, Abraham Ackerman Jr., blacksmith,
of Bergen Co., New Jersey to Hendrick Beer, of
same, £39, line of Hendrick Bear. Signed Abraham
Ackerman Jr. Wit: Abraham L. Ackerman and
Reynier van Giesen.

1 Mar 1759, Reynier & Hester van Giesen, of
Hackensack, Bergen Co., New Jersey to Trustees
of Hackensack and Schralinburg; Jacob Outwater,
Jacob Kip, Lawrence Ackerman, Hartman Brinkerhof
and elders of Dutch Reformed Church of
Hackensack ...also Peter Durie, Carl Debaun,
Roelif Martese, Peter Day Demarest, Elders and
Minister Johannis Schuyler of Dutch Reformed
Church of Chralengburgh, £100, 4 acres...corner
to Lowrence Ackerman...granted from John Berry
to Garret van Dien 26 May 1695...sold 23 Feb
1742 to Cornelius van Dien, who sold through his
executors Hendrick Kip and Reynier van Giesen 20
Apr 1757 to Hendrick van Dien who sold 20 Jul
1757 to Reynier van Giesen. Signed Reynier van
Giesen and Hester (x) van Giesen. Wit: Hendrick
Banta and Albert Huysman.

6 Nov 1788, Mary Moore, widow and William
Augustine Moore, coach maker, both of New York
City to Nicholas Vreeland, of Bergen, Bergen

Co., New Jersey, £104.75, 45.5 acres...corner to Jacob van Wagener and Doctor Bard. Signed Mary Moore and William A. Moore. Wit: Jasper Pryor and Jacob van Wagener.

6 Nov 1788, Mary Moore, widow and William Augustine Moore, coach maker, both of New York City to Jacob Newkerk, of Bergen, Bergen Co., New Jersey, £87, 25 acres...corner to Edmond William Kingsland and Jasper Pryor. Signed Mary Moore and William A. Moore. Wit: Jasper Pryor and John Day.

6 Nov 1788, Mary Moore, widow and William Augustine Moore, coach maker, both of New York City to Jasper Pryor, yeoman, of Bergen, Bergen Co., New Jersey, £87, 25 acres...corner to Hallimign van Houten. Signed Mary Moore and William A. Moore. Wit: Hallimign van Houten and Jacob van Wagener.

6 Nov 1788, Mary Moore, widow and William Augustine Moore, coach maker, both of New York City to Hallimign van Houten, yeoman, of Bergen, Bergen Co., New Jersey, £155, 50 acres...corner to Jasper Pryor. Signed Mary Moore and William A. Moore. Wit: Jacob van Wagener, Isaac Blanch and Jasper Pryor.

23 May 1788, Edmond William & Mary Kingsland, of New Barbadoes, Bergen Co., New Jersey to Garret J. van Reypen and Levines Winne, both yeoman, of Bergen, Bergen Co., New Jersey, £170, 62.5 acres ...Penhorns Creek. Signed Edmond William Kingsland and Mary Kingsland. Wit: Nicholas (x) Vreeland and William Kingsland.

6 Nov 1788, Mary Moore, widow and William Augustine Moore, coach maker, both of New York City to Jacob van Wagener, of Bergen, Bergen Co., New Jersey, £160, 40 acres...Pinhorns Creek. Signed Mary Moore and William A. Moore. Wit: Jasper Pryor and Hallimigh van Houten.

1 Sep 1784, Peter Stuyversant, of Bergen Twp., Bergen Co., New Jersey to Casparus Pryor, of

same, £140, 8.47 acres...corner to Nicholas Tourse and John van Wagener...half of tract purchased 18 Aug 1784, of Robert William Leake, attorney for John George Leake, of Great Britain. Signed Peter (x) Stuyversant. Wit: John van Horne, Jacob van Wagener and Nicholas Terhune.

Jan 1789, Sheriff of Bergen Co., New Jersey to collect £21.1 from William Drummond for Jacobus Post and Peter Post.

Jan 1789, Sheriff of Bergen Co., New Jersey to collect £21.35 from John van Giesen for Nehemiah Wade.

Jan 1789, Sheriff of Bergen Co., New Jersey to collect £22.65 from Simon van Winkle Jr. and Jacob van Winkle for Peter J. Mead.

13 Aug 1784, George Leslie, yeoman, of Kendekemeck, Bergen Co., New Jersey to Helmegh van Houten, husbandman, of Bergen Twp., Bergen Co., New Jersey, £123, 20.7 acres...corner to Edmond Kingsland. Signed George Leslie. Wit: Jores Demoldt and Zacharias Sickels.

16 Oct 1785, Josiah & Elizabeth Hornblower, gentleman, of Second River, Essex Co., New Jersey to Helmegh van Houten, husbandman, of Bergen Twp., Bergen Co., New Jersey, £124, 20.7 acres...bounded by John van Wagener, Job Smith and heirs of William Earle. Signed Josiah Hornblower and Elizabeth Hornblower. Wit: John van Houten and Edmond William Kingsland.

Mar 1789, Sheriff of Bergen Co., New Jersey to collect £26.15 from Isaac Hawlenbeck for Abraham W. D. Peyoter.

27 Jun 1787, Nicose J. & Margaret Kip, of Hackensack, Bergen Co., New Jersey to John van Reypen, blacksmith, of Parschneiss, Bergen Co., New Jersey, £240, 125 acres...corner to estate of John Hennion, Edward Marselius and Ezekiel Harrah. Signed Nicholas (x) Kip and Margareth

(x) Kip. Wit: Joost Demarest and Joan Kip.

3 Jun 1779, Henderius Kuyper, Garret Lydecker and James Bourd, commissioners, of Bergen Co., New Jersey to William Clark, £638.3, 74.5 acres...corner to Josiah Hornblower, Simon van Emburgh and Arent Schuyler...seized of Abraham van Emburgh, late of New Barbadoes, Bergen Co., New Jersey, for joining the army of the King. Signed Henderius Kuyper, Garret Lydecker and James Bourd. Wit: Hendrick Bardan and Hendrick Denny.

14 Jun 1788, William & Elizabeth Clark, of Bergen Co., New Jersey to Arent Schuyler, of same, £360, 74.5 acres...bounded by Simon van Emburgh. Signed William Clark and Elizabeth Clark. Wit: John Zabriskie and G. Mead

# Chapter 6

## Bergen County
## Courthouse
## Deed Records
## Volume F

### Recorded
### in
### 1789-1792

27 Oct 1758,, Peter Adolph, Bergen, Bergen Co., New Jersey to Andries van Reypen, £60, corner to Peter Marselius. Signed Peter Adolph. Wit: Robert Sickels and Zacharias Sickels.

4 Dec 1788, Mayor General Frederick William Baron de Steuben, of New York City to John Zabriskie Jr., of New Barbadoes, Bergen Co., New Jersey, £1200, in New Barbadoes Twp. Signed Steuben ??. Wit: Benjamin Malhu and William H. Robinson.

Mar 1789, Sheriff of Bergen Co., New Jersey to collect £50 from Peter van Zile for Cornelius Haring.

Mar 1789, Sheriff of Bergen Co., New Jersey to collect £100 from Helmegh Post for John Ackerman.

Mar 1789, Sheriff of Bergen Co., New Jersey to collect £63.55 from Richard Day for John Shaw.

Mar 1789, Sheriff of Bergen Co., New Jersey to collect £600.65 from Wert Guilson Bertholf, deceased, in the hands of James Bertholf, executor for Archibald Campbell.

Mar 1789, Sheriff of Bergen Co., New Jersey to collect £19.85 from Abraham Post for John

Benson.

Mar 1789, Sheriff of Bergen Co., New Jersey to collect £206.8 from John Manntius Quackenhus for Dutch Church of Hackensack.

28 Feb 1771, John van Boskerk, sheriff, of Bergen Co., New Jersey to Cornelius Lozier, of Paramus, Bergen Co., New Jersey, £62, 60 acres...in Preckness...bounded by Abraham Spear and Benjamin Spear...purchased from Abraham Spear by Barent Spear, deceased, in hands of Amos Spear. Signed John van Boskerk. Wit: Francis Hogelandt and Daniel Durie.

6 Nov 1783, John Day, surveyor, of Bergen Co., New Jersey to Matthias P. Newkerk, of Bergen Precinct, Bergen Co., New Jersey, £220, 25 acres ...in corporation of Bergen. Signed John Day. Wit: John Outwater and Daniel van Reypen.

27 Apr 1789, Peter A. & Hester Degroot, of Hackensack Precinct, Bergen Co., New Jersey to Wiert & Leah Banta, £0.5 and love and affection, bounded by Seba Banta, Hendrick Banta, Bellemans Kill and William Lozier. Signed Peter Degroot. Wit: Jacob Demarest and Joost Zabriskie.

25 Jun 1781, Henry Jo van Houten, of Saddle River, Bergen Co., New Jersey and Cornelius H. van Houten, of Achqueghenanck, Essex Co., New Jersey to Cornelius Jo van Houten, of Saddle River, Bergen Co., New Jersey, £0.25, 160 acres ...bounded by John Cadmus...John Cor. van Houten, deceased and Helmegh Cor. van Houten, deceased, were joint tenants...said Helmegh Jo. van Houten, Cornelius Kol. van Houten and Cornelius Jo. van Houten heirs of John and Helmegh van Houten. Signed Henry Jo van Houten and Cornelius H. van Houten. Wit: Peter H. Peterson and Hessel Peterson.

29 Apr 1786, John Sickels, of Bergen, Bergen Co., New Jersey to Jacob Brewer, of same, £126, 14 acres...bounded by Garret van Reypen, Signed John Sickels. Wit: Garret van Reypen and John

Day.

13 Aug 1768, Daniel Haring, Sr., yeoman, of Schralenburgh, Bergen Co., New Jersey to Cornelius Haring, yeoman, of Bergen Co., New Jersey, £50, 10.5 acres...corner to Jan Durie and Jan Durie Sr. Signed Daniel Haring. Wit: David Durie and Johannis Bogart.

4 Jun 1784, Jacob C. Haring, of Dutchess Co., New York to Cornelius D. Haring, of Parkack, Bergen Co., New Jersey, £50, willed by Daniel Haring to said Jacob C. Haring. Signed Jacob C. Haring. Wit: Arendt van Hask and Hendrick Haring.

1 May 1786, Cornelius Haring, John Haring and John Neafie, all of Franklin Twp., Bergen Co., New Jersey to David Baldwin, of Harrington Twp., Bergen Co., New Jersey, £39, 39 acres...in Harrington Twp....division between Thomas van Boskerk, Jacob van Horne and Albert Zabriskie... bounded by Abraham Ackerman. Signed Cornelius Haring, John Haring and John Neafie. Wit: John Hopper and John Benson.

Jun 1789, Sheriff of Bergen Co., New Jersey to collect £21.5 from John Drummond for Anne Roach and John H. Garretson, executors of Doctor Nicholas Roach.

25 May 1781, John Ja. Mead, of Prequanack, Bergen Co., New Jersey to Manemanus Meyer, minister, of same, £36.8, 11.5 acres. Signed John Ja. Mead. Wit: Abraham Ryerse and Samuel Burham.

9 Dec 1772, James Bourd, of Ringwood, Bergen Co., New Jersey to Joseph Bourd, of same, £6, willed to said James Bourd by Cornelius Bourd, who purchased of James Alexander. Signed James Bourd. Wit: David Bourd and Mary (x) Bourd.

1 Feb 1764, Nicholas Gouverneur, of New York City, David Ogden Sr., Samuel Gouverneur and David Ogden, of Newark, Essex Co., New Jersey to

Joseph Bourd, of Ringwood, Bergen Co., New Jersey, £26.75, 27.86 acres...on road from Ringwood Furnace to Pompten. Signed Nicholas Gouverneur, David Ogden, David Ogden Jr. and Samuel Gouverneur. Wit: John Young and Margret Gouverneur.

10 Jan 1755, James Bourd of Ringwood, Bergen Co., New Jersey to Elizabeth Bourd, of same, £0.25, 37 acres...willed to said James Bourd, (eldest son) by Cornelius Bourd. Wit: David Bourd and Joseph Woolcox.

9 Dec 1772, James Bourd, of Ringwood, Bergen Co., New Jersey to Joseph Bourd, of same, £0,25, 147 acres...patented 13 Apr 1749. Signed James Bourd. Wit: David Bourd and Elizabeth Bourd.

8 Nov 1788, James & Sarah Thompson, of Pennsylvania to Richard Bergen, of Kings Co., New York, £625, 18 acres & 100 acres...in New Barbadoes Precinct... bounded by William Ernis ...sold 26 Apr 1738 by Warner & Mary Richards to John Richards...2nd tract sold 28 Apr 1833 by Warner & Mary Richards to John Richards... bounded by Harp Garrabrants, deceased, Hendrick Volk and William Ernis. Signed James Thompson and Sarah Thompson. Wit: Tunis Bergen, Arvn Ryerse, and Samuel W. Stockton.

3 Dec 1787, Benjamin & Elizabeth vander Linde, of Paramus, Bergen Co., New Jersey to Michael Ryers, of Harrington Precinct, Bergen Co., New Jersey, £49.5, 16.5 acres...corner to John Ryers ...line of Fredrick van Reypen. Signed Benjamin vander Linde and Elizabeth vander Linde. Wit: Albert Ackerman and Lewis Concklin.

3 Jul 1784, Rev. Benjamin & Elizabeth vander Linde, of Paramus, Bergen Co., New Jersey to John Ryers, of Harrington Precinct, Bergen Co., New Jersey, £13.5, 3 acres...corner to Cornelius Smith. Signed Benjamin vander Linde and Elizabeth vander Linde. Wit: Albert Ackerman, John Ackerman and Abraham Manning.

2 Aug 1784, Cornelius Haring, commissioner, of Bergen Co., New Jersey to Garret Lydecker, £3712, 180 acres...corner to John Benson and John G. Benson...line of Hellabrant Lozier, deceased...seized of Garret Lydecker, Min., late of Hackensack Precinct, Bergen Co., New Jersey, for joining the Army of the King. Signed Cornelius Haring. Wit: John Benson and John G. Benson.

4 Apr 1770, John Hendrickse & Cornelish Banta, farmer, of Tieneck, Bergen Co., New Jersey to Garret G. Lydecker, of english neighborhood, Bergen Co., New Jersey, £670.9, 57.24 acres & 1.91 acres...bounded by Albert H. Banta, Hendrick R. Bogart, John Ackerson...2nd tract corner to John Terhune, Roelif Bogart, Roelif vander Linde. Signed John H. (x) Banta and Cornelish (x) Banta. Wit: Siebe Banta and David Archibald.

2 Sep 1785, John G. & Maria Benson, yeoman, of Hackensack Precinct, Bergen Co., New Jersey to Garret Lydecker, £4.15, 1.35 acres...bounded by said Lydecker. Signed John Benson and Maria (x) Benson. Wit: Cornelius Haring and John Benson.

8 Mar 1775, Thomas Hughes, of Sing Sing, Westchester Co., New York and Gustavus Kingsland, of Bergen Co., New Jersey to Christopher Ureance, of Bergen Co., New Jersey, £6, one ninth part of fishery. Signed Thomas Hughes and Gustaves Kingsland. Wit: Henry King and William Dow.

23 Apr 1787, William Ernis to Casparus Degraw, £80, bounded by Warner Richards and James Ernis. Signed William (x) Ermis. Wit: Peter Degraw and Harp van Reypen.

8 Sep 1789, Nehemiah & Jane Wade, of Bergen Co., New Jersey to Isack Smith, of same, £95, 19 acres...in Bergen Precinct...lately laid out to Joseph Sackett Jr...corner to heirs Samuel Sackett, deceased. Signed Nehemiah Wade and Jane Wade. Wit: David Godwin and William Reaxing.

26 Mar 1768, Jacobus Outwater, carpenter, of Bergen Co., New Jersey to John Richards, gentleman, of Bergen Co., New Jersey and John Morris Scott, of New York City, £300, patented by said Outwater...part sold 1 Mar 1767, by said Outwater to Jacob Titsort, who sold 10 Dec 1767 to said Richards and Scott...said Outwater sold 24 Mar 1767 to Derick Brinkerhof, Jacobus Brinkerhof, Hendrick Kip and Peter Kip. Signed Jacobus (x) Outwater. Wit: John Outwater and Abram Lozier.

1 May 1789, Egbert & Sarah van Zile, farmer, of Franklin Twp., Bergen Co., New Jersey to Jacobus Ackerman, of Harrington Twp., Bergen Co., New Jersey, £100, 10.5 acres...where Edward Earle now lives...bounded by Cornelius Lozier. Signed Egbert (x) van Zile and Sarah (x) van Zile. Wit: Edward Earle and Jeso Chapple and Abraham Westervelt.

25 Apr 1789, Andrew A. & Mary Hopper, of Franklin Twp., Bergen Co., New Jersey to John Pulisfelt, weaver, of same, £250, 40 acres & 15 acres...corner to Abraham J. Ackerman...line of William Ackerman and David Ackerman. Signed Andrew A. Hopper and Mary Hopper. Wit: Sarah (x) Stevens and Abraham Westervelt.

12 Aug 1788, Daniel & Elisabeth van Reypen, of Bergen Twp., Bergen Co., New Jersey to Jasper Pryor, of same, £46, 4.5 acres...Ahasisnus Creek. Signed Daniel van Reypen and Elisabeth (x) van Reypen. Wit: Augustine Darcy and John van Boskerk.

29 Apr 1789, Derick Lefferts, of New York City to Adolph Waldron, gentleman, of Brooklyn, Long Island, Queens Co., New York, £1200, 11.75 acres & 9 acres & 4.25 acres & 6 acres & 4 acres...in New Barbadoes...corner to late Daniel Isaac Brown...2nd track line of late David Bardan ...3rd track between Jacob Roome and Cornelius Bogart...2nd tract purchased 13 Jul 1765 from Jacob & Elizabeth Roome...3rd tract purchased 1 Apr 1768 by William Provoost from Samuel &

Catharine Lydecker with John & Lamitye Romine...4th track line of Hendrick Bardan, purchased 4 Jun 1776 from John Fisher and Cornelius Lozier...5th tract bounded by William Provoost, Nicasie Kip and Jacob Zabriskie, purchase 12 Sep 1774, by William Provoost from James & Ann Lawrence. Signed Derick Lefferts. Wit: Nancy Lefferts and James J. Beckman.

4 Nov 1779, Henderius Kuyper and James Bourd, commissioners, of Bergen Co., New Jersey to Adolphus Waldron, £6575, 304 acres...line of Roelif van Houten...seized of Hendrick Dooremus, late of Saddle River Twp., Bergen Co., New Jersey, for offending his allegiance. Signed Henderius Kuyper and James Bourd. Wit Garret Lydecker and Adam Boyd.

6 May 1784, Cornelius Haring, commissioner, of Bergen Co., New Jersey to William Jackson Jr., of Bergen Twp., Bergen Co., New Jersey, £502, 23 acres...bounded by Jacobus Bogart...seized of William Bayard, late of Bergen Twp, Bergen Co., New Jersey, for joining the army of the King. Signed Cornelius Haring. Wit: Peter S. Demarest and Benjamin Blacklidge.

10 May 1784, Cornelius Haring, commissioner, of Bergen Co., New Jersey to William Jackson Jr., of Bergen Twp., Bergen Co., New Jersey, £550, 75 acres...seized of William Bayard, late of Bergen Twp, Bergen Co., New Jersey, for joining the army of the King. Signed Cornelius Haring. Wit: Peter S. Demarest and Benjamin Blacklidge.

1 Sep 1789, Johannes Rutan, farmer, of Franklin Twp., Bergen Co., New Jersey to Adam Snyder, blacksmith, of same, £32.5, 6.75 acres...corner to Cornelius J. Bogart...line of Adam van Norden and John Cairns. Signed Johannes (x) Rutan. Wit: John Ryers and Abraham Westervelt.

9 Apr 1785, Cornelius Bogart, miller, of Paramus, Bergen Co., New Jersey to John Pulisfelt, of same, £6, 0.5 acres...line of Abraham Hopper. Signed Cornelius Bogart. Wit:

David (x) Ackerman and Abraham Ackerman.

Oct 1789, Sheriff of Bergen Co., New Jersey to collect £55.7 from William Earnest Baron van Rottenburgh for Jacob Bamper.

Oct 1789, Sheriff of Bergen Co., New Jersey to collect £26.25 from John van Houten for James S. Bogart.

15 Dec 1789, Jacob Terhune, Elias Provoost, Albert Zabriskie, Hendrick Bardan, Solomon Freligh, Peter Zabriskie, Isaac van Saen, Nicose Brinkerhof and Jacobus Huysman, named elders and deacons of the Dutch Reformed Church of Hackensack, Bergen Co., New Jersey. Signed Jacob Terhune, Elias Provoost, Albert Zabriskie, Hendrick Bardan, Solomon Freligh, Peter Zabriskie, Isaac van Saen, Nicose Brinkerhof and Jacobus Huysman.

15 Dec 1789, Solomon Freligh, Jacob Bogart, David Durie, David Demarest, James Christie, Isaac van Voorhees, Simon Demarest, Peter Cole and Dawer Westervelt, named elders and deacons of the Dutch Reformed Church of Hackensack, Bergen Co., New Jersey. Signed Solomon Freligh, Jacob Bogart, David Durie, David Demarest, James Christie, Isaac van Voorhees, Simon Demarest, Peter Cole and Dawer Westervelt.

22 Dec 1789, Hendrick Berry, Hartman Brinkerhof, Roelif Terhune, Michase Terhune and George van Giesen, named elders and deacons of the Dutch Reformed Church of Hackensack, Bergen Co., New Jersey. Signed Hendrick Berry, Hartman Brinkerhof, Roelif Terhune, Michase Terhune and George van Giesen.

22 Dec 1789, Abraham Demarest, Richard Heathen, Albert Bogart and John Demott, named elders and deacons of the Dutch Reformed Church of Hackensack, Bergen Co., New Jersey. Signed Abraham Demarest, Richard Heathen, Albert Bogart and John Demott.

14 Nov 1789, Sheriff of Bergen Co., New Jersey to collect £8 from Moses Westfield for Job Smith.

27 Oct 1789, Sheriff of Bergen Co., New Jersey to collect £45.65 from Reuben Carter for Roelif van Brunt.

5 Mar 1788, Peter Ward, sheriff of Bergen Co., New Jersey to Jonas Wade, of Essex Co., New Jersey, £225, 120 acres...in Bergen Twp...to pay judgement obtained by Matthias Ogden against Daniel Baldwin, Hasakiak Thompson and Matthias Halsted. Signed Peter Ward. Wit: Nehemiah Ward and Cornelius D. Bourd.

14 Dec 1784, Catharine van Houten, (widow of Helmegh van Houten, deceased), Affey Dooremus, Yannaty van Houten, Peyntie van Houten, Fythe van Houten and Mathew & Gentry Cranck, heirs of Helmegh van Houten, deceased to John Dooremus, of Bergen Co., New Jersey, £30, 6 acres. Signed Catrena (x) van Houten, Affey (x) Dooremus, Yannaty (x) van Houten, Printkey (x) van Houten, Fythe (x) van Houten, Mathew (x) Cranck and Gentry (x) Cranck. Wit: Samuel van Saen and Nicholas Kip.

25 Aug 1755, Giles Mead, yeoman, of Bergen co., New Jersey to Teunis Day, yeoman, of same, £52, 34 acres...line of George Ryerse. Signed Giles Mead. Wit: George Vreeland and John Vreeland.

1 May 1754, Lewis Morris Ashfield (eldest son of Richard Ashfield, deceased, of New York) to Derick Day, £15, the sale between Rip van Dam and Richard Ashfield contained more acres than stated ie. 710 acres. Signed Lewis M. Ashfield. Wit: Anthony Dennis and Teunis Jaroleman.

7 Nov 1789, Henry & Caty Kip, of Preckness, Bergen Co., New Jersey to George H. Dooremus, of same, £107, 6 acres. Signed Henry Kip and Caty Kip. Wit: Cornelius Kip and George Dooremus.

1 May 1790, John Kersout, of Sataway Bridge,

Bergen Co., New Jersey to Garret G. van Wagener, of Stotterdam, Bergen Co., New Jersey, £85, 34.35 acres...corner to Martin J. Ryerson. Wit: Jacob Terhune.

Mar 1790, sheriff of Bergen Co., New Jersey to collect £40 from Barnardus Verbrick for Peter Zabriskie.

23 Mar 1790, sheriff of Bergen Co., New Jersey to collect £15.1 from Cornelius vander Vorst for Samuel Garretson.

13 Dec 1784, Peter & Martina Zabriskie, of New Barbadoes Precinct, Bergen Co., New Jersey to William Jones, of Island of Santa Croiz, West Indies, £1500, 242 acres & 12 acres...in Saddle River Precinct...line of Jacob Hopper, heirs of Johannes Post, Thomas van Reypen and Hartman Cadmus...corner to land late of Elias Vreeland...line of Staats Bush and Marinus van Winkle...line of Albert Terhune...2nd tract sold to said Zabriskie by Hendrick Kip, Jacob Kip and others. Signed Peter Zabriskie and Martina Zabriskie. Wit: John Smith and Peter Wilson.

19 Apr 1790, William George Jones, of Saddle River Precinct, Bergen Co., New Jersey to James Huysman, of New Barbadoes Precinct, Bergen Co., New Jersey, £150, 35.5 acres...bounded by Jacob and Cornelius Hopper...purchased by said Jones from Peter Zabriskie. Signed William George Jones. Wit: James Reading and Nehemiah Wade.

19 Apr 1790, William George Jones, of Saddle River Precinct, Bergen Co., New Jersey to Thomas van Reypen, of same, £135.35, 20.25 acres... corner to Richard Terhune. Signed William George Jones. Wit: James Reading and Nehemiah Wade.

19 Apr 1790, William George Jones, of Saddle River Precinct, Bergen Co., New Jersey to Cornelius Hopper, of New Barbadoes Precinct, Bergen Co., New Jersey, £123.75, 24.75 acres ...bounded by Cornelius Post, Jacob Hopper and James Huysman. Signed William George Jones. Wit:

James Reading and Nehemiah Wade.

19 Apr 1790, William George Jones, of Saddle River Precinct, Bergen Co., New Jersey to Richard Terhune and John Terhune, of New Barbadoes Precinct, Bergen Co., New Jersey, £307.55, 64.75 acres...line of Marinus van Winkle. Signed William George Jones. Wit: James Reading and Nehemiah Wade.

20 Apr 1790, Peter Zabriskie, of New Barbadoes Precinct, Bergen Co., New Jersey to James Huysman, of same, £150, 30.5 acres...along Saddle River...part of tract mortgaged by William George Jones to Peter Zabriskie 13 Dec 1784. Signed Peter Zabriskie. Wit: James Reading and Nehemiah Wade.

20 Apr 1790, Peter Zabriskie, of New Barbadoes Precinct, Bergen Co., New Jersey to Richard Terhune and John Terhune, of New Barbadoes Precinct, Bergen Co., New Jersey, £307.55, 64.75 acres. Signed Peter Zabriskie. Wit: James Reading and Nehemiah Wade.

20 Apr 1790, Peter Zabriskie, of New Barbadoes Precinct, Bergen Co., New Jersey to Cornelius Hopper, of same, £123.75, 24.75 acres...part of tract mortgaged by William George Jones to Peter Zabriskie 13 Dec 1784. Signed Peter Zabriskie. Wit: James Reading and Nehemiah Wade.

20 Apr 1790, Peter Zabriskie, of New Barbadoes Precinct, Bergen Co., New Jersey to Thomas van Reypen, of Saddle River Precinct, Bergen Co., New Jersey, £135.35, 20.25 acres...part of tract mortgaged by William George Jones to Peter Zabriskie 13 Dec 1784. Signed Peter Zabriskie. Wit: James Reading and Nehemiah Wade.

2 Jul 1784, Cornelius Haring, commissioner, of Bergen Co., New Jersey to Peter Ward, of Saddle River Precinct, Bergen Co., New Jersey, £800, 100 acres...corner to Jacobus Bogart and Jacobus Pulisfelt...seized from Christian Pulisfelt, late of Franklin Twp., Bergen Co., New Jersey,

for joining the army of the King. Signed
Cornelius Haring. Wit: John Neafie and Petrus
Haring.

23 Mar 1790, sheriff of Bergen Co., New Jersey
to collect £106.5 from Ely B. van Rottenburgh
for Garret J. Hopper.

23 Mar 1790, sheriff of Bergen Co., New Jersey
to collect £107.7 form Ernst Baron van
Rottenburgh for Albert Wilson.

23 Mar 1790, sheriff of Bergen Co., New Jersey
to collect £25.35 from William Ernst Baron van
Rottenburgh for Peter Tebow.

9 Apr 1786, Enoch Smith, of Bergen Co., New
Jersey, Joseph Smith Jr. and Morris Smith, both
of New York to Abel Smith, £0.5, corner to Job
Smith...part of farm of Phillip Smith Sr.,
deceased. Signed Enoch Smith, Joseph Smith and
Movris Smith. Wit: Joseph Smith and Israel Wood.

23 Mar 1790, sheriff of Bergen Co., New Jersey
to collect £60 from Barnardus Verbrick for John
Perry.

23 Mar 1790, sheriff of Bergen Co., New Jersey
to collect £25.85 from John van Houten for Tunis
Ryerson, John Wright, Jacob Bardan and Peter
Day.

23 Mar 1790, sheriff of Bergen Co., New Jersey
to collect £49.7 from Cornelius van Houten for
Jacob van Wagener.

12 Jun 1790, Henry Harris, innkeeper, of Saddle
River Twp., Bergen Co., New Jersey to Jacob
Ackerman, miller, of same, £48, livestock and 5
acres where said Harris lives. Signed Henry (x)
Harris. Wit: Jacob Mae Nash and W. McElse.

Jun 1790, sheriff of Bergen Co., New Jersey to
collect £14.85 from Richard Ryerson for Phebe
Camp.

10 Jun 1790, sheriff of Bergen Co., New Jersey to collect £200 from Richard Earle and John Earle for George Ogilvie.

Jun 1790, sheriff of Bergen Co., New Jersey to collect £200 from John Earle and Richard Earle for Barent Roorbach.

10 Jun 1790, sheriff of Bergen Co., New Jersey to collect £50 from Cornelius van Houten for John van Houten.

11 Jun 1790, sheriff of Bergen Co., New Jersey to collect £340 from David Lozier and John van Wagener for Nicolas Lozier.

12 Jan 1775, Jacob Zabriskie, miller, of New Hamburgh, Bergen Co., New Jersey to Christian Zabriskie, of Paramus, Bergen Co., New Jersey, £1000, 150 acres...corner to Albert Zabriskie ...line of Andreas Zabriskie. Signed Jacob Zabriskie. Wit: George Dooremus and John Dooremus.

Jun 1790, sheriff of Bergen Co., New Jersey to collect £39.6 from Giles Mead for Jacob J. Bardan.

Jun 1790, sheriff of Bergen Co., New Jersey to collect £10 from Richard H. van Houten for Thomas van Reypen.

Jun 1790, sheriff of Bergen Co., New Jersey to collect £60 from Samuel Demarest and David Demarest for Jacob Hopper.

Jun 1790, sheriff of Bergen Co., New Jersey to collect £8.6 from John M. Quackenhus for John Earle.

Jun 1790, sheriff of Bergen Co., New Jersey to collect £6.65 from John Vreeland for John M. Quackenhus.

15 Dec 1789, Richard & Jane Stanton, of Bergen Co., New Jersey to John Dooremus, of same, £90,

12 acres...both sides of Krakeil Val Being Brook. Signed Richard Stanton and Jane Stanton. Wit: Abraham Ryerson and Albert (x) Stagg.

Jun 1790, sheriff of Bergen Co., New Jersey to collect £64 from Daniel Wandle for Samuel Gale.

Jun 1790, sheriff of Bergen Co., New Jersey to collect £200 from Peter Banta and Siebe Banta for Stephen Bourdett.

Jun 1790, sheriff of Bergen Co., New Jersey to collect £14.1 from William M. Bell for Robert Robertson.

1 May 1787, John Stevens, James Packer and Walter Rutherford, proprietors of eastern New Jersey to Cornelius Haring, of Bergen Co., New Jersey, £100, 80.59 acres...formerly John Fox's, now David Christie's. Signed John Stevens, James Packer and Walter Rutherford. Wit: Cornelius Best and Gilbert Sherer.

24 Aug 1790, Effie Dooremus, (widow of Hendrick Dooremus, late of Saddle River Twp., Bergen Co., New Jersey) to Adolphus Waldron, of New Barbadoes Precinct, Bergen Co., New Jersey, £100, 300 acres...bounded by Theumis Hennion... corner to Roelif van Houten and Nicolas Kip. Signed Aagye Dooremus. Wit: Martin Shaw, Nicholas Kip and Alex B. Waldron.

Oct 1790, sheriff of Bergen Co., New Jersey to collect £20.4 from James vander Voch for Robert Johnson and Lewis Ogden.

Oct 1790, sheriff of Bergen Co., New Jersey to collect £62.6 from John van Houten for Hannah Baldwin.

Oct 1790, sheriff of Bergen Co., New Jersey to collect £40 from John Bardan for David Simmons.

27 Oct 1790, sheriff of Bergen Co., New Jersey to collect £87.5 from Samuel Verbrick and Roelif Verbrick for Peter Zabriskie.

27 Oct 1790, sheriff of Bergen Co., New Jersey to collect £81 from William Bell, executor of estate of Yoost B. Zabriskie for Ralph Thurman and Richard Thurman.

1 Oct 1785, Garret & Catharine van Reypen Jr., of Bergen, Bergen Co., New Jersey to Jacob Everson, of same, £250, 2 one acre lots...corner to Abraham Dedrix, Mathew Newkerk and Hendrick Newkerk. Signed Garret van Reypen and Catherine van Reypen. Wit: Hellemige van Houten and Cujuthine Davey.

12 Jan 1791, Henry Barcoff, of Franklin Precinct, Bergen Co., New Jersey to John Rose, of same, £50, chattel goods. Signed Henry (x) Barcoff. Wit: Albert Wilson and Josiah (x) Ackhart.

18 Jan 1791, Elders and deacons of the Dutch Reformed Congregation at Ramapaugh, Bergen Co., New Jersey name their church. Peter Light, John Haring, Aavies (x) Pulisfelt, Hendrick BulsTelt, William Ackhart, Hendrick (x) Traphagen, Jonathan (x) van Gelder and James Christie.

13 Apr 1790, Anthony & Hettie Bartrim, blacksmith of Saddle River Twp., Bergen Co., New Jersey to Abraham C. Lines, carpenter, of Franklin Twp., Bergen Co., New Jersey, £28, 9 acres...in Franklin Twp. Signed Anthony Bartrim and Hettie (x) Bartrim. Wit: Jacobus (x) Lines and John Collins.

14 Feb 1790, Peter & Celena Degroot Sr., farmer, of english neighborhood, Bergen Co., New Jersey to Jacob Degroot, of same, £1300, 125 acres & 4 acres... bounded by Garret Lydecker and Samuel Cowerover ...part of tract granted to John Johnson and Johanna Cowerover 20 Apr 1725...2nd tract bounded by Hendrick Banta. Signed Peter Degroot. Wit: John Degroot and John Daily.

22 Feb 1791, Jacob Degroot, farmer, of english neighborhood, Hackensack Precinct, Bergen Co.,

New Jersey to John Degroot, of same, £200, 60 acres...bounded by John Brinkerhof and Samuel Edsall. Signed Jacob Degroot. Wit: John Daily and Christian Bourdett.

22 Feb 1791, Jacob Degroot, farmer, of english neighborhood, Hackensack Precinct, Bergen Co., New Jersey to John Degroot, of same, £1330, 120 acres & 4 acres. Signed Jacob Degroot. Wit: John Daily and Christian Bourdett.

22 Feb 1791, John Degroot, farmer, of english neighborhood, Hackensack Precinct, Bergen Co., New Jersey to Jacob Degroot, of same, £1330, 300 acres & 40 acres...bounded by John Brinkerhof and Samuel Edsall. Signed John Degroot. Wit: John Daly and Christian Bourdett.

13 Apr 1784, Jacob Lozier, of Hackensack Twp., Bergen Co., New Jersey to John Merurau, of Richmond Co., New York, £450, 52 acres...line of Benjamin Westervelt. Signed Jacob Lozier. Wit: John Outwater and John J. Demarest.

29 Jan 1785, Jacobus Brinkerhof, Hendrick Brinkerhof, Albert Brinkerhof and George Brinkerhof Jr., all of Bergen Co., New Jersey to John Mercerau, of same, £89, 4.5 acres...in Hackensack Twp...bounded by Lawrence J. van Boskerk, John Bogart and Roelif Bogart. Signed James Brinkerhof, Henry Brinkerhof and Albert Brinkerhof. Wit: John Bogart and Paul vander Vorst.

Jan 1791, sheriff of Bergen Co., New Jersey to collect £140 from James Bertholf for Mary Shaw.

Jan 1791, sheriff of Bergen Co., New Jersey to collect £400 from Peter Cadmus for Archibald Campbell.

Jan 1791, sheriff of Bergen Co., New Jersey to collect £124 from Peter B. Westervelt for Thomas Harris.

23 Mar 1791, Doctor Phillip Day, of Bergen Co.,

New Jersey to Isaac Hawlenbeck Jr., of same, £80, 4 acres. Signed Phillip Day. Wit: Anthony Bartrim and Nehemiah Wade.

15 Aug 1763, Jacobus Laroe and Jacob & Mary Cough to Weybrough Bertholf, Samuel Laroe, in his will dated 29 Apr 1760 devised his real estate and the parties on the 12 May 1762 agreed to divide the said estate, which division was made by George Ryerson on a may showing 40 acres, 87 acres and 120 acres. Signed Jacobus Laroe, Jacobus Hock and Mary (x) Cough.

Mar 1791, sheriff of Bergen Co., New Jersey to collect £140 from James Bertholf for Mary Shaw.

Mar 1791, sheriff of Bergen Co., New Jersey to collect £400 from Peter Cadmus for Archibald Campbell.

Mar 1791, sheriff of Bergen Co., New Jersey to collect £124 from Peter B. Westervelt for Thomas Harris.

13 Apr 1791, John B. & Elizabeth Westervelt, of Sirawlingburgh, Hackensack Precinct, Bergen Co., New Jersey to James Thompson, of New York City, £142, 15.5 acres...line of Peter Ja Demoot, Garret Banta. Signed John B. Westervelt and Elizabeth (x) Westervelt. Wit: Robert Yales, James Thompson Jr., James Quackinbush and Johanes Westervelt.

1 Dec 1786, Hendrick H. Banta, farmer, of the english neighborhood, Bergen Co., New Jersey to Jacob Snyder, carpenter and John van Blerkum, cordwinder, both of North River, Bergen Co., New Jersey, £120, 15.5 acres...line of Garret Banta and Peter J. Degroote. Signed Hendrick H. (x) Banta. Wit: John Fairbarin and John Day.

8 Oct 1790, Jacob & Margaret Snyder, carpenter and John van Blerkum, cordwinder, both of North River, Hackensack Precinct, Bergen Co., New Jersey to John B. Westervelt, of Sirawlingburgh, Hackensack Precinct, Bergen Co., New Jersey,

£142, 15.5 acres...line of Garret Banta and
Peter J. Degroote. Signed Jacob Snyder, Margaret
(x) Snyder and John van Blerkum. Wit: Sarah
Smith and John Day.

19 Apr 1791, Margaret Snyder, wife of Jacob
Snyder and Sarah van Blerkum, wife of John van
Blerkum release their right of dowry in sale to
John B. Westervelt. Signed Margaret (x) Snyder
and Sarah (x) van Blerkum. Wit: Henry van Allen
and Abraham Westervelt.

3 Jun 1790, Samuel Sackett, gentleman, of Long
Island, New York and Augustus Sackett, of New
York City to Paul Saunier, of Bergen Co., New
Jersey, £200, 9.1 acres & 32 acres...adjoining
Doctor Joseph Sackett. Signed Samuel Sackett and
Augustus Sackett. Wit: Mary Shackerly and James
Ellis.

Mar 1791, sheriff of Bergen Co., New Jersey to
collect £15 from Mathew Cronkhite for Tunis
Ryerson.

Mar 1791, sheriff of Bergen Co., New Jersey to
collect £100 from Samuel B. Demarest for John
Zabriskie.

Mar 1791, sheriff of Bergen Co., New Jersey to
collect £46.25 from Jacob Brower Jr. for Peter
Ustick, executor of estate of Peter Brewer.

Mar 1791, sheriff of Bergen Co., New Jersey to
collect £90.65 from Richard H. van Houten for
John Everson.

Mar 1791, sheriff of Bergen Co., New Jersey to
collect £15.65 from Francis Cook for Peter
Schuyler.

Mar 1791, sheriff of Bergen Co., New Jersey to
collect £100 from John van Allen and Peter van
Allen for Peter Tebow.

Mar 1791, sheriff of Bergen Co., New Jersey to
collect £58 from Jacob Meyer and Jacob Parcel

for John van Boskerk.

Mar 1791, sheriff of Bergen Co., New Jersey to collect £44.7 from Jacob Lozier for John Earle.

Mar 1791, sheriff of Bergen Co., New Jersey to collect £22.7 from Henry Hennion for John Earle.

Mar 1791, sheriff of Bergen Co., New Jersey to collect £18.75 from William Drummond for John Earle.

Mar 1791, sheriff of Bergen Co., New Jersey to collect £26 from Jacobus Laroe for Jacobus Cough and Samuel Laroe.

4 Mar 1791, John Outwater and Henry Berry, commissioners of Bergen Co., New Jersey to Peter Zabriskie, executor of will of Jacob Zabriskie, £171, 52 acres...in Bergen Twp. Signed John Outwater and Henry Berry. Wit: Archibald Campbell and Michael B. Terhune.

7 Jan 1791, Daniel van Reypen of Bergen, Bergen Co., New Jersey to Garret Odell, of New Barbadoes Precinct, Bergen Co., New Jersey, £75, 17.5 acres...bounded by Garret J. van Reypen and George Dooremus. Signed Daniel van Reypen. Wit: George Dooremus and John D. Bardan.

Mar 1791, sheriff of Bergen Co., New Jersey to collect £500 from John van Wagener and David Lozier for Peter Zabriskie.

7 May 1791, John & Marya Meyer, yeoman, of Slatterdam, Bergen Co., New Jersey to Cornelius J. van Houten, yeoman, of same, £600, 106 acres ...bounded by Lucas van Saen, Lawrence Cornelius, John Ackerman, Henry Ackerman and Phillip van Bussen. Signed John (x) Meyer and Maria (x) Meyer. Wit: Cornelius Lozier and Hessel Peterson.

3 Nov 1779, Henderius Kuyper and James Bourd, commissioners, of Bergen Co., New Jersey to Hendrick Bogart, £1457.55, 100 acres...bounded

by the Ramapo Patent...seized of Jacobus Fox,
late of Franklin Twp., Bergen Co., New Jersey.
Signed Henderius Kuyper and James Bourd. Wit:
John Day and Richard Day.

10 Jun 1791, John & Phebe Day, of New York City
to Mathew P. Newkerk, of Bergen Twp., Bergen
Co., New Jersey, £150, 20 acres...in Bergen Twp.
...line of John H. van Houten. Signed John Day
and Phebe Day. Wit: Henry Post and Garret van
Reypen.

11 Oct 1791, John & Henderikia Outwater, of New
Barbadoes Precinct, Bergen Co., New Jersey to
Samuel Berry, yeoman, of same, £80.4, 11 acres
...corner to Abraham and Peter Allen...line of
Nicawsey Terhune. Signed John Outwater and
Henderichia (x) Outwater. Wit: Abraham Allen and
Jacob Outwater.

11 Jun 1791, John & Phebe Day, of New York City
to Jacob Newkerk, of Bergen Twp., Bergen Co.,
New Jersey, £188, 25 acres...corner to Mathew P.
Newkerk and John Stevens. Signed John Day and
Phebe Day. Wit: Henry Post and Garret van
Reypen.

3 May 1791, Anthony & Williamphey Mandeville, of
Pompton Plains, Pequanack Twp., Morris Co., New
Jersey to John G. Ryerson, of Saddle River Twp.,
Bergen Co., New Jersey, £450, 50 acres & 10
acres...in Franklin Twp...corner to Henry
Brown...2nd tract in Saddle River Twp...
adjoining Joseph Kerbride. Signed Anthony
Mandeville and Williamphey (x) Mandeville. Wit:
Martin G. Ryerson and Charles A. Obrign.

1 Jun 1791, Samuel P. & Wilhelmina Demarest, of
New Bridge, Bergen Co., New Jersey to John
Zabriskie Jr., of same, £116.2, 11 acres...
corner to John Demarest and David Demarest.
Signed Samuel P. Demarest and Wilhelmina
Demarest. Wit: John Seaman and Cornelius
Houghland.

11 May 1791, Harmanus van Norden, was at the

house of Henry Harris, at Slotterdam, Bergen Co., New Jersey, on 1 Jan 1791 and bite the ear of Jacob Mackness.

10 May 1791, James Demarest, of Bergen Co., New Jersey was at the house of Henry Harris, at Slotterdam, Bergen Co., New Jersey, on 1 Jan 1791 and saw a fight between Harmanus van Norden and Jacob Mackness and said Mackness had the rim of his right ear torn off. Signed James Demarest.

10 May 1791, Henry Harris, of Bergen Co., New Jersey reports the ear affair. Signed Henry (x) Harris.

Jun 1791, sheriff of Bergen Co., New Jersey to collect £146.65 from Henry Kip for Richard Day.

Jun 1791, sheriff of Bergen Co., New Jersey to collect £20.75 from William Hammel for John Earle.

Jun 1791, sheriff of Bergen Co., New Jersey to collect £5 from Peter P. van Blerkum for Richard Day.

Jun 1791, sheriff of Bergen Co., New Jersey to collect £61.65 from James Ceard for Dederick Tice.

Jun 1791, sheriff of Bergen Co., New Jersey to collect £12 from Dederick Tice for Adrian P. Post.

2 Sep 1785, John Day, yeoman, of Bergen Co., New Jersey to John H. van Houten, of Bergen Twp., Bergen Co., New Jersey, £112, 14 acres...corner to Garret van Reypen and Helmegh van Houten ...bounded by Mathew Newkerk purchased 1 Jan 1780 from Hendrius Kuyper, deceased. Signed John Day. Wit: John van Houten and Zacharias Sickels.

20 May 1784, John Day, yeoman, of Bergen Co., New Jersey to Helmegh van Houten, of same, £139.25, 25 acres...bounded by Abraham Sickels,

George Demott, Daniel van Reypen and his brother Garret van Reypen, Garret van Reypen Jr. and Johannes Sickels. Signed John Day. Wit: John van Houten and Zacharias Sickels.

Jun 1790, sheriff of Bergen Co., New Jersey to collect £53.3 from John Drummond for Abraham Ogden.

13 Jul 1790, John & Mary van Houten, of Saddle River Precinct, Bergen Co., New Jersey to Martin Ryerson, of same, £100, 48 acres...in Franklin Twp...one half of tract patented by the heirs of Anthony Sharp at the request of Isaac and Joseph Sharp, the other half by Phillip Schuyler, Isaac Schuyler, Peter Schuyler, Casparous Schuyler and Arent Schuyler to Peter van Houten and John van Houten on 20 Oct 1780. Signed John van Houten and Mary van Houten. Wit: Isaac Hawlenbeck and Garret Hawlenbeck.

1 Apr 1778, Peter & Charity van Allen, of Compton, Bergen Co., New Jersey to Martin John Ryerson, of same, £200, 13 acres...formerly sold by Garret Post to Jacob Mead who sold to said van Allen. Signed Peter van Allen and Charity (x) van Allen. Wit: Philip Schuyler and Robert Clark.

1 Apr 1778, Peter & Charity van Allen, of Compton, Bergen Co., New Jersey to Martin John Ryerson, of same, £500, 1 acre...corner to Guilliam Bertholf. Signed Peter van Allen and Charity (x) van Allen. Wit: Philip Schuyler and Robert Clark.

1 Mar 1790, Peter & Rachel van Houten, of Compton, Bergen Co., New Jersey to Martin John Ryerson, of same, £800, 135 acres in three tracts. Signed Peter (x) van Houten and Rachel (x) van Houten. Wit: Garret Post and Isaac Hawlenbeck.

8 Dec 1775, William van Emburgh, yeoman, of Hackensack, Bergen Co., New Jersey to his two brothers, Simon van Emburgh and James van

Emburgh, both of New Barbadoes Neck, Bergen Co., New Jersey, willed by his father Gilbert van Emburgh. Signed William van Emburgh. Wit: William Dow and Aury King.

25 Jun 1785, Richard Day, sheriff of Bergen Co., New Jersey to Anne Harris, £670.3, 102 acres... bounded by Abraham Lozier, Elias Day, Garret Lydecker, Hellabrant Lozier, Peter Lozier, John Westervelt and Dower Westervelt...17 acres... same area...33 acres...same area...7 acres... same area...Anne Baldwin, executor of estate of Stephen Baldwin, deceased, recovered in court against Anne Harris, executor of estate of John Lozier, deceased, £151.1, and lands of said John Lozier were sold by sheriff to pay debt. Signed Richard Day. Wit: James Hordie and Peter Wilson.

24 Sep 1787, Hellabrant Lozier, of Bergen Co., New Jersey to Anne Harris, late Anne Lozier, and executor of estate of John Lozier, deceased, £0.25, bounded by heirs of Jacob Westervelt... Hellebrant Lozier, deceased, grandfather of said Hellebrant Lozier and father-in-law of said Anne Harris willed to his two sons Peter and John Lozier and to his two grandchildren Hellebrant Lozier and Peter Lozier. Signed Hellebrant Lozier. Wit: Elias Day and Abram Lozier.

31 May 1791, Helmegh van Houten, of Bergen Co., New Jersey to Elizabeth Post, (wife of Abraham Post), of same, £28.5, 7 acres...bounded by heirs of George Dooremus. Signed Helmegh (x) van Houten. Wit: Henry B. Spear and Cornelius Hennion.

18 Oct 1791, Michael Simmons, of Bergen, Bergen Co., New Jersey to Jacob Pryor Jr., of same, £25, 1 acres...bounded by Nicholas Tourse, Peter Kuyper and Casparus Pryor.

Oct 1791, sheriff of Bergen Co., New Jersey to collect £104,85 from Cornelius A. van Houten for Ann Basset.

16 Dec 1760, Garret & Mary Hennion, yeoman, of

Bergen Co., New Jersey to Henry Powleson, cordwinder, of same, £185, 50 acres...corner to Statts Degroot..line of Stephen Bourdett...part of farm Samuel Moore sold to said Hennion containing 90.75 acres. Signed Garret Hennion and Mary (x) Hennion. Wit: Thomas Smith and William Wentworth.

16 Apr 1788, John van Giesen, of Bergen Co., New Jersey to Marcelius M. van Giesen, of New York City, by John van Blerkum, his guardian, £0.25, 136 acres except 6 acres sold to Cornelius Neafie and 46.7 acres and 20.52 acres and 15.85 acres ... willed to said John van Giesen by Derick van Giesen. Signed John van Giesen. Simon van Winkle Jr. and Henry Wormold.

27 Dec 1758, John Jacobusse, (elder son of Roelif Jacobusse) and Gertruy Jacobusse, (widow and mother of said John), both of Pequaneck, Bergen Co., New Jersey to Jacobus Jacobusse, yeoman, of Wormek, Essex Co., New Jersey, £150, 200 acres except 5 acres sold to Jacobus Bergs and 50 acres...purchased of Thomas Juriansen, 27 Dec 1758, who purchased 5 May 1713. Signed John (x) Jacobusse and Gertruy (x) Jacobusse. Wit: Jacobus Barquo and Mary Barquo.

22 Aug 1791, Nicholas & Alida Bogart, of Nermitage, Bechmans Town, Dutchess Co., New York to Isaac vander Beck Jr., of New Barbadoes, Bergen Co., New Jersey, £350, corner to Adolph Waldron, Jacob Zabriskie, David Bardan, Roland Hill and Doctor William Ja van Emburgh. Wit: James Kent and John C. Peers.

Oct 1791, sheriff of Bergen Co., New Jersey to collect £9.35 from Peter van Blerkum for John W. Christie.

Oct 1791, sheriff of Bergen Co., New Jersey to collect £20.6 from Christian Tise for Isaac Hawlenbeck.

24 Dec 1791, Hendrick & Yannetye Brinkerhof, yeoman, of Hackensack Precinct, Bergen Co., New

Jersey to Roelif Demarest, blacksmith, of same, £1000, 150 acres...line of Samuel C. Demarest, John Jo. Huyler, W. Helmus Huyler and John Banta, deceased...bounded by Johannes P. Westervelt, Johannes Banta and Jacob Quackinbush. Signed Henry Brinkerhof and Yannetye (x) Brinkerhof. Wit: Benjamin Blacklidge and Benjamin Blacklidge.

6 Oct 1789, Richard G. van Houten, of Bergen Co., New Jersey to Elias Vreeland, of Essex Co., New Jersey, £13.5, 12 acres...Derick van Houten willed 16 May 1769 to his two sons Garrabrant van Houten and Helmegh van Houten and to son Richard van Houten 12 acres. Signed Richard van Houten. Wit: Mary Benson and John Benson.

27 Apr 1790, Elias S. Vreeland, of Essex Co., New Jersey to Jacob Smith, of same, £20, 12 acres...purchased of Richard G. van Houten. Signed Elias S. (x) Vreeland. Wit: John Benson Jr. and John Moore Jr.

19 May 1791, Jacob Smith, of Aquacknonch Twp., Essex Co., New Jersey to Richard Day, of Preakness, Bergen Co., New Jersey, £30, 12 acres ...purchased of Elias S. Vreeland. Signed Jacob Smith. Wit: John Benson Jr. and John Moore Jr.

8 Jun 1776, Michael G. & Jannica Vreeland, of Bergen Twp., Bergen Co., New Jersey to John Vreeland, (son of Helmagh Vreeland), carpenter, of same, £80, 5 acres...corner to James Collard ...part of tract sold 25 Jun 1737 by John G. Vreeland, of Bergen Co., New Jersey to Michael G. Vreeland, of Achqueckenonk, Essex Co., New Jersey. Signed Michael G. (x) Vreeland and Jannica (x) Vreeland. Wit: Daniel Sickels and Robert Morris.

1 Jan 1789, Capt. Aaron & Ann Gilbert, of Closter, Bergen Co., New Jersey to Daniel A. Vervalen, of same, £190.75, 34.5 acres...corner to Cornelius Talman, deceased...bounded by Jacob Parcel and Martin Paulisen. Signed Aaron Gilbert and Ann Gilbert. Wit: Isaac Morris and David

Haring.

Jan 1792, sheriff of Bergen Co., New Jersey to collect £10.6 from Jacobus S. Bogart for Catherine Goelet.

Jan 1792, sheriff of Bergen Co., New Jersey to collect £107.75 from Peter van Blerkum for Lewis Meidebarger.

Chapter 7

Bergen County
Courthouse
Deed Records
Volume G

Recorded
in
1792-1794

2 Jul 1791, Adam Boyd, sheriff, of Bergen Co., New Jersey to Jonas Wade, of Essex Co., New Jersey, £0.5, 120 acres...corner to Cornelius Haring...seized from Matthias Halsted...said Wade, recovered in court 1789 against Matthias Halsted £162.8. Signed Adam Boyd. Wit: Catharine Boyd and Nehemiah Wade.

26 Jan 1792, Archibald Campbell, of New Barbadoes, Bergen Co., New Jersey to John Spear, of Essex Co., New Jersey, £40, 75 acres... bounded by William King and Capt. William Davis ...line of Thomas Cadmus...formerly land of Gilbert van Emburgh who willed 16 Jun 1779 to said Campbell. Signed Archibald Campbell. Wit: Abraham Allen and Reynier Earle.

12 Mar 1792, Peter Zabriskie, (executor of will of Jacob Zabriskie), of Bergen Co., New Jersey to James van Horne, of same, £225, 52 acres. Signed Peter Zabriskie. Wit: John van Bueren and Nehemiah Wade.

18 Apr 1789, Walter Rutherford, James Parker and John Stevens to John Benson, of Franklin Twp., Bergen Co., New Jersey, £40, 25.87 acres... corner to John Haring. Signed Walter Rutherford, James Parker and John Stevens. Wit: Azariah Dunham and James Dunham.

15 Aug 1791, Teunis Hennion, farmer, of Pucanas, Bergen Co., New Jersey to Edo Marselius, farmer, of Pucanas, Bergen Co., New Jersey, £153, 106 acres...line of David D. Hennion, David J. Hennion and Theunis Hennion. Signed Teunis (x) Hennion. Wit: John J. Hennion and Brian van Houten.

1 May 1791, Jonas vander Vorst, blacksmith, of Bergen Co., New Jersey to David Lozier, miller, of same, £100, chattel goods. Signed Jonas vander Vorst. Wit: Daniel Salter and Catime (x) Salter.

31 May 1790, Archibald Campbell, of Bergen Co., New Jersey to Jeremiah Pope, of same, £50, 5 acres...corner to John Demarest...purchased from Harmanus Brass, of New Barbadoes Twp., Bergen Co., New Jersey, 23 Feb 1786. Signed Archibald Campbell. Wit: William Soarner and Robert Campbell.

21 Oct 1736, Walter Briggs, carpenter, of Bergen Co., New Jersey to Hendrick Hendrickse Banta, yeoman, of same, £60, 60 acres...line of Mattys DeMott and James Duncan...formerly belonging to Richard Baker. Signed Walter Briggs. Wit: Guryda Lydecker and Maria Lydecker.

13 Dec 1785, William Rutan, yeoman, of Scrawlenburgh, Bergen Co., New Jersey to his son Paulus Rutan, for love and affection, 30 acres. Signed William (x) Rutan. Wit: David Bye and James Canness.

25 Mar 1764, Henry & Mary Powleson, of New York City to Catharine Lynson, of same, £155, 50 acres ...where Garret Hennion now lives...corner to Garret Benson...patented as 90 acres by Maj. John Berry... part of the farm Samuel Moore sold to Garret Heanyon ...2 acres was sold to Thomas Allen. Signed Henry Powleson and Mary (x) Powleson. Wit: Charles Hade Fullwood and William Wentworth.

1 May 1792, Isaac Delemater, yeoman, of

Harrington Twp., Bergen Co., New Jersey to Johannes Westervelt, mason, of Bergen Co., New Jersey, £30, corner to Garret Ackers and Johannes Waldron. Signed Isaac Delemater. Wit: Isaac Morris and Stephen Westervelt.

2 Nov 1779, Henderius Kuyper and James Bourd, commissioners, of Bergen Co., New Jersey to Henry Wisner, £778.1, 200 acres...line of Cornelius Blauvelt and Cornelius Haring... seized of Abraham and John C. Haring, late of Harrington Twp., Bergen Co., New Jersey, for offending loyalty to the state of New Jersey. Signed Henderius Kuyper and James Bourd. Wit: John Day and John A. Hopper.

20 Jan 1791, Abraham Garrabrants, Garrabrant Garrabrants, Cornelius Garrabrants, Francis & Catharine Spear to Phillip van Cortlandt, £137, 14.25 acres...corner to John van Emburgh. Signed Abraham Garrabrants, Carrabrant Garrabrants, Cornelius Garrabrants and Francis (x) Spear. Wit: John Peck, Anthony King, John Kedney and Gerard Hoeghoost.

12 May 1786, Cornelius & Anne Cooper, of New Barbadoes Precinct, Bergen Co., New Jersey to Reverend Solomon Freligh, of same, £115, corner to Poules vander Beck. Signed Cornelius Cooper and Anne Cooper. Wit: Peter Wilson and Alexander Brookschank.

4 May 1791, Johannes van Wagener and Helmegh van Wagener, both of Saddle River Precinct, Bergen Co., New Jersey to Hendrich van Wagener, of same, £5, 141 acres and 15 acres and 6 acres and 12.5 acres and 7 acres...line of Hennes van Wagener ...second parcel in line of Hannes Diedericks... purchased from Abraham Cadmus, 18 May 1789, and sold by Catharine van Wagener to Johannes van Wagener same day. Signed Johannes van Wagener and Helmegh van Wagener. Wit: Peter Line and John Outwater.

21 Aug 1792, Cornelius & Mattye van Houten, of Saddle River Twp., Bergen Co., New Jersey to Edo

Marselius Jr., of same, £60, 10 acres...corner to Johannes A. van Houten. Signed Cornelius van Houten and Mattye (x) van Houten. Wit: Isaac van Saen and Albert Zabriskie.

23 Dec 1771, Reverend Garret & Elizabeth Lydecker, of the english neighborhood, Bergen Co., New Jersey to Elizabeth Lydecker and Rachael Lydecker, of same, £30, line of Cornelius Lydecker. Signed Garret Lydecker and Elizabeth Lydecker. Wit: Johannes Benson and John Day.

21 Jul 1792, Abraham & Caty Willis, of Acquacknonk Twp., Essex Co., New Jersey to the society for establishing useful manufacturing in the state of New Jersey, £84, 28 acres...two tracts in Saddle River Twp., Bergen Co., New Jersey, returned 24 May 1791 to John Johnston and were surveyed at request of Abraham Godwin and said Willis became a joint partner. Signed Abraham Willis and Caty Willis. Wit: William Hallen and Thomas Marshallen

28 Sep 1791, John & Marytie Brewer, of Bergen Co., New Jersey to John Zabriskie Jr., of same, £53, line of heirs of Elizabeth Seaman. Signed John Brewer and Marytie (x) Brewer. Wit: John Heathen and Cornelius Houghland.

5 Jan 1792, Barent Cole, of Bergen Co., New Jersey to John Zabriskie Jr., of same, £37.75, 4 acres...in New Barbadoes Precinct...line of Isaac van Saen, David Dideson and Jacob Bogart. Signed Barent Cole. Wit: Abraham Collins and William Cairns.

28 Feb 1790, George Ryerse, of Bergen Co., New Jersey to his son John Ryerse, of same, £0.25, 10 acres...line of John van Winkle...formerly belonging to Henry Mead. Signed George Ryerse. Wit: Samuel Jones and Phineas Jones.

1 Apr 1786, George Ryerse, of Bergen Co., New Jersey to his son John Ryerse, of same, for love and affection, 25.5 acres. Signed George Ryerse.

Wit: Thomas Jones and George S. Ryerse.

13 Sep 1792, Cornelius & Yannetie van Boskerk yeoman, of Harrington Precinct, Bergen Co., New Jersey to David Baldwin, carpenter, of Pamerpough, Bergen Co., New Jersey, £600, 210 acres...line of Thomas van Boskerk and Cornelius Bogart. Signed Cornelius (x) van Boskerk and Yannetie (x) van Boskerk. Wit: David Archibald and Abraham van Boskerk.

8 Mar 1787, Cornelius Haring, agent of forfeited estates of Bergen Co., New Jersey to John Stephens, £300, 54.93 acres...corner to James Alexander and Robert Hunter Morris...line of John Romine...seized of John F. Ryerson, late of Saddle River Precinct, Bergen Co., New Jersey, for joining the army of the King. Signed Cornelius Haring. Wit: John Haring and John Benson.

1 Dec 1792, John & Rachel Stephens, of Hoboken, Bergen Co., New Jersey to Richard Degraw, of same, £74.9, 54.93 acres and 229.14 acres and 20 acres ...first tract purchased of Cornelius Haring...second tract corner to John Ryerson and Cornelius Garretson...third tract adjoining the second. John Stephens and Rachel Stephens. Wit: Mary Thompson and Petrus Haring.

13 Nov 1792, Hassel & Catharine Ryerson, of Weigheaw, Bergen Co., New Jersey to John Ryerson, of same, yeoman, £10, 18 acres...corner to George Ryerson. Signed Hassel Ryerson and Catharine (x) Ryerson. Wit: James Ludlow and Sally van Allen.

3 May 1781, John Ja. Mead, of Paquanck, Bergen Co., New Jersey to Garret Jacobusse, of Pompton, Bergen Co., New Jersey, £20, 17.72 acres... line of George Ryerson...conveyed to said John and Henry Mead, by their father Jacob Mead, deceased, 4 Jul 1774. Signed John Mead. Wit: Henry Mead and Abraham Ryerse.

18 Mar 1786, Henry Mead, of Pacquanach, Bergen

Co., New Jersey to Garret Jacobusse, of Bergen Co., New Jersey, £55.2, 5.52 acres...line of George Ryerse. Signed Henry Mead. Wit: John Day and Benjamin Day.

1 May 1762, Isaac & Leya Bogart, miller, of Bergen Co., New Jersey to Simon Simson, of Staten Island, New York, £580, grist mill and 4 acres...line Hendrick Brinkerhof, deceased and Benjamin Westervelt. Signed Isaac Bogart and Leya (x) Bogart. Wit: Gyllejaem Bogart and Guilliam Bertholf.

13 Apr 1791, Abraham Hopper, of Bergen Co., New Jersey to Albert Wilson, of Harrington Precinct, Bergen Co., New Jersey, £6, 11 acres...formerly land of Capt. Pryor...purchased of Hendrick Hopper and Samuel Bush. Signed Abraham Hopper. Wit: John (x) Neart and James Wilson.

1 Dec 1792, Jonas vander Vorst, of Bergen Co., New Jersey to Cornelius Cooper, of same, £20, 6 acres of rye. Signed Jonas vander Vorst. Wit: William Ross Smith and Nick Wade.

20 Apr 1793, Abraham & Mary Lozier, of Hackensack Precinct, Bergen Co., New Jersey to Gasye (now wife of Jacobus Bogart), £485, 54 acres...line of Johannes Bogart, Jacob Lozier, John Zabriskie, Cornelius van Aerlandt. Signed Abraham Lozier and Mary Lozier. Wit: Derick Lozier and Johannes Bogart.

13 Nov 1773, John S. Earle, merchant, of Hackensack, New Barbadoes Precinct, Bergen Co., New Jersey to Geashe Bogart, wife of Jacobus Bogart, of Hackensack Precinct Bergen Co., New Jersey, £115, 10 acres...line of John Zabriskie and Jacobus P. Demarest...corner to Andrew van Boskerk. Signed John Earle. Wit: Johannes Bogart and Peter Valleau.

7 Nov 1792, Garrabrant Juriansen, of New Barbadoes Precinct, Bergen Co., New Jersey to James D. Christie, of same, £30, 2 acres...line of John Juriansen. Signed Garrabrant Juriansen.

Wit: Richard Benson and Casparus Degraw.

26 Oct 1792, Albert & Mary Wilson, yeoman, of Harrington Twp., Bergen Co., New Jersey to Cornelius Bogart, yeoman, of same, £345, 2 acres and 1 acre...corner to David Ackerman. Signed Albert Wilson and Mary (x) Wilson. Wit: Andries Zabriskie and Albert Ackerman.

21 Feb 1785, William & Alana Nagel, yeoman, of Harrington Twp., Bergen Co., New Jersey to Gerardus Riker, farmer, of same, £700, 170 acres and 3.5 acres...corner to Aury Juriansen, (formerly land of Guesslocert Nagel, deceased), John Juriansen and Garrabrant Juriansen... bounded by David Nagel. Signed William Nagel and Alana (x) Nagel. Wit: David Haring, Daniel Derick and David Demarest.

20 Apr 1793, Gerardus & Margaret Riker, yeoman, of Closter, Harrington Twp., Bergen Co., New Jersey to Thomas Lawrence, of (at the present) Cobus Hill, Albany Co., New York and John Lawrence, yeoman, of Rochland, Orange Co., New York, £830, 170 acres and 3.5 acres...purchased of William Nagel. Signed Gerardus Riker and Margaret (x) Riker. Wit: John Lawrence Jr. and Thomas Lawrence.

11 Jan 1786, John Stevens, James Parker and Walter Rutherford, three of the general proprietors of New Jersey to Jacob Debane, £312, 156.78 acres...corner to John Verway. Signed John Stevens, James Parker and Walter Rutherford. Wit: Edward Haswell and John Thompson.

1 Jul 1776, Margaret Ogilvie, widow of New York City, George & Ann Ogilvie, gentleman, of Newark, New Jersey and Barent & Mary Roorbach, gentleman, of Newark, New Jersey, (which Margaret, George and Mary of heirs of Reverend John Ogilvie, deceased), to Richard Earle and John Earle, both yeoman, of Bergen Co., New Jersey, £864, 232 acres and 139 acres...in Bergen Twp...corner to Isaac and George van

Giesen. Signed Margaret Ogilvie, George Ogilvie, Anne Ogilvie, Barent Roorbach and Mary M. Roorbach. Wit: Jane Perce, Mary Sendorf, Hanna Gramm and Ahp B. Macashorter.

5 Apr 1793, Barent Cole, of Bergen Co., New Jersey to John Zabriskie Jr., of same, £63.45, 4.5 acres...in New Barbadoes Precinct...line of Isaac van Saen. Signed Barent Cole. Wit: Peter Zabriskie and Guilliam Demarest.

29 Sep 1790, John Earle, of Bergen Twp., Bergen Co., New Jersey to Matthias P. Newkerk and Hendrick Newkerk, of same, £190, John Earle held by release from Richard Earle, 28 Sep 1790...adjoining a meadow which Edward Earle, father of said Richard and John Earle held by release from John Earle and Phillip Earle, deceased, 5 Sep 1755. Signed John Earle. Wit: Daniel Sickels and John Day.

25 Sep 1784, John Day, of Bergen Twp., Bergen Co., New Jersey to Peter Stuyversant, of same, £230, 27 acres...corner Jacob Newkerk and Nicholas Tourse. Signed John Day. Wit: Matthias (x) Newkerk and Jacob (x) Newkerk.

18 Aug 1784, Robert William Leake late of Albany Co., New York, presently living in England to Peter Stuyversant, of Bergen Co., New Jersey, £280, 14.25 acres... whereas Robert Leake, deceased, of New York City, willed to Robert William Leake, who gave power of attorney to John George Leake. Signed Robert William Leake, by John George Leake. Wit: John Brown Jr. and Augustine Darcy.

4 Aug 1784, Peter van Allen, of Bergen Co., New Jersey to Abraham Manning, of same, £150, 25 acres...purchased by John Bardan, John Bogart and Girbert van Blerkum from Andrew Johnson and Mr. Leslie. Signed Peter van Allen. Wit: James S. Bogart and Cornelius vander Hoof.

23 Jan 1788, Jebe M. & Leah Banta and Nicholas Banta, of the english neighborhood, Bergen Co.,

New Jersey to Jacob Degroot, of same, £120, 15 acres...corner to Phillip Dusell...line of Peter Degroot, Hendrick Banta and John Faboucough. Signed Sebe M. (x) Banta and Leah (x) Banta. Wit: Jacob P. Romine and John Day.

6 May 1793, Walter & Catharine Rutherford, of New York City and James & Rachel Drummond, (by Walter Rutherford, their attorney) to Abraham Rutan, of Franklin Twp., Bergen Co., New Jersey, £146.4, 61 acres...corner to Garret A. Hopper. Signed Walter Rutherford and Catharine Rutherford. Wit: Abraham Westervelt and Andrea Hopper.

21 Aug 1793, Enoch Vreeland, Richard van Horne and Hendrick Kip settle a line of division between them an John van Winkle and Walling van Winkle. Signed Enoch Vreeland, Richard van Horne, Hendrick Kip, John (x) van Winkle and Walling van Winkle.

6 May 1793, Walter & Catharine Rutherford, of New York City and James & Rachel Drummond, (by Walter Rutherford, their attorney) Garret A. Hopper, of Franklin Twp., Bergen Co., New Jersey, £146.4, 41 acres...in Bergen Twp. Signed Walter Rutherford and Catharine Rutherford. Wit: Abraham Westervelt and Andrea Hopper.

27 May 1785, Walling van Vorst, of Bergen Co., New Jersey to Peter Kip, of same, £900, 100 acres...willed to Walling van Vorst by his father Garret van Vorst, which by release from his brother Cornelius van Vorst...except 3 acres sold to Hermanus van Thustien. Signed Walling (x) van Vorst. Wit: Isaac van Reypen and Charles Slade Fullwood.

14 Sep 1793, Edmond & Mary Kingsland, Burnett Richards, all of Bergen Co., New Jersey and John Gill, of Philadelphia, Pennsylvania to William & Margaret Hornblower, of Essex Co., New Jersey, 57 acres and 119 acres...corner to Richard Bergen. Signed Edmond William Kingsland, Mary Kingsland, Burnett Richards and John Gill. Wit:

Samuel Duffield, John Duffield, Burnett N. Kingsland and William Kingsland.

7 Oct 1793, William & Margaret Hornblower, of Essex Co., New Jersey to Richard Bergen, of New Barbadoes Neck, Bergen Co., New Jersey, £615, 119 acres and 57 acres...purchased of Edmond & Mary Kingsland, Burnett Richards and John Gill. Signed William Hornblower and Margaretta Hornblower. Wit: Josiah Hornblower and William King.

11 Nov 1793, David & Phebe Halsey, of Paterson, Bergen Co., New Jersey to Gilbert Cooper, of Paterson, Essex Co., New Jersey, £260, 6 acres ...bounded by Garret van Houten...purchased by said Halsey from John F. Post, 26 Sep 1793. Signed David Halsey and Phebe Halsey. Wit: Helmegh van Giesen and Peter van Houten.

10 Jan 1791, John Earle, of Bergen Precinct, Bergen Co., New Jersey to Richard Earle, of same, £432, 139 acres...corner to Thomas Fredericksen, Elias D. Kuyper and George van Giesen. Signed John Earle. Wit: John Outwater and Thomas Brinkerhof.

5 Feb 1793, Philip A. Schuyler, of New Barbadoes Neck, Bergen Co., New Jersey and Jacob Mark, of New York City, report the conditions of the copper mine they purchased from Arent F. Schuyler, of New Barbadoes Neck, Bergen Co., New Jersey, 4 Feb 1793...to be called the New Jersey Copper Mine and other articles of Inc. Signed Philip A. Schuyler and Jacob Mark. Wit: Nicholas Roosevelt, William Davis and James Brown.

4 Feb 1793, Arent F. Schuyler, of New Barbadoes Neck, Bergen Co., New Jersey to Philip A. Schuyler, gentleman, of New Barbadoes Neck, Bergen Co., New Jersey and Jacob Mark, merchant, of New York City, mineral rights to his farm... devised to Col. John Schuyler, deceased by his father, Capt Arent Schuyler, deceased...land purchased by Col. John Schuyler from Col. William Kingsland...line of Gilbert van Emburgh.

Signed Arent F. Schuyler, Philip A. Schuyler and Jacob Mark. Wit: Nicholas Roosevelt, William Davis and James Brown.

19 Feb 1793, Jacob & Elizabeth Roome and Rachel Jacobusse, all of Saint John, Saint John Co., New Brunswick to Cornelia Benson, of the english neighborhood, Bergen Co., New Jersey, £25, house and 2 acres...line of the late Cornelius Lydecker. Signed Jacob Roome, Elizabeth Roome and Rachel Jacobusse. Wit: Isaac Lawton and Thomas Lawton.

1 Nov 1793, Hannah Campbell, (widow of George Campbell), of New Barbadoes Precinct, Bergen Co., New Jersey to Simon Simmons, of same, £43.3, 7.87 acres...line of Doctor van Bueren, the widow of Doctor McKnight and Edward William Kingsland...Thomas Francis Outwater willed one tenth of his estate to Hannah Outwater, now Hannah Campbell. Signed Hannah (x) Campbell. Wit: John Outwater and Abraham Allen.

19 Dec 1788, Job Smith, of Bergen Precinct, Bergen Co., New Jersey to his son Job Smith Jr., of same, £10, 5 acres...between Daniel Smith and Job Smith...bounded by Richard and John Earle. Signed Job Smith. Wit: Daniel Smith and John Outwater.

20 Jan 1792, Cornelius R. & Matie van Houten, of Totoway, Bergen Co., New Jersey to Alexander Phenix Waldron, of New Barbadoes, Bergen Co., New Jersey, £75, 15.1 acres. Signed Cornelius R. van Houten and Matie (x) van Houten. Wit: Philip Querau and Casparus Zabriskie.

15 Feb 1794, Alexander P. Waldron, of New Barbadoes, Bergen Co., New Jersey to White Matlack, of New York City, £205, 15.1 acres. Signed Alexander P. Waldron. Wit: Nehemiah Wade, John Grigg and Jacob Terhune.

7 Feb 1794, Alexander P. Waldron, of New Barbadoes, Bergen Co., New Jersey to White Mattack, of New York City, £205, mineral rights

...Garrabrant van Houten, deceased, willed to his daughter Matie, wife of Cornelius R. Van Houten one fourth part of all mines and minerals found on his land. Signed Alexander P. Waldron. Wit: Nehemiah Wade, John Grigg and Jacob Terhune.

29 May 1789, John Ogden, of Essex Co., New Jersey and Moses Ogden, (oldest son and heir of Uzal Ogden, deceased, late of Essex Co., New Jersey) to Peter Schuyler and Phillip Schuyler, (son of Isaac Schuyler), of Bergen Co., New Jersey, £20, 20.15 acres...re-establish deed destroyed by fire between the said John Ogden and Uzal Ogden, deceased to Peter Schuyler and Isaac Schuyler... line of heirs of Gauen Saunier, surveyed at request of David Ogden, now owned by John Hennion. Signed John Ogden and Moses Ogden. Wit: Ebenezer Smith and Zephaniah Grant.

15 Oct 1787, John & Phebe Day, of Bergen Co., New Jersey to Peter Stuyversant, of Bergen Co., New Jersey, £93, 15 acres...line of Seil Marselius and Jacob Newkerk. Signed John Day and Phebe Day. Wit: Peter Day and Hannah Gilbert.

29 Apr 1786, Hartman Sickels, of Bergen, Bergen Twp., Bergen Co., New Jersey to Peter Stuyversant, of Bergen Co., New Jersey, £38.25, 4.25 acres...corner to Garret & Sarah vander Hoof and Helmegh van Houten. Signed Hartman Sickels. Wit: Abraham Pryor and Jacob Brown.

26 Apr 1787, John Winne, of Bergen, Bergen Co., New Jersey to Peter Stuyversant, of Bergen Co., New Jersey, £50, 1 acre...bounded by Dutch Reformed Church. Signed John (x) Winne. Wit: Zacharias Sickels and Daniel van Reypen.

20 Feb 1790, Jacob Zabriskie, of New Hamburgh, Bergen Co., New Jersey to Leah Slutt, of New York, £100, 5 acres...corner to Albert van Voorhees, Stephen Terhune and Samuel Provoost. Signed Jacob Zabriskie. Wit: Benjamin Bertholf and Samuel Provoost.

20 Feb 1790, Jacob Zabriskie, miller, of New Hamburgh, Bergen Co., New Jersey to Garret Zabriskie, yeoman, of same, £1000, 25 acres and 40 acres... corner to Leah Slutt, Stephen Terhune, Albert van Voorhees and Nicasie Kip. Signed Jacob Zabriskie. Wit: Benjamin Bertholf and Samuel Provoost.

28 Mar 1794, Adam Boyd, sheriff of Bergen Co., New Jersey to William Colfax, £218, 45.37 acres and 37.9 acres and 10.49 acres and 15.5 acres and 41.8 acres and 13.15 acres and 6.86 acres and 15.92 acres and 19.17 acres and 10.84 acres and 14 acres... corner to Joseph Bartrim and David Ogden...where Adam Belcher formerly lived ...sold to pay debt of John Jay and Anna van Horne, who recovered in court against Benjamin Woodruff, executor of estate of Benjamin Woodruff, of Long Pond, Franklin Twp., Bergen Co., New Jersey, £300.95. Signed Adam Boyd. Wit: Casparus van Vorst and Abraham Westervelt.

3 Feb 1794, Archibald & Catharine Campbell, of New Barbadoes Precinct, Bergen Co., New Jersey to John Cassady, of same, £80, lot in town of Hackensack...line of Patrick McFadden. Signed Archibald Campbell and Catharine Campbell. Wit: John van Bueren and Robert Campbell.

14 Mar 1794, Edward & Catharine Eckerson, cordwinder, of Harrington, Bergen Co., New Jersey to David Eckerson, of Orange Co., New York, £595

25 Jan 1788, Abraham & Mary Ackerman, of Franklin Twp., Bergen Co., New Jersey to Jacobus vander Linde, of Hackensack Precinct, Bergen Co., New Jersey, £57.5, 15.75 acres...line of John Romine. Signed Abraham (x) Ackerman and Mary (x) Ackerman. Wit: Adam Snyder and Abraham Westervelt.

2 May 1794, Jacob & Alltie Campbell, mariner, of Hackensack Precinct, Bergen Co., New Jersey to Doctor Beckman van Bueren, yeoman, of same, £125, 10 acres...line of Jacob Quackinbush and

Abraham Brown. Signed Jacob Campbell and Alltie (x) Campbell. Wit: Jacob Terhune and David Terhune.

7 Mar 1794, Christopher Juriansen, John Juriansen, Powles & Nieltya Powleson, Rolof & Sarah van Wagener and Garrabrant Juriansen, all of New Jersey to Richard Bergen, of same, £50, 15 acres...line of John Sip. Signed Neallie (x) Juriansen, Rulof (x) van Wagener, Garrabrant Juriansen, Christopher Juriansen, John (x) Juriansen and Paul Powleson. Wit: John Outwater and Abraham Cark.

25 Jun 1793, John & Marretye Benson, of english neighborhood, Bergen Co., New Jersey to Garret G. Lydecker, of same, £1300, 125 acres...line formerly surveyed for Samuel Edsall, now belonging to heirs of John Degroot and Ryithe Lydecker. Signed Johannes Benson and Marretye Benson. Wit John Westervelt and John Day.

6 May 1794, Jacob & Alleda Campbell, of Hackensack Precinct, Bergen Co., New Jersey to Doctor Beckman van Bueren, yeoman, of same, £130, 2 acres...bounded by Joost Demarest. Signed Jacob Campbell. Wit: Archibald Wade.

7 Nov 1790, John & Attia van Wagener, of Tenafly Neck, Bergen Co., New Jersey to John van Horne, of Bergen Twp., Bergen Co., New Jersey, £522, 12.75 acres...bounded by Nicholas Vreeland. Signed John van Wagener and Altia (x) van Wagener. Wit: Garret van Reypen and Jacob Outwater.

25 Apr 1794, Andrew & Maria Haspending, merchant, of New Burgh, Ulster Co., New York to Abraham Prine, of Bergen, Bergen Co., New Jersey, £280, 5 acres...in Bergen Twp...corner to John Collard. Signed Andrew Haspending and Maria Haspending. Wit: Abraham Westervelt and Cornelia Zabriskie.

30 Apr 1750, Magdalena Valleau, widow, of Hackensack, Bergen Co., New Jersey to elders and

deacons of Peremus Church, for 3 seats in the church, 45 acres...corner to land formerly belonging to John van Boskerk, now Johannes Davidie Ackerman. Signed Magdalena Valleau. Wit: Theodore Valleau and Stephen Bourdett.

23 Sep 1778, John & Mary Haring, of Orange, Orange Co., New York to John Durie, (son of John P. Durie), of Harrington Twp., Bergen Co., New Jersey, £1300, 112 acres...bounded by Garret Ackerson, John Fleerboom, Jacobus Fleerboom, Teunis Blauvelt and Joseph Blauvelt. Signed John Haring and Mary Haring. Wit: Cornelius C. Roosevelt and Joseph (x) Blauvelt.

1 Feb 1794, Abraham & Elizabeth van Emburgh, of New Barbadoes Precinct, Bergen Co., New Jersey to Jotham Baldwin, of same, £30, 12 acres... line of Peter Ackerman and Jacob Hopper. Signed Abraham van Emburgh and Elizabeth van Emburgh. Wit: Archibald Campbell and Isaac Ward.

19 apr 1785, Harmanus & Catharine Brass, of New Barbadoes Precinct, Bergen Co., New Jersey to Christopher Pope, of same, £40, line of John Varick, Peter Zabriskie. Signed Harman Brass and Catharine (x) Brass. Wit: Peter Zabriskie and John Dunlap.

23 Mar 1794, John Mehelm, of Bedminster, Somerset Co., New Jersey and Magnus Beckman, of New York City, (excutors of will of Samuel Beckman) to William McEwen, of Bedminster, Somerset Co., New Jersey, £300, 20 acres...in Hackensack Precinct...formerly belonged to Lawrence van Boskerk...line of John van Boskerk. Signed John Mehelm and Magnus Barkman. Wit: Jacob Coff and Robert Gault.

23 Apr 1794, William & Martha McEwen, of Bedminster, Somerset Co., New Jersey to Magnus Beckman, of New York City, £300, 20 acres. Signed William McEwen and Martha McEwen. Wit: Jacob Coff and Robert Gault.

1 Sep 1794, Isaac Roosevelt, of New York City to

Johannes Blauvelt, of Hackensack Precinct, Bergen Co., New Jersey, £668, 55 acres...line of Roelif Westervelt. Signed Isaac Roosevelt. Wit: Robert Campbell and Richard Varick.

13 Aug 1794, William Colfax, of Saddle River Twp., Bergen Co., New Jersey to William Burton, £80, 31 acres and 10.03 acres...corner to heirs of William Earle...sold by James Dunham to Patrick Hanly, who sold to said Colfax...2nd tract corner to Doctor Stimus. Signed William Colfax. Wit: Jonathan Dodd and Cornelius Hennion.

30 Sep 1794, Benjamin & Elizabeth Vincent, of Bergen Co., New Jersey to William Scott, glasser of Essex Co., New Jersey, £100, 16 acres...in Saddle River Twp...corner to Ezekiel Stymather. Signed Benjamin Vincent and Elizabeth Vincent. Wit: Jonathan Dodd and John Wright.

1 May 1788, Cornelius Haring, agent of forfeited estates, of Bergen Co., New Jersey to Isaac Nicoll, of Hackensack Precinct, Bergen Co., New Jersey, £48, 5 acres...corner to John Romine... seized of Albert Zabriskie, late of Hackensack Precinct, Bergen Co., New Jersey, for joining the army of the King. Signed Cornelius Haring. Wit: David P. Haring and Petrus Haring.

5 Jun 1784, Albert & Lena Banta, of Hackensack Precinct, Bergen Co., New Jersey to Jacob Demott, of same, £500, line of Walter Briggs, James Duncan and Mattys Demott...sold to Hendrick Hendrickse Banta, father of said Albert Banta, by Walter Briggs, 21 Oct 1736 and willed to said Albert Banta 8 Dec 1758, and confirmed by indenture from Samuel Durie, Hendrick Banta and Weyntye Banta, 4 Jan 1762. Signed Albert Banta and Lena (x) Banta. Wit: John Stagg and Casparus Westervelt.

2 Jan 1789, Peter Ward, sheriff of Bergen Co., New Jersey to Catharine Kuyper, of Hackensack Precinct, Bergen Co., New Jersey, £55, 10 acres and 11.4 acres and 6.15 acres and 10 acres...in

the english neighborhood, Hackensack Precinct, Bergen Co., New Jersey...corner to Garret Benson, William Lee, Michael Vreeland and Cornelius van Vorst...purchased from Stephen Bourdett, 28 Feb 1759...second tract purchased from Cornelius Garrabrants...3rd and fourth tracts corner to Kile van Kull and Anthony White...James Bourd recovered in court against Catharine Kuyper, executor of estate of Hendrickus Kuyper £60. Signed Peter Ward. Wit: Abraham Westervelt and John van Houten.

10 Dec 1724, Jacob van Wagener, of Noster Dam, Pomery Pough, Bergen Co., New Jersey to Garret van Wagener, of Slatter Dam, Saddle River Precinct, Bergen Co., New Jersey, £200. Signed Jacob (x) van Wagener. Wit: Peter Cole and Garret Vreeland.

15 Jun 1763, John Zabriskie, Joost Zabriskie, Jacobus Hendrickse Brinkerhof, Jacob van Wagener, Samuel Demarest, Wiert Banta, David Banta, Hendrick Banta, Garret Diedericks, Jacob Banta and Johannis Terhune, all of Hackensack, Bergen Co., New Jersey to Christian Zabriskie, of same, £100. Signed John Zabriskie, Joost Zabriskie, Jacobus Hendrickse Brinkerhof, Jacob van Wagener, Samuel Demarest, Wiert Banta, David Banta, Hendrick Banta, Garret Diedericks, Jacob Banta and Johannis Terhune. Wit: Isaac van Giesen and Guilliam Bertholf.

16 May 1774, Albert Zabriskie, Nicholas Zabriskie, John Zabriskie, Jacob Zabriskie, Peter Zabriskie and Joost Zabriskie, six of the sons of John Zabriskie, deceased to Christian Zabriskie, also a son of the said John Zabriskie, £200, line of Hendrick Brinkerhof and John Ackerson in his will dated 13 Oct 1765, farm to said Christian Zabriskie. Signed Albert (x) Zabriskie, Nicholas (x) Zabriskie, John Zabriskie, Jacob Zabriskie, Peter Zabriskie and Joost Zabriskie. Wit: Robert Morris and John Joost Zabriskie.

21 Jan 1773, David & Hila Banta, of New York

City to Christian Zabriskie, of Hackensack, Bergen Co., New Jersey, £10, bounded by Abraham Lydecker, Derick Banta and Stephen Bourdett. Signed David Banta and Hila (x) Banta. Wit: William Bogart and John Zabriskie Jr.

17 Feb 1767, Joost Zabriskie, yeoman, of Hackensack, Bergen Co., New Jersey to Christian Zabriskie, of same, £50, corner to Jacob Banta, deceased and heirs of Hendrick Brinkerhof...2nd tract corner to Joris Brinkerhof and Hendrick Brinkerhof...devised by John Zabriskie, deceased. Signed Joost Zabriskie. Wit: Jacob Zabriskie and John Zabriskie Jr.

21 Jan 1755, Johannis Duchse Banta and Derick Johannes Banta, both yeoman, of Bergen Co., New Jersey to Peter Zabriskie, of same, £150, 5 acres. Signed Johannes (x) Banta and Derrick (x) Banta. Wit: Joost Zabriskie and Guilliam Bertholf.

29 May 1756, Peter Zabriskie to Christian Zabriskie, yeoman, of Hackensack, Bergen Co., New Jersey, £150. Signed Peter Zabriskie. Wit: Joost Zabriskie and Guilliam Bertholf.

## Chapter 8

### Bergen County
### Courthouse
### Deed Records
### Volume H

Recorded
in
1794-1795

23 Jun 1784, Garret & Ledey **Lydecker**, of the english neighborhood, Bergen Co., New Jersey to Albert **Zabriskie**, of Tuneck, Bergen Co., New Jersey, £775, 1.91 acres and 6.15 acres and 1.77 acres...in Hackensack Precinct...where Daniel **Christie** now lives...bounded by Albert H. **Banta**, Roelif **Bogart** and John **Bogart**...2nd tract corner to Johannis **Peck** and Daniel **Demarest** Signed Garret **Lydecker** and Ledey (x) **Lydecker**. Wit: David **Benson** and Abraham (x) **Blauvelt**.

21 Feb 1756, Samuel **Demarest**, blacksmith, of Hackensack, Bergen Co., New Jersey to Christian **Zabriskie**, yeoman, of Bergen Co., New Jersey, £150, two tracts...corner to heirs of Garret **Benson**...2nd tract purchased by said Samuel **Symese Demarest** and Christian **Zabriskie** from heirs of Lucas van **Horne**. Signed Samuel **Demarest**. Wit: John **Zabriskie** and John **Zabriskie** Jr.

17 Feb 1767, Joost **Zabriskie**, yeoman, of Hackensack, Bergen Co., New Jersey to Christian **Zabriskie**, yeoman, of Bergen Co., New Jersey, £500, 68 acres...line of heirs of John **Zabriskie**, deceased and heirs of Hendrick **Brinkerhof**, deceased. Signed Joost **Zabriskie**. Wit: Jacob **Zabriskie** and John **Zabriskie** Jr.

15 Apr 1793, James & Rachel Demarest, carpenter, of Orange Twp., Orange Co., New York to Jeremiah Pope, of New Barbadoes Twp., Bergen Co., New Jersey, £140, 14 acres...in New Barbadoes Twp. ...corner to Thomas Outwater and land formerly belonging to Elias Williams and Jacobus Ackerman. Signed James Demarest and Rachel Demarest. Wit: John Cassady and Jasper Demarest.

10, Jan 1795, Henry & Mary Denny, hatter, of New York City to Abraham Wilson, merchant, of same, £160, in town of Hackensack...line of Patrick MacFerren and widow Dugan. Signed Henry Denny and Mary Denny. Wit: James L. Bogart and John Westervelt.

13 Apr 1786, Richard van Giesen, of Bergen Co., New Jersey to John van Giesen, of same, £1.2, 1 acre. Signed Derick van Giesen. Wit: William Yeomans and Richard van Giesen.

20 Jan 1795, John & Hannah Cassady, of Warick, Orange Co., New York to Thomas Gardner, of New York City, £300, in town of New Barbadoes...line of Patrick McFadden. Signed John Cassady and Hannah Cassady. Wit: Robert Campbell and Patrick McFadden.

26 Mar 1794, Robert Morris, of New Brunswick, Middlesex Co., New Jersey to Albert Terhune, of Bergen, Bergen Co., New Jersey, £412.1, 157 acres...line of James Debane. Signed Robert Morris. Wit: Jacob Debane and John Puffering.

2 Jan 1792, Marcelius van Giesen, of New York City to Benjamin Day, of same, £654.6, 1224 acres...in town of Saddle River...line of John van Giesen, Cornelius Neafie and Garret van Houten. Signed Marcelius van Giesen. Wit: John Day and P. V. van Emburgh.

1 Dec 1786, Cornelius Haring, agent of forfeited estates, of Bergen Co., New Jersey to Martin Hoffman and Josiah Ogden Hoffman, (sons of Nicholas Hoffman), £220, 535 acres...in Hackensack Precinct...one half formerly

belonging to Abraham Gouverneur, of New York City, deceased and the other half to David Ogden and Abraham Ogden...seized of Nicholas Hoffman, late of New York City, for joining the army of the King. Signed Cornelius Haring. Wit: Isaac Blanch and Richard Blanch.

13 Mar 1794, John & Hannah Cassady, of New Barbadoes Precinct, Bergen Co., New Jersey to Bernard Hart, of New York City, £385, 15 acres ...in town of New Barbadoes...corner to the children of the widow Huyler, Lawrence Ackerman and John Varick. Signed John Cassady and Hannah Cassady. Wit: Robert Campbell and George Campbell.

28 Mar 1795, Abraham & Catharine Collins, of Bergen Co., New Jersey to John E. Seaman, of New York City, £700, at New Bridge...land of said Catharine Collins's former husband, John Zabriskie, deceased. Signed Abraham Collins and Catharine Collins. Wit: Robert Campbell and Nehemiah Wade.

20 Apr 1795, John E. Seaman to his brother, Edward Seaman, Jr., £533.3, bounded by Isaac van Zane and John Terhune...willed to Elizabeth Zabriskie, mother of said John E. Seaman and daughter of grandfather, John Zabriskie, of New Bridge, Bergen Co., New Jersey, in his will dated 27 Jun 1774, he also willed to his son John Zabriskie Jr....formerly purchased of Peter van Voorhees, Daniel van Voorhees and Abraham Brower. Signed John E. Seaman. Wit: Robert Campbell and Thomas Howard.

20 Apr 1795, Edmund Seaman, Jr., of Bergen Co., New Jersey to John E. Seaman, of New York City, £666.65, his interest in estate of John Zabriskie Jr., deceased, of New Bridge, Bergen Co., New Jersey. Signed Edmund Seaman Jr. Wit: Robert Campbell and Thomas Howard.

1 Mar 1792, Isaac & Rachel vander Beck Jr., of New Barbadoes Precinct, Bergen Co., New Jersey to Abraham Collins, of same, £56.2, 5.75 acres

...corner to Hendrick Kip. Signed Isaac vander Beck Jr. and Rachel vander Beck. Wit: Thomas Rozell and Mary Rossel.

10 Feb 1795, James Drummond and Rachel Drummond, heirs of the Earl of Perth, by their attorney Walter Rutherford to Michael Fisher, of Bergen Co., New Jersey, £148, 197 acres. Signed Walter Rutherford. Wit: George Turnbull and Conradt (x) Boss.

1 Jan 1795, Elisha & Catharine Boudinot, of Newark, Essex Co., New Jersey to Michael Fisher, of Bergen Co., New Jersey, £148.2, 197 acres. Signed Elisha Boudinot and Catharine Boudinot. Wit: William P. Smith.

26 Oct 1793, John & Cornelia Smith, yeoman, of Bergen Co., New Jersey to John Butler, bricklayer, of Richmond, New York, £200, 11.4 acres...corner to Jacob van Wagener...formerly belonging to Job Smith, deceased, who willed to his son the said John Smith. Signed John Smith and Cornelia Smith. Wit: Israel Oakley and Peter Lozier.

11 Mar 1795, Abraham & Mariah Brown, of Hackensack Precinct, Bergen Co., New Jersey to John Christeen, blacksmith, of New Barbadoes, Bergen Co., New Jersey, £250, 6 acres...corner to Beckman van Bueren. Signed Abraham Brown and Mariah (x) Brown. Wit: Lucas van Saen and John Brown Jr.

14 Sep 1790, William Burnet, of South Amboy, Middlesex Co., New Jersey to Peter van Zile, of Franklin Twp., Bergen Co., New Jersey, £144.3, 155.52 acres...corner to survey of James Alexander and Robert Hunter Morris dated 12 Jun 1753. Signed William Burnet. Wit John Thompson and Abraham Willis.

1 Aug 1792, William Burnet, of South Amboy, Middlesex Co., New Jersey to John Johnston, of Perth Amboy, Middlesex Co., New Jersey, of the second part, (executor of the will dated 2 May

1761, of Andrew **Johnston**, late of Perth Amboy, Middlesex, Co., New Jersey), and Albert van **Zile** of Franklin Precinct, Bergen Co., New Jersey, of the third part, £135.1, 108 acres...in Franklin Precinct...two tracts of land patented 14 Mar 1700 by Michael **Hawden**, containing 600 acres and sold to the said Andrew **Johnston** and George **Willock**. Signed William **Burnet** and John **Johnston**. Wit: Cornelius **Hennion**, John **Thompson**, (for Johnston), Alche van **Voorhees** and John **Thompson**, (for Burnet).

16 Jul 1794, Bernard **Hart**, of New York City to Martin **Hoffman**, of same, £242.5, 18 acres...in town of New Barbadoes...line of Lawrence **Ackerman**, John **Varick** and Archibald **Campbell**. Signed Bernard **Hart**. Wit: Gabriel W. **Ludlow** and Mat. W. **Howell**.

26 Mar 1795, Abraham **Montanye**, farmer, of the english neighborhood, Bergen Co., New Jersey to David H. **Mellows**, yeoman, of New York City, £2050, 200 acres...line of John **Smith** and Peter **Demarest**...bounded by Garret **Lydecker** and Benjamin **Westervelt**. Signed Abraham **Montanye**. Wit: Peter **Arell**, Jacob **Degroot** and John J. **Montanye**.

12 Mar 1774, Jacobus Gust **Jacobusse**, of Pequaneck, Saddle River Twp., Bergen Co., New Jersey to Theunis **Ryerse** Jr., blacksmith, of Prakence, Saddle River Twp., Bergen Co., New Jersey, £26, 12 acres...corner to Jacob **Mead**. Signed Jacobus G. (x) **Jacobusse**. Wit: George **Ryerse** and Elizabeth **Ryerse**.

21 Sep 1793, David P. & Hester **Demarest**, of Hackensack Precinct, Bergen Co., New Jersey to Ceasar **Mestayer** and Mary Magdalena **Mestayer**, both of New Barbadoes Precinct, Bergen Co., New Jersey, £700, 19 acres...corner to Peter **Demarest** and Giliam **Bogart**...bounded by John **Anderson** purchased from David & Catharine **Demarest**, 20 Mar 1765. Signed David **Demarest** and Hester **Demarest**. Wit: Robert **Campbell** and Peter **Christie**.

1 Aug 1792, William Burnet, of South Amboy, Middlesex Co., New Jersey to John Johnston, of Perth Amboy, Middlesex Co., New Jersey, of the second part, (executor of the will dated 2 May 1761, of Andrew Johnston, late of Perth Amboy, Middlesex, Co., New Jersey), and John Willis of Franklin Precinct, Bergen Co., New Jersey, of the third part, £282.35, 209 acres. Signed William Burnet and John Johnston. Wit: Cornelius Hennion, John Thompson, (for Johnston), Alche van Voorhees and John Thompson, (for Burnet).

24 May 1783, Johannis S. van Winkle, of Bergen Co., New Jersey to Simeon J. van Winkle, of Essex Co., New Jersey, £500, 100 acres and 212 acres...corner to Hannes Bricker...2nd tract line of Peter Garretson and Derick Barentsen. Signed John S. (x) van Winkle. Wit: Robert Blair and Charles Slade.

26 Oct 1774, Simeon van Winkle, of Essex Co., New Jersey to John van Winkle, of Bergen Co., New Jersey, £144, 212 acres...line of Peter Garretson. Signed Simeon (x) van Winkle. Wit: Hessel Peterson and Jacobus Post.

1 Jun 1743, Garret Garretson, yeoman, of Bergen Co., New Jersey to Simeon van Winlke, of Essex Co., New Jersey, £215, 212 acres...said Garret Garretson, Derick Barentsen, Peter Garretson, Johannes Garretson and Abraham Garretson purchased from Richard Ashfield and Derick Barentse, Peter Garretson, Johannes Garretson and Abraham Garretson sold 9 Feb 1732 to said Garret Garretson. Signed Garret (x) Garretson. Wit: Casparus Schuyler and George Vreeland.

1 Jul 1766, Abraham & Sarah Rutan, yeoman, of Saddle River, Bergen Co., New Jersey to Johannis van Winkle, yeoman, of same, £300, 100 acres... corner to Hannes Bricker. Signed Abraham (x) Rutan and Sarah (x) Rutan. Wit: Isaac Kingsland and Guilliam Bertholf.

26 May 1791, Adam Boyd, sheriff of Bergen Co., New Jersey to Joost A. Zabriskie, of New

Barbadoes Precinct, Bergen Co., New Jersey, £151, 0.25 acres...in New Barbadoes Precinct ...Ralph Thurman and Richard Thurman recovered in court £81 from William M. Bell, executor of estate of Joost C. Zabriskie. Signed Adam Boyd. Wit: Jacob van Houten and Catharine Boyd.

5 Dec 1792, John Johan & Antye Demarest, tanner, of New Barbadoes Twp., Bergen Co., New Jersey to Joost Alb. Zabriskie, of same, £100, 0.75 acres. Signed John Demarest and Anne Demarest.

9 Mar 1792, Cornelius & Ann Cooper, of New Barbadoes, Bergen Co., New Jersey to Nehemiah Wade, of same, £45, 1.5 acres...corner to Reverend Solomon Freligh. Signed Cornelius Cooper and Ann Cooper. Wit: Jacob Brower and James Hodge.

17 Oct 1791, John & Mary van Houten, farmer, of Bergen Co., New Jersey to John Neafie, £430, 105 acres and 52 acres...bounded by Martin J. Ryerson and Gabriel Ogden. Signed John van Houten and Mary van Houten. Wit: Nehemiah Wade and Wallace D. Nicoll.

10 Jun 1769, Weart H. & Hannah Banta, carpenter, of Hackensack, Bergen Co., New Jersey to Jacobus Roosevelt, of New York City, £190, 60 acres... corner to Samuel Demarest Sr. Signed Wert Banta and Hannah Banta. Wit: Andrew Barbene and James Hearny.

1 Aug 1794, Robert Campbell, of New Barbadoes Precinct, Bergen Co., New Jersey to Isaac Roosevelt, of New York City, £140, 56 acres... line of Roelif Westervelt. Signed Robert Campbell. Wit: James Roosevelt and Richard Varick.

2 May 1795, David P. Demarest, of Bergen Co., New Jersey to David Anderson and Abraham van Boskerk release of bond for £400. Signed David P. Demarest. Wit: Jacob Terhune and Catharine Terhune.

1 Feb 1795, John & Sarah Terrill and John M. & Rachel Clark, of Elizabeth, Essex Co., New Jersey to Samuel Berry, of New Barbadoes Precinct, Bergen Co., New Jersey, £95.7, 8.5 acres...in New Barbadoes Precinct...line of Enoch G. Vreeland. Signed John Terrill, Sarah Terrill, John M. Clark and Rachel Clark. Wit: John Outwater and John Vryper.

12 Jun 1787, David Brown, of Bergen Co., New Jersey to John Brown, of same, £25, chattel goods. Signed David Brown. Wit: John Yertes and Simon Dooremus.

1 Apr 1794, Reuben & Catharine Carter, of Barbadoes Neck, Bergen Co., New Jersey to David Tuttle, of same, £80.4, 2 acres. Signed Reuben Carter and Catharine (x) Carter. Wit: William Budd and William S. Pennington.

17 Jun 1795, William S. & Phebe Pennington, of Newark, Essex Co., New Jersey to William Budd, of New Barbadoes, Bergen Co., New Jersey, £278, 21.39 acres...corner to Francis Tuers...line of Enoch and Peter Sandford...bounded by Sarah Sandford. Signed William S. Pennington and Phebe Pennington. Wit: Anamas Baldwin, Cornelius van Reypen and Daniel van Reypen.

22 Aug 1795, John & Caty Neafie, of Franklin Twp., Bergen Co., New Jersey to Albert Zabriskie, of Harrington Twp., Bergen Co., New Jersey, £179.65, 108.4 acres...in Harrington Twp ...corner to John van Horne...part of 322 acres returned 14 Feb 1796 to Richard Morris trustee of Robert Hunter Morris, deceased...said Richard Morris sold to said Neafie 1 Aug 1795. Signed John Neafie and Caty (x) Neafie. Wit: Abraham Willis and Abraham Westervelt.

1 May 1786, Cornelius Haring, John Haring and John Neafie, all of Franklin Twp., Bergen Co., New Jersey to Jacob van Horne, of Harrington Twp., Bergen Co., New Jersey, £34.7, 34.72 acres... in Harrington Twp...line of George Hackinback and John van Boskerk. Signed

Cornelius Haring, John Haring and John Neafie. Wit: Peter Ward and John Hopper.

22 Aug 1795, Catharine Neafie, wife of John Neafie, for £0.25, releases her dower rights. Signed Catharine (x) Neafie. Wit: Abraham Willis and Abraham Westervelt.

15 May 1785, Richard Day, sheriff of Bergen Co., New Jersey to Aaron Burr, of New York City, £520, 98 acres and 151.74 acres...corner to Benjamin Odle, ...2nd tract corner to Henry Hopper, Peter Dubois and John Hopper...Anne Baldwin recovered £470 in court of Joseph Brown executor of estate of James Marcus Provoost. Signed Richard Day. Wit: William Treson,y John Bartow Provoost and John Cleves Seymmes.

9 Jul 1794, William Cutting, of New York City to William M. Bell, of Franklin Precinct, Bergen Co., New Jersey, £981, 98 acres and 151.74 acres ...in Franklin Precinct ...corner to Benjamin Odle...2nd tract in lin of Henry Hopper, Kingsland's patent and John Hopper. Signed William Cutting. Wit: Alexander C. McWhorter and John Wells.

17 Feb 1767, Helmegh van Houten, of Bergen Precinct, Bergen Co., New Jersey to Roelif Westervelt, of the english neighborhood, Bergen Co., New Jersey, £107.85, 25 acres...corner to land formerly belonging to Jacob Banta...line of Cornelius Brinkerhof, Michael Smith, Abraham Montanye...purchased from John Christeen 11 Sep 1761. Signed Helmegh van Houten. Wit: Johannis van Houten and Lois Marselius.

27 Apr 1756, Samuel & Sarah Moore Sr. and Samuel & Hester Moore Jr., all of Bergen Co., New Jersey to Benjamin Westervelt, yeoman, of same, £560, 150 acres...in Hackensack Precinct...line of John Moore and Garret Hennion...bounded by Thomas Moore. Signed Samuel Moore, Sarah Moore, Samuel Moore and Hester (x) Moore. Wit: Garret Benson and Guilliam Bertholf.

1 Nov 1795, Brian van Horne, Nicholas & Janetie Tuers and John & Allia Marselius, all of Bergen, Bergen Co., New Jersey to Daniel van Ryper, of same, £10, lately owned by Garret van Ryper. Signed Brian (x) van Horne, Nicholas Tuers, Janetie (x) Tuers, John Marselius and Allia (x) Marselius. Wit: John van Horne and Zacharias Sickels.

20 May 1790, George Ryerson, Richard Ryerson, Martin Ryerson and Francis Ryerson, all of Bergen Co., New Jersey are bound to each other by £200 to decide the division of their lands by Daniel Donetson, Joost Beam, Abraham Ryerson and Conrad Beam. Signed Joost Beam, Daniel Donetson, Abraham (x) Ryerson and Conrad (x) Beam.

16 Apr 1795, Benjamin Day power of attorney to John Day, of Saddle River Twp., Bergen Co., New Jersey, to sell land in Saddle River Twp., 124 acres...purchased of Marcelius M. van Giesen, 3 Jan 1792 ...bounded by John van Giesen and Garret van Houten, deceased...second tract purchased of Richard Day, John Day, Philip Day, Peter Day and David Day Mar 1795. Signed Benjamin Day. Wit: Henry Mead, Rachael Mead and Margaret Jacobusse.

28 Jan 1795, John & Helena van Dalson, of Hackensack Twp., Bergen Co., New Jersey to John van Boskerk, of Bergen Twp., Bergen Co., New Jersey, £144, 12 acres...in Bergen Twp...bounded by former property of Henricus Kuyper, deceased, now of John Vreeland...line of Thomas Brown and Peter van Boskerk. Signed John van Dalson and Helena (x) van Dalson. Wit: Solomon Freligh and William Christie.

1 May 1754, Lewis Morris Ashfield, eldest son of Richard Ashfield, deceased, of New York to Cornelius Kip, Cornelius Dooremus and Hendrick Dooremus, £60, 829 acres...Kip van Dam and Richard Ashfield sold to Cornelius Kip and George Dooremus...said George Dooremus was the father of Cornelius Dooremus and Hendrick Dooremus. Signed Lewis M. Ashfield. Wit: Anthony

Dennis and Teunis Jaroleman.

5 Oct 1795, Isaac & Rachel vander Beck, of New Barbadoes Precinct, Bergen Co., New Jersey to Jacob vander Pool, of same, £50, corner to Rowland Hill. Signed Isaac vander Beck and Rachel vander Beck. Wit: Henry Bartrim and Anne P. (x) vander Beck.

6 May 1795, Trustees of Liberty Hall of Schralenburgh, Harrington Twp., Bergen Co., New Jersey, named. Signed Daniel Demarest, Abraham Demarest, Benjamin Blacklidge, Solomon Freligh, David Durie and Isaac Kip.

7 May 1795, Trustees of School House in Closter named. Signed Isaac Nagel, David Nagel and Abraham Ferdon.

1 Jan 1791, John & Elshe Drummond, of Saddle River Precinct, Bergen Co., New Jersey to Robert Drummond, of same, £10, 10.16 acres...where John van Ryper now lives...line of Garret Thibow... formerly property of widow Elizabeth Firm. Signed John Drummond and Elshe (x) Drummond. Wit: Cornelius Hennion and Abraham Spear.

1 Jun 1792, John & Elsey Earle, Clausia Earle and Mary Earle, all of Bergen Corporation, Bergen Co., New Jersey to John Smith, farmer, of same, £1300, 189.5 acres...line of Daniel Smith and John Leake...bounded by Edward Earle. Signed John Earle, Elsey Earle, Clausia (x) Earle and Elsey (x) Earle. Wit: Job Smith and Byneon Earle.

7 Mar 1795, John & Cornelia Smith, of Bergen Corporation, Bergen Co., New Jersey to John Stevens, of Hoboken, Bergen Corporation, Bergen Co., New Jersey, £250, 189.5 acres...line of Daniel Smith and John Leake...bounded by Edward Earle. Signed John Smith and Cornelia Smith. Wit: John Seely and Joseph Smith.

10 Mar 1795, John George Leake, of New York City to John Stevens, of same, £4000, 400 acres and

25 acres and 35.5 acres and 8.75 acres and 13 acres...on Island of Seacaucus ...corner to late Edward Earle and Daniel Smith ...2nd tract corner to Philip Earle...purchased by Robert Leake, deceased, (father of said John George Leake) and Andrew & Rachel Teed, 7 Mar 1762 ...3rd tract conveyed to John Earle by his brother Richard Earle...5th tract...line of Hartman Brinkerhof. Signed John George Leake. Wit: Isaac Mead and John Seely.

1 May 1787, Ichabod Grumman, of Bergen Co., New Jersey to George McIntire, of same, £0.25, 11.4 acres...corner to Kile van Kull and Cornelius van Vorst. Signed Ichabod Grumman. Wit: Andrew Gautier, Daniel Smith and John Chetwood.

5 Mar 1796, Commissioners of the Loan Office, of Bergen Co., New Jersey to John van Bueren and Robert Campbell, of Bergen Co., New Jersey, £162, 106 acres...corner to Abraham and Jacob Stagg. Signed John Outwater and Henry Berry. Wit: John Westervelt and George Ryerson.

1 Mar 1796, Commissioners of the Loan Office, of Bergen Co., New Jersey to John van Bueren and Robert Campbell, of Bergen Co., New Jersey, £140, 45 acres...in Franklin Twp...corner to Johannes van Zile. Signed John Outwater and Henry Berry. Wit: John Westervelt and George Ryerson.

9 Mar 1792, Cornelius & Ann Cooper, New Barbadoes Precinct, Bergen Co., New Jersey to Nehemiah Wade, of same, £45, 1.5 acres...corner to Reverend Solomon Freligh and Isaac Bardan. Signed Cornelius Cooper and Ann Cooper. Wit: Jacob Brewer and James Hodge.

23 Feb 1796, Edmund & Elizabeth Seaman Jr., of New Barbadoes Twp., Bergen Co., New Jersey to John Anderson, of same, £1500, 74.5 acres and 38.5 acres and 24.5 acres...2nd tract bounded by Jacob van Saen, Peter Wilson and William Williams...3rd tract bounded by Luke van Saen and Albert J. van Voorhees. Signed Edmund Seaman

Jr. and Elizabeth (x) Seaman. Wit: Nehemiah Wade and Jacob Terhune.

5 Mar 1796, Commissioners of the Loan Office, of Bergen Co., New Jersey to John van Bueren and Robert Campbell, of Bergen Co., New Jersey, £100, 106 acres...in Hackensack Precinct ...corner to Abraham and Jacob Stagg...line of Samuel Brewer. Signed John Outwater and Henry Berry. Wit: John Westervelt and George Ryerson.

14 Mar 1796, Robert Campbell, of Bergen Co., New Jersey to Roelif Demarest, $50.00, quit claim. Signed Robert Campbell. Wit: Isaac Kip and Jacob Terhune.

14 Mar 1796, John & Catharine van Bueren, of Hackensack, Bergen Co., New Jersey to Roelif Demarest, of Hackensack Precinct, Bergen Co., New Jersey, $500.00, 106 acres...purchased with Robert Campbell from the commissioners of Bergen Co., New Jersey. Signed John van Bueren and Catharine van Bueren. Wit: Peter Demarest and Isaac Kipp.

15 Jul 1784, Cornelius Haring, agent of forfeited estates in Bergen Co., New Jersey to Peter Ward, of Saddle River Precinct, Bergen Co., New Jersey, £765, 63 acres...in Franklin Twp...line of Simon van Winkle and Peter van Zile...seized of Robert Drummond, late of Essex Co., New Jersey, for joining the army of the King. Signed Cornelius Haring. Wit: John Hopper and Petrus Haring.

15 Aug 1793, William M. Bell, sheriff of Bergen Co., New Jersey to Peter Ward, of Bergen Co., New Jersey, £20, 179 acres and 147 acres and 116 acres...in Franklin Twp...Abraham Lott recovered in court, £82.95 of John Johnson. Signed William M. Bell. Wit: Ann Zabriskie and John DeHensck.

29 Feb 1796, Richard Bergen, of New Barbadoes Neck, Bergen Co., New Jersey to Casparus Degraw, of same, £9, 0.5 acres. Signed Richard Bergen. Wit: James Ernis and Nassel Juriansen.

1 Apr 1795, Jacob & Margret Snyder, of Saddle River Precinct, Bergen Co., New Jersey to Harmanus Brass, yeoman, of same, £88, 17.6 acres. Signed Jacob Snyder and Margret (x) Snyder. Wit: Henry van Allen and Thomas Snyder.

23 Mar 1796, Harmanus & Ann Brass, of Saddle River Precinct, Bergen Co., New Jersey to Richard Degraw, of same, £90, 17.6 acres... bounded by Francis van Winkle, Andrew Snyder and Garrabrant Garretson. Signed Harmanus Brass and Ann (x) Bross. Wit: Jacob Snyder and Margaret (x) Snyder.

6 Nov 1790, John P. Garretson, of Saddle River Precinct, Bergen Co., New Jersey to Jacob Snyder, of Hackensack Precinct, Bergen Co., New Jersey, £150, 50 acres...corner to Francis van Winkle. Signed John P. Garretson. Wit: Abraham Willis and Nassel Ryerson.

12 Oct 1784, Coonrat & Clorche Lines, (alias Rutan), of Wyoming, Pennsylvania to Daniel Lines, of Franklin Twp., Bergen Co., New Jersey, £150, 71.51 acres...corner to survey returned to Richard Ashfield and deeded to Anthony Beam... formerly belonging to Coonrat Lines, deceased. Signed Coonrat (x) Lines and Clorche (x) Lines. Wit: John Collins and Jacob Beam.

19 Jun 1795, Albert & Rachel van Zile, of Franklin Twp., Bergen Co., New Jersey to Abraham van Zile, of same, £1, 106.24 acres...corner to Martin Holmes...part of the farm of the late Peter van Zile. Signed Albert van Zile and Rachel van Zile. Wit: John Willis and John Willis Jr.

16 Jan 1796, Benjamin Seaman, (a grandchild of John Zabriskie) to his brother Edmund Seaman, £533.3, bounded by Isaac van Zane and John Terhune...willed to Elizabeth Zabriskie, mother of said John E. Seaman and daughter of grandfather, John Zabriskie, of New Bridge, Bergen Co., New Jersey, in his will dated 27 Jun 1774, he also willed to his son John Zabriskie

Jr....formerly purchased of Peter van Voorhees, Daniel van Voorhees and Abraham Brower. Signed Benjamin Seaman. Wit: Robert Campbell and Charles S. Ogden.

13 Mar 1796, Hessel Ryerson, of Saddle River Twp., Bergen Co., New Jersey to John G. Ryerson, of same, £0.25, 77.6 acres and 12 acres and 50.6 acres...whereas John Ryerson, deceased, willed 4 Dec 1779, devised to his son, said Hessel Ryerson, one fourth part and to his grandson, John G. Ryerson, son of George Ryerson, one third part...land surveyed by Abraham Willis. Signed Hessel Ryerson. Wit: Richard Day and Abraham Willis.

16 Mar 1787, Simon van Ness, of Morris Co., New York to Peter S. Roome, of same, £200, 69.37 acres and 15.2 acres and 105 acres. Signed Simon van Ness. Wit: Henry Doyle and Isaac Hawlenbeck.

18 Apr 1796, Caleb & Patience Wade, of Bergen Co., New Jersey to Jonas Wade, of Essex Co., New Jersey, £450, 6.75 acres...line of William Clark, Doctor van Boskerk, Richard Eaton and Peter Christie. Signed Caleb Wade and Patience (x) Wade. Wit: Lucas van Boskerk and Phebe Wade.

18 Apr 1796, Thomas & Sarah Lawrence, blacksmith, of Bergen Co., New Jersey to Cornelius Meyer, of same, £350, 20 acres...in Hackensack Twp...line of Jacob Quackinbush. Signed Thomas Lawrence and Sarah Lawrence. Wit: Walter D. Nicoll, Sarah Nicoll and Margret Nicoll.

18 Apr 1796, Isaac & Deborah Nicoll, of Bergen Co., New Jersey to Thomas Lawrence, of same, £2500, 100 acres...by farm of said Nicoll. Signed Isaac Nicoll and Deborah Nicoll. Wit: I. Lawrence Jr. and Walter D. Nicoll.

1 May 1790, John J. Post, yeoman, of Franklin Precinct, Bergen Co., New Jersey to John Bantow, yeoman, of same, £200, 125 acres and 100 acres ...line of Daniel Rutan...2nd tract corner to

land purchased by Peter Post, now owned by Jacob vander Beck. Signed John J. Post. Wit: John R. van Voorhees and David Spear.

20 Mar 1792, Johannes & Catharine Terhune, of Bergen Co., New Jersey to Joost Zabriskie, of same, £16, 2 acres...in New Barbadoes Precinct ...corner to Cornelius Bogart. Signed Johannes Terhune and Catharine (x) Terhune. Wit: Frances Zabriskie and Sarah (x) Huyler.

13 Apr 1796,, John & Caty van Cleave, of the english neighborhood, Bergen Co., New Jersey to William Danielsen, of Corporation of Bergen, Bergen Co., New Jersey, £177, 4.5 acres...line of Peter Degroot. Signed John van Cleave and Caty (x) van Cleave. Wit: John Day and William Lozier.

25 Feb 1796, Garret Vreeland, of Corporation of Bergen, Bergen Co., New Jersey to John Vreeland, of same, division of lands they jointly own... corner to Michael Vreeland, Nicholas Vreeland, Michael Cornelius Vreeland, Daniel van Reypen, Thomas Brown, George Vreeland, Jacob van Wagener, deceased. Signed John Vreeland. Wit: Henry Cole and Thomas Cubberly.

25 Feb 1796, John Vreeland, of Corporation of Bergen, Bergen Co., New Jersey to Garret Vreeland, of same, division of lands they jointly own. Signed Garret Vreeland. Wit Henry Cole and Thomas Cubberly.

29 Jan 1793, Marynes van Winkle, of New Barbadoes Precinct, Bergen Co., New Jersey to Thomas van Ryper, of Saddle River Precinct, Bergen Co., New Jersey, £3.6, 1 acre...in Saddle River Precinct...corner to Samuel Reading. Signed Marines (x) van Winkle. Wit: Cusparus Burk and Garret Burk.

27 Dec 1776, Johannis & Hester Dedrix, of Corporation of Bergen, Bergen Co., New Jersey to Daniel Dedrix, of same, £15, 7 acres. Signed Johannis Dedrix and Hester (x) Dedrix. Wit:

Elbert Post and David Campbell.

15 Feb 1764, Johannes Diedericks, Garret Diedericks, Cornelius Diedericks, Abraham Diedericks, Johannes & Anntye Vreeland and Margaret van Ryper, widow, all heirs of Wander Diedericks, of Bergen Co., New Jersey to Daniel Diedericks, of Bergen Co., New Jersey, £7, in town of Bergen, bounded by Frederick Thomas, Garret Garretson, Lawrence Arentson Toor and John Arentson Toor...purchased by said Wander Diedericks from Cloes Arentson Toor and John Arentson Toor, executors of estate of Englebert Steenhuys. Signed Johannes Diedericks, Garret Diedericks, Cornelius (x) Diedericks, Abraham Diedericks. Aatie (x) Vreeland, Johannis Vreeland and Margaret (x) van Ryper.

1 Aug 1755, Johannes Diedericks, Garret Diedericks, Cornelius Diedericks, Johannes & Anntye Vreeland and Margaret Juriansen, widow, all of Bergen Co., New Jersey to Abraham Diedericks, £14, in Bergen Twp...between Peter Marselius and Haun van Houten ...bounded by Johannes Juriansen. Signed Johannes Diedericks, Garret (x) Dedrix, Cornelius (x) Dedrix, Anntye (x) Vreeland, Margaritie (x) Juriansen and Johannis (x) Vreeland. Wit: Johannis Marselius and Peter Marselius.

1 Aug 1755, Johannes Diedericks, Garret Diedericks, Abraham Diedericks, Johannes & Anntye Vreeland and Margaret Juriansen, widow, all of Bergen Co., New Jersey to Cornelius Diedericks, £14, between Hendrick van Winkle and Garret Juriansen, son of Jursoa Garretson, deceased...line of Johannes van Wagener. Signed Johannes Diedericks, Garret (x) Dedrix, Abraham Diedericks, Anntye (x) Vreeland, Margaritie (x) Juriansen and Johannis (x) Vreeland. Wit: Johannis Marselius and Peter Marselius.

18 Jun 1785, Akeyea Fielding, of Pamrepe, Bergen Co., New Jersey to Egbert Post, of same, £304, 32 acres...line of Michael Vreeland and Cornelius van Boskerk. Signed Akeyea (x)

Fielding. Wit: Daniel van Reypen and John Day.

26 Sep 1794, Daniel Smith, farmer, of Corporation of Bergen, Bergen Co., New Jersey to Egbert Post, of same, £60, 6 acres. Signed Daniel Smith. Wit: John Kelly and Zacharias Sickels.

26 Sep 1794, Catharine Kuyper, (widow and executor of estate of Hendrick Kuyper, of Bergen Twp., Bergen Co., New Jersey), of Bergen Co., New Jersey to Egbert Post, of Bergen Twp., Bergen Co., New Jersey, £68, 6 acres...corner to the widow Brown. Signed Catharine Kuyper. Wit: Zacharias Sickels and Cornelius Garrabrants.

26 Sep 1794, John van Dalsem, yeoman, of Bergen Co., New Jersey to Egbert Post, of Bergen Twp., Bergen Co., New Jersey, £68, 6 acres...corner to Catharine Kuyper. Signed John van Dalsem. Wit: Zacharias Sickels and Cornelius Garrabrants.

14 Sep 1795, William Colfax, of Saddle River Twp., Bergen Co., New Jersey to Nicholas Cocoro, of same, £160, 42.51 acres...corner to Garrabrant and Helmegh van Houten. Signed William Colfax. Wit: Richard Day and John Neafie.

5 May 1796, Derick Banta, of Tenafly, Hackensack Precinct, Bergen Co., New Jersey to John P. Durie, of Harring Town, Bergen Co., New Jersey, £464.65, corner to Dower R. Westervelt, Daniel Romine, John P. Bogart, John Lozier and Elias Day. Signed Derick (x) Banta. Wit: John J. Westervelt and Benjamin Blacklidge.

1 May 1796, John S. & Rachel Banta, of Tenafly, Hackensack Precinct, Bergen Co., New Jersey to John P. Durie, of Harring Town, Bergen Co., New Jersey, £1735.35, 56 acres and other tracts... line of Roelif and John Brinkerhof, Daniel Romine, Derick Banta, Dower R. Westervelt, John T. Bogart, John J. Bogart and John Blauvelt. Signed John S. Banta and Rachel Banta. Wit: John J. Westervelt and Benjamin Blacklidge.

2 Feb 1790, Garret Lydecker, of the english neighborhood, Bergen Co., New Jersey to John Smith, of same, £18, 2.5 acres...corner to the heirs of Albert G. Lydecker. Signed Garret Lydecker. Wit: John Day and Garret G. Lydecker.

29 Apr 1793, Garret A. & Martyntye Lydecker, of Franklin Twp., Bergen Co., New Jersey, John A. & Annye Lydecker, Abraham A. & Rebecca Lydecker, of Clarkstown, and Cornelius A. & Margaret Lydecker, of Orange Town, Orange Co., New York to John M. Smith, of english neighborhood, Bergen Co., New Jersey, £57.4, 5.65 acres... east side of Overpeck Creek, english neighborhood, Bergen Co., New Jersey...line of Garret G. Lydecker. Signed Garret A. Lydecker, Martyntye Lydecker, John Lydecker, Annie Lydecker, Abraham Lydecker, Rebekah Lydecker, Cornelius Lydecker and Margaret Lydecker. Wit: Petrus Haring, James Demarest, Abraham Demarest and Petrus Haring.

5 May 1794, Albert C. & Seintie Zabriskie, of Hackensack Precinct, Bergen Co., New Jersey to John Smith, of same, £500, 52.75 acres...corner to Samuel James Moore. Signed Albert C. Zabriskie and Seintie Zabriskie. Wit: Abel Smith and Benjamin Westervelt.

19 Mar 1792, Jacob & Margaret Snyder, carpenter, of Saddle River Precinct, Bergen Co., New Jersey to Francis van Winkle, farmer, of same, £21, three eighth parts of land in agreement made 25 May 1784 between John C. Garretson, John J. Ryerson and said van Winkle. Signed Jacob Snyder and Margaret (x) Snyder. Wit: George Ryerson and Thomas C. Mills.

7 Apr 1795, John van Bueren, of Bergen Co., New Jersey to Nicholas Squire, of same, £425, 44 acres...line of Thomas Harrison, deceased and Isaac Kingsland, deceased. Signed John van Bueren. Wit: Nehemiah Wade and Richard Zabriskie.

3 May 1796, Mary Ryerson, (widow of Thurnis

Ryerson), of Totowa, Bergen Co., New Jersey to
John Dooremus, of same, £650, 74 acres and 35
acres...line of Garret van Houten, deceased.
Signed Mary Ryerson. Wit: John Outwater and
Abraham Westervelt.

3 May 1796, Mary Ryerson, (widow of Thurnis
Ryerson), of Totowa, Bergen Co., New Jersey to
Richard Ryerson, of Preakness, Bergen Co., New
Jersey, £400, 36.3 acres...line of Isaac vander
Beck. Signed Mary Ryerson. Wit: Cornelius
Hennion and John Hopper.

17 Apr 1794, Richard & Hannah Day, and Samuel &
Leah van Saen, all of Bergen Co., New Jersey to
Elizabeth van Winkle, of same, £125, 30 acres
...in Saddle River Twp...line of John van Winkle
and Mathew & Gentry Cronkhite. Signed Richard
Day, Hannah Day, Samuel (x) van Saen and Leah
(x) van Saen. Wit: Frans Romine and Abraham
Ryerson.

## Chapter 9

## Bergen County
## Courthouse
## Deed Records
## Volume J

## Recorded
## in
## 1795-1798

8 Sep 1795, Petrus Haring, Jacob Terhune and Abraham Westervelt, judges of Superior Court, nominate John Haring, John W. Hopper and Henry Wammamaker to partition the lands of Aury J. Ackerman, 118.51 acres...in Franklin Twp., Bergen Co., New Jersey. Signed Petrus Haring, Jacob Terhune and Abraham Westervelt.

23 Mar 1796, assigning of lots, house of Archibald Campbell, innkeeper, New barbadoes Precinct, Bergen Co., New Jersey...lot 1, 29 acres, to heirs of Andrew Johnston...lot 2, 30 acres, to James Parker...lot 3, 30 acres, to Isaac Sharp. Signed John Haring, John Hopper, John D. Haring Sr. and Henry Wammamaker.

21 Apr 1772, Nathaniel Davenport, of New Foundland, Bergen Co., New Jersey to Cornelius Davenport and John M. Davenport, of same, £165, 93.24 and 24 acres and 11.58... three tracts...in Saddle River Precinct...3rd tract corner to Humphry Davenport. Signed Nathaniel Davenport. Wit: John Davenport and Abraham Smith.

4 Jun 1796, John Davenport and Leonard Davenport, of New Foundland, Morris Co., New Jersey and Abraham Davenport, (heir of John Davenport, deceased), of Pequanack, Morris Co., New Jersey to John and Cornelius Davenport, of

Saddle River Twp., Bergen Co., New Jersey, £0.25, 105 acres...to correct error in deed.. whereas John Davenport sold to Humphry Davenport 105 acres 24 Dec 1751 in Morris Co., New Jersey who willed it to his sons John and Cornelius Davenport. Signed John Davenport and Leonard (x) Davenport. Wit: David Marinus and Jacob Davenport.

4 Jun 1796, Samuel Seward, of Saddle River Twp., Bergen Co., New Jersey to Cornelius Davenport, of same, £12.3, 11.1 acres...purchased of Samuel Cole. Signed Samuel Seward. Wit: John Welling, Jacob Davenport and David Marinus.

9 Jan 1796, Stephen Bogart, yeoman, of Franklin Twp., Bergen Co., New Jersey to John Haring, yeoman and Abraham Rutan, yeoman, of same, £9.25, line of heirs of Jacobus van Voorhees and Andrew Hopper. Signed Stephen Bogart. Wit: Cornelius Bogart and Garret D. Ackerman.

20 Oct 1795, Elizabeth van Emburgh, of New York City to Henry Kark, of New Barbadoes Neck, Bergen Co., New Jersey, £20, 1 acres...line of Joseph Kingsland. Signed Elizabeth van Emburgh. Wit: Gilbert van Emburgh and Abraham van Emburgh.

12 Jul 1796, Elizabeth Harrison, widow, of Barbadoes Neck, Bergen Co., New Jersey to Abraham van Emburgh, of same, £34, 1.15 acres. Signed Elizabeth Harrison. Wit: John Ferdon and Henry Kark.

26 Sep 1793, David & Ellener Brower, of New Barbadoes Precinct, Bergen Co., New Jersey to Theodorus Brower, of New York City, £50, 5 acres ...line of John Bardan and Peter Wilson. Signed David Brower and Elenner (x) Brower. Wit: John van Norden and Peter Brower.

6 Sep 1796, George & Elizabeth van Giesen, of New Barbadoes Precinct, Bergen Co., New Jersey to Elbert Anderson, of Hackensack Precinct, Bergen Co., New Jersey, $3000.00, 114 acres.. in

Bergen Twp...bounded by John Leake...adjudged to Garret van Giesen, Isaac van Giesen and George van Giesen. Signed George van Giesen and Elizabeth van Giesen. Wit: Edward Mitchell and Lawrence A. Ackerman.

21 Nov 1788, Richard & Hannah Day, of Saddle River Twp., Bergen Co., New Jersey to William Reed, of same, £19.4, 4.36 acres. Signed Richard Day and Hannah Day. Wit: Eliza van Giesen amd Benjamin Day.

1 Jul 1796, Isaac & Rachel vander Beck, of Hackensack Twp., Bergen Co., New Jersey to John Clem, of same, £800, 3.25 acres...line of Adolph Waldron. Signed Isaac vander Beck Jr. and Rachel vander Beck. Wit: Nehemiah Wade and Jacob Terhune.

24 May 1796, Henry Mead, of Saddle River Twp., Bergen Co., New Jersey to Egbert and Peter Sanders, of same, £700, 100 acres...between William Ryerson and John Day...purchased of John Westervelt, sheriff of Bergen Co., New Jersey for judgement in favor of Peter Demarest against estate of Peter van Blerkum. Signed Henry Mead. Wit: David Demarest and Philip Day.

15 Sep 1796, Benjamin Day, of Onondaga Co., New York to John Day, of Bergen Co., New Jersey, £150, 124 acres...corner to John van Giesen and heirs of Garret van Houten. Signed Benjamin Day. Wit: N. Wade, Richard Day and William Shaw.

31 Dec 1787, Garrabrant Juriansen and John Juriansen, both of New Barbadoes Precinct, Bergen Co., New Jersey to Christopher Juriansen, of same, £10, 65 acres...line of Hendrick Kip...2nd tract line of Jurie Juriansen and Garrabrant Garrabrants. Signed Garrabrant Jurianse and John (x) Jurianse. Wit: John Outwater and Casparus Degraw.

13 Sep 1793, Hannah van Norstrandt, (widow and executor of estate of Christopher van Norstrandt, deceased), of New Barbadoes

Precinct, Bergen Co., New Jersey to Christopher
Juriansen, of same, £304, 34.5 acres...land
previously sold to pay debts. Signed Hannah (x)
van Norstrandt. Wit: Gilm Outwater and John
Outwater.

1 Nov 1793, John & Susannah Fell, of Bergen Co.,
New Jersey to John H. Thompson, merchant, of New
York City, £2000, 220.08 acres...corner to Peter
Dubois. Signed John Fell and Susannah Fell. Wit:
John Moore and Neweri Barlton.

4 Apr 1796, John & Charity Collard, of Bergen
Twp., Bergen Co., New Jersey to John Post,
carpenter, of same, £350, 5 acres...line of
Peter Stuyversant and John van Horne. Signed
John Collard and Charity (x) Collard. Wit:
Daniel Sickels, Joseph Waldron and Daniel van
Reypen.

22 Sep 1796, Isaac Nicoll, agent of forfeited
estates, of Bergen Co., New Jersey to Abraham
van Emburgh, £81.5, 40 acres...line of William
Davis...seized of Abraham van Emburgh, late of
New Barbadoes Twp., Bergen Co., New Jersey, for
joining the army of the King. Signed Isaac
Nicolel. Wit: Richard Zabriskie and John
Outwater.

21 Apr 1749, William Berry, yeoman, of Middlesex
Co., New Jersey to Isaac Vreeland, of New
Barbadoes, Bergen Co., New Jersey, £12, one
fourth part of what was willed by his
grandfather, John Berry...line of his brother,
John Berry and Derick Terhune. Signed William
Berry. Wit: Simon Vreeland and Paulus vander
Beck.

13 Aug 1796, Jacob Spear, of Saddle River Twp.,
Bergen Co., New Jersey to his son Benjamin
Spear, of same, for love and affection, 60 acres
...corner to David Brower. Signed Jacob Spear.
Wit: David J. Hennion and Cornelius Hennion.

1 May 1796, Peter Hun, yeoman, of Franklin Twp.,
Bergen Co., New Jersey to John A. van Voorhees,

of same, £22.15, 5 acres...line of John and William Albertson. Signed Peter Hun. Wit: Jacob Hun and Albert van Voorhees.

21 May 1796, John D. Ackerman, yeoman, of New Barbadoes Precinct, Bergen Co., New Jersey and James & Rachel McColly, of Saddle River Precinct, Bergen Co., New Jersey to John A. van Voorhees, of Franklin Twp., Bergen Co., New Jersey, £10, quit claim their interest...John van Voorhees willed to his son Adam van Voorhees 137 acres, and after the death of said Adam van Voorhees, the land would pass to his four daughters, Helena, wife of Garret Ackerman, Elizabeth, wife of Peter Post, Margaret, wife of Johannes Lance and Rachel, wife of David G. Ackerman and said Rachel died, leaving children, the said John D. Ackerman and the said Rachel, wife of James McColly. Signed John D. (x) Ackerman, James (x) McColly and Rachel (x) McColly. Wit: Anthony Bartrim and Nartman Crins.

12 Mar 1786, Garret van Giesen and Isaac van Giesen, both of Bergen Co., New Jersey to George van Giesen, of same, £5, line of Lawrence Ackerman and Lawrence A. Ackerman, (who sold to Reynier van Giesen, who willed and was father to the parties of these presents). Signed Isaac van Giesen and Garret van Giesen. Wit: Simon Simmons and John Cassady.

1 May 1794, Nancy Terhune, widow, and William & Elizabeth Hammel, of New Barbadoes Precinct, Bergen Co., New Jersey to George van Giesen, of same, £329, 0.29 acres...corner to Isaac Ward, Isaac vander Beck and Adam Boyd. Signed Ann Terhune, William Hammel and Elizabeth (x) Hammel. Wit: Isaac Ward and Peter Zabriskie.

20 Mar 1795, Richard Day, Philip Day, John Day, Peter Day and Benjamin Day to David Day, £0.5, 40 acres...in Saddle River Twp. Signed Richard Day, Philip Day, John Day, Peter Day and Benjamin Day. Wit: Garret Jacobusse and Mary Jacobusse.

17 Jun 1795, William S. & Phebe Pennington, of
Newark, Essex Co., New Jersey to John Sandford,
of same, £100, 10 acres...in New Barbadoes...
corner to Isaac Gouverneur. Signed William S.
Pennington and Phebe Pennington. Wit: Anamas
Baldwin and Cornelius van Reypen.

10 Oct 1792, Mary McKnight, (widow and devise of
Charles McKnight, doctor), of New York City to
John Varick Jr., of New Barbadoes, Bergen Co.,
New Jersey, £ 19.5 acres...corner to George
Campbell, deceased and Enoch Vreeland...
purchased of John Morris Scott, 20 Sep 1779.
Signed Mary McKnight. Wit: Robert Ross and
Benjamin Day.

10 Sep 1796, Judges of Superior Court name John
W. Hopper, William M. Bell and Henry Wammamaker
to divide the 179 acres in Franklin Twp., Bergen
Co., New Jersey claimed by Peter Ward. Signed
Peter Haring, Jacob Terhune and Abraham
Westervelt.

2 Jan 1797, Division of 179 acres is to John
Johnson, surviving heir of Andrew Johnson,
deceased. Signed John Hopper, William M. Bell
and Henry Wammamaker.

2 Jun 1785, John & Catharine Neafie, cordwinder,
of Franklin Twp., Bergen Co., New Jersey to John
van Horne, yeoman, of same, £500, 175 acres...
line of John Romine and Isaac Ronkling. Signed
John Neafie and Catharine Neafie. Wit: John
Hogan and Joost Beam.

31 May 1768, Garret van Wagener, yeoman, of
Essex Co., New Jersey to Catrina Zabriskie, of
New York City, £0.25 and tender regard for his
daughter and grandchildren, Joost Zabriskie,
Christina Zabriskie, Catrina Zabriskie and Sarah
Zabriskie...to Catrina Zabriskie, one negro
woman named Peggy and to each of the grandchildren, a negro child which are the children
and grandchildren of said Peggy. Signed Garret
van Wagenings. Wit: David Marinus and Benjamin
Dubois.

10 Apr 1784, Wilhelmus Vreeland, (executor of estate of Andres van Boskerk, of Bergen Co., New Jersey), farmer, of Staten Island, New York to Israel Oakley, farmer, of Bergen Co., New Jersey, 60 acres. and 12.9 acres...bounded by Kile van Kull...willed to Margaret van Boskerk, wife of said Andres van Boskerk, and upon her death to be sold at auction by his good friends and executors, Helmegh Vreeland and William Douglas, deceased. Signed Wilhelmus Vreeland. Wit: Abraham Bancker and Eden Vreeland.

28 Jul 1789, John Bard Sr., practitioner of Physic, of New York City to Jacobus van Boskerk, of Constable Nook, Bergen Co., New Jersey, £0.25, 54.16 acres. Signed John Bard. Wit: Samuel Bard and John van Boskerk.

29 Jul 1789, John Bard Sr., practitioner of Physic, of New York City to Jacobus van Boskerk, of Constable Nook, Bergen Co., New Jersey, £232, 54.16 acres. Signed John Bard. Wit: Samuel Bard and John van Boskerk.

13 Jan 1797, Israel & Elizabeth Oakley, farmer, of Bergen Co., New Jersey to Abraham van Boskerk, of New York City, £3350, 60 acres and 12.9 acres...bounded by Kile van Kull...2nd tract bounded by Jacobus van Boskerk...formerly belonging to Andreas van Boskerk, deceased. Signed Israel Oakley and Elizabeth (x) Oakley. Wit: Abraham Bancker and John Oakley.

6 Mar 1797, John B. & Elizabeth van Horne, carpenter, of Harrington, Bergen Co., New Jersey to Catherina Ackerman, wife of Peter A. Ackerman, of Franklin Twp., Bergen Co., New Jersey, £777, 77.77 acres...bounded by Stants Storm, Thomas van Boskerk, Albert Zabriskie and Andrew H. Hopper. Signed John van Horne and Elizabeth van Horne. Wit: James Perry and James Demarest.

10 Sep 1793, Edmund William & Mary Kingsland, of Bergen Co., New Jersey, William & Margaret Hornblower, of Essex Co., New Jersey and John

Gill, of Philadelphia, Pennsylvania to Burnel Richards, of Bergen Co., New Jersey, 57 acres and 119 acres...line of Richard Bergen. Signed Edmund William Kingsland, Mary Kingsland, William Hornblower, Margaret Hornblower and John Gill. Wit: Samuel Duffield, John Duffield, William Kingsland and Burnel R. Kingsland.

5 Apr 1797, Peter & Blandena Cadmus, of Newark Twp., Essex Co., New Jersey to John Christian Frederick Rommel, late of Germany, £1800, 40 acres...in New Barbadoes Neck...corner to Philip A. Schuyler, deceased, Benjamin Sandford, Arent Schuyler, Joseph Fielts, John Fielts and Simon van Emburgh. Signed Peter Cadmus and Blandena Cadmus. Wit: John Rutan and Abraham Cadmus.

12 Dec 1769, Isaac Bogart, of Campgaw, Bergen Co., New Jersey to John van Allen, £350, 139 acres minus 19 acres...in Saddle River Precinct...bounded by William Hopper and Hendrick Laroe, deceased...purchased from William Kingsland, sheriff of Bergen Co., New Jersey, who sold the lands of Johannes Laroe to satisfy a judgement of Abraham Gouverneur. Signed Isaac Bogart. Wit: Hessel Dooremus and Guilliam Bertholf.

4 Jan 1796, Jacobus & Leah Bertholf and Oseltie Bertholf, all of New Barbadoes, Bergen Co., New Jersey to Mary Ryerson, of Saddle River Twp., Bergen Co., New Jersey, £660, 30 acres lot in town of Hackensack...bounded by Paulus vander Beck and Isaac van Giesen. Signed James Bertholf, Leah (x) Bertholf and Oseltie Bertholf. Wit: Nehemiah Wade and Isaac vander Beck Jr.

24 Feb 1796, Marcelius M. van Giesen, merchant, of New York City to Ralph Post, Cornelius van Giesen, Casparus Egbert, Peter Egbert and Cornelius Brooks, all farmers, of New Jersey, £427.5, 47.5 acres...corner to John Benson. Signed Marcelius M. van Giesen. Wit Garret Stephens and Walling Egbert Jr.

17 Jan 1797, John & Maltye van Giesen, of Totawa, Bergen Co., New Jersey to Roelif Post, of Essex Co., New Jersey, £144, 18 acres... corner to John van Houten. Signed John van Giesen and Maltye van Giesen. Wit: Peter van Ryper and John van Giesen.

23 May 1797, Albert & Rachel van Zile, of Franklin Twp., Bergen Co., New Jersey to Cornelius van Horne, of same, £512, 106 acres ...line of John Banta part of farmer of Peter van Zile who willed to said Ablert van Zile 7 Apr 1795. Signed Albert van Zile and Rachel van Zile. Wit: John Willis Jr. and Abraham Willis.

28 Mar 1797, commissioners of the loan office of Bergen Co., New Jersey to Thomas Howard, of Hackensack Precinct, Bergen Co., New Jersey, £350, 12 acres...corner to John Demarest, David Demarest and Samuel Demarest. Signed John Outwater and Henry Berry. Wit: John A. Westervelt and Isaac van Voorhees.

27 Apr 1797, Mary Ryerson, widow, of Saddle River Twp., Bergen Co., New Jersey to Michael Price, of New Barbadoes Twp., Bergen Co., New Jersey, £900, 30 acres...bounded by the estate of Isaac van Giesen...purchased from James Bertholf. Signed Mary Ryerson. Wit: Nehemiah Wade and John Outwater.

21 Jan 1797, John & Rachel van Horne, yeoman, of Franklin Twp., Bergen Co., New Jersey to John M. Hogencamp, of Orange Town, Orange Co., New York, £754, 146 acres...line of John Waldron. Signed John van Horne and Rachel (x) van Horne. Wit: George G. Dooremus and James Demarest.

13 Sep 1758, William & Gane van Alah and David & Catrena Hennion to Lambartus Laroe, of Ramapork, Bergen Co., New Jersey, £170, 100 acres...corner to Dolf Shut. Signed William (x) van Alah, Gane (x) van Alah, David (x) Hennion and Catrena (x) Hennion. Wit: Abel Noble and Timothy Rose.

3 Sep 1796, Daniel Smith, of Bergen Twp., Bergen

Co., New Jersey to his son Daniel Smith Jr., of same, for love and affection, 65 acres...corner to James J. Bogart and Robert Neil....purchased of Daniel Baldwin. Signed Daniel Smith. Wit: William Labagh and Robert Earle.

1 May 1797, Lucas & Lenah van Saen, of New Barbadoes Precinct, Bergen Co., New Jersey to Cornelius Nelene, of same, £130, 10 acres...in Saddle River Precinct...line of John van Houten, deceased. Signed Lucas van Saen and Lenah (x) van Saen. Wit: John Romine and Garret Zabriskie.

13 Mar 1797, Jacob D. Gremow, of Bergen Co., New Jersey to Daniel Smith, of same, £80, bounded by M. Bayard and John van Horne. Signed Jacob D. Gremow. Wit: Henry Cole and Joseph Smith.

23 Nov 1756, John van Reypen, carpenter, of Saddle River, Bergen Co., New Jersey to Jacobus Post, carpenter, of same, £525, 125 acres... corner to Isaac van Reypen...line of the widow of Derick B. van Horne, George Ryerse and Tunia Thomas van Reypen...purchased of Helmogh Sip, who purchased of Thomas van Reypen, 10 Jan 1749. Signed John van Reypen. Wit: John Post and George Ryerse.

10 Jun 1797, Robert Morris, of New Brunswick, New Jersey to Cornelius Demarest, late of Paramus, Bergen Co., New Jersey, now of New York City, £153.3, 51.93 acres...map made in 1760 by George Ryerson, Jonathan Hampton and Benjamin Morgan. Signed Robert Morris. Wit: Daniel Demarest and James C. Jarvis.

3 Jul 1794, John & Naomi Day, of the english neighborhood, Bergen Co., New Jersey to Christeen Bourdett, of Fort Lee, Bergen Co., New Jersey, £450, 50 acres...corner to heirs of John Degroot, Hartman Brinkerhof and Samuel Ellis. Signed John Day and Naomi (x) Day. Wit: Jacob Degroot and Jacob Edsall.

27 Jul 1796, Christeen & Clashee Bourdett, of Hackensack Precinct, Bergen Co., New Jersey to

Albert Anderson, of New York City, £750, 52 acres...corner to the heirs of John Degroot ...line of Hartman Brinkerhof, John Day and Samuel Ellis. Christeen Bourdett and Clashee Bourdett. Wit: Stephen Bourdett and Stephen Bourdett.

15 Aug 1763, Jacobus Laroe and Johannes & Weybrough Bertholf to Mary Cough, division of property...Samuel Laroe willed 29 Apr 1760 divided his real estate between the three parties of these presents ...on 12 May 1762, George Ryerson made the division...to Mary Cough tract in Saddle River Precinct containing 57 acres...also tract of 10 acres. Signed Jacobus Laroe, Johannes (x) Bertholf and Weybrough (x) Bertholf. Wit: Jonathan Rose and Quilliam Bertholf.

17 Apr 1797, Peter Sanders, of Saddle River Twp., Bergen Co., New Jersey to Peter Courter, of same, £175, 25 acres...line of William Ryerson and Henry Mead...being a legacy given to the said Peter Courter by Egbert Sanders, deceased. Signed Peter (x) Sanders. Wit: Justus Burnet and Robert Gould.

31 Mar 1788, Enoch & Phebe Smith, of Secoakes, Bergen Co., New Jersey, Joseph & Nancy Smith and Morris & Elizabeth Smith, of New York to Job Smith, of Secoakes, Bergen Co., New Jersey, £1600, 200 acres...Pinhoun Creek...line of Daniel Smith...part of the farm of Philip Smith, late of Secoakes, Bergen Co., New Jersey. Signed Enoch Smith, Phebe (x) Smith, Joseph Smith, Nancy Smith, Morris Smith and Elizabeth Smith. Wit: John Day, Abel Smith and Abel J. Smith.

11 Feb 1794, Daniel Smith, of Bergen Twp.,, Bergen Co., New Jersey to Job Smith, of same, for one lot of cedar swamp given to him by indenture by Job Smith, the elder, late of Bergen Twp., Bergen Co., New Jersey, 20 acres ...line of Reynier Earle. Signed Daniel Smith. Wit: James Lee and John Outwater.

11 Dec 1794, William & Mary Crolius, (heirs of Joseph Dobbs, deceased), John & Catherine Remmey and Catherine Dobbs, widow of William Dobbs to Adam D. Morant, baker, of New York City, power of attorney. Signed William Crolius, Mary Crolius, John Remmey, Catherine (x) Remmey and Catherine (x) Dobbs. Wit: Willet Cole and William Dyke.

15 Mar 1783, John & Elizabeth Ackerman, of Harrington Precinct, Bergen Co., New Jersey to Abraham Terhune, of same, £700, 50 acres...line of Jacobus Bogart, David Ackerman and Abraham Rutan. Signed John G. Ackerman and Elizabeth (x) Ackerman. Wit: Garret Ackerman and Cornelius Bogart.

4 Oct 1714, Elias & Mary Boudinot, merchant, of New York City to Harper Garrabrants, of New Barbadoess Neck, Bergen Co., New Jersey, £295, 200 acres...line of John Juriansen and John Berry. Signed Elias Boudinot and Marie Catherine Boudinot. Wit: Isaac Woodruff, of Essex Co., New Jersey.

21 Feb 1795, John & Sarah Terrill, John M. & Rachel Clark, of Elizabeth, Essex Co., New Jersey to Garrabrant Garrabrants, of New Barbadoes Precinct, Bergen Co., New Jersey, £105.7, 8.5 acres...line of Enoch Vreeland, Benjamin Zabriskie, Casparus Zabriskie and Philip Berry. Signed John Terrill, Sarah Terrill, John M. Clark and Rachel Clark. Wit: John Outwater and Jacob van Ryper.

3 Feb 1796, George G. & Abigail Ryerson, Martin G. & Nanthe Ryerson, John G. & Elenor Ryerson, Theunis G. & Alana Ryerson, Francis G. & Grela Ryerson, Dederick & Jenny Tise, Mary Ryerson, Anthony & Hester Bartrim and Abraham & Anna Luke, all of Bergen Co., New Jersey to Richard G. Ryerson, of same, £0.25, formerly belonging to George F. Ryerson, deceased...was awarded to party of second part by Abraham Ryerson, Daniel Dennison, Joost Beam and Conrad Beam. Signed George G. Ryerson, Abigail Ryerson, Martin G.

Ryerson, Agnes (x) Ryerson, John G. Ryerson, Nelly Ryerson, Theunis Ryerson, Alana Ryerson, Francis G. Ryerson, Grela Ryerson, Dederick Tise, Jenny Tise, Marie (x) Ryerson, Abraham Luke, Anna (x) Luke, Anthony Bartrim and Hester Bartrim. Wit: James Lines and John Collins.

P. 189, shows a map with Richard Ryerson, 11 acres next to Abraham Decker with 50.75 acres. A second map shows Richard Ryerson with 84 acres next to George Ryerson with 84 acres, Francis Ryerson with 38 acres and Martin Ryerson with 90 acres.

1797, Sarah Campbell and Jacob & Saley Haring, all of Bergen Co., New Jersey to (torn page), £15, all the interests of David Campbell, deceased. Signed Sarah Campbell, Jacob (x) Haring and Saley (x) Haring. Wit: Jasper Demarest and John van Voorhees.

2 Oct 1797, Thomas Howard, of New Barbadoes Twp., Bergen Co., New Jersey to Stephen Rudd, of New York City, £350, in Hackensack Twp...corner to John Demarest. Signed Thomas Howard. Wit: Nehemiah Wade and R. S. Beckman.

7 Nov 1797, Jesse Woodward, of Saint John, New Brunswick, Nova Scotia, Benjamin R. & Sarah Westervelt, of Hackensack Twp., Bergen Co., New Jersey, John & Mary Lozier, of Harrington Twp., Bergen Co., New Jersey, Thomas & Hester van Boskerk, of Harrington Twp., Bergen Co., New Jersey, Abraham & Jane van Boskerk, of Harrington Twp., Bergen Co., New Jersey, Elizabeth Bileston, of Hackensack Twp., Bergen Co., New Jersey and Edward & Ruth Bileston to Thomas Dugan, of New York City, £1200, 20 acres...in Hackensack Twp., at Fort Lee, where Stephen Bourdett, deceased, lived...line of Peter Bourdett...all estate rights the parties of the first part along with widow Eleanor Bourdett, wife of Stephen Bourdett had in the estate of said Stephen Bourdett. Signed Eleanor Bourdett, John Lozier, Mary Lozier, Benjamin R. Westervelt, Sarah Westervelt, Abraham van

Boskerk and Jane van Boskerk. Wit: John Day and John Dudley.

8 Jul 1795, John George Leake, of New York City to Jeremiah Yeomans, of Bergen Co., New Jersey, £25, 10 acres...in Bergen Twp. Signed John George Leake. Wit: Andrew Engle and Janet Engle.

26 May 1746, Roelif van Houten, Derick van Houten and Jacob van Houten, all yeoman, of Bergen Co., New Jersey to Reynier van Giesen and Derick van Giesen, both of same, division of jointly held lands, 40.75 acres...corner to George Willock and Maj. Anthony Brackholst... purchased from Andrew Johnston, Thomas Lawrence and Robert Herde. Signed Roelif van Houten, Derick van Houten and Jacob van Houten. Wit: Luke Ryerse and George Ryerse.

14 Nov 1795, William & Hester Colfax, of Saddle River Twp., Bergen Co., New Jersey to Peter Schuyler, of same, £220, 44 acres. Signed William Colfax and Esther Colfax. Wit: Philip J. Schuyler and L. Jackson.

1 May 1786, Cornelius Haring, John Haring and John Neafie, all of Franklin Twp., Bergen Co., New Jersey to Thomas van Boskerk, of Harrington Twp., Bergen Co., New Jersey, £45, 75 acres...in Harrington Twp. Signed Cornelius Haring, John Haring and John Neafie. Wit: Peter Ward and John Hopper.

1 Dec 1774, Burnet Richards, mariner and John Richards, of New Barbadoes Neck, Bergen Co., New Jersey to Garrabrant Garrabrants, farmer, of same, £84, 42 acres. Signed Burnet Richards and John Richards. Wit: Roger Kingsland.

28 May 1796, Derick Banta, of New Barbadoes Twp., Bergen Co., New Jersey to John Banta, of same, £866.65, 11 acres...in Hackensack Precinct...corner to John Demarest, David Demarest and Samuel Demarest...2nd tract in New Barbadoes Precinct...line of John Zabriskie Jr., John Brower and heirs of Elizabeth Seaman...3rd

tract corner to John Zabriskie Jr...4th tract corner to Luke van Saun and Isaac van Saun...line of Jacob Bogart...and all land forfeited by John Zabriskie that he purchased of Maj. Gen. Frederick William Baron de Steuben. Signed Derick (x) Banta. Wit: Nehemiah Wade and Cornelius Houghland.

19 Sep 1797, John G. Ryerson, of Newark Twp., Essex Co., New Jersey to Abraham Ackerman, of Paterson Twp., Essex Co., New Jersey, £165, 72.82 acres...Pumpton Twp., Bergen Co., New Jersey...corner of a farm formerly belonging to George F. Ryerson, deceased...2nd tract of 11 acres...corner to Abraham Luke. Signed John G. Ryerson. Wit: John J. Westervelt and Adam Boyd.

11 Apr 1791, Peter & Nieshe van Allen, of New York City to William van Allen, of same, £470, 110 acres...in Harrington Precinct ...two fifths of 282 acre tract sold by Oliver Delaney and Henry Cuyler to States Storm, Nov 1772...line of Doctor Johnson. Signed Peter van Allen and Nieshe (x) van Allen. Wit: John van Allen and Henry Briksman.

1 May 1767, Albert van Voorhees and John van Voorhees, (sons of William van Voorhees, deceased), of Saddle River Precinct, Bergen Co., New Jersey to their brother, Abraham van Voorhees, of same, 91.25 acres... William van Voorhees devised to his five sons, Jacobus van Voorhees, John van Voorhees, Abraham van Voorhees, Albert van Voorhees and William van Voorhees and said Jacob van Voorhees, deceased, and eldest son did devised 13 Apr 1758 to his brothers John van Voorhees and Albert van Voorhees his share and said parties of the first part sold one third part of this tract. Signed Albert van Voorhees and Yan van Voorhees. Wit: Roelif Westervelt and Quilliam Bertholf.

1 May 1787, John Stevens, James Parker and Walter Rutherford, general proprietors of New Jersey to Abraham van Voorhees, of Bergen Co., New Jersey, £112.5, 50.04 acres...part of

Romopogh Tract. Signed John Stevens. Wit: Cornelius Best and Gilbert Sherer. Signed James Parker. Wit: John Thompson and Gilbert Sherer. Signed Walter Rutherford. Wit: John Rutherford and Gilbert Sherer.

1 Aug 1794, James Parker, Bower Reed and Abraham Ogden, (executors of the wills of Henry Cuyler, the elder and Henry Cuyler, the younger) to Abraham van Voorhees, of Franklin Twp., Bergen Co., New Jersey, £104, 104.09 acres ...line of John and William Albertson...Henry Cuyler, the elder willed 24 Aug 1770 to his two sons Henry Cuyler and Barnt R. Cuyler and John Smith, of Perth Amboy. Signed James Parker and Abraham Ogden. Wit: Edward J. Ball and William Courter.

10 Feb 1797, James Parker, Andrew Bell and John Rattoone, all of Perth Amboy, Middlesex Co., New Jersey to Abraham van Voorhees, of Franklin Twp., Bergen Co., New Jersey, £247.2, 104.09 acres...in Franklin Twp...line of John and William Albertson...parties of first part with John Haring sell at public auction at house of Capt. John Hopper, in Franklin Twp., Bergen Co., New Jersey. Signed James Parker, Andrew Bell and John Rattoone. Wit: Lambert Barberie and Thomas Paul.

15 Dec 1797, Abraham van Voorhees, farmer, of Franklin Twp., Bergen Co., New Jersey to Peter W. Winter, (son of William Winter, the carpenter, now living), yeoman, of same, £351.25, 104.09 acres...line of John and William Albertson. Signed Abraham (x) van Voorhees. Wit: Peter A. Westervelt and Abraham Westervelt.

16 Mar 1723, George Ryerson, Pockquanack, Bergen Co., New Jersey and Jurian Westervelt, of Hackensack, Bergen Co., New Jersey to Francis Ryerson, of New York City, correction of jointly owned lands surveyed by James Alexander, Paulus vander Beck and Andreas van Boskerk. Signed George Ryerson and Jurian Westervelt. Wit: Paulus vander Beck and Edmund Kingsland.

6 Mar 1797, Elias & Mary Day, of Tenafly, Hackensack Precinct, Bergen Co., New Jersey to John Becker and Richard Scott, both of Bergen Co., New Jersey, £100, 7 acres...corner to Benjamin Westervelt. Signed Elias Day and Mary (x) Day. Wit: John G. Benson and Simon Campbell.

22 Apr 1796, William S. & Phebe Pennington, of Newark, Essex Co., New Jersey to David Sayre, of same, £96.85, 8.8 acres...corner to John Sandford. Signed William S. Pennington and Phebe Pennington. Wit: William P. Smith and Abigail (x) Crane.

1 Jan 1798, John & Elizabeth Travis, merchant, of Philadelphia, Pennsylvania to John Old, iron master, of Ringwood, New Jersey, £9000, 16 acres...line of Cornelius Bourd...William M. Bell, sheriff of Bergen Co., New Jersey sold 6 Jan 1796 to said John Travis...2nd tract, 40 acres...3rd tract, 3.57 acres...4th tract, 6.4 acres...5th tract, 6.5 acres...line of Walter Erwin...willed by Cornelius Bourd, 1 Feb 1764 to Joseph Bourd, who sold to Nicholas Gouverneur, Samuel Gouverneur, David Ogden Sr. and David Ogden Jr., who sold 5 Jul 1764 to Peter Hasenclever...Jonathan Davis and Joseph Bartrim were executors of will of Cornelius Bourd and sold to Walter Erwin, of Ringwood, 6 May 1754, 73 acres...15 acres.... two tracts surveyed for Cornelius Bourd 18 Feb 1739, sold to Joseph Wilcox, of Newark, New Jersey, who sold to Jacob Mead, who sold to Yelles Mead, 11.37 acres and 15 acres...65.63 acres, sold to Peter Hasenclever, and Joseph & Phebe Wilcox 18 Dec 1754...5975 acres returned to Jonah Ogden...11,386.02 acres sold 31 Dec 1754 to Peter Hasenclever by Oliver Delaney, Henry Cayler Jr. and Walter Rutherford...193.96 acres sold by Walter & Catherine Rutherford to Peter Hasenclever, 5 Aug 1765...several tracts surveyed by James Alexander, deceased, and returned to Jonah Ogden, John Ogden, David Ogden, David Ogden and Uzal Ogden containing 100.11 acres. Signed John Travis and Elizabeth Travis. Wit: Charles Christie and Thomas

Cadwalader.

20 Jan 1798, Richard & Mary Earle, of Bergen, Bergen Co., New Jersey to Andrew Engle, of same, $875.00, 110 acres...line of Hendrick van Giesen and Isaac van Giesen. Signed Richard Earle and Mary Earle. Wit: Albert C. Zabriskie and John Paulisen.

22 Sep 1783, Daniel Smith, yeoman, of Bergen Precinct, Bergen Co., New Jersey to his son John Smith, of same, £50, 50 acres...line of Job Smith. Signed Daniel Smith. Wit: John Outwater and John Hennion.

3 Sep 1796, Daniel Smith, of Seacawkus, Bergen Twp., Bergen Co., New Jersey to his son, John Smith, of same, £1000 or $2500.00, 40 acres... line of Job Smith, the second...division line between Pinhorne and Earle. Signed Daniel Smith. Wit: William Labagh and Robert Earle.

16 Apr 1796, Egbert & Sarah van Zile, of New York City to Cornelius Wortendyke, of Harrington Twp., Bergen Co., New Jersey, £324, 37.5 acres...in Franklin Twp...line of Harmanus van Zile. Signed Egbert (x) van Zile and Sarah (x) van Zile. Wit: Abraham Westervelt and Ralph Westervelt.

21 Mar 1748, Robert & Phebe Hallet, of Orange Co., New York to Jacob Concklin, of Westchester Co., New York, £332, 166 acres...in Orange Co.???...line of Henry Ludlow. Signed Robert Hallet and Phebe Hallet. Wit: James Hallet and Edward Briges.

4 May 1773, Jacob & Hester Concklin, of Orange Co., New York to Jacob Concklin Jr., of same, £600, 166 acres...in Orange Twp., Orange Co., New York...except 61 acres purchased by Daniel Haring. Signed Jacob Concklin and Hester Concklin. Wit: William Bell and Abraham Maby.

26 May 1790, Daniel & Elizabeth Haring, yeoman, of Harrington Twp., Bergen Co., New Jersey to

Jacob Concklin, of same, £200, 61.5 acres...in Harrington Twp ...corner to John Gisner and John Ryker. Signed Daniel Haring and Elizabeth (x) Haring. Wit: Thomas Eckerson and Jacob Outwater.

20 Jul 1796, John Geiner Sr., yeoman, of Harrington, Bergen Co., New Jersey to Jacob Concklin, of same, £875, 79 acres...part in Orange Twp., Orange Co., New York and part in Harrington, Bergen Co., New Jersey. Signed John Geiner. Wit: Peter Maby and Jasper Maby.

3 Aug 1796, John Geiner Sr., yeoman, of Harrington, Bergen Co., New Jersey to Elizabeth Concklin, wife of Jacob Concklin, of same, £100, 31 acres...part in Orange Twp., Orange Co., New York and part in Harrington, Bergen Co., New Jersey. Signed John Geiner. Wit: Abraham Y. Blauvelt and Petrus Haring.

24 Feb 1797, Peter & Sally Maby, of Harrington, Bergen Co., New Jersey to Jacob Concklin, of same, £720, 40 acres...bounded by John Riker and Henry Ludlow. Signed Peter Maby and Sarah Maby. Wit: Abraham Y. Blauvelt and Petrus Haring.

25 Jul 1791, Roelif H. & Anantie van Houten, of Bergen Co., New Jersey to Jacob van Ryper, of same, £200, 22 acres...corner to John van Winkle...part of tract willed to said Roelif H. van Houten by his father Helmegh van Houten. Signed Roelif van Houten and Anantie (x) van Houten. Wit: Abraham Ryerson and Henry Hennion.

8 Oct 1791, Jacob & Manacha van Ryper, of Preakness, Bergen Co., New Jersey to Richard van Reypen, of Bergen Co., New Jersey and Michael Vreeland, of Essex Co., New Jersey, £150, 22 acres...corner to John van Winkle.

11 Apr 1796, Joost & Mary Cough, of Saddle River Twp., Bergen Co., New Jersey to Cornelius Meyer, of same, £30, 5.8 acres...corner to Herman van Bussen and John Garretson...purchased of Abraham Toor. Signed Joost Cough and Mary (x) Cough. Wit: John McCarty and Caspar Post.

21 Apr 1794, Cornelius Post, Casparus Cough and Caty Brown, (daughter of Elias Cough), of Saddle River Precinct, Bergen Co., New Jersey to Cornelius Meyer, of same, £350, 56.64 acres ...line of Jacob Turse, Abraham Turse and Merynes van Winkle...said Post and Cough name executors of Elias Cough, late of Saddle River Twp., Bergen Co., New Jersey in Orphans Court. Signed Cornelius Post, Casparus Kaugh Jr. and Caty (x) Brown. Wit: John Bertholf, George Taylor, Garret C. Post and Abraham M. van Roden.

10 Feb 1795, Henry & Margaret Traphagen, yeoman, of Franklin Twp., Bergen Co., New Jersey to Lewis Lacolamb, of Brooklyn, Kings Co., New York, £880, 220 acres. Signed Henry (x) Traphagen and Margaret (x) Traphagen. Wit: Henry H. Traphagen and Abraham Westervelt.

1 Jul 1797, Lewis Lacolamb, of Philadelphia, Pennsylvania power of attorney to Lewis Cadignan, of Bergen Co., New Jersey. Signed Lewis Lacolambe. Wit: Charles Pantgiband and Charles Riddie.

12 Mar 1798, Lewis Lacolamb, late of Franklin Twp., Bergen Co., New Jersey to Charles Pantgiband, of same, £1861.5, 219 acres ...purchased of Henry & Margaret Traphagen. Signed Lewis Lacolamb, by his attorney, Lewis Cadignan. Wit: Zane Wade and Nehemiah Wade.

3 Mar 1798, Henry Harris, of Saddle River Twp., Bergen Co., New Jersey to John D. Bardan, of same, £18, yoke of oxen. Signed Henry (x) Harris. Wit: John Bardan and Daniel (x) Haring.

14 Mar 1795, Daniel Smith, farmer, of Seacauke, Bergen Co., New Jersey to Charles Henry Lambert Mary Trierdhommel DeBorre, gentleman, of same, £500, 11.4 acres...line of Kile van Kull... purchased of Hendericus & Catharine Kuyper 7 Mar 1765...10 acres...line of Anthony White. Signed Daniel Smith. Wit: Boonen Graves and John H. Remsen.

16 Sep 1797, Cornelius Davenport, of Onondaga Co., New York power of attorney to Charles A. Hricos. Signed Cornelius (x) Davenport. Wit: Peter (x) Davenport and John M. Gaugy.

22 Apr 1797, William S. & Phebe Pennington, merchant, of Newark, Essex Co., New Jersey to Benjamin Sandford, of New Barbadoes, Bergen Co., New Jersey, £152.9, 12.7 acres...corner to Francis Tuers and Reuben Carter. Signed William S. Pennington and Phebe Pennington. Wit: William P. Smith and Abigail (x) Crane.

22 Apr 1797, Matthew D. & Martha Coe, yeoman, of Franklin Twp., Bergen Co., New Jersey to William J. Blank, of same, £54, 6.75 acres...line of Joseph Halsted. Signed Matthew D. Coe and Martha Coe. Wit: Jacob Romine and Anna (x) Osborne.

12 Apr 1798, Andrew & Hannah Gautier, yeoman, of Bergen Co., New Jersey and Thomas & Elizabeth Gautier, yeoman, of Bergen Co., New Jersey to Jasper Zabriskie, of same, £900, 27 acres... corner to Thomas Brown...24.7 acres corner to Lawrence Brown, son of Thomas Brown...24.7 acres, for total of 77 acres. Signed Andrew Gautier, Hannah Gautier, Thomas Gautier and Eliza Gautier. Wit: Daniel van Reypen and Abraham van Boskerk.

15 Apr 1793, James & Rachel Demarest, carpenter, of Orange Twp., Orange Co., New York to Caleb Williams, of Hackensack, New Barbadoes Twp., Bergen Co., New Jersey, £400, 2 acres...line of Elias Provoost. Signed James Demarest and Rachel Demarest. Wit: John Cassady and Jasper Demarest.

13 Mar 1798, John Kingston, of Saddle River Twp., Bergen Co., New Jersey to Gilbert Lake, of same, £20.35, livestock. Signed John Kingston. Wit: Cornelius Post and Samuel (x) Toers.

5 May 1798, John & Johanna vander Beck, of New Barbadoes Twp., Bergen Co., New Jersey to John Marker, of same, £144, lot in town of New Barbadoes...bounded by Archibald Campbell and

Thomas Chapple. Signed John vander Beck and Johanna (x) vander Beck. Wit: Robert Campbell and Isaac P. vander Beck.

20 Apr 1798, Derick Banta, yeoman, of New Barbadoes Precinct, Bergen Co., New Jersey to Luke van Boskerk, of same, $7250.00, 11 acres... corner to John Demarest, Samuel Demarest and David Demarest...2nd tract corner to John Zabriskie Jr and heirs of Elizabeth Seaman... 3rd tract of 7 acres...corner to Lucas van Saen, Isaac van Saen and Jacob Bogart...4th tract granted to Maj. Gen. Frederick William Baron de Steuben....total of 60 acres. Signed Derick (x) Banta. Wit: John Haring and Roelif Verbrick.

21 Nov 1797, Samuel & Vroutye Wood, of Bergen Co., New Jersey to Cornelius Meyer, of Bergen, Bergen Co., New Jersey, £525, 10.5 acres...in Hackensack Twp. Signed Samuel Wood and Vroutye (x) Wood. Wit: Benjamin Westervelt and Abraham Demarest.

2 May 1792, Joize Roiz Silva, merchant, of New York City to Samuel Demarest, of Bergen Co., New Jersey, £420,three tracts held in trust for Mary Duffy...1st tract, 4.25 acres...corner to the father of Samuel Demarest, Peter Demarest...line of David Samuel Demarest and Peter John Demarest...2nd tract, 10.4 acres...corner to Jacobus P. Demarest and John P. Demarest...3rd tract, 19.21 acres...corner to Lawrence van Boskerk.

23 Sep 1786, William & Mary Earle, of Bergen Woods, corporation of Bergen, Bergen Co., New Jersey to John Delemater, of same, £40, 3 acres. Signed William Earle and Mary Earle. Wit: Isaac Hamman and Henry (x) Banta.

24 May 1792, James & Cornelia Brinkerhof, Sebe & Bailtic Brinkerhof, Albert Brinkerhof and George Brinkerhof, all of New Barbadoes Precinct, Bergen Co., New Jersey to Adam Boyd, of same, £153, 25 acres. Signed Balsha (x) Brinkerhof,

Albert Brinkerhof, George Brinkerhof, Jacobus
Brinkerhof, Cornelia Brinkerhof and Siba
Brinkerhof. Wit: John P. Bogart and Derick
Brinkerhof.

2 May 1795, David P. Demarest, of Bergen Co.,
New Jersey to David Anderson and Abraham van
Boskerk, release of their bond dated 1 May 1793,
of £400. Signed David P. Demarest. Wit:
Catherine Terhune and Jacob Terhune.

7 Feb 1798, John S. & Rachel Banta, yeoman, of
New Barbadoes Precinct, Bergen Co., New Jersey
to Derick Banta, yeoman, of same, $7825.00, 11
acres...in Hackensack Precinct...corner to John
Demarest, Samuel Demarest and David Demarest...
2nd tract, in New Barbadoes Precinct...corner to
John Zabriskie Jr. and John Brower...3rd tract,
7 acres...corner to Luke van Saun, Isaac van
Saun and Jacob Bogart. Signed John S. Banta and
Rachel Banta. Wit: Elbert J. Haring and John
Haring.

5 Apr 1794, Jacob & Susanna Hallet, merchant, of
New York City to John J. Ackerman, Richard
Cooper and Gilyaem J. Bogart, all yeoman, of
Harrington, Bergen Co., New Jersey, £777, 129.5
acres...in Harrington Twp...corner to Andrias
Waldron, heirs of David Ackerman, Jacob Hopper,
Peter DeBaun and Peter Demarest. Signed Jacob
Hallet and Susanna Hallet. Wit: William van
Boskerk and Jacob W. Hallet.

19 May 1797, John Johnston, (executor of estate
of Andrew Johnston), of Perth Amboy, Middlesex
Co., New Jersey to James van Gelder, of Franklin
Twp., Bergen Co., New Jersey, £57, 33 acres...
Andrew Johnston made his will 2 May 1761. Signed
John Johnston. Wit: John Haring and Edward John
Ball.

19 May 1797, John Johnston, (executor of estate
of Andrew Johnston), of Perth Amboy, Middlesex
Co., New Jersey to Jacob Young and Henry
Pulisfelt, both of Franklin Twp., Bergen Co.,
New Jersey, £229, 114.47 acres...corner to

Abraham van Gelder. Signed John Johnston. Wit: John Haring and Edward John Ball.

18 May 1798, Isaac & Reyne Moses, merchant, of New York City to John Hibbard, of same, £500, 4 acres...corner to the old farm of Peter Demarest, deceased, John Peter Demarest, David Samuel Demarest and David P. Demarest...2nd tract, 10.34 acres...corner to Jacobus P. Demarest...3rd tract, 19.21 acres...line of Richard Heathen...purchased of Jose Roir Silva 24 Dec 1794. Signed Isaac Moses and Reyne Moses. Wit: Thomas S. Ogden and William Ogden.

14 Jul 1798, Jacob & Sarah Haring, of Harrington, Bergen Co., New Jersey to William Williams, of New Barbadoes, Bergen Co., New Jersey, $500.00, all those tracts willed to said Haring by Jacob Fleerboom. Signed Jacob (x) Haring and Sarah (x) Haring. Wit: Nehemiah Wade and Francis Wade.

15 Dec 1797, William van Allen, of Harrington Twp., Bergen Co., New Jersey to Abraham DeBaun, of same, £0.5, 110 acres...corner to Doctor Johnson...two fifths part of 282 acre tract sold by Oliver Delaney and Henry Cuyler to States Storm. Signed William van Allen. Wit: Nehemiah Wade and Jane Wade.

4 Aug 1798, election of trustees of Academy in New Barbadoes Twp., Bergen Co., New Jersey. Signed Solomon Freligh, John van Bueren, Isaac vander Beck Jr., Robert Campbell and Nehemiah Wade.

1 May 1798, John T. & Elizabeth Stagg, of New York City to John Moffat, of Paterson, Essex Co., New Jersey, £130, 3 acres...in Saddle River Twp... corner to Isaac vander Beck, John R. Ludlow, Hassel Ryerson. Signed John T. (x) Stagg and Elizabeth Stagg. Wit: J. Romine and Christopher Stagg.

21 May 1791, Peter Helmag & Leah van Houten, John C. & Antye Westervelt, Cornelius H. &

Styntia Dooremus, all of Saddle River Twp., Bergen Co., New Jersey and John H. & Margaret Garretson, of Acquacknonk Twp., Essex Co., New Jersey to Jurie S. van Reypen, of Saddle River Twp., Bergen Co., New Jersey, £500, all interest in the estate of their grandfather...Simon J. van Reypen, willed to said Jurie S. van Reypen and his four daughters, the said Leah, Antye, Styntia and Margaret, also their interest in the estate of their grandfather, Yurrie Peterson. Signed Peter H. van Houten, Leah van Houten, John C. Westervelt, Anne Westervelt, Cornelius Dooremus, Stynlia (x) Dooremus, John H. Garretson and Margaret Garretson. Wit: Albert Wright and Hessel Peterson.

18 Oct 1798, Michael & Helena Price, gentleman, of New Barbadoes Twp., Bergen Co., New Jersey to his daughter Elizabeth Moore, wife of Lewis Moore, of same, for love and affection, 90 acres ...bounded by Powles vander Beck and Isaac van Saen, deceased. Signed Michael Price. Wit: Stephen Price and Henry vander Beck.

15 Dec 1794, Casparus Schuyler, of Pompton,, Bergen Co., New Jersey to Gabriel Ogden, of same, £60, 60 acres. Signed Casparus Schuyler. Wit: Charles Ogden and Joseph Curtis.

18 Apr 1797, Charles & Ann Ogden, of Newark, Essex Co., New Jersey to Martin J. Ryerson, of Pompton, Bergen Co., New Jersey, £815.65, 170 acres...at Pompton...line of Peter and John van Houten...purchased from Rev. Uzal & Mary Ogden 27 Nov 1788...purchased of Peter & Mary Schuyler 21 Mar 1797. Signed Charles Ogden and Ann Ogden. Wit: Joseph Robert Murden and Margaretta Johnston.

18 Apr 1797, Moses & Mary Ogden, of Newark Essex Co., New Jersey to Martin J. Ryerson, of Pompton, Bergen Co., New Jersey, £815.65, 170 acres...at Pompton...line of Peter and John van Houten...purchased from Rev. Uzal & Mary Ogden 27 Nov 1788...purchased of Peter & Mary Schuyler 21 Mar 1797. Signed Moses Ogden and Mary Ogden,

Wit: Esther F. Caldwell and Elizabeth G. Ogden.

7 Feb 1787, John H. van Wagener, of Bergen Co., New Jersey to Jacob & Mary van Ness, Abraham & Cattalya Cadmus and John & Anna Diedericks, all heirs of Helmegh van Wagener, £0.25, 95.25 acres and 20 acres. Signed John van Wagener. Wit: Abraham Ryerson and Joseph Bartrim.

20 Aug 1798, Aaron J. Westervelt, of Hackensack Twp., Bergen Co., New Jersey to Andrew Ten Eyck, of New York, £240, 4 acres...corner to Joost Demarest and Hendrick van Voorhees...2nd tract, 1.5 acres...adjoining David S. Demarest...1.75 acres...corner to John Zabriskie. Signed Aaron J. Westervelt. Wit: Jesse Woodhull and Isaac Nicoll.

15 Aug 1763, John & Weybrough Bertholf and Jacob & Mary Cough to Jacobus Laroe, agreement on division of land...Samuel Laroe, willed 29 Apr 1760 that his estate be divided between the parties of these presents. Signed Johannes (x) Bertholf, Weybrough (x) Bertholf, Jacob Cough and Mary (x) Cough.

## Chapter 10

### Bergen County Courthouse Deed Records Volume K

Recorded in 1798-1800

26 Nov 1793, John & Lenah Eckerson, David & Anganietye Eckerson, Jacob & Annatie Eckerson, Thomas & Cornelia Eckerson, Peter & Matye Demarest, Samuel & Elizabeth Banta, Johannis M. & Maria Meyer, John J. Meyer, Jacob J. Meyer, Lidia vander Hoof, Maria Demarest, Rachel Ramsey, (the last seven being children of Sarah Meyer, formerly Sarah Eckerson), Maria Eckerson, Yanitye Eckerson and Martye Eckerson, (the last three being children of Peter Eckerson, deceased) (and all children of Thomas Eckerson Sr., deceased) to Edward Eckerson, of Harrington, Bergen Co., New Jersey, £520.6, 110.5 acres...corner to John Banta, Frederick Wortendyke, Hendrick Storm and John A. Banta. Signed Hendrick Eckerson, Maria (x) Eckerson, Peter (x) Demarest, Matye (x) Demarest, Samuel (x) Banta, Elizabeth (x) Banta, Mary (x) Meyer, Thomas (x) Meyer, Cornelius Meyer, John (x) Eckerson, Lenah (x) Eckerson, David Eckerson, Aganietye (x) Eckerson, Jacob Eckerson, Hannah (x) Eckerson, Thomas (x) Eckerson, Cornelia (x) Eckerson and John (x) Meyer. Wit: Benjamin Blacklidge, David Jacob Thomas Eckerson, Thomas Meyer, Cornelius Meyer, Abraham Debaun, Jacob Eckerson, Peter Eckerson, Jacob Romine and Samuel Forger.

3 Nov 1798, Peter Zabriskie, of New Barbadoes Twp., Bergen Co., New Jersey to Morris Earle, of

same, £150, lot in Town of Hackensack. Signed Peter Zabriskie. Wit: James Chapple and Nehemiah Wade.

19 Dec 1798, Michael Vreeland, of Hackensack Twp., Bergen Co., New Jersey took his slave, Phillis was found fit and above age 21 and under age 40. Signed Jacob Terhune, Jacobus Demarest, Nicholas Westervelt and Richard (x) Vreeland.

18 Oct 1798, Guilliam & Ann Outwater, Jacob & Maritie Outwater, John Outwater, Attia Outwater and Catalina Outwater, of Bergen Twp., Bergen Co., New Jersey to James Kells, of same, £19.5, corner to Nicholas Vreeland. Signed Guilliam (x) Outwater, Anne (x) Outwater, Jacob Outwater, Maritie (x) Outwater, Attia (x) Outwater, Catalina (x) Outwater and John Outwater. Wit: Henry Brinkerhof and Zacharias Sickels.

8 Sep 1796, Abraham Wilson to Ralph Thurman, merchant, of New York City, $450.00. Signed Abraham Wilson. Wit: Philip Wilson, Peter A. Wilson and Eglinton M. Boyle.

18 Jul 1796, Andrew & Hannah Gautier, of Bergen Co., New Jersey to Peter Post, of same, £110, 6.9 acres...line of Kile van Kull. Signed Andrew Gautier and Hannah Gautier. Wit: Richard van Reypen and Klaas (x) Vreeland.

8 Jan 1799, John & Johannah Bayard, of New Brunswick, New Jersey to Peter Post, of Bergen Twp., Bergen Co., New Jersey, £114, 11.4 acres ...corner to Kile van Kull. Signed John Bayard and Johannah Bayard. Wit: Jane Kirkpatrick and Anna Maria Bayard.

13 Nov 1797, Helena Bogart, gentlewomen, of New York City, late of New Barbadoes, Bergen Co., New Jersey Henry Traphagen, teacher in the Academy at Hackensack, Bergen Co., New Jersey, £300, in New Barbadoes Precinct...corner to Peter Zabriskie. Signed Helena Bogart. Wit: Thomas Mackaness and Edward Dunscomb.

25 Feb 1799, William Jackson and Abraham Pryor, of Bergen Co., New Jersey to Elders and Deacons of the Reformed Dutch Church, of Bergen, New Jersey, £0.2, four tracts...corner to Tulman van Meets patent, Fytis Hartmann...line of Derick Clausant... commissioners for lands of Rev. William Jackson, Jacob van Wagener, Garret NewKerk, Zacharias Sickels, Abraham Diedericks, Johannes van Wagener, George Cadmus, Abraham Pryor and Hendrick Kuyper...said William Jackson and Abraham Pryor being the surviving elders and deacons. Signed Abraham Pryor and William Jackson. Wit: John Sickels and Nicholas Toris.

26 Feb 1799, Reformed Dutch Church names Elders and Deacons. John Cornelius, Matthew (x) Newkerk, Joseph van Winkle, Daniel Sickels, John Dedrix, Jacob van Wagener, John Vreeland, John van Horne and Jury van Winkle.

15 Aug 1798, Thomas Howard, gentleman, of New York City to John D. Hibbard, of same, £180, 9 acres...corner to Stephen Rudd. Signed Thomas Howard. Wit: Silvester van Boskerk and Henry Provoost.

4 Dec 1788, Capt. David & Rhoda Lyons, of Elizabeth Town, New Jersey to Francis Tuers, of Barbadoes Neck, Bergen Co., New Jersey, £320, adjoining Col. Philip Cortlandt and Josiah Hornblower. Signed David Lyons and Rhoda Lyons. Wit: James Brown and William Davey.

25 May 1795, Andrew & Susannah Bell, of Perth Amboy, New Jersey to Thomas Meyer, of Ramahogh, Bergen Co., New Jersey, £22.75, 39 acres...in Franklin Twp...corner to lot of 25 acres said Bells sold to John McCall. Signed Andrew Bell and Susannah Bell. Wit: John Haring and John Rattoone.

20 Mar 1797, Peter & Myntie Debaun, of Franklin Twp.., Bergen Co., New Jersey to Peyathes Gutchens, of same, £26.25, 5 acres. Signed Peter Debaun and Myntie (x) Debaun. Wit: John Terhune and Albert J. Terhune.

28 Mar 1798, William & Joanna Budd and Jobiah & Mary Aber, all of New Barbadoes, Bergen Co., New Jersey to John Rutan, of same, £242, 16.14 acres ...line of the widow Frances Tuers and Sarah Sandford. Signed William Budd, Jabiah (x) Aber, Joanna (x) Budd and Mary Aber. Wit: John van Emburgh and Derick Rutan.

29 Apr 1799, Petrus Demarest, yeoman, of Franklin Twp., Bergen Co., New Jersey to his two sons, Daniel Demarest, of New York City and Guilliam Demarest, of Franklin Twp., Bergen Co., New Jersey, for love and affection, 100 acres... line of Albert Smith, Morris Sharp, James Anderson, Conrad Knight and Samuel Banta. Signed Petrus Demarest. Wit: Peter van Boskerk and Abraham Westervelt.

29 Apr 1799, Petrus Demarest, yeoman, of Franklin Twp., Bergen Co., New Jersey to his two sons, Daniel Demarest, of New York City and Guilliam Demarest, of Franklin Twp., Bergen Co., New Jersey, for love and affection, chattel goods. Signed Petrus Demarest. Wit: Peter van Boskerk and Abraham Westervelt.

31 Mar 1798, John Springer, of Bergen Co., New Jersey to William Crum, of New York City, £160, 100 acres...line of David Eckerson. Signed John Springer. Wit: Peter A. Hopper and Abraham Westervelt.

2 Jul 1798, John Johnson, of the english neighborhood, Bergen Co., New Jersey to Abraham vander Beck, of Bergen Co., New Jersey, £100, 3 acres...corner to Samuel Moore and the widow Demarest. Signed John Johnson. Wit: Nehemiah Wade and Adam Boyd.

27 Nov 1798, Abraham vander Beck, of Bergen Co., New Jersey to Elizabeth Johnson, of same, £0.25, 3 acres...corner to Samuel Moore and the widow Demarest. Signed Abraham vander Beck. Wit: Nehemiah Wade and Jane Wade.

6 May 1799, formed Academy of Bergen, Daniel van

Reypen chosen moderator; the following were chosen: Daniel Sickels, John Dedrix, Nicholas Tuers, Daniel Dedrix, Jacob van Wagener, Jury van Winkle and Daniel van Winkle Jr. Signed Daniel van Reypen, John Cornelius, John van Horne, Peter Sip, Jacob van Wagener, Daniel Sickels, Michael Demott, Daniel Dedrix, John Dedrix, Cornelius van Reypen, Michael Simmons, Jury van Winkle, Daniel van Winkle Jr., Nicholas Tuers, Joseph van Winkle, Cornelius van Vorst, Garret J. van Reypen, Daniel van Winkle and Eden Winner. The Trustees of the Academy are: Nicholas Tuers, Jacob van Wagener, Daniel Sickels, Daniel Derick, Daniel van Winkle Jr., Jury van Winkle and John Dedrix.

22 Mar 1799, Jacob & Catharine Blank Sr., of Franklin Twp., Bergen Co., New Jersey to Jacob & Mary Blank Jr., of Orange Co., New York, $1250.00, 188.44 acres, the first 100 acres sold to said Jacob & Mary Blank by Elshe Hopper 9 Apr 1796. Signed Jacob Blank Sr. and Catharine (x) Blank. Wit: Abraham (x) Quackinbush and Abraham Westervelt.

26 Feb 1795, John & Catharine Rose, yeoman, of Franklin Twp., Bergen Co., New Jersey to Mathew D. Coe, yeoman, of New Palts, Ulster Co., New York, £800, 206 acres. Signed John (x) Rose and Catharine (x) Rose. Wit: John Haring and Benjamin Westervelt.

18 May 1799, Abraham & Ann Debaun, of Harrington Twp., Bergen Co., New Jersey to William van Allen, of same, £0.5, 110 acres or two fifths of 282 acres...line of Oliver Delaney, Staats Storm and Dob. Johnson. Signed Abraham Debaun and Ann (x) Debaun. Wit: James Demarest and Yan Debaun.

15 Feb 1793, Stephen & Anna Bogart, of Bergen Co., New Jersey to James Bogart, of same, £1200, 117 acres...corner to Johannes and Jacob Ackerman, John Romine...part of 217.5 acres formerly belonging to Roelif Romine and mapped by Alexander McDowell...willed by Roelif Romine to the heirs of his son John Romine...also 184

acres...given by John Romine Jr. to Roelif Romine who willed to the heirs of his son John Romine...bounded by Roelif van Houten...also 10 acres...between Jacob Garretson and Cornelius van Houten...purchased by John R. Romine and Jacob Ackerman from Jacob Mead. Signed Stephen J. Bogart and Anna (x) Bogart. Wit: Henry van Winkle and Daniel (x) Smith.

7 Feb 1795, John van Dalson, Matthew G.& Caty Newkerk, Hendrick & Jane Newkerk, of Bergen Co., New Jersey to James van Boskerk, of same, £131.1, 11.4 acres...corner to Kile van Kull and Thomas Brown...purchased by Garret Newkerk from Garret & Catharina Kuyper. Signed Matthew Newkerk, Caty (x) Newkerk, Henry Newkerk, Jane Newkerk, Jan van Dalson and Helena (x) Christie. Wit: Joseph Quinby, Stephen Vreeland, William Christie and James S. Cannon.

13 Apr 1776, Johannis C. & Elizabeth Westervelt, of Slattesdam, Saddle River Precinct, Bergen Co., New Jersey to John F. Ryerson, John Garretson, Garret van Wagener, Derick Romine, John R. Bardan, Urey Westervelt, Elenor Ryerson, Cornelius Westervelt, Hessel Ryerson, George Ryerson, John Lambert, John Hopper and Peter Hopper, all of same and Henry Garretson, of Essex Co., New Jersey, £0.25, to be used for a school...along M. Ryerson Mill Dam. Signed John C. Westervelt and Elizabeth (x) Westervelt. Wit: Marmaduke Ackerman and David Archibald.

27 May 1773, Levinnes Winne, of Bergen, Bergen Co., New Jersey to Johannis Winne, of same, 24 acres...corner to Garret Sip. Signed Levinnes (x) Winne. Wit: Benjamin Westervelt and John Day.

7 Oct 1795, Hannah Westervelt, (widow of Christopher van Norstrandt, now married to John Westervelt), of Franklin Twp., Bergen Co., New Jersey to Jacob van Norstrandt, of New Barbadoes Precinct, Bergen Co., New Jersey, £252.5, 50 acres...in New Barbadoes Precinct...corner to John van Winkle. Signed Hannah (x) Westervelt.

Wit: Jane van Ryper and Luke Westervelt.

7 Oct 1795, Hannah Westervelt, (widow of Christopher van Norstrandt, now married to John Westervelt), of Franklin Twp., Bergen Co., New Jersey to Casparus van Iderstine, of New Barbadoes Precinct, Bergen Co., New Jersey, £22, 2.75 acres...between John van Winkle and Christopher Juriansen. Signed Hannah (x) Westervelt. Wit: Jane van Ryper and Luke Westervelt.

28 Mar 1763, Peter & Halamar Degroot, of Hackensack, Bergen Co., New Jersey to Luke Peterson, of same, £30, 10 acres...corner to Hendrick Sebe Banta and Michael Vreeland. Signed Peter Degroot and Halamar (x) Degroot. Wit: Hendrick (x) Banta and John Day Jr.

27 May 1799, John Marselius, of Bergen, Bergen Co., New Jersey to John Heavner, of same, £20, 1.5 acres...line of Matthew P. Newkerk. Signed John Marselius. Wit: Isaac van Ryper and John Stuyversant.

13 Apr 1799, Jacob Degroot, of Hackensack Twp., Bergen Co., New Jersey to Luke Peterson, of same, $445.00, 31 acres...line of Henry Banta. Signed Jacob Degroot. Wit: John Day and Isaac Hamman.

27 Sep 1786, Peter Zabriskie, of New Barbadoes Precinct, Bergen Co., New Jersey to his daughter, Anna Zabriskie, for love and affection, line of Hendrick Bush, deceased. Signed Peter Zabriskie. Wit: Elias Provoost and Peter Wilson.

13 May 1792, Abraham Pryor, Hartman Pryor and Arionca Rap, (wife of Adam Rap), all of Bergen Twp., Bergen Co., New Jersey to Casparus Pryor, of same, £0.5, 2 rods...line of John Kelly. Signed Abraham Pryor, Hartman Pryor and Arionca (x) Rap. Wit: Matthew Necker and Zacharias Sickels.

1 May 1799, Adam & Arionca Rap, of Bergen Twp., Bergen Co., New Jersey to Jasper Pryor, of same, $350.00, 1 acre...corner to John van Horne.

1 May 1799, Egbert & Sarah Post, of Ramespough, Bergen Co., New Jersey to Adam Rap, of Bergen, Bergen Co., New Jersey, £220, bounded by Nicholas Vreeland, John Vreeland and John van Horne. Signed Egbert Post and Sarah (x) Post. Wit: George Vreeland and Casparus Pryor.

5 May 1790, Garret Banta, John Demott and Cornelius Dooremus surveyed a tract of land, meet at house of Abraham Allen and Jan Holder. Signed Garret Banta, John Demott and Cornelius Dooremus.

27 May 1799, John Marselius, of Bergen, Bergen Co., New Jersey to John Heavner, of same, £150, 3 acres...line of Josiah Hornblower and Matthew P. Newkerk. Signed John Marselius. Wit: John Stuyversant and Isaac van Ryper.

20 May 1799, Daniel Lewis Sr., of Pompton, Bergen Twp., Bergen Co., New Jersey to Daniel Lewis Jr., of same, 14 acres...corner to Anthony Beam, Abraham Lewis and Cornelius Lewis, deceased. Signed Daniel (x) Lewis Sr. Wit: Richard Lines and John Collins.

18 Aug 1797, Samuel Helm, boatman, of New York City to Hendrick Banta, yeoman, of Hackensack Precinct, Bergen Co., New Jersey, £20, in New Barbadoes Precinct...corner to Peter P. Demarest, John van Boskerk, Jacob Zabriskie, Hendrick van Voorhees. Signed Samuel Helm. Wit: John Huyler and Benjamin Blacklidge.

1 May 1799, Samuel & Sarah Reading, of Newark, Essex Co., New Jersey to Richard Ackerman, of Saddle River Twp., Bergen Co., New Jersey, £1200, 15 acres...line of Thomas van Ryper, Arent Schuyler, the widow Lenah Banta and Joshua Bush...6.1 acres...corner to first lot...line of Marinus van Winkle. Signed Samuel Reading. Wit: Nehemiah Wade and Jacob Terhune.

29 Jul 1799, William & Margaret Williams, of New Barbadoes Twp., Bergen Co., New Jersey to Jacob Day, carpenter, of New York City, £65, 88 acres ...line of William Ellis, deceased, Cornelius Bogart, John Day and Michael Vreeland...to a place which Daniel Day, one of the heirs of William Day was entitled...purchased from Daniel Day 1 May 1799. Signed William Williams and Margareth Williams. Wit: Richard Terhune and Jacob Terhune.

21 Jul 1799, Burnet Richards, of New Barbadoes Neck, Bergen Co., New Jersey to Richard Bergen, of same, $1312.00, 57 acres...in New Barbadoes Twp...line of William & Margaret Hornblower, Doctor Hugh Williams, John Gill...29 acres, adjoining...currently property of Edmund William Kingsland, deceased...one fourth of property corner to Samuel Lewis. Signed Burnet Richards. Wit: John Outwater and Nicholas Outwater.

21 Jul 1799, Richard & Elizabeth Bergen, New Barbadoes Neck, Bergen Co., New Jersey to Gerard Bancker, of New York City, $5900.00, 172.6 acres ...between Richard Bergen and Casparus Degraw...bounded by John Ernis, Garret and Jacob Bogart and Doctor Hugh Williams...60 acres adjoining Rev. Uzal Ogden...3 acres adjoining. Signed Richard Bergen and Elizabeth Bergen. Wit: Nicholas Outwater and John Outwater.

22 Apr 1797, Marseles Marselius, of Bergen, Bergen Co., New Jersey to William Coulter, of Bergen Twp., Bergen Co., New Jersey, £100, line of Henry Cole. Signed Seil Marselius. Wit: John Marselius and Thomas Boyd.

1 Jul 1784, Cornelius Haring, agent for forfeited estates of Bergen Co., New Jersey to Capt. Giles Mead, of Hackensack Precinct, Bergen Co., New Jersey, £400, 6.75 acres...line of Doctor van Boskerk and Richard Eaton...seized of Edmund Simmons, late of Bergen Co., New Jersey, for going behind enemy lines. Signed Cornelius Haring. Wit: Isaac Blanch.

26 Oct 1790, Giles Mead, farmer, of Bergen Co., New Jersey to Caleb Wade Jr., tanner and cordwinder, of Essex Co., New Jersey, £150, 6.75 acres...in Hackensack Precinct...corner to William Clark, Richard Eaton, Peter Christie and Doctor van Boskerk. Signed Giles Mead. Wit: Nehemiah Wade and William Ross Smith.

6 Aug 1799, David & Deborah vander Pool, of Hackensack Twp., Bergen Co., New Jersey to William Nicoll, New York City, $1250.00, 6.75 acres...corner to William Clark, Richard Eaton, Peter Christie and Doctor van Boskerk. Signed David vander Pool and Deborah vander Pool. Wit: Isaac Nicoll and Nehemiah Wade.

9 Apr 1796, Jonas Wade, of Essex Co., New Jersey to David vander Pool, of same, £450, 6.75 acres ...tract of land belonging to Caleb Wade Jr...in Hackensack Precinct, Bergen Co., New Jersey... corner to Doctor van Boskerk, Richard Eaton and Peter Christie. Signed Jonas Wade. Wit: Caleb Wade and David vander Pool Jr.

29 Apr 1799, Conrad Lines, of Pompton, Bergen Twp., Bergen Co., New Jersey to Peter Ryerson, of same, £25, 24 acres...corner to Anthony Beam, Abraham Lines and Cornelius Lines, deceased. Signed Conrad (x) Lines. Wit: Abraham Lines and John Collins.

14 May 1799, Daniel Lines Jr., of Pompton, Bergen Twp., Bergen Co., New Jersey to his daughter Catherine Ryerson, for love and affection, chattel goods. Signed Daniel (x) Lines Jr. Wit: Richard Lines, Jury Lines and John Collins.

20 Sep 1797, Jacob & Anne Moore, farmer, of Hackensack Twp., Bergen Co., New Jersey to Cornelius Lydecker, farmer, of same, £100, 5 acres...in the english neighborhood...line of Albert Westervelt. Signed Jacob Moore and Anne (x) Moore. Wit: Jacob Nagel and Garret Banta.

1 Jan 1799, James & Jane McCurdy, (Jane is one

of the daughters and heirs of Martin Ryerson), of Bergen Co., New Jersey to Benjamin Helm, of Essex Co., New Jersey, £0.25, 56.4 acres...56 acres...line of Garrabrant van Houten, Helmegh van Houten, deceased...53.51 acres, part of 107 acres, adjoining...35.7 acres, part of 39 acres...13 acres...41 acres...35 acres. Signed James McCurdy and Jane McCurdy. Wit: Benjamin Helm, John Benson and Abraham van Houten.

2 Jan 1799, Benjamin & Elizabeth Helm, of Essex Co., New Jersey to James McCurdy, of Bergen Co., New Jersey, £0.25, 56.4 acres...56 acres, part of 107 acres...53.51 acres...35.7 acres...13 acres...41 acres...35 acres. Signed Benjamin Helm and Elizabeth Helm. Wit: John Benson and Abraham van Houten.

3 Sep 1799, John M. & Rachel Clark, of Essex Co., New Jersey and John & Sarah Terrill, of Middlesex Co., New Jersey to Philip Berry, of Bergen Co., New Jersey, $165.00, 15 acres ...corner to land purchased by the parties of the first part from the heirs of Thomas van Ryper, who purchased from Indians...purchased from the heirs of Nicholas Roosevelt who obtained it from Henry Berry. Signed John Terrill, Sarah Terrill, John M. Clark and Rachel Clark. Wit: Joseph Hurbbut and Jacob Terhune.

3 Sep 1799, John M. & Rachel Clark, of Essex Co., New Jersey and John & Sarah Terrill, of Middlesex Co., New Jersey to Henry Berry, of New Barbadoes Precinct, Bergen Co., New Jersey, $165.00, 17.5 acres...adjoining land purchased by Philip Berry 3 Sep 1799. Signed John Terrill, Sarah Terrill, John M. Clark and Rachel Clark. Wit: Joseph Hurbbut and Jacob Terhune.

3 Sep 1799, John M. & Rachel Clark, of Essex Co., New Jersey and John & Sarah Terrill, of Middlesex Co., New Jersey to Theodore van Winkle and Tunis van Iderstine, of Bergen Co., New Jersey, $125,00, 12.5 acres...adjoining the previous tracts. Signed John Terrill, Sarah Terrill, John M. Clark and Rachel Clark. Wit:

Joseph Hurbbut and Jacob Terhune.

3 Sep 1799, John M. & Rachel Clark, of Essex Co., New Jersey and John & Sarah Terrill, of Middlesex Co., New Jersey to Thomas van Ryper, of Saddle River, Bergen Co., New Jersey, £240, 24 acres...adjoining the previous tracts. Signed John Terrill, Sarah Terrill, John M. Clark and Rachel Clark. Wit: Joseph Hurbbut and Jacob Terhune.

8 Jun 1798, George G. & Abigail Ryerson, of Pompton, Bergen Twp., Bergen Co., New Jersey to Ferres Doty, of same, £85, 6 acres...former line of Conrad Lines. Signed George G. Ryerson. Wit: William Colfax and Henry van Winkle.

11 Nov 1789, John Benson, John Outwater and Abraham Westervelt, judges of Bergen Co., New Jersey survey 12 acres in Saddle River Precinct for the heirs of John Ryerson. Survey done by Jacobus Post, Christian A. Zabriskie and John Benson Jr. Map on p. 169 shows land of John G. Ryerson. No. 1, Gartia Garretson, wife of John Garretson; No. 2, Blandenah the wife of James van Bueren, deceased; No. 3, George Ryerson; No. 4, Elizabeth Jaroleman, wife of John Jaroleman; No. 5, Lenah Ryerson, widow of Richard Ryerson; No 6, Jane Vreeland, the wife of Mycal Vreeland; No. 7, Hessel Ryerson; No. 8, Antia Hall, widow of Thomas Hall; No. 9, John Ryerson, deceased brother to George and Hessel Ryerson; No. 10, Hessel Ryerson; No. 11, George Ryerson; No. 12, John Ryerson, deceased brother of George and Hessel Ryerson. Bounded by Henry Dooremus, John G. Ryerson, Jacobus Post, Christian Post and John Benson. Signed Jacobus Post, Christian Zabriskie and John Benson Jr.

11 Nov 1789, John & Johannah Bayard, of New Brunswick, New Jersey division of land with William & Euphonica Patterson 7.4 acres...corner to Kile van Kull...6.8 acres...corner to Hendrick Kuyper. Signed Elisha Boudinot, Samuel Ogden and John G. Cumming. Wit: William P. Smith.

11 Nov 1789, Elisha Boudinot, Samuel Ogden and John G. Cumming, commissioners, division of land to John & Johannah Bayard and William & Euphonica Patterson...previously described. Signed Elisha Boudinot, Samuel Ogden and John G. Cumming. Survey notes by Samuel Hayes.

16 Sep 1799, George van Boskerk, of New Barbadoes Precinct, Bergen Co., New Jersey to John Hibbard, of Hackensack Precinct, Bergen Co., New Jersey, $200.00, 4 acres...corner to John Cooper and Lucas van Boskerk. Signed George van Boskerk. Wit: Richard J. Cooper and Catharine Berry.

23 May 1799, Josiah & Deborah Johnson, yeoman, of Hackensack Precinct, Bergen Co., New Jersey to John Hibbard, of same, £120, 12 acres... corner to Guilliam Demarest, David Anderson, William Challen. Signed Josiah Johnson and Deborah Johnson. wit: Peter Christie and Abraham Collins

21 Sep 1799, Thomas & Mary Hazard, gentleman, of New York City to Andrew van Horne, of Bergen Co., New Jersey, $8000.00, 60 acres...part of the estate of Andries van Boskerk...12 acres allotted to Margaret van Boskerk, wife of said Andries van Boskerk...corner to Jacobus van Boskerk. Signed Thomas Hazard and Mary Hazard. Wit: Samuel West and Abraham van Boskerk.

28 Mar 1797, John & Myntie van Allen, of Saddle River Twp., Bergen Co., New Jersey to John Quackenhus, of Orange Co., New York, £1825, 50 acres...corner to Cornelius Westervelt...115 acres...corner to John Ryerse, John J. Ryerson, deceased and Doctor Styles. Signed John (x) van Allen and Myntie (x) van Allen. Wit: Jacob Ackerman and Thomas Wills.

15 Apr 1799, Cornelius van Horne, farmer, of Bergen, Bergen Co., New Jersey to Richard Cadmus and Jasper Cadmus, both farmers, of same, $1935.52, 17.14 acres...corner to Andres van Horne...3 acres...line of Thomas Hazard and

Peter van Boskerk...2.8 acres. Signed Cornelius van Horne. Wit: Andres van Horne and Bernard Spring.

17 Jul 1799, George & Effy Cadmus, yeoman, of Bergen, Bergen Co., New Jersey to Richard Cadmus and Jasper Cadmus, of same, $200.00, 7.5 acres ...line of Peter van Boskerk and Thomas Hazard.

19 Sep 1799, Andres & Baffie van Horne, of Bergen Twp., Bergen Co., New Jersey to Richard Cadmus and Jasper Cadmus, of same, $5500.00, 53.5 acres...bounded by Peter Cole and Peter van Buskerk...30 acres...corner to Cornelius van Boskerk. Signed Andres van Horne and Baffie (x) van Horne. Wit: Samuel West and Abraham van Boskerk.

15 Oct 1799, George & Rachel van Boskerk, of New Barbadoes Twp., Bergen Co., New Jersey to Henry Traphagen Jr., of same, £40, 5.25 acres...corner to Lawrence A. Ackerman, John Earle, Elias Provoost. Signed George van Boskerk and Rachel van Boskerk. Wit: Patrick Creyan and Anthony R. Gale.

14 Oct 1799, William Colfax, of Saddle River, Bergen Co., New Jersey to Daniel Tichiner, of Long Pond, Bergen Co., New Jersey, £175, 21.7 acres...13 acres...corner to Joseph Bartrim. Signed William Colfax. Wit: Thomas J. Gillenland and James Tichiner.

14 Feb 1735, Abraham & Rachel Garretson, of Haghquagemunek, Bergen Co., New Jersey to John & Vroutie Bardan, of Hackensack, Bergen Co., New Jersey, exchange of land containing 400 acres for 239 acres...between Peter Garretson and Hans Neafie...40 acres...corner to the heirs of Derick Barentsen and Richard Ashfield...obtained from the brother of said Abraham Garretson, Garret Garretson...Garret & Neshe Garretson, parents of said Abraham Garretson sold to him 10 Jun 1720 and brother sold 19 Feb 1730. Signed Abraham (x) Garretson and Rachel (x) Garretson. Wit: Jacob Outwater and David Demarest.

13 Nov 1782, Garret van Wagener, of Saddle River Twp., Bergen Co., New Jersey to John D. Bardan, of same, £245, 50 acres. Signed Garret (x) van Wagener. Wit: Jacob D. Bardan and John Bogart.

3 Oct 1785, Jacob D. Bardan, of Saddle River, Bergen Co., New Jersey to his brother John D. Bardan, of same, for consideration, 40 acres ...between John R. Bardan and Garret van Wagener...corner to the heirs of Derick Barentsen...sold 25 Mar 1768 by Reynier Bardan to Derick Bardan, father of said Jacob and John Bardan. Signed Jacob D. Bardan. Wit: George Dooremus and Jacob Demarest.

8 Jul 1797, Richard J. & Margaret van Horne, Thomas & Antye van Horne, Garret D. & Elizabeth Ackerman and Henry & Nashie Harris, all of Bergen Co., New Jersey to John D. & Catrina Bardan, of same, $1.00, 47 acres...line of Richard Vreeland and John vander Beck...John van Horne, father of the above Richard, Thomas, Elizabeth, Nashie and Catrina willed 25 Apr 1794 to said Catrina. Signed Richard J. van Horne, Margaret van Horne, Thomas van Horne, Antye (x) van Horne, Garret D. (x) Ackerman, Elizabeth (x) Ackerman, Henry (x) Harris and Nashie Harris. Wit: Thomas Wills and John Benson.

11 Feb 1792, James & Gertrude Parker, of Perth Amboy, Middlesex Co., New Jersey to David D. Ackerman, of Franklin Twp., Bergen Co., New Jersey, £181, corner to Col. Richard Townly. Signed James Parker and Gertrude Parker. Wit: Eliza Parker and Edward John Ball.

11 Apr 1796, Cornelius Westervelt, John Westervelt and Stephen Westervelt, all of Saddle River Precinct, Bergen Co., New Jersey to David D. Ackerman, of Franklin Precinct, Bergen Co., New Jersey, £12, 8 acres. Signed Cornelius Westervelt, John Westervelt and Stephen Westervelt. Wit: Jacob D. Ackerman and John H. (x) Garretson.

28 Sep 1797, Nicholas & Jane van Blerkum, of

Aquackanonk Twp., Essex Co., New Jersey and Isaac & Caty Kip, of Brooklyn, Long Island, New York to Garret van Vorst, of New Barbadoes Twp., Bergen Co., New Jersey, £5.5, 7.4 acres...in Saddle River Twp...corner to the heirs of John van Winkle, Marinus van Winkle and Thomas van Ryper. Signed Nicholas van Blerkum, Jane (x) van Blerkum and Caty (x) Kip.

3 Apr 1793, James & Sarah Hodge, of Albany, New York to John vander Beck, of Bergen Co., New Jersey, £47.5, in New Barbadoes Precinct... bounded by Thomas Chapple. Signed James Hodge and Sarah Hodge. Wit: William Ross Smith and Simon Simonson.

9 Oct 1784, Joris & Lena Brinkerhof, of New Barbadoes Precinct, Bergen Co., New Jersey to John Banta, of same, £31.5, 4.5 acres...corner to land Joris Brinkerhof sold to John Chapple. Signed Joris Brinkerhof and Mardalena Brinkerhof. Wit: Peter Wilson and John Chapple.

9 Oct 1784, Joris & Lena Brinkerhof, of New Barbadoes Precinct, Bergen Co., New Jersey to John Chapple, of same, £31.5, 14.5 acres... corner to Nicause Brinkerhof, John Banta and Abraham Allen. Signed Joris Brinkerhof and Mardalena Brinkerhof. Wit: Peter Wilson and John Banta.

14 Aug 1794, Abraham Allen, Peter Allen and Sarah Allen, (mother of said Abraham and Peter and widow of Abraham Allen), all of Bergen Co., New Jersey to John Chapple, of same, £28, 4 acres...in New Barbadoes Precinct...line of Seba Brinkerhof, John Banta and John Earle. Signed Abraham Allen, Peter Allen and Sarah (x) Allen. Wit: John Outwater and Guilliam Outwater.

15 Feb 1787, John & Mary Banta, of New Barbadoes Precinct, Bergen Co., New Jersey to John Chapple, of same, £10.5, 1.5 acres...line of Nicause Brinkerhof and Thomas Chapple. Signed John Banta and Mary (x) Banta. Wit: John Board and Elias Provoost.

17 Jan 1800, Jeremiah Pope, of Bergen Twp., Bergen Co., New Jersey to William van Emburgh, of same, $600.00, 21 acres...line of the heirs of Archibald Campbell. Signed Jeremiah Pope. Wit: John Outwater and William van Emburgh.

18 Jan 1800, William van Emburgh, of New Barbadoes Twp., Bergen Co., New Jersey to Mary Pope, wife of Jeremiah Pope, of same, $600.00, 21 acres...line of the heirs of Archibald Campbell. Signed William van Emburgh. Wit: John Outwater and Jeremiah Pope.

20 Jan 1800, Jeremiah Pope, of New Barbadoes Twp., Bergen Co., New Jersey to Petertie Fritch, wife of John Fritch, of New York City, for love and affection, chattel goods. Signed Jeremiah Pope. Wit: Simon Simonson.

21 Sep 1799, John Benson, Abraham Westervelt and William Colfax, judges of Bergen Co., New Jersey to John G. Benson, Albert Zabriskie and John Brinkerhof, instructions to survey land in Bergen Twp. that John van Wagener willed 24 Nov 1792 to his two daughters, Antie and Leah van Wagener and Altie van Wagener willed 27 May 1794 to her two daughters Antie and Leah van Wagener, of which David & Leah Lozier, of Hackensack Twp., Bergen Co., New Jersey now claim an equal one half part. Signed John Benson, Abraham Westervelt and William Colfax.

21 Sep 1799, Survey completed. Signed Albert Zabriskie, John G. Benson and John Brinkerhof. Lot No. 1 allotted to Quilliam & Antie Outwater, 77 acres...line of Cornelius Bogart and Hendrick Zabriskie. Lot No. 2 allotted to David & Leah Lozier, 10 acres...line of Derick Westervelt, Jacob and Derick Brinkerhof. Lot No. 3 allotted to Guilliam & Antie Outwater, 6 acres...line of John van Horne. Lot No. 4 allotted to David & Leah Lozier, 6 acres...line of John van Horne. Lot No. 5 allotted to David & Leah Lozier, 4 acres...line of John van Horne. Lot No. 6 allotted to Guilliam & Antie Outwater, 4 acres ...line of John van Horne. Lot No. 7 allotted to

David & Leah Lozier, 6 acres...line of John van Horne and Hendrick Brinkerhof. Lot No. 8 allotted to Guilliam & Antie Outwater, 5 acres ...line of John van Horne and Hendrick Brinkerhof. Lot No. 9 allotted to David & Leah Lozier, 6 acres...line of Hendrick Brinkerhof. Lot No. 10 allotted to Guilliam & Antie Outwater, 6 acres...line of Hendrick Brinkerhof. Lot No. 11 allotted to David & Leah Lozier, 25 acres...corner to John Vreeland and Nicholas Vreeland. Lot No. 12 allotted to Guilliam & Antie Outwater, 25 acres...line of Thomas Gautier. Lot No. 13 allotted to Guilliam & Antie Outwater, 20 acres...corner to Nicholas and John Vreeland. Lot No. 14 allotted to David & Leah Lozier, 20 acres...corner to John Vreeland. Lot No. 15 allotted to David & Leah Lozier, 7 acres ...line of Nicholas Vreeland. Lot No. 16 allotted to Guilliam & Antie Outwater, 7 acres ...line of John van Horne. Lot No. 17 allotted to David & Leah Lozier, 12 acres...corner to Nicholas Vreeland. Lot No. 18 allotted to Quilliam & Antie Outwater, 12 acres. Lot No. 19 allotted to Guilliam & Antie Outwater, corner to Nicholas Vreeland. Lot No. 20 allotted to David & Leah Lozier. Lot No. 21 allotted to Guilliam & Antie Outwater, 2 acres. Lot No. 22 allotted to David & Leah Lozier, 2 acres.

6 Nov 1799, Guilliam & Antie Outwater, of Bergen Co., New Jersey to David & Leah Lozier, of same, $1.00, lots of land in survey performed by Albert Zabriskie, John G. Benson and John Brinkerhof to divide the estate of John van Wagener. Signed Guilliam (x) Outwater and Antie (x) Outwater. Wit: Nehemiah Wade and Alexander James.

26 Nov 1799, David & Leah Lozier, of Bergen Co., New Jersey to Guilliam & Antie Outwater, of same, $1.00, lots of land in survey performed by Albert Zabriskie, John G. Benson and John Brinkerhof to divide the estate of John van Wagener. Signed David Lozier and Leah (x) Lozier. Wit: Nehemiah Wade and Alexander James.

24 Jan 1800, Hendrick & Martie Spear, of Harrington Twp., Bergen Co., New Jersey to Abraham Whitten, of same, $458.00, 23 acres... line of Martin Hogencamp...5 acres...bounded by Doctor Outwater, Cornelius J. Blauvelt, Samuel Haring and Martin Hogencamp. Signed Henry Spear and Martie (x) Spear. Wit: Elizabeth Haring and Peter Haring.

22 Mar 1798, Joseph van Winkle, of Bergen Twp., Bergen Co., New Jersey to Casparus Pryor, of same, £100, 5 acres...corner to Jacob Newkerk, Cornelius van Vorst and Jacob Marselius. Signed Joseph van Winkle. Wit: Jasper Pryor and Jacob Pryor.

29 Aug 1799, Walter & Jannekie Clendenny, of Bergen Twp., Bergen Co., New Jersey to Jasper Pryor, farmer, of same, $162.50, 4 acres...line of Hendrick Brinkerhof. Signed Walter Clendenny and Jannekie (x) Clendenny. Wit: Joseph Waldron and Zacharias Sickels.

3 Sep 1799, Paul & Margaret Saunier, of Bergen Twp., Bergen Co., New Jersey to Peter Sickels, farmer, of same, $230.00, 4 acres...corner to Nathaniel Earle. Signed Paul Saunier and Margaret (x) Saunier. Wit: David (x) Carr and Zacharias Sickels.

7 Jul 1789, John George Leake, gentleman, of New York City to Aaron Devone, carpenter, of same, £10, 1 acres...in Bergen Twp. Signed John George Leake. Wit: William Day and Catharine (x) Eaton.

15 Nov 1794, John George Leake, gentleman, of New York City to Aaron Devone, of Bergen, Bergen Co., New Jersey, £410, 50 acres...line of Cornelius Huyler, Jacob Garrabrants and Johannaton Yeomans. Signed John George Leake. Wit: Christian Mestell.

14 Jan 1800, Nathaniel & Jane Day, of New York City to Jacob Day, of same, $125.00, their rights to any claim of the estate of William Day in Hackensack Twp. of 88 acres...corner to

William Ettis, deceased, Cornelius Bogart, Michael Vreeland and John Day. Signed Nathaniel (x) Day and Jane Day. Wit: Daniel van Reypen and Jane van Reypen.

12 Feb 1800, Isaac & Rachel vander Beck Jr., of Bergen Co., New Jersey to Casparus Bogart, of New Barbadoes Twp., Bergen Co., New Jersey, $1345,00, bounded by Thomas Rozell. Signed Isaac vander Beck and Rachel vander Beck. Wit: Francis Wade and Nehemiah Wade.

8 Feb 1800, Mary Westervelt, widow, John & Winetye Westervelt, all of Harrington, Bergen Co., New Jersey to Doctor Jacob Outwater, of Orange Town, Rockland Co., New York, $550.00, 7.63 acres...corner to Abraham Blauvelt, Jacob Wortendyke, deceased and Abraham J. Haring... 7.69 acres adjoining. Signed Mary (x) Westervelt, John Westervelt and Winetye (x) Westervelt. Wit: Jacob J. Blauvelt and John David Haring.

25 Apr 1799, Abraham & Minetye van Roden, of Franklin Twp., Bergen Co., New Jersey to Tunis Bardan, of Acquacknonk Twp., Essex Co., New Jersey, £300, in Saddle River Twp...purchased of Cornelius & Matteyntye Mayes 19 May 1789. Signed Abraham van Roden and Minetye (x) van Roden. Wit: Adrian van Reypen and Encreas Gould.

22 Feb 1800, John J. & Mary Durie, of Harrington, Bergen Co., New Jersey to Fredrick G. Haring, of same, $775.00, 20 acres...corner to Cornelius Eckerson and Abraham Eckerson. Signed John Durie and Mary (x) Durie. Wit: Jacob Marselius and John David Haring.

5 May 1776, Sarah Sandford, of New Barbadoes Neck, Bergen Co., New Jersey to Peter Sandford, of same, £25, 8 acres...corner to Timothy Davis, David Post and Abraham Tuers. Signed Sarah (x) Sandford. Wit: James Davis and William Dow.

6 Dec 1780, Catherine Post, of New Barbadoes Neck, Bergen Co., New Jersey to Peter Sandford,

of same, £12, 11 acres...corner to Samuel
Pennington, Rachel Sandford, Abraham Tuers and
Timothy Davis. Signed Catherine (x) Post. Wit:
William Dow and John (x) Jenkins.

17 Dec 1796, Mary Pennington, widow, of New Oak
Twp., Essex Co., New Jersey to John P. Sandford,
of same, £149.85, 11 acres...in Bergen
Twp...corner to the widow Davis, the widow Tuers
and Benjamin Sandford. Signed Mary (x)
Pennington. Wit: Aaron Pennington and Abraham
Tuers.

13 Mar 1799, Benjamin & Mary Sandford, farmer,
of New Barbadoes Twp., Bergen Co., New Jersey to
Thomas Sandford, of same, $150.00, 3 acres...
line of Peter Sandford, Abraham Sandford,
Elizabeth Robertson and Elijah Sandford. Signed
Benjamin Sandford and Mary Sandford. Wit: Peter
P. Sandford and Zacharias Sickels.

14 Aug 1799, Elizabeth Robertson, of New
Barbadoes Twp., Bergen Co., New Jersey to
William Whitfield, of same, $185.60, 4 acres...
corner to Thomas Sandford and Elijah Sandford.
Signed Elizabeth (x) Robertson. Wit: John
Machett and Peter P. Sandford.

24 Dec 1793, John George Leake, of New York City
to Jacob Garrabrants Jr., of same, £208, 26
acres...in Bergen Twp...corner to Johnnaten
Yeomans. Signed John George Leake. Wit:
Alexander Thompson and Michael Casey.

5 Apr 1799, Jacob Blank Jr., farmer, of Orange
Co., New York is bound to Jacob & Catharine
Blank Sr., of Franklin Twp., Bergen Co., New
Jersey, for $1000.00 for deed 22 Mar 1799 for
chattel goods. Signed Jacob Blank Jr. Wit:
Abraham (x) Quackinbush and Abraham Westervelt.

5 Apr 1799, David A. & Mary Haring and James &
Elizabeth Powleson, of Harrington Twp., Bergen
Co., New Jersey to Johannes H. Blauvelt, farmer,
of same, $900.00, 50 acres...tract which Fredrie
Vervalen, deceased purchased in partnership with

Wilhelmus Ferdon of Henry Ludlow and surveyed by John J. Haring, deceased, in 1773. Signed David A. Haring, Mary Haring, James Powleson and Elizabeth (x) Powleson. Wit: Benjamin Blacklidge and Petrus Haring.

8 Jul 1799, Albert C. Zabriskie, sheriff, of Bergen Co., New Jersey to Caleb Russell, of Morristown, Morris Co., New Jersey, $1000.00, 7 acres...in Pompton Twp...surveyed by Abraham Ogden...Ralph Burnet obtained judgement against Mathias Wynants and Martin Ryerson, executors of the estate of Josiah Stagg for £121.95. Signed Alberg C. Zabriskie. Wit: David B. Ogden and Sylvester D. Russell.

7 Mar 1800, William & Ann Westervelt, of Hackensack, Bergen Co., New Jersey to George van Boskerk, of same, £150, corner to Peter Wilson. Signed William Westervelt and Ann Westervelt. Wit: Caleb Williams and John Mackrel.

9 Jan 1794, Jacob Berry and John Berry, both of New Barbadoes Precinct, Bergen Co., New Jersey to John Crain, of Essex Co., New Jersey, £260, (at 8 shillings to the dollar), 20 acres... obtained by will to the said Jacob and John Berry from their father Abraham Berry. Signed Jacob Berry and John Berry. Wit: John Outwater and John Crane.

17 Feb 1800, Henry & Elshe Bardan, of New Barbadoes Twp., Bergen Co., New Jersey to David Anderson, of same, $625.00, 2 acres...corner to Benjamin van Norden, Isaac vander Beck, Capt. John D. Bardan and Henry Bardan. Signed Henry Bardan and Elshe Bardan. Wit: Nehemiah Wade and Garret Myer.

17 Mar 1800, Hendrick & Marrettye Spear and Abraham & Caty Whitten, of Harrington, Bergen Co., New Jersey to John F. Haring, of same, $515.00, 21 acres...line of Abraham Delemater and Martin Hogencamp. Signed Hendrick Spear, Abraham Whitten, Caty Whitten and Marrettye (x) Spear. Wit: Peter A. (x) Haring and Cornelius

Quackinbush.

25 Mar 1800, Casparus & Elenor Degraw, of New Barbadoes Twp., Bergen Co., New Jersey to Gerard Bancker, of same, $325.00, 1.75 acres...line of the heirs of James Ernis, deceased. Signed Casparus Degraw and Elenor Degraw. Wit: Garrabrant Yurianse and Theodorus van Winkle.

8 Feb 1800, Mary Westervelt, of Harrington, Bergen Co., New Jersey to Daniel Blauvelt, of same, $1046.00, 25.75 acres. Signed Mary (x) Westervelt. Wit: Isaac T. Blauvelt and John David Haring.

8 Feb 1800, Mary Westervelt and John & Winetye Westervelt, all of Harrington, Bergen Co., New Jersey to Abraham Haring, of same, $1124.50, 43.25 acres...corner to John A. Blauvelt, Leonard Degraw and Daniel Blauvelt. Signed Mary (x) Westervelt, John Westervelt and Winetye (x) Westervelt. Wit: Isaac T. Blauvelt and John David Haring.

24 Mar 1800, John van Boskerk, of New York City to James Campbell, of New Barbadoes Twp., Bergen Co., New Jersey, $400.00, 7 acres...line of John Terhune. Signed John van Boskerk. Wit: John Batholf and Hendrick Barr.

22 Feb 1800, Thomas & Abby Volk, of Harrington, Bergen Co., New Jersey to Samuel Cole, of same, $1250.00, 20 acres...line of Henry Volk and Leonard Degraw. Signed Thomas Volk and Abby Volk. Wit: Petrus Haring and John David Haring.

6 Mar 1800, Samuel & Sarah Cole, of Harrington Twp., Bergen Co., New Jersey to Jacob J. Cole, farmer, of same, $250.00, 5 acres...line of Abraham Demarest and Johannes van Horne. Signed Samuel Cole and Sarah (x) Cole. Wit: Peter Cole and Petrus Haring.

7 Mar 1800, Samuel & Sarah Cole, of Harrington Twp., Bergen Co., New Jersey to Christian van Horne, $250.00, .25 acres...line of Henry Volk.

Signed Samuel Cole and Sarah (x) Cole. Wit: Peter Cole and Petrus Haring.

17 Mar 1800, Thomas P. & Margaret Stebena Banta, of Franklin Twp., Bergen Co., New Jersey to Robert Fredericksen, of Rockland, New York, $425.00, 23.78 acres...line of Peter Demarest, Albert Wilson, Albert van Dun and Conrad Knact. Signed Thomas P. Banta and Margaret Banta. Wit: Albert Wilson and John (x) Pane.

18 Mar 1800, Stephen & Mary Westervelt, of Saddle River Twp., Bergen Co., New Jersey to Jacob Ackerman, of same, $1138.00, 43.09 acres ...line of John van Wagener, John U. Westervelt, Peter Hopper and Jacob Demarest. Signed Stephen Westervelt and Mary Westervelt. Wit: David Marinus and Abraham Willis.

19 Mar 1800, Stephen & Mary Westervelt, of Saddle River Twp., Bergen Co., New Jersey and Cornelius Westervelt, of Essex Co., New Jersey to John van Wagener, of Saddle River Twp., Bergen Co., New Jersey, $150.00, 2.69 acres... line of Garret van Wagener and John U. Westervelt. Signed Stephen Westervelt, Mary (x) Westervelt and Cornelius Westervelt. Wit: David Marinus and Abraham Willis.

19 Jun 1794, Ann D. Visme, of New York City to William M. Bell, sheriff, of Bergen Co., New Jersey, £450, 36 acres. Signed Ann Devisme. Wit: J. B. Provoost and J. Fred Provoost.

15 Apr 1800, school board election. Signed James D. Demarest, William Westervelt, Isaac Ryerse and John Quackinbush.

11 Apr 1800, Jeremiah & Anna van Boskerk, of Saddle River Twp., Bergen Co., New Jersey to Charity Stockholm, of same, $1137.50, 40 acres ...line of Joost Cough and Doctor John Garretson. Signed Jeremiah van Boskerk and Anna (x) van Boskerk. Wit: Alexander James and C. Greudhornme Devone.

8 May 1738, Jacob & Martintie Outwater, shoemaker, of Hagquagemonck, Bergen Co., New Jersey to Reynier Bardan, of Hackensack, Bergen Co., New Jersey, weaver, £377, 30 acres... between Peter Garretson and Hans Neafie...line of John Bardan ....Garret & Netie Garretson, of Pomerpogh, Bergen Co., New Jersey sold 10 Jun 1729 to Abraham & Rachel Garretson, who sold a portion to said Jacob Outwater, 14 Feb 1735. Signed Jacob Outwater and Martintie ((x) Outwater. Wit: David Demarest and Isaac vander Beck.

19 Apr 1800, Isaac & Anny Sherwood Jr., of Franklin Twp., Bergen Co., New Jersey to David Ackerman, of same, $812.50, 32.5 acres...bounded by John Westervelt, John van Horne and the heirs of Albert Ackerman. Signed Isaac Sherwood Jr. and Anna Sherwood. Wit: Elizabeth Haring and Petrus Haring.

20 Dec 1799, Daniel van Ryper, Cornelius van Ryper and Richard van Ryper, of Bergen Twp., Bergen Co., New Jersey to John Brower, of same, £210, 10 acres...line of Garret van Ryper. Signed Daniel van Ryper, Cornelius van Ryper and Richard van Ryper. Wit: Abraham Pryor and Peter Brower.

29 Apr 1800, Garret J. & Lenah van Ryper, of Bergen Twp., Bergen Co., New Jersey to Jacob Brower, of same, $500.00, 8 acres...line of John Brower. Signed Garret J. van Ryper and Lenah van Ryper. Wit: John Outwater and John Dedrix.

29 Mar 1800, John J. & Rachel Banta, of New Barbadoes Twp., Bergen Co., New Jersey to Abraham Haring, of Harrington Twp., Bergen Co., New Jersey, $700.00, 28 acres...line of Taddus van Iderstine, David van Bussen and Theodous van Winkle...2 acres adjoining. Signed John J. Banta and Rachel Banta. Wit: Alexander James and Theodorus van Winkle.

4 Apr 1800, Richard J. & Margarity van Horne, of New Barbadoes Twp., Bergen Co., New Jersey to

John J. Banta, of same, $500.00, 180 acres... line of lot of land sold by Maj. John Berry to Garret van Vorst...between George Brinkerhof and Samuel Berry...line of Enoch George Vreeland and John van Winkle. Signed Richard J. van Horne and Margarity van Horne. Wit: Alexander James, James van Winkle and Theodorus van Winkle.

5 May 1796, James Drummond, by Walter Rutherford, his attorney, of New York Co., New York to George Lawrence, of Franklin Twp., Bergen Co., New Jersey, £320.1, 123 acres. Signed Walter Drummond. Wit: Daniel van Ryper and Abraham Forshear.

## Chapter 11

### Bergen County
### Courthouse
### Deed Records
### Volume L

Recorded
in
1800-1800

12 May 1800, Thomas Day, of Bergen Co., New Jersey to Michael Day, of New York City, $125.00, 88 acres...in Hackensack Twp...lately belonging to William Ellis, deceased...line of Cornelius Bogart, Michael Vreeland and John Day. Signed Thomas Day. Wit: Nehemiah Wade and Jacob Degroot.

1 Mar 1800, John & Elizabeth Clem, of New Barbadoes Twp., Bergen Co., New Jersey to John Anderson, of same, $3750.00, 3.25 acres... bounded by Adoph Waldron and Isaac vander Beck. Signed John Clem and Elizabeth Clem. Wit: David Godwin and Jacob Terhune.

29 Apr 1793, Garret Alb. & Martyntye Lydecker, of Franklin Twp., Bergen Co., New Jersey, John Alb. & Annie Lydecker, Abraham & Rebecca Lydecker, of Clerkstown and Cornelius Alb. & Margaret Lydecker, of Orange Town, Orange Co., New York to John Demott, of the english neighborhood, Hackensack Twp. Bergen Co., New Jersey, £1250, 21.22 acres...corner to the heirs of John Degroot...0.75 acres...7 acres...line of Derick Vreeland, Samuel Moore and John Benson. Signed Garret A. Lydecker, Martyntye Lydecker, Abraham Lydecker, Rebeckah Lydecker, John Lydecker, Anna Lydecker, Cornelius Lydecker and Margaret Lydecker. Wit: Petrus Haring, James Demarest, Cornelius Garret Lydecker and Albert

Westervelt.

4 Apr 1800, Hendrick & Marettye Spear and
Abraham & Caty Whitten, of Harrington, Bergen
Co., New Jersey to Abraham Delemater, of same,
$125.00, 2 acres. Signed Abraham Whitten, Henry
Spear, Caty Whitten and Marettye (x) Spear. Wit:
Cornelius Quackinbush and Martynes Hogencamp.

23 Apr 1800, Hendrick & Marettye Spear and
Abraham & Caty Whitten, of Harrington, Bergen
Co., New Jersey to Thomas Outwater, of Orange
Town, Rockland Co., New York, $187.50, 5 acres
...corner to Cornelius J. Blauvelt, Daniel
Haring and Peter Perry. Signed Abraham Whitten,
Henry Spear, Caty Whitten and Marettye (x)
Spear. Wit: Petrus Haring, Elizabeth Haring and
John D. Haring.

24 Mar 1800, Martin J. & Altye Hogencamp, of
Harrington, Bergen Co., New Jersey to Abraham
Delemater, of Harrington Twp., Bergen Co., New
Jersey, $20.00, 0.5 acres...corner to Peter
Perry. Signed Martin J. Hogencamp and Altia
Hogencamp. Wit: Petrus Haring and James
Demarest.

22 Feb 1800, Willeinfrie Rutan, widow of Jacobus
Rutan and Abraham J. Rutan, both of Harrington,
Bergen Co., New Jersey to Henry O. Zabriskie, of
New Barbadoes, Bergen Co., New Jersey, $350.00,
13 acres...line of Jacob J. Zabriskie, Jacob
Bogart and Jacobus A. Bogart as surveyed by
Jacobus van Boskerk, deceased. Signed
Willeinfrie (x) Rutan and Abraham J. Rutan. Wit:
Anne (x) Westervelt and Abraham Westervelt.

10 May 1796, Albert Zabriskie, blacksmith, of
Harrington Twp., Bergen Co., New Jersey to Henry
A. Zabriskie, of New Barbadoes Precinct, Bergen
Co., New Jersey, £60, line of Jacob Zabriskie,
John Cooper and Herman Lutkins. Signed Albert
Zabriskie. Wit: Ralph A. Westervelt and Abraham
Westervelt.

1 May 1800, John & Elizabeth Bogart, of

Hackensack Twp., Bergen Co., New Jersey to John Demarest, of same, $1500.00, 43 acres...line of Peter Lozier, Richard Cooper, Daniel Demarest and John Anderson. Signed John Bogart. Wit: John Dudley and Isaac Kip.

1 May 1800, Jacob & Sarah Demarest, of Hackensack Twp., Bergen Co., New Jersey to John Bogart, of same, $1500.00, 43 acres...line of Peter Lozier, Richard Cooper, Daniel Demarest and John Anderson. Signed Jacob Demarest and Sarah (x) Demarest. Wit: Peter J. Demarest and John Peak.

15 Nov 1799, Joseph & Catlyntie Whitten, of Franklin Twp., Bergen Co., New Jersey to James T. Blauvelt, of Harrington, Bergen Co., New Jersey, $3000.00, 30 acres...corner to Andreas Snyder, Abraham Haring, John Archibald, Andrew Snyder and Thomas Snyder. Signed Joseph Whitten and Catlyntie (x) Whitten. Wit: Abraham A. Haring and John David Haring.

23 Dec 1799, Abraham & Caty Whitten, of Franklin Twp., Bergen Co., New Jersey to George Snyder, of same, $1000.00, 54.75 acres...corner to James Blauvelt, Abraham Bogart and Joseph Whitten. Signed Abraham Whitten and Caty Whitten. Wit: Abraham A. Haring and James Blauvelt.

14 Jan 1800, Joseph Whitten, of Franklin Twp., Bergen Co., New Jersey to George Snyder, of same, $125.00, 7.25 acres. Signed Joseph Whitten. Wit: James Blauvelt and Henry Spear.

1 Mar 1800, Joseph & Catlyntie Whitten, of Franklin Twp., Bergen Co., New Jersey to John Potter, of same, $320.00, 18 acres...in Saddle River Twp...corner to Adam van Norden, Jacob Ackerman and Cornelius Lozier. Signed Joseph Whitten and Catlyntie (x) Whitten. Wit: David Haring and Albert Terhune.

26 Feb 1800, Joseph & Catlyntie Whitten, of Franklin Twp., Bergen Co., New Jersey to Mannon Chapple, of same, $94.50, 3.25 acres...in Saddle

River Precinct...line of Johannes Myer and Simon van Winkle. Signed Joseph Whitten and Catlyntie (x) Whitten. Wit: George Snyder and John David Haring.

22 Apr 1800, John & Margaret Ridgway, blacksmith, of Saddle River Precinct, Bergen Co., New Jersey to John Powleson, wheelwright, of Franklin Twp., Bergen Co., New Jersey, £32.5, 2 acres. Signed John (x) Ridgway and Margaret (x) Ridgway. Wit: John C. Stagg and William (x) Decker.

10 May 1800, John G. Benson, Jacob Degroot, of the english neighborhood, Bergen Co., New Jersey, Jacob Lozier, baker, of New York City and Abraham Lozier, cabinet maker, of New York City to John Day, of the english neighborhood, Bergen Co., New Jersey, $2012.50, 57.5 acres ...corner to Cornelius Bogart and heirs of Jacob Edsall. Signed John G. Benson, Jacob Degroot, Jacob Lozier and Abraham Lozier. Wit: Albert A. Westervelt and Johannah Degroot.

5 May 1789, Hessel Ryerson, of Saddle River Precinct, Bergen Co., New Jersey to John Westervelt, of same, £80, 18 acres...line of Cornelius Westervelt. Signed Hessel Ryerson. Wit: John Outwater and Samuel Barhans.

25 May 1799, John George Kanous, of Pompton, Twp., Bergen Co., New Jersey to Jacob Kanous, of same, £282, 30 acres...line of John Felter Smith ...20.35 acres adjoining...10.9 acres adjoining ...20.75 acres adjoining. Signed John George Kanous. Wit: Henry van Winkle and Thomas Gillenland.

10 Apr 1800, John & Margaret Ridgway, blacksmith, of Saddle River Precinct, Bergen Co., New Jersey to James Blauvelt, of Franklin Twp., Bergen Co., New Jersey, $50.00, 6.75 acres ...corner to Cornelius Ja Bogart and John Carnes. Signed John (x) Ridgway and Margaret (x) Ridgway. Wit: John A. Rutan and John Pulis.

25 Feb 1800, Cornelius & Yarmerbey van Boskerk, of Bergen Precinct, Bergen Co., New Jersey to David Baldwin, of Harrington Twp., Bergen Co., New Jersey, $5000.00, 239.25 acres ...corner to Thomas L. van Boskerk, Fredrick van Reypen and Cornelius Bogart. Signed Cornelius (x) van Boskerk and Yarmerbey (x) van Boskerk. Wit: John David Haring and Abraham Westervelt.

3 Mar 1800, Henry & Catharine Wittsee, of New York City to James Kane, $152.50, 11.1 acres ...corner to Jacob Romine. Signed Henry (x) Wittsee and Catharine Wittsee. Wit: John Keating.

17 May 1793, Andrew Bell, of Perth Amboy, New Jersey to Richard Degraw, of Bergen Co., New Jersey, £27,3, 45.41 acres...corner to Jacob van Winkle. Signed Andrew Bell. Wit: John Thompson, Richard Carman and Helmegh van Winkle.

7 Apr 1800, Andrew Bell, of Perth Amboy, New Jersey to Richard Degraw, of Saddle River, Bergen Co., New Jersey, $22.00, 9.72 acres... corner to John F. Ryerson. Signed Andrew Bell. Wit: Helmegh van Winkle and Robert Rattoone.

15 Mar 1800, David & Annatye Campbell, of Harrington, Bergen Co., New Jersey to Joseph Jorden, of same, $50.00, 4 acres...line of David Demarest and Bannadus Vervalen. Signed David Campbell and Annatye (x) Campbell. Wit: Benjamin Blacklidge and Seba Bogart.

3 May 1800, Bannadus & Marrety Vervalen, yeoman, of Harrington, Bergen Co., New Jersey to Joseph Jorden, painter, of same, $34.37, 2.75 acres... line of David Demarest and Garret Auryansen. Signed Bannadus Vervalen and Marrety (x) Vervalen. Wit: Benjamin Blacklidge and Benjamin Blacklidge.

13 Feb 1800, Bannadus & Marrety Vervalen, yeoman, of Harrington, Bergen Co., New Jersey to David Anderson, of New York City, $175.00, 0.5 acres...corner to land late the property of

Margaret Valentine. Signed Bannadus Vervalen and
Marrety (x) Vervalen. Wit: Benjamin Blacklidge,
Benjamin Blacklidge, Isaac Blanch and Thomas
Blanch Jr.

28 Feb 1763, Cornelius Bogart, merchant, of
Paramus, Bergen Co., New Jersey to Joost
Zabriskie, of Hackensack, Bergen Co., New
Jersey, line of Abraham Westervelt and Jacob
Zabriskie. Signed Cornelius Bogart. Wit: Jacob
Zabriskie and Guilliam Bertholf.

1 May 1793, Cornelius Bogart, yeoman, of
Harrington Twp., Bergen Co., New Jersey to his
grandsons Andrew Zabriskie and Cornelius
Zabriskie, of New Barbadoes Precinct, Bergen
Co., New Jersey, for love and affection, line of
Joost Zabriskie. Signed Cornelius Bogart. Wit:
Christian A. Zabriskie and John van Blerkum.

2 Jan 1800, John D. & Aghy Terhune, of New
Barbadoes Twp., Bergen Co., New Jersey to
Christian A. Zabriskie, of same, $2500.00, 68.61
acres...line of Casparus Bogart and heirs of
Stephen Terhune. Signed John D. Terhune and Aghy
(x) Terhune. Wit: Abraham Willis and David
Terhune.

21 Mar 1761, Christian & Leah Zabriskie, yeoman,
of Bergen Precinct, Bergen Co., New Jersey to
Andreas G. Zabriskie, yeoman, of same, £75, 15
acres...line of Lucas Bogart, Hendrick C.
Zabriskie and Albert C. Zabriskie. Signed
Christian (x) Zabriskie and Leah (x) Zabriskie.
Wit: Yan vander Beck and Paulus Livesey.

13 Dec 1774, Hendrick C. & Mary Zabriskie,
yeoman, of Paramus, New Barbadoes Precinct,
Bergen Co., New Jersey to Andreas Zabriskie, of
same, £105, 15 acres...line of Lucas Bogart,
Hendrick C. Zabriskie and Albert C. Zabriskie.
Signed Hendrick C. Zabriskie and Mary (x)
Zabriskie. Wit: David Terhune and Christian J.
Zabriskie.

2 May 1800, Abraham & Elizabeth Forshear, of

Franklin Twp., Bergen Co., New Jersey to Thomas
Ackerson, of Harrington Twp., Bergen Co., New
Jersey, £252, 47.65 acres...corner to William
Forshear, John DeBaun and Garret Hopper. Signed
Abraham Forshear and Elizabeth (x) Forshear.
Wit: Abraham Rutan and Abraham Westervelt.

5 Mar 1800, Samuel Cobb and Ebenezer Farrand, of
Hanover Twp., Morris Co., New Jersey to John
Peter Tennet, of Pompton Twp., Bergen Co., New
Jersey, £15, 10 acres...line of John T.
Seahulfter. Signed Samuel Cobb and Ebenezer
Farrand. Wit: Henry Shumaker and Anthony (x)
Merian.

8 Apr 1800, Capt. Abraham & Sarah Haring, of
Harrington, Bergen Co., New Jersey to John A.
Blauvelt, of same, $562.25, 20 acres...line of
Daniel Blauvelt. Signed Abraham Haring and Sarah
Haring. Wit: Petrus Haring and John David
Haring.

21 May 1800, John Auryansen, of Harrington,
Bergen Co., New Jersey to his son Daniel
Auryansen, of same, $200.00, line of Garret
Auryansen. Signed Yan Auryansen. Wit: John David
Haring and Abraham Nagel.

8 Mar 1800, James D. & Mary Demarest, of
Harrington, Bergen Co., New Jersey to Garret F.
Haring, of same, $447.54, 16.75 acres...line of
Garret Blauvelt, Cornelius Quackinbush and
Christian Campbell. Signed James Demarest and
Mary Demarest. Wit: Petrus Haring and John David
Haring.

20 Mar 1800, James D. & Mary Demarest, of
Harrington, Bergen Co., New Jersey to Christian
Campbell, of same, $447.54, 16.75 acres...corner
to Cornelius Quackinbush and Garret F. Haring.
Signed James Demarest and Mary Demarest. Wit:
Petrus Haring and John David Haring.

20 Mar 1800, James D. & Mary Demarest, of
Harrington, Bergen Co., New Jersey to Cornelius
Quackinbush, of same, $1105.12, 33.5 acres...

bounded by Christian Campbell, Garret Blauvelt, Garret F. Haring and Christian Blauvelt. Signed James Demarest and Mary Demarest. Wit: Petrus Haring and John David Haring.

20 Mar 1800, Jacob J. & Elizabeth van Houten, of Acquacknonk, Essex Co., New Jersey to John H. Garretson, of same, $200.00, 12.5 acres...in Saddle River Twp ...corner to Derick G. van Houten, Adrian A. van Houten, widow Burham and Michael Ortley. Signed Jacob J. (x) van Houten and Elizabeth (x) van Houten. Wit: John G. Garretson and Abraham Willis.

3 Apr 1800, Samuel Cobb, of Morris Co., New Jersey to William Drummond, of Saddle River Twp., Bergen Co., New Jersey, £9.4, 9.43 acres ...line of David Hennion. Signed Samuel Cobb. Wit: James Ackerman and James Ackerman Jr.

3 Apr 1800, Samuel Cobb, of Morris Co., New Jersey to William Drummond, of Saddle River Twp., Bergen Co., New Jersey, £19.05, 19.08 acres...corner to James Parker. Signed Samuel Cobb. Wit: James Ackerman and Abraham (x) Spear.

7 Apr 1800, John A. & Cornelia Blauvelt, of Harrington, Bergen Co., New Jersey to John Ferdon, of same, $540.52, 21.5 acres...corner to Derick Haring, Thomas Blauvelt and Garret Auryansen. Signed John a. Blauvelt and Cornelia (x) Blauvelt. Wit: Petrus Haring and John David Haring.

3 Apr 1797, John & Nelly Garretson, of New York City to Paul Durie, Miller, of Harrington Twp., Bergen Co., New Jersey, £250, 25 acres... reference a deed from Henry Ellison to Simon Durie 22 Dec 1785. Signed John Garretson and Nelly Garretson. Wit: John Outwater and Thomas Outwater.

2 May 1799, Thomas & Margaret Johnson, of Brooklyn, Kings Co., New York to Paul Durie, of Harrington Twp., Bergen Co., New Jersey, $625.00, 25 acres...reference a deed from Henry

Ellison to Simon Durie 22 Dec 1785. Signed Thomas Johnson and Margaret Johnson. Wit: Lawrence Brower and Benjamin Rhodes.

14 Jan 1800, Elizabeth Durie and Paul & Anatta Durie, of Harrington Twp., Bergen Co., New Jersey to Richard Blanch, Thomas Blanch Jr. and Isaac Blanch, all of same, £525, 25 acres... corner to Cornelius Acker. Signed Elizabeth Durie, Paul Durie and Anatta Durie. Wit: George G. Brinkerhof and Jacob Marselius.

1 Nov 1793, James Parker and Abraham Ogden, two of executors of the estate of Henry Cuyler, the elder and Henry Cuyler, the younger To Abraham Fashun, of Franklin Twp., Bergen Co., New Jersey, £53.25, 30 acres...corner to John Fell. Signed James Parker and Abraham Ogden. Wit: David A. Ogden and David B. Ogden.

6 Feb 1796, William M. Bell, sheriff of Bergen Co., New Jersey to John Travis, merchant, of Philadelphia, Pennsylvania, £900, 16 acres, and 40 acres, and 3.57 acres, and 6.5 acres, and 73 acres, and 15 acres, and 11.37 acres, and 15 acres, and 65.63 acres, and 6018.88 acres, and 5937.38 acres, and 193.96 acres, and 100.11 acres, and 55.62 acres, and 98.27 acres, and 18.87 acres, and 91.76 acres, and 5319.13 acres, and 68.66 acres...purchased 26 Feb 1767, from Peter Hawenclever by Rev. Thomas Dampin, John Eleves and Richard Willis, trustees for Mary Crofts, Patrick Crawford and Gilbert Meason, John Duval, William Robinson, Neal Ward, Mary Sleack, Lucy Sleack, William Berry, Hutchinson Muse, Robert Muse, Richard Ackerson, the said Peter Hawenclever as partners with Andrew Seton and Richard Crofts, The said Andrew Sitors and William Robinson as assignees of the estate of the said Andrew Seton and the said Charles Crofts of the second part and David Gramm, George Jackson, Arthur Foust, the said Richard Willis and Richard Ackerson, of the third part...deed 23 Aug 1793 between Thomas Boyd and George Jackson and Robert Muse...John Jacob Fresch won in court £4000 from George Jackson

and Robert Muse. Signed William M. Bell. Wit:
Petrus Haring and Alexander C. McWhorter.

22 Apr 1800, Guilliam J. & Cathyntie Bogart, of
Harrington, Bergen Co., New Jersey to John C.
Westervelt, of same, $100.94, 4 acres...corner
to John Haring. Signed Guilliam J. Bogart and
Cathyntie (x) Bogart. Wit: Daniel J. (x) van
Horne and John David Haring.

16 Jun 1800, Gerard & Catharine Bancker, farmer,
of Bergen Co., New Jersey to Susan Ayesagg, wife
of Benjamin Ayesagg, farmer, of same, $3525.00,
88.73 acres...in New Barbadoes Twp...line of
Doctor Hugh Williams, Richard Bergen and Rev.
Uzal Ogden....and 60 acres adjoining...whereas
Richard & Elizabeth Bergen, of New Barbadoes
Neck sold to said Bancker 26 Jul 1799. Signed
Gerard Bancker and Catharine Bancker. Wit: Elias
Provoost and Jacob Zabriskie Jr.

1 May 1800, Jacob D. & Magdalena Demarest, of
Bergen Co., New Jersey to George Warren Chapman,
doctor, $206.25, 1 acres...corner to
Schrawlenburgh Church. Signed John D. Demarest
and Magdalena (x) Demarest. Wit: Nehemiah Wade
and Francis Wade.

16 Mar 1787, Doctor John & Catharine van
Blerkum, of New Barbadoes Precinct, Bergen Co.,
New Jersey to Echie Fielding, widow, of Bergen
Precinct, Bergen Co., New Jersey, £1100, 65
acres...bounded by John Richards, deceased,
Isaac vander Beck, Ane van Winkle, Tade van
Iderstine, John Vreeland and John Outwater
...formerly belonging to Isaac Vreeland,
deceased and by Enoch Vreeland, John Vreeland
and Abraham Vreeland, deceased, sold 25 May 1761
to Simon Vreeland. Signed John van Blerkum and
Caty van Blerkum. Wit: John Christie and Enoch
Vreeland.

2 Feb 1800, Adrian van Houten, of Saddle River
Twp., Bergen Co., New Jersey to Evert H. Venese
of Caldwell Twp., Essex Co., New Jersey and
Eldrick Yorkes, of Acquacknonk Twp., Essex Co.,

New Jersey, $893.00, 35 acres...adjoining John J. Ryker, Jacob Smith and Rudolph Jacobus... formerly belonging to Rudolph van Houten, who divided between his three sons Robert, John and Cornelius van Houten, Robert died and willed to his son, the said Adrian van Houten. Signed Adrian van Houten. Wit: Jacob Smith, Jacob van Winkle and John Parker.

15 Jan 1800, Abraham & Hester Kip, of New Barbadoes Twp., Bergen Co., New Jersey to Albert Bogart, of Harrington Twp.,, Bergen Co., New Jersey, $45.50, 0.5 acres...line of John Bogart, Guilliam Bogart,, Hendrick Bogart and Cornelius D. Haring. Signed Abraham Kip and Hester (x) Kip. Wit: Nathan Gotrius and Aaron (x) Toers.

10 Aug 1700, Peter & Nancy Ward, of Bergen Co., New Jersey to James Thin, of Franklin Twp., Bergen Co., New Jersey, $250.00, 23.85 acres... purchased from William & Elizabeth Teusbury, 15 May 1798. Signed Peter Ward and Nancy Ward. Wit: John Felter and Cornelius Carr.

3 Apr 1800, James & Eleanor Terhune, of New Barbadoes Twp., Bergen Co., New Jersey to John S. Banta, of same, $1200.00, 5 acres...line of Peter Terhune, Nicanse Terhune and 14 acres adjoining. Signed James Terhune and Eleanor (x) Terhune. Wit: Alexander James and Theodorus van Winkle.

31 Mar 1800, Daniel & Elizabeth Blauvelt, of Harrington,, Bergen Co., New Jersey to Wilhelmus Ferdon, of same, $275.00, 8.5 acres...line of John van Dalson, deceased, David A. Haring and Johannes Ferdon. Signed Daniel Blauvelt and Elizabeth (x) Blauvelt. Wit: Petrus Haring and John David Haring.

21 Apr 1800, William van Dalson and Henry van Dalson, (executors of estate of John van Dalson), both of Bergen Co., New Jersey to Wilhelmus Ferdon, yeoman, $75.00, 2.75 acres... line of Samuel Vervalen. Signed William van Dalson and Henry van Dalson. Wit: Roelif Newkerk

and Abraham Haring.

2 May 1800, Samuel & Mary Vervalen, of Orange Town, Rockland Co., New York to Wilhelmus Ferdon, of Harrington, Bergen Co., New Jersey, $75.00, 2 acres...line of William H. Ferdon and Thomas Eckerson. Signed Samuel (x) Vervalen and Mary (x) Vervalen. Wit: Benjamin Blacklidge and Peter Blacklidge.

14 Jun 1800, Albert & Hannah Wright, cordwinder, New Barbadoes Precinct, Bergen Co., New Jersey to David Terhune, of same, £75, 1.5 acres... line of Albert van Voorhees. Signed Albert Wright and Hannah (x) Wright. Wit: Garret Zabriskie and Jacob C. Zabriskie.

26 Sep 17794, Robert Montgomery, of Upper Freehold Twp., Monmouth Co. New Jersey heir to William Burnet, late of South Amboy, Middlesex Co., New Jersey to Peter Ward, of Franklin Twp., Bergen Co., New Jersey, £58.35, 33.35 acres... corner to Magdelen Valleau. Signed Robert Montgomery. Wit: William Pular and John Haring.

10 Apr 1795, Augustine Reid, of Roxbury, Morris Co., New Jersey to Peter Ward, of Franklin Twp., Bergen Co., New Jersey, £23.4, one fifth of 190.87 acres...line of Le Roux. Signed Augustine Reid. Wit: Walter Rutherford and Valentine Sillcock.

12 Jun 1795, Lewis Morris, of Morris, West Charter Co., New York to Peter Ward, of Franklin Twp., Bergen Co., New Jersey, £21.25, three equal undivided tenth parts of 190.87 acres. Signed Lewis Morris. Wit: James Morris and John Shults.

5 May 1798, William & Elizabeth Teusbury, (late Elizabeth van Horne, executor of estate of James van Horne), of Middlesex Co., New Jersey to Peter Ward, of Franklin Twp., Bergen Co., New Jersey, £260, 5 equal twenty fourth parts of 44 acres and 229 acres and 200 acres and 194 acres and 116 acres and 230 acres. Signed William

Teusbury and Elizabeth Teusbury. Wit: Abraham Schuyler and John Maby.

7 Jun 1798, Gertrude Parker, (widow of James Parker), of Perth Amboy, Middlesex Co., New Jersey to Peter Ward, of Franklin Twp., Bergen Co., New Jersey, $328.68, 93.17 acres...in Franklin Twp. Signed Gertrude Parker. Wit: Elizabeth Parker and James Parker.

1 Feb 1799, Joseph & Elizabeth Sharp, of Hardiston Twp., Sussex Co., New Jersey to Peter Ward, of Franklin Twp., Bergen Co., New Jersey, £87, 5 sevenths of the one equal undivided half part 183.5 acres. Signed Joseph Sharp and Elizabeth Sharp. wit: David Ford and Matthias Little.

16 Apr 1799, Gouverneur Morris, of West Chester Co., New York to Peter Ward, of Franklin Twp., Bergen Co., New Jersey, $59.37, one tenth part of 190.87 acres. Signed Gouverneur Morris. Wit: James Morris and John Shults.

24 Feb 1800, John M. & Rachel Clark, of Essex Co., New Jersey to Albert C. Zabriskie, of Hackensack Twp., Bergen Co., New Jersey, $200.00, 5 acres...line of Henry J. Brinkerhof and John Terrill. Signed John M. Clark. wit: John Outwater and Jacob Outwater.

15 Feb 1800, Jacob & Elizabeth Outwater and Nicholas & Rachel Outwater, of New Barbadoes Twp., Bergen Co., New Jersey to Jacob Brinkerhof, James Brinkerhof and Cornelius Brinkerhof, sons of George Brinkerhof, $1612.00, former property of George Brinkerhof, deceased, (father of the parties) who purchased of John Berry. Signed Jacob Outwater, Elizabeth Outwater, Nicholas Outwater and Rachel Outwater. Wit: Henry Berry and John Outwater.

15 Feb 1800, Jacob & Elizabeth Outwater and Nicholas & Rachel Outwater, of New Barbadoes Twp., Bergen Co., New Jersey to Jacob Brinkerhof, James Brinkerhof and Cornelius

Brinkerhof, sons of George Brinkerhof, all of their interest in the estate of their father George Brinkerhof. Signed Jacob Outwater, Elizabeth Outwater, Nicholas Outwater and Rachel Outwater. Wit: Henry Berry and John Outwater.

2 May 1800, Peter & Elizabeth Christie, of Bergen Co., New Jersey to William Ely, of same, £528.5, 37.75 acres...in Hackensack Precinct... corner to Josiah Johnson, Wert Banta and Guilliam Demarest...formerly the property of David Demarest. Signed Peter Christie and Elizabeth Christie. Wit: Jacobus J. Demarest and Paulus Paulisen.

9 Dec 1799, Daniel & Elizabeth Corson, yeoman, of Hackensack, Bergen Co., New Jersey to John J. Ackerman, yeoman, of same, $5550.00, 126 acres ...line of John C. Bogart, heirs of John J. Bogart, Jacob Lozier, heirs of Guilliam Bogart, the elder and John Ackerman. Signed Daniel Corson and Elizabeth Corson. Wit: Benjamin Buckbee and John C. Bogart.

24 Mar 1800, Martin J. & Altia Hogencamp, yeoman, of Harrington Twp., Bergen Co., New Jersey to Daniel J. Haring, of same, $780.00, 23.23 acres...line of Fredrick Haring, Henry Spear, Abraham Whitten and Abraham Delemater. Signed Martin J. Hogencamp and Altia Hogencamp. Wit: Petrus Haring and James Demarest.

24 Mar 1800, Martin J. & Altia Hogencamp, yeoman, of Harrington Twp., Bergen Co., New Jersey to Peter Perry, yeoman, of Orange Twp., Rockland Co., New York, $2960.00, 74 acres... corner to Doctor Thomas Outwater, Abraham Delemater, Daniel Haring, Leander Degraw, John Bryne and Abraham J. Haring. Signed Martin J. Hogencamp and Altia Hogencamp. Wit: Petrus Haring and James Demarest.

18 Jun 1800, Mary Hopper, Garret A. Ackerman and John A. Westervelt, (administrators of the estate of Andrew A. Hopper, of Bergen Co., New Jersey) to Christian A. Zabriskie, of Bergen

Co., New Jersey, $1420.00, 40 acres...corner to the house of Peter van Boskerk...line of Thomas van Boskerk and Peter Ackerman. Signed Mary Hopper, Garret A. Ackerman and John A. Westervelt. Wit: Isaac Sherwood Jr. and Abraham D. Terhune.

1 Jun 1763, Cornelius & Elizabeth Bogart, merchant, of Paramus, Bergen Co., New Jersey to Joost Zabriskie, cordwinder, of Hackensack, Bergen Co., New Jersey, £293.25, 46.75 acres... corner to John Romine and Derick Terhune. Signed Cornelius Bogart and Elizabeth Bogart. Wit: Hendrick (x) van Giesen and Guilliam Bertholf.

26 Jun 1773, John & Juliana Romine, goldsmith, of New York City to Joost Zabriskie, of Hackensack Precinct, Bergen Co., New Jersey, £750, 8.25 acres...corner to William Provoost, Johannes Terhune and Cornelius Bogart...and 35 acres...line of Nicanse Kip, Joris van Giesen ...and 6.25 acres. Signed John Romine and Juliana (x) Romine. Wit: William vander Water and Edmund Seaman.

12 Apr 1800, Henry Bogart, of Harrington, Bergen Co., New Jersey to Guilliam Bogart, of same, $1.00, 27.5 acres...willed by John Bogart to his sons the said Henry and Guilliam. Signed Hendrick Bogart. Wit: Abraham David Haring and John David Haring.

1 Jul 1800, Christian A. & Maria Zabriskie, merchant, of Bergen Co., New Jersey to Garret A. Ackerman, farmer, of same, $425.00, 40 acres... line of Peter Ackerman, Thomas van Boskerk and Garret Ackerman...part of the farm of Andrew Hopper, deceased. Signed Christian A. Zabriskie and Mary Zabriskie. Wit: Jane Bogart and Abraham Westervelt.

20 Aug 1783, Peter A. Cathelinty Westervelt, of Harrington Twp., Bergen Co., New Jersey to Stephen A. Westervelt and Albert A. Westervelt, £280.3, 173 acres...line of Barnet Cole and Samuel P. Demarest...said Peter, Stephen and

Albert are sons of Albert Westervelt, deceased.
Signed Peter A. Westervelt and Cathelinty (x)
Westervelt. Wit: Cornelius D. (x) Haring and
Cornelius Haring.

1 May 1800, John & Maria Westervelt, of
Slotterdam, Saddle River Twp., Bergen Co., New
Jersey to Richard Degraw, of same, $3525.00,
141.14 acres...line of John Earle, Lawrence van
Orden, widow Burham, Michael Ortley...18.81
acres, adjoining. Signed John Westervelt and
Mary Westervelt. Wit: John G. Garretson and
Jacob (x) van Saun.

5 May 1800, Jacob Degraw, of Saddle River Twp.,
Bergen Co., New Jersey to Richard Degraw, of
same, £0.25, 4 acres...line of Abraham Houseman,
deceased...formerly belonging to Leonard and
John Degraw, deceased...and 7.68 acres...
bounded by Robert Morris, John Pulis and Simon
van Winkle...purchased by John Degraw, deceased
from George Vreeland...3 acres adjoining. Signed
John Degraw. Wit: John Westervelt and Francis D.
Ryerson.

2 May 1800, Abraham & Mary Rutan, wheelwright,
of Franklin Twp., Bergen Co., New Jersey to
Jacobus Degroot, of same, $247.50, 18 acres...
line of Carl DeBaun, Abraham and Nicholas Raye.
Signed Abraham Rutan and Mary (x) Rutan. Wit:
Abraham Westervelt and Abraham Forshear.

2 May 1800, Abraham & Mary Rutan, wheelwright,
of Franklin Twp., Bergen Co., New Jersey to
Abraham Raye and Nicholas Raye, yeoman, of same,
$55.00, 4 acres...line of Carl DeBaun and
Jacobus Degroot. Signed Abraham Rutan and Mary
(x) Rutan. Wit: Abraham Westervelt and Abraham
Forshear.

2 May 1800, Abraham & Elizabeth Forshear,
yeoman, of Franklin Twp., Bergen Co., New Jersey
to William Forshear, hatter, of same, $868.37,
49.65 acres...corner to Thomas Ackerson, John
DeBaun, James Mourison and Abraham Rutan. Signed
Abraham Forshear and Elizabeth (x) Forshear.

Wit: Abraham Rutan and Abraham Westervelt.

2 May 1800, Abraham & Elizabeth Forshear, yeoman, of Franklin Twp., Bergen Co., New Jersey to Abraham Rutan, wheelwright, of same, $581.25, 21 acres...line of James Mourison. Signed Abraham Forshear and Elizabeth (x) Forshear. Wit: Abraham Westervelt and Annie (x) Westervelt.

15 Apr 1800, Jacob & Sally vander Beck to John H. Garretson, $1500.00, 32 and 19.57 acres... bounded by Herman vander Beck. Signed Jacob vander Beck and Sarah (x) vander Beck. Wit: Herman vander Beck and T. Willis.

16 Apr 1800, Isaac & Rachel vander Beck, of New Barbadoes Twp., Bergen Co., New Jersey to John Fine, of Paterson, Essex Co., New Jersey, $260.31, 12.25 acres...line of Doctor John Condict, Haramanus van Blerkum and James McCurdy ...part of 39 acres surveyed for Martin F. Ryerson. Signed Isaac vander Beck and Rachel vander Beck. Wit: David Godwin and Peter John Roebuck.

13 Apr 1800, Guilliam Bogart, of Harrington Twp., Bergen Co., New Jersey to Henry Bogart, of same, $1.00, 31.75 acres...line of Albert Bogart...and 15 acres...willed to said Guilliam and Henry by their father John Bogart. Signed Guilliam Bogart. Wit: Abraham David Haring and John David Haring.

29 May 1797, Lawrence & Mary van Boskerk, carpenter, of Saddle River Precinct, Bergen Co., New Jersey to John Felter, carpenter, of same, £1200, 25 acres...in Harrington Twp...line of Albert Zabriskie...purchased of John A. van Boskerk, Thomas A. van Boskerk and Annatie van Boskerk...2.25 acres...corner to Andrew Terhune ...purchased of Peter & Myntie DeBaun. Signed Lawrence van Boskerk and Mary (x) van Boskerk.

10 May 1798, Lawrence & van Boskerk, carpenter, of Saddle River Precinct, Bergen Co., New Jersey

to John Felter, farmer, of same, £500, 216.58 acres. Signed Lawrence van Boskerk. Wit: John T. Hudson and John Haring.

1 May 1800, Jacob Ja Brower, yeoman, of Bergen Co., New Jersey to John George Leake, gentleman, of New York City, $250.00, 14 acres...corner to John Sickels, Daniel Dedrix and Garret van Ryper.

13 Jun 1800, Aury Banta, farmer, of Saratoga Co., New York to John George Leake, gentleman, of New York City, $78.12, 6.25 acres...line of David B. Ogden, Hendrick Banta and Belloman Degroot. Signed Aury Banta. Wit: A. Engle and Rachel (x) Farcle.

11 Apr 1800, Charity Stockholm, widow, of Bergen, Bergen Co., New Jersey to Peter Samuel Der Vorst (de Mumorus), of same, $1200.00, line of Cornelius Garrabrants, Jasper Zabriskie and Anthony White. Signed Charity Stockholm. Wit: Alexander James.

14 Jan 1800, Edward & Eleanor Nicoll to Charles Prendhomme DeBaun, gentleman, $1000.00, 11.4 acres...in Bergen Precinct...line of Kile van Kull...and 10 acres adjoining. Signed Edward Nicoll and Eleanor Nicoll. Wit: Daniel J. Ebbets and Samuel Gale.

11 Jan 1800, Peter & Sarah Post, farmer, of Bergen Point, Bergen Co., New Jersey to Charles Prendhomme DeBaun, gentleman, of same, £554, 11.4 acres...line of Kile van Kull...and 6.8 acres adjoining. Signed Peter Post and Sarah Post. Wit: John Butler.

16 Jan 1800, John & Judith Butler, of Bergen Co., New Jersey to Charles Prendhomme DeBaun, gentleman, of same, $20.00, one eighteenth part of 10 acres...line of Kile van Kull. Signed John Butler and Judith Butler. Wit: Daniel Butler and E. J. Dupont.

21 Mar 1800, Jacob & Kitty van Horne, of Bergen

Co., New Jersey to Charles Prendhomme DeBaun, gentleman, of same, $20.00, line of Kile van Kull...purchased of Abraham Post. Signed Jacob van Horne and Cattrin van Horne. Wit: Benjamin Cole and Andrew van Horne.

6 Jan 1800, Jasper & Jenny Zabriskie, of Bergen Point, Bergen Co., New Jersey to Charles Prendhomme DeBaun, gentleman, of same, £9, one eighteenth part of 10 acres...line of Kile van Kull. Signed Jasper Zabriskie and Jenny (x) Zabriskie. Wit: Benjamin Zabriskie and Michael Zabriskie.

8 Jan 1800, Abraham & Naomi Spear, of Bergen Point, Bergen Co., New Jersey to Charles Prendhomme DeBaun, gentleman, of same, £6.75, one eighteenth part of 10 acres...line of Kile van Kull. Signed Abraham (x) Spear and Naomi (x) Spear.

1 Feb 1800, Andrew & Hannah Gautier, of Morris Co., New Jersey to Charles Prendhomme DeBaun, gentleman, of Bergen Co., New Jersey, $22.50, one eighteenth part of 10 acres...line of Kile van Kull. Signed Andrew Gautier and Hannah Gautier. Wit: Bridget Osborne and John Turner.

19 Apr 1800, Matthus Newkerk, of Bergen, Bergen Co., New Jersey to Charles Prendhomme DeBaun, gentleman, of Bergen Co., New Jersey, £9, one eighteenth part of 10 acres...line of Kile van Kull...said Matthus Newkerk is the attorney for William van Dalson and Henry van Dalson, executors of the estate of John van Dalson, wit: Richard Blauvelt and Abraham Haring. Signed Matthew Newkerk. Wit: John van Cleave and Daniel van Reypen.

1 Jan 1800, John Noble & Sally Cumming, of Newark, Essex Co., New Jersey to John Harvey Bureaux, of Bergen Point, Bergen Co., New Jersey, $1350.00, 6.8 acres...corner to Hendrick Kuyler...and 6.8 acres adjoining...and 11.4... line of Kile van Kull...11.4 acres...6.8 acres ...described in deed by heirs of Anthony White.

Signed John N. Cumming and Sally Cumming. Wit: Charles Prendhomme DeBaun and Alexander Clemmes.

9 Jan 1800, Charles Prendhomme DeBaun, of Bergen Point, Bergen Co., New Jersey to John Harvey Bureaux, of same, $3000.00, annexed to a deed executed by Hendrick & Catharine Kuyler to Daniel Smith 10 Nov 1765. Signed Charles Prendhomme DeBaun.

2 Sep 1799, John Marselius, farmer, of Bergen, Bergen Co., New Jersey to Marsel Marselius, £10 and love and affection, adjoining John Diedericks. Signed John Marselius. Wit: Michael Simmons and Abraham (x) Devone.

2 Sep 1799, John Marselius, farmer, of Bergen, Bergen Co., New Jersey to Cornelius Marselius, £10 and love and affection, line of Peter Sip and George DeMott. Signed John Marselius. Wit: Michael Simmons and Abraham (x) Devone.

5 Jun 1800, John & Elizabeth Fleerboom, cordwinder, of Harrington, Bergen Co., New Jersey to John C. Haring, yeoman, of same, £25, 4 acres...corner to John Maby and Peter Bogart. Signed John (x) Fleerboom and Elizabeth (x) Fleerboom. Wit: Abraham Westervelt and Anne Westervelt.

1 May 1800, Joseph van Winkle, of Bergen Precinct, Bergen Co., New Jersey and Peter Wilson, of New York City, (executors of the estate of Henry van Winkle, of New Barbadoes Precinct) to Isaac vander Beck Jr., of New Barbadoes Precinct, Bergen Co., New Jersey, £1100, 22 acres...line of Adolphus Waldron and Henry Bardan...and 2 acres...line of Nicholas Bogart and Joost Zabriskie...will of Henry van Winkle dated 23 Jan 1785. Signed Joseph van Winkle and Peter Wilson. Wit: Daniel van Reypen and Richard van Reypen.

9 Apr 1800, Henry & Antye Verbrick, of Franklin Twp., Bergen Co., New Jersey to Jacob Terhune, of New Barbadoes, Bergen Co., New Jersey,

$325.00, 45.75 acres...corner to Nicause Brinkerhof. Signed Henry Verbrick and Ann Verbrick. Wit: Roelif Verbrick and Jane Terhune.

3 Mar 1800, Hendrick van Voorhees, Nicause van Voorhees, Isaac van Voorhees and Jacob van Voorhees, all of New Barbadoes Precinct, Bergen Co., New Jersey to Jacob Terhune, of same, $300.00, corner to heirs of Derick Terhune. Signed Hendrick van Voorhees, Nicasue van Voorhees, Isaac van Voorhees and Jacob van Voorhees. Wit: Isaac van Saun and Albert Zabriskie.

24 Feb 1800, John M. & Rachel Clark, of Essex Co., New Jersey to Albert van Voorhees, of New Barbadoes Twp., Bergen Co., New Jersey, $200.00, 5 acres...corner to Albert C. Zabriskie. Signed John M. Clark. Wit: John Outwater and Jacob Outwater.

7 Mar 1800, Joseph & Sally Crane Jr., of Newark Twp., Essex Co., New Jersey to Cornelius Toers, of New Barbadoes Neck, Bergen Co., New Jersey, £21, 1.9 acres...line of the widow Elizabeth Davis. Signed Joseph Crane Jr. and Sally Crane. Wit: John Sandford and Ebenezer Smith.

12 Aug 1799, Sarah Sandford, of New Barbadoes Neck, Bergen Co., New Jersey to Ebenezer Smith, of Newark Twp., Essex Co., New Jersey, $250.00, 10 acres...line of Cornelius Toers, Franke Toers and William J. Cumming. Signed Sarah (x) Sandford. Wit: Peter P. Sandford and Cornelius Toers.

18 Jan 1800, Henry & Elenah Aster, of Orange Town, Rockland Co., New York to William Concklin, of Ramapough, Bergen Co., New Jersey, £1170, 240.7 acres. Signed Henry Aster and Elenah (x) Aster. Wit: William Concklin Jr. and Peter (x) Ramsey.

7 Jun 1792, Evert Bancker, merchant, of New York City to John Earle, yeoman, of Bergen Co., New Jersey, £512, 167 acres...line of Doctor John

Bard. Signed Evert Bancker. Wit: William vander Water and Israel Wood.

22 Apr 1800, John & Gatia van Boskerk, yeoman, of New Barbadoes Precinct, Bergen Co., New Jersey to Richard J. Cooper, of same, $312,50, 5 acres...line of Jacob van Voorhees, John van Boskerk and the heirs of Samuel Helm. Signed John van Boskerk and Gatia van Boskerk. Wit: Peter Cooper and John Gunter.

22 Jul 1800, John Demarest, of Hackensack Twp., Bergen Co., New Jersey to Roelif Bogart, of same, £452.5, 25 acres...line of Richard Cooper and Peter Lozier. Signed John Demarest. Wit: Sarah Nicoll and Walter D. Nicoll.

24 Jun 1800, Jacob T. DeBaun, of New Barbadoes Precinct, Bergen Co., New Jersey to John Ackerman, of Harrington Precinct, Bergen Co., New Jersey, $562.48, 19.75 acres...corner to Jacob Hopper, Petrus DeBaun and John Lozier. Signed Jacob T. DeBaun. Wit: Richard J. Cooper and Ann Cooper.

18 Mar 1800, John Day and Thomas Day, both of Morris Co., New Jersey to Richard Day, Philip Day, John Day, Peter Day, Benjamin Day and David Day, all of Bergen Co., New Jersey, £0.25, 134 acres...line of William Ryerson. Signed John Day and Thomas Day. Wit: Abraham Ryerson and Hessel Hopper.

18 Mar 1800, Richard Day, Philip Day, John Day, Peter Day, Benjamin Day and David Day, (all sons of Thunis Day, deceased), all of Bergen Co., New Jersey to John Day and Thomas Day, both of Morris Co., New Jersey, £0.25, 134 acres...in Saddle River Twp...line of Roelif Jacobus and William Ryerson. Signed Richard Day, Philip Day, Peter Day, John Day, Peter Day and Benjamin Day. Wit: Abraham Ryerson and Hessel Hopper.

18 Mar 1800, John Day of Morris Co., New Jersey to Thomas Day, of same, £0.25, 67 acres...in Saddle River Twp...part of a larger tract

formerly belonging to William Bayard. Signed John Day. Wit: Abraham Ryerson and Hessel Hopper.2

18 Mar 1800, Thomas Day, of Morris Co., New Jersey to John Day, of same, £0.25, 67 acres...in Saddle River Twp...part of a larger tract formerly belonging to William Bayard. Signed Thomas Day. Wit: Abraham Ryerson and Hessel Hopper.

6 May 1800, Richard Degraw, of Saddle River Twp., Bergen Co., New Jersey to John Degraw, of same, £0.25, 47 acres...line of Nicause Terhune, John van Blerkum, George Ryerson, Francis Ryerson and Simon van Winkle...and 5.22 acres, adjoining...and 12 acres.. one half of land formerly belonging to Leonard and John Degraw, deceased...and 5.22 acres, adjoining...and 12 acres...line of John Bardan...purchased by John Degraw, deceased from George Vreeland. Signed Richard Degraw. Wit: John Westervelt and Francis D. Ryerson.

6 May 1800, Richard & Ann Degraw, of Saddle River Twp., Bergen Co., New Jersey to John Degraw, of same, $750.00, 15 acres...in New Barbadoes Twp...line of Abraham Houseman. Signed Richard Degraw and Ann Degraw. Wit: John Westervelt and Francis D. Ryerson.

1 May 1800, Abraham & Catharine Quackinbush, taylor, of Franklin Twp., Bergen Co., New Jersey to Lewis S. Concklin, carpenter, of same, $325.00, 18 acres...corner to David Ackerman, Peter Ackerman and Garret J. Hopper. Signed Abraham A. Quackinbush and Catharine Quackinbush. Wit: Abraham Westervelt and Isaac Sherwood.

14 Mar 1800, Lenah Neafie, (heir of Derick Day, late of Morris Co., New Jersey) to John Day and Thomas Day, of Morris Co., New Jersey, $1.50, 1223 acres...in Saddle River Twp...line of William Ryerson and Roelif Jacobus...purchased by said Derick Day and Hartman Vreeland, of late

of Essex Co., New Jersey. Signed Lena Neafie.
Wit: Simon Dooremus and John Day.

8 Mar 1800,, John Conselyea, (executor of the
estate of Abraham D. Brower, late of Bergen Co.,
New Jersey) to Henry J. Vreeland, of New
Barbadoes Twp., Bergen Co., New Jersey, $313.00,
2 acres...line of George van Boskerk decided at
the house of John Hopper, innholder, in Hopper
Town, Bergen Co., New Jersey. Signed John
Conselyea. Wit: Philip Berry and Josiah Johnson.

31 May 1800, Abigail Day, widow, of New York
City to Henry Day, of the english neighborhood,
Bergen Co., New Jersey, $750.00, 5.5 acres...in
hackensack Precinct...line of William Lozier,
Philip Durcell, John van Cleave and Peter A.
Degroot. Signed Abigail (x) Day. Wit: John Day
and Jacob Degroot.

11 Apr 1797, Enoch Sandford, of New Barbadoes
Neck, Bergen Co., New Jersey to William
Sandford, of New York City, £115, 5.5 acres...
line of Thomas Turner (who purchased of
Peregrine Sandford) and Michael Sandford. Signed
Enoch (x) Sandford. Wit: John Dodd and Elijah
Sandford.

18 Jul 1799, Sarah Sandford, of New Barbadoes
Twp., Bergen Co., New Jersey to Cornelius Tuers,
of same, £89.75, 8 acres...line of Francis
Tuers. Signed Sarah (x) Sandford. Wit: Abraham
Tuers and Zacharias Sickels.

13 Aug 1796, William S. & Phebe Pennington, of
Newark, Essex Co., New Jersey to Samuel Ogden,
of same, £180, 18.75 acres...in New Barbadoes
Neck...line of Francis Tuers and Sarah Sandford.
Signed William S. Pennington and Phebe
Pennington. Wit: Luther Goble and Sally Wheeler.

8 Aug 1796, Mary Pennington, William S. & Phebe
Pennington, of Newark, Essex Co., New Jersey to
Samuel Ogden, of same, £400, 22.27 acres...in
New Barbadoes Neck...line of Elizabeth Davis,
Jacob Ogden, Reuben Carter and Robert Kennedy.

Signed Mary (x) Pennington, William S.
Pennington and Phebe Pennington. Wit: Jonathan
Beach and Aaron Pennington.

28 Jan 1800, Reuben & Catharine Carter, of New
Barbadoes, Bergen Co., New Jersey to John N.
Cumming, of Newark, Essex Co., New Jersey,
$2000.00, 25.27 acres...line of Jacob Ogden,
Mary Pennington (sold by her to Benjamin
Sandford) and Peter Sandford...and 16.98 acres
...line of Samuel Ogden and Jacob Ogden...and 32
acres...line of Jacob Ogden and Zacharias
Sickels. Signed Reuben Carter and Phebe (x)
Carter. Wit: James Hedden and John vander Pool.

10 Jun 1800, Court appoints George J. Dooremus,
Abraham Ryerson and Henry Wammamaker to divide
land in line of Richard G. van Houten, Cornelius
van Houten, Peter Day, Richard Day and Roelif
Jacobus. Signed John Benson, John Outwater and
Abraham Westervelt.

9 Aug 1800, At the house of Thomas van Horne,
innkeeper, Saddle River Twp., Bergen Co., New
Jersey, land divided to John Day, David Day,
Richard Day, Benjamin Day and Philip Day. Signed
Abraham Ryerson, Henry Wammamaker and George
Dooremus.

5 Mar 1800, Albert C. Zabriskie, Sheriff, of
Bergen Co., New Jersey to Albert Wyhoff, of New
York City, $10.00 560 acres...mortgaged by
Andrew Bell...James R. Smith and Albert Wyhoff
won in court $1340.15 from Charles & Jane
Trelease. Signed Albert C. Zabriskie. Wit:
Alexander McWhorter and David B. Ogden.

20 Apr 1800, Guilliam & Cattyntie Bogart, of
Harrington, Bergen Co., New Jersey to John
Lozier, of same, $309.37, 12.25 acres...corner
to Richard Cooper and Petrus DeBaun. Signed
Guilliam Bogart and Cattyntie (x) Bogart. Wit:
Daniel (x) van Horne and John David Haring.

29 Apr 1800, Guilliam & Cattyntie Bogart, of
Harrington, Bergen Co., New Jersey to John

Lozier, of same, $309.37, 12.25 acres...line of John D. Ackerman, Jacob DeBaun and Richard Cooper. Signed Guilliam Bogart and Cattyntie (x) Bogart. Wit: Daniel (x) van Horne and John David Haring.

13 Aug 1800, John S. & Rachel Banta, of New Barbadoes, Bergen Co., New Jersey to Albert Ackerman, of Franklin Twp., Bergen Co., New Jersey, $4500.00, 180 acres...between George Brinkerhof and Samuel Berry...line of Enoch George Vreeland and John van Winkle...sold by Maj. John Berry to Garret van Vorst, deceased. Signed John S. Banta and Rachel Banta. Wit: Robert Campbell and Henry P. Kip.

3 May 1800, John & Elizabeth Earle, of New Barbadoes Twp., Bergen Co., New Jersey to Marregretie Romine, wife of Daniel Romine, of same, $3125.00, 9.9 acres...line of heirs of George van Giesen, Lawrence P. Ackerman...and 22 acres, adjoining...and 0.5 acres, adjoining. Signed John Earle and Elizabeth Earle. Wit: John Demott and Jacob Demott.

1 May 1800, Daniel J. & Margaret Romine, of New Barbadoes Twp., Bergen Co., New Jersey to Jacob Demott, of Hackensack Twp., Bergen Co., New Jersey, $3890.00, 70.4 acres...line of John Durie and John Demott...and 30.7 acres, adjoining. Signed Daniel J. Romine and Margaret Romine. Wit: John Earle and Jacob C. Banta.

9 Apr 1791, Margaret & Daniel Romine, of New Barbadoes Twp., Bergen Co., New Jersey to John & Sinety Demott, of the english neighborhood, Bergen Co., New Jersey, (the said Margaret and Sinety are daughters of Morta Roeliffe, deceased, late of Tenafly, Bergen Co., New Jersey), £140, 31 acres...line of widow Banta ...and 70 acres bounded by John Banta...and 40 acres, adjoining. Signed Daniel Romine and Margretye Romine. Wit: Michael Vreeland and John Day.

9 Apr 1800, John & Sinety Demott, of english

neighborhood, Bergen Co., New Jersey to Daniel & Margaret Romine, of New Barbadoes Twp., Bergen Co., New Jersey, (the said Margaret and Sinety are daughters of Morta Roeliffe, deceased, late of Tenafly, Bergen Co., New Jersey), 31 acres...line of heirs of Johannes Banta...and 70 acres bounded by John Banta...and 40 acres, adjoining. Signed John Demott and Franseynlie Demott. Wit: Michael Vreeland and John Day.

18 Apr 1800, Richard & Margaret van Horne, of New Barbadoes Twp., Bergen Co., New Jersey to Pryntie van Winkle, of Saddle River Twp., Bergen Co., New Jersey, $90.62, 7.5 acres...George Wagener road...line of Thomas van Horne and John Westervelt. Signed Richard van Horne and Margaret van Horne. Wit: Henry Berry and John Outwater.

1 May 1800, John C. & Annatie Banta, of Franklin Twp., Bergen Co., New Jersey to Ludwig Bush, of same, $1875.00, 115 acres...line of Abraham Hand, Daniel J. Romine, Henry Powleson, Peter Brush and Jacob C. van Ryper. Signed John Banta and Annatie (x) Banta. Wit: Peter Ackerman and Abraham Westervelt.

## Chapter 12

## Bergen County Courthouse Deed Records Volume M

### Recorded in 1800-1801

10 May 1800, Arent J. & Swan Schuyler, Robert & Jane Kennedy, John & Mary Schuyler, all of New Barbadoes Twp., Bergen Co., New Jersey, Adomial Schuyler, Henry S. Johns, John Kennedy, of the Kingdom of Great Britain to Christian A. Zabriskie, of New Barbadoes Twp., Bergen Co., New Jersey, $420.00, 5.5 acres...in Saddle River Twp. Signed Arent J. Schuyler, Swan Schuyler, John Schuyler, Mary Schuyler, Jane Kennedy, Robert Kennedy, Adomial Schuyler, by attorney, Henry S. Johns, by attorney and Robert Watts, by attorney. Wit: James Brown and Peter J. Schuyler.

13 Oct 1797, Jacob Bardan, Rebecka Bardan, Garret Garretson, Mary Garretson, of Saddle River Twp., Bergen Co., New Jersey, Peter Ramsey, Jane Ramsey, Henry Edtsler, Ellen Edtsler, of Franklin Twp., Bergen Co., New Jersey, John Ja Ryerson and Margaret Ryerson, of Long Island, New York, (all heirs of Jacob Ryerson) to John Westervelt, of Franklin Twp., Bergen Co., New Jersey, £450, 149 acres...line of John Ryerson, William Colfax and Anthony Bartrim...and 2 acres, adjoining...part of 140 acres purchased by Ryer Ryerson, deceased of George Willock, Andrew Johnston and Mary Johnston 19 May 1727 who sold part to his son Jacob Ryerson 1 Oct 1746. Signed Jacob (x) Bardan, Rebecca Bardan, Garret Garretson, Mary

(x) Garretson, Peter (x) Ramsey, Jane (x) Ramsey, Henry Aster, Ellen (x) Aster, Garret Garretson for John J. Ryerson and Margaret Ryerson. Wit: Jacob Ackerman and Uriah van Ryper.

1 Apr 1800, John D. & Uschelshe Pake, of Harrington, Bergen Co., New Jersey to Abraham Demarest, of same, £80, 4 acres...corner to Garret Demarest and Jacob Haring. Signed John D. Pake and Uschelshe (x) Pake. Wit: Richard Blanch and Cornelius van Horne.

9 Apr 1800, Jacobus D. Demarest, John D. Demarest, both of Harrington, Bergen Co., New Jersey and Peter D. Demarest, of Hackensack Precinct, Bergen Co., New Jersey to Abraham D. Demarest, of Harrington, Bergen Co., New Jersey, $1.00, several tracts...line of Albert Bogart, Nicholas Baldwin, Jacob Quackinbush and Tunis Quackinbush. Signed Jacobus Demarest, Peter Demarest and John Demarest. Wit: Albert Bogart and John David Haring.

11 Feb 1800, Walter and John Rutherford, trustees appointed by Gen. John Reed, John Stark & Susannah Robertson, of New York City to Thomas, George and Andrew Snyder, of Bergen Co., New Jersey, $2025.00, 162 acres. Signed Walter Rutherford, John Rutherford, John Stark Robertson and Susannah Robertson. Wit: James Morris and Agnes McDongall.

21 Apr 1800, Walter and John Rutherford, trustees appointed by Gen. John Reed, John Stark & Susannah Robertson, of New York City to Cornelius Wortendyke, of Tapan, New Jersey, £393, 131 acres. Signed Walter Rutherford, John Rutherford, John Stark Robertson and Susannah Robertson. Wit: James Morris, Morgan Lewis and Materoin Livingston.

1 May 1800, Andrew & Rachel Snyder, of Franklin Twp., Bergen Co., New Jersey to Thomas & Mary Snyder, of same, 67 acres and 3.21 acres. Signed Andrew (x) Snyder and Rachel (x) Snyder. Wit:

1 May 1800, Thomas & Mary Snyder, of Franklin Twp., Bergen Co., New Jersey to Andrew & Rachel Snyder, of same, 67 acres and 3.21 acres. Signed Thomas Snyder and Mary (x) Snyder. Wit: Anne Westervelt and Abraham Westervelt.

5 Apr 1800, Peter Hopper, farmer, of Saddle River Twp., Bergen Co., New Jersey to Garret P. Hopper, farmer, of same, $431.00, 10.12 acres... corner to Jacob Ackerman and Peter P. vander Beck...and 15 acres...corner to lot surveyed for John Ryerson Jr. and Derick Ryerson 6 Mar 1749. Signed Peter Hopper. Wit: Jacob Ackerman and Thomas Wills.

1 May 1800, John & Ann Westervelt, of Saddle River Twp., Bergen Co., New Jersey to John Ridgway, of same, $300.00, 15.1 acres...line of Thomas van Horne. Signed John Westervelt and Ann Westervelt. Wit: Eliza Westervelt and Thomas Wills.

1 May 1800, John & Ann Westervelt, of Saddle River Twp., Bergen Co., New Jersey to Jacob van Saun, of same, $179.00, 9.55 acres...line of Thomas van Horne and Richard van Horne. Signed John Westervelt and Ann Westervelt. Wit: Jacob Ackerman and Thomas Wills.

28 Nov 1795, Thomas Duncan, gentleman, of New York City to Cary Ludlow, of same, £280, 40 acres...at Slotterdam, Bergen Co., New Jersey ...bounded by Richard Yates, Simon van Ryper and Yurrie Peterson. Signed Thomas Duncan. Wit: Abraham Ludlow and William C. Ludlow.

1 May 1800, Cary & Hester Ludlow to Isaac Kip, of Slotterdam, Bergen Co., New Jersey, $875.00. Signed Cary Ludlow and Hester Ludlow. Wit: George Ludlow and Abraham Ludlow.

1 May 1800, George & Caty Lawrence, of Franklin Twp., Bergen Co., New Jersey to Henry Tise, of same, $415.00, 35 acres...bounded by Benjamin

Westervelt and Nicholas Meysinger. Signed George
Lawrence and Caty (x) Lawrence. Wit: Abraham
Westervelt.

14 Apr 1800, Andrew Hennion, yeoman, of Franklin
Twp., Bergen Co., New Jersey to Peter & Caty
Hennion, $200.00, 13.35 acres...line of Garret
Hopper, Jacob Hopper and Abraham Pulisfelt.
Signed Andrew Hennion. Wit: Henry van Allen and
Abraham Tise.

13 Mar 1800, Andrew Hennion, yeoman, of Franklin
Twp., Bergen Co., New Jersey to Felter Sevin,
yeoman, of same, $900.00, 40 acres...corner to
Garret W. Hopper. Signed Andrew Hennion. Wit:
Peter (x) Hennion and Abraham Westervelt.

1 May 1800, George & Caty Lawrence, of Franklin
Twp., Bergen Co., New Jersey to David Forshear,
of same, $1008.50, 88.51 acres...corner to
Nicholas Meysinger, William Concklin and John
Haring. Signed George Lawrence and Caty (x)
Lawrence. Wit: Abraham Westervelt and Abraham
Forshear.

15 Apr 1800, Jacob H. & Ann Zabriskie,
carpenter, of Franklin Twp., Bergen Co., New
Jersey to Jacob vander Beck, farmer, of Saddle
River Precinct, Bergen Co., New Jersey, £628 or
$1570.00, 92 acres...line of John Haring...and
6.75 acres...and 4 acres. Signed Jacob H.
Zabriskie. Wit: Harm vander Beck and W. Wills.

31 May 1800, Elizabeth Davis, of Newark Twp.,
Essex Co., New Jersey to Zacharias Sickels, of
New Barbadoes Twp., Bergen Co., New Jersey,
$470.00, 2.35 acres...line of Samuel Ogden...
and 4 acres. Signed Elizabeth (x) Davis. Wit:
Josiah James and Smith Ward.

1 May 1800, David & Polly Forshear, of
Harrington Twp., Bergen Co., New Jersey to Isaac
Maby, yeoman, of same, £305, 31.2 acres...line
of John Forshear and Isaac Rose. Signed David
(x) Forshear and Mary Forshear. Wit: Anne (x)
Westervelt and Abraham Westervelt.

1800, Isaac & Sally Maby, of Harrington Twp., Bergen Co., New Jersey to Peter J. Maby, farmer, of same, £150, 5 acres...corner to Minden Maby, Peter Bogart and Margaret Then...and 3 acres, adjoining...line of William Holdrum...and 11 acres, adjoining. Signed Isaac Maby and Sally (x) Maby. Wit: Isaac DeBaun.

1 May 1800, Henry J. & Mary Zabriskie, of New Barbadoes Twp., Bergen Co., New Jersey to Thomas Wammamaker and Henry Brawn, both of Franklin Twp., Bergen Co., New Jersey, $375.00, 20 acres ...corner to Abraham Zabriskie and Michael Marsan. Signed Henry Zabriskie and Mary Zabriskie. Wit: Peter Ackerman and Abraham Westervelt.

3 Apr 1800, Andries & Sarah van Deen, yeoman, of Franklin Twp., Bergen Co., New Jersey to David Au. Demarest, yeoman, of Harrington Twp., Bergen Co., New Jersey, $1650.00, 37 acres...corner Hendrick van Voorhees, John Zabriskie and Richard Cooper...and 6.48 acres...line of John Lozier and John van Boskerk. Signed Andries van Deen and Sarah van Deen. Wit: John van Wagener and Helmegh van Wagener.

28 Apr 1800, Crynes & Susan Bertholf, of Franklin Twp., Bergen Co., New Jersey to Albert Alyee, of same, $2600.00, 50 acres...line of Jacobus J. Bogart and Jacobus Pulisfelt. Signed Corynes Bertholf and Susan Bertholf. Wit: Abraham Westervelt and Henry van Allen.

10 Jul 1800, Nicholas J. Roosevelt, of New Barbadoes Neck, Bergen Co., New Jersey to Arent J. Schuyler, of Bergen Co., New Jersey, $2000.00, 8.94 acres. Signed Nicholas J. Roosevelt. Wit: Jacob Mark and Lewis Mark.

8 Sep 1800, John & Elizabeth van Horne, carpenter, of Franklin Twp., Bergen Co., New Jersey to James W. Ackerman, yeoman, of same, $362.25, 14.49 acres...line of William Ackerman and heirs of Albert Ackermam...part of farm formerly belonging to Albert Ackerman. Signed

John van Horne and Elizabeth van Horne. Wit: Isaac Sherwood and James Demarest.

8 Sep 1800, John & Elizabeth van Horne, carpenter, of Franklin Twp., Bergen Co., New Jersey to John D. Ackerman, yeoman, of New York City, $1145.31, 31.89 acres...bounded by David Ackerman and heirs of Albert Ackerman. Signed John van Horne and Elizabeth van Horne. Wit: Isaac Sherwood and James Demarest.

27 Oct 1800, John & Elizabeth van Horne, carpenter, of Franklin Twp., Bergen Co., New Jersey to John D. Ackerman, yeoman, of New York City, $1500.00, 31 acres...bounded by John D. Ackerman and heirs of Albert Ackerman. Signed John van Horne and Elizabeth van Horne. Wit: James W. Ackerman and Hendrick Banta.

29 Apr 1800, John Westervelt and John Osborne (administrators of the estate of Lawrence van Boskerk), of Saddle River Twp., Bergen Co., New Jersey to Casparus van Vorst, of New Barbadoes Twp., Bergen Co., New Jersey, $3300.00, 141.14 acres...corner to widow Burham and Lawrence van Norden...and 18.81 acres...line of Martin F. Ryerson. Signed John Westervelt and John (x) Osborne. Wit: Henry van Vorst and Walling van Winkle.

1 May 1800, Casparus & Margaret van Vorst, of New Barbadoes Twp., Bergen Co., New Jersey to John Westervelt, of Saddle River Twp., Bergen Co., New Jersey, $3300.00, 141.14 and 18.81 acres...former property of Lawrence van Boskerk. Signed Casparus van Vorst and Margaret (x) van Vorst. Wit: Henry van Vorst and Walling van Winkle.

31 Oct 1800, Mary Ryerson, (administrator of the estate of Martin F. Ryerson), late of Bergen Co., New Jersey to Richard J. Terhune, of New Barbadoes Twp., Bergen Co., New Jersey, $441.25, 32.09 acres...in Saddle River Twp...line of Richard G. van Houten and Richard Day. Signed Mary Ryerson. Wit: Theunis Ryerson and Jacob

Terhune.

31 Oct 1800, Richard J. & Polly Terhune, of Bergen Co., New Jersey to Mary Ryerson, of Saddle River Twp., Bergen Co., New Jersey, $441.25, 32.09 acres...in Saddle River Twp...line of Richard G. van Houten and Richard Day. Signed Richard Terhune and Polly Terhune. Wit: Theunis Ryerson and Jacob Terhune.

1 Sep 1800, John & Gatia van Boskerk, yeoman, of New Barbadoes Precinct, Bergen Co., New Jersey and Jacob & Elizabeth van Voorhees, yeoman, of Harrington, Bergen Co., New Jersey to John Lozier, of Harrington, Bergen Co., New Jersey, £58.4, 5 acres...corner to Henry Cooper and David A. Demarest. Signed John van Boskerk, Gatia van Boskerk, Jacob van Voorhees and Elizabeth van Voorhees. Wit: James van Voorhees and John Johnson.

2 Apr 1800, Albert Terhune, farmer, of New Barbadoes Twp., Bergen Co., New Jersey to James Terhune, of same, $2000.00, 83 acres...line of George and Albert Brinkerhof, Nehemiah Wade, Seba Brinkerhof and Abraham W. Depeyster. Signed Albert Terhune. Wit: Richard Terhune and Jacob van Houten.

10 Apr 1798, Joseph Elizabeth Sharp, to James Mourison, of Franklin Twp., Bergen Co., New Jersey, £168, five fourteenths of 231.3 acres. Signed Joseph Sharp and Elizabeth Sharp. Wit: Mathias Little and Hannah Soloman.

26 Jul 1800, John & Janne Moore, millwright, of Franklin Twp., Bergen Co., New Jersey to James Mourison, yeoman, of same, $892.52, five equal undivided tenth parts of 238 acres. Signed John Moore and Janne (x) Moore. Wit: Peter Westervelt and Abraham Westervelt.

18 Jul 1794, Peter Knott, yeoman, of Monmouth Co., New Jersey to Johann Pulisfelt, of Franklin Twp., Bergen Co., New Jersey, £50, 50 acres... purchased of John Meyer. Peter Knott. Wit: John

Johnston and John Haring.

26 Apr 1800, Johannis & Mary Myer, of Franklin Twp., Bergen Co., New Jersey to John D. Pulis, of same, $431.25, 34.5 acres...bounded by Jacobus Bogart, Crynes Bertholf and Martin Myer. Johannis (x) Myer and Maria (x) Myer. Wit: Martin Myer and Cornelius van Horne.

7 Mar 1800, George & Dorcas McIntire, farmer, of Bergen Point, Bergen Co., New Jersey to Charles Prendhomme DeBaun, of same, $22.00. Signed George McIntire and Dorcas McIntire. Wit: Eleanor van Rath and Andrew van Horne.

23 May 1800, Thomas & Elisa Gautier, of Bergen, Bergen Co., New Jersey to Charles Prendhomme DeBaun, of Bergen Point, Bergen Co., New Jersey, $22.00, 10 acres. Signed Thomas Gautier and Eliza Gautier. Wit: Thomas Cubberly and Jacob Cubberly.

26 May 1800, Jacob A. & Deghea Ackerman, miller, of Saddle River Twp., Bergen Co., New Jersey to John G. Ryerson, farmer, of same, $360.00, 24 acres...line of Jacob D. Bardan, Lawrence van Norden, Margaret Burham, Cornelius Westervelt, Simon van Winkle...purchased of John C. Westervelt who purchased of Uriah Westervelt. Signed Jacob Ackerman and Deghea (x) Ackerman. Wit: John Marinus and Thomas Wills.

5 May 1800, John & Jane Kip, of New Barbadoes Twp., Bergen Co., New Jersey to Lucas van Saun, of same, $1000.00, 20 acres...corner to Nicholas Kip, Isaac Kip, James Terhune...and 4 acres... line of Guilliam and James Terhune. Signed John Kip and Jane (x) Kip. Wit: John D. Bardan and Nicholas Romine.

8 Jun 1800, Luke & Margaret Wessels, of Acquacknonk Twp., Essex Co., New Jersey to Richard Bergen, of New Barbadoes Twp., Bergen Co., New Jersey, £97.8, 16.3 acres. Signed Lucas Wessels and Margaret Wessels. Wit: Abraham Willis and Jacob C. Vreeland.

13 Oct 1800, Samuel & Mary Scott Smith, (said Mary is only surviving executor of estate of Mary McKnight, late of New York City and widow of Charles McKnight, deceased), attorney, of Hawestraw, Rockland Co., New York to Barnet Cole, of New Barbadoes Twp., Bergen Co., New Jersey, $150.00, 32.5 acres...in New Barbadoes Twp...said Mary McKnight in her will dated 23 Dec 1794, named as excutors her brother Lewis A. Scott, of New York City, Peter Jay Mumo, of New York City and her daughter, Mary Scott McKnight, now Mary Scott Smith. Signed Samuel Smith and Mary Scott Smith.

19 Aug 1800, Edward William Kingsland, of New Barbadoes Precinct, Bergen Co., New Jersey to Barnet Cole, of same, $150.00, one half of 32 acres...James Outwater sold to John Richards, late of New Barbadoes Twp., Bergen Co., New Jersey and John Harris Schott, of New York City and John Richards had his land seized and sold to Edward William Kingsland. Signed Edward William Kingsland. Wit: Peter Allen and John Outwater.

14 Apr 1800, Peter & Catharine Wilson, doctor of law, Columbia College, New York City to John D. Bardan, of New Barbadoes Precinct, Bergen Co., New Jersey, £125, line of Adophus Waldron. Signed Peter Wilson and Catharine Wilson. Wit: Peter van Voorhees and Nicholas Lozier.

19 Apr 1798, Lucas & Hannah van Boskerk, of Harrington Twp., Bergen Co., New Jersey to Jacob van Voorhees, of same, £3400, line of John van Boskerk, Johannes van Houten, Cornelius Cooper ...except 2 acres sold to James Applebee, now belonging to Peter Demarest...2nd tract of 45 acres...part of tract David Johannes Ackerman purchased from Abraham Brower...line of Peter Demarest, heirs of Samuel Helm...3rd tract of 16.4 acres...under hand of Peter Demarest and Daniel Demarest, 24 Aug 1752 and the right of Peter Durie...corner to Richard P. Cooper, John Lozier, Andries van Dun. Signed Lucas van Boskerk and Hannah van Boskerk. Wit: Charles

Slade Fullwood and Jacob P. DeBaun.

2 Sep 1800, John J. & Gatia van Boskerk, of Kennakamack, Bergen Co., New Jersey to Jacob van Voorhees, yeoman, of same, £0.25, 5 acres... corner to Derick Cooper. Signed John J. van Boskerk and Gatia van Boskerk. Wit: James van Voorhees and John Johnson.

1 Apr 1800, Rachel Cooder, (widow of John Cooder and daughter of Samuel Ellis, deceased), of Bergen Co., New Jersey to John Fish, son of said Rachel, of same, $1.00 and love and affection, in Newburgh, New York...devised to said Rachel by Samuel Ellis. Signed Rachel (x) Cooder. Wit: Christian Bourdett and Michael Freeland.

3 May 1800, John & Mary Johnson, of Franklin Twp., Bergen Co., New Jersey to John DeBaun and David Cole, of same, £650, 101.75 acres...line of Abraham Rutan. Signed John Johnson and Mary (x) Johnson. Wit: Samuel Johnson and Andrew Blanch.

4 Oct 1800, Jacob & Nelly Dooremus, of Acquacknonk Twp., Essex Co., New Jersey to Simon Jn. van Winkle, of same, $212.25, 18.5 acres... in New Barbadoes Twp...line of Richard Benson... purchased by Rev. Uzal Ogden of Burnet Richards 28 Jul 1795...surveyed and divided 9 Dec 1762 by Azariah Dunnom and Josiah Hornblower by agreement 4 Jan 1762 between Burnet Richards, William Kingsland, John Richards, Yerrye Yurianse, John Morinscott, Walling van Winkle, Helmegh Sip, Hendrick Kip, John van Vorst and Garrabrant Yurianse, John van Winkle, Johannis Sip and Christopher van Norstrandt and again by the said Jacob Dooremus purchased of Rev. Uzal & Marytie Ogden, 6 Sep 1799. Signed Jacob Dooremus and Nelly (x) Dooremus. Wit: John S. van Winkle and Encuas Gould.

25 Nov 1800, Jacobus J. & Elizabeth Demarest, yeoman, and John J. & Craltye Paulisen, yeoman, all of Hackensack Precinct, Bergen Co., New Jersey to William Ely, yeoman, of same, $1.00,

13.75 acres...between John Demarest and Josiah Johnson ...and 15 acres...line of Albert N. van Voorhees ...said William, Elizabeth and Craltye are the grand children and only heirs of Peter P. Demarest. Signed Jacobus J. Demarest, Elizabeth Demarest, John Paulisen and Ellenor Paulisen. Wit: Nicholas Degroot and Josiah Johnson.

18 Jun 1800, Richard & Elizabeth Bergen, of New Barbadoes Twp., Bergen Co., New Jersey to Luke Wessels, of Acquacknonk Twp., Essex Co., New Jersey, £36.65, 6.11 acres...corner to lot said Wessels purchased of Burnet Richards. Signed Richard Bergen and Elizabeth Bergen. Wit: Jacob E. Vreeland and Alexander Willis.

13 May 1800, Harmanus & Patte van Zile, of Bergen Twp., Bergen Co., New Jersey to Henry Massacar, of Franklin Twp., Bergen Co., New Jersey, £525, 56 acres...between Cornelius Acker and Cornelius Wortendyke...line of Isaac van Blerkum, James Cane, Theodous Perhamus, Morter Groff, Abraham Lozier. Signed Harmanus (x) van Zile and Paty (x) van Zile. Wit: John A. Boyd and David P. Haring.

5 Nov 1800, William & Mary Ely and Jacobus & Elizabeth Demarest, all of Hackensack Precinct, Bergen Co., New Jersey to Ellenor Paulisen, wife of John Paulisen, of same, $5.00, 13.75 acres and 7 acres...bounded by John Hebberd, Jacobus Demarest, Albert van Voorhees and Elizabeth Demarest. Signed William Ely, Mary Ely, Jacobus J. Demarest and Elizabeth Demarest. Wit: Josiah Johnson and Nicholas Degroot.

1 Dec 1800, Adrian P. Post and Nashie Post, (administrators of estate of Peter P. Post) to Garret Eckerson, of Harrington Twp., Bergen Co., New Jersey, $142.50, 3.75 acres...line of Henry Storm court decided 27 Aug 1800 at the house of William Williams, at New Barbadoes, Bergen Co., New Jersey. Signed Adrian Post and Nashie Post. Wit: Nehemiah Wade and Francis Wade.

25 Jun 1800, John & Elsey Earle, of Bergen Twp., Bergen Co., New Jersey to Peter Sip, of same, $1087.50, 38.5 acres...purchased of Evert Bancker. Signed John Earle and Elsey Earle. Wit: Henry Labagh and John Outwater.

8 Sep 1800, Jacob En & Maritie Vreeland, of Acquacknonk Twp., Essex Co., New Jersey to Enoch Vreeland, of New Barbadoes Twp., Bergen Co., New Jersey, $78.75, 6 acres...line of Doctor Williamson. Signed Jacob E. Vreeland and Mary Vreeland. Wit: John van Bueren and Abraham Willis.

18 Jun 1800, Richard & Elizabeth Bergen, of New Barbadoes Twp., Bergen Co., New Jersey to Jacob En Vreeland, of Acquacknonk Twp., Essex Co., New Jersey, £37, 6.18 acres...corner to Luke Wessels. Signed Richard Bergen and Elizabeth Bergen. Wit: Lucas Wessels and Abraham Willis.

2 Aug 1800, Edmund William Kingsland, of New Barbadoes Neck, Bergen Co., New Jersey to Jacob E. Vreeland, of Acquacknonk Twp., Essex Co., New Jersey, £100, 24 acres...line of Hue Williamson. Signed Edmund William Kingsland. Wit: William Kingsland and Henry Kingsland.

11 Feb 1800, Walter Rutherford and John Rutherford, of New York City, trustees of Gen. John Reed, of Kingdom of Great Britain thereto appointed John Stark & Susannah Robertson to Uriah van Ryper, of Bergen Co., New Jersey, £138, 49.32 acres...corner to lot formerly belonging to John Albertse Bardan. Signed Walter Rutherford, John Rutherford, John Stark Robertson and Susannah Robertson. Wit: Mary R. Clarkson, Daniel van Ryper, John Shults (for John Rutherford) and Mary Chidlaw.

21 Jul 1800, Deborah van Boskerk, widow of Cornelius van Boskerk, late of Casbletbeen, Richmond Co., New York to Thomas M. Daniel Jr., of Bergen Co., New Jersey, $62.50, 1.125 acres ...formerly belonging to Philip Smith, and devised to Deborah van Boskerk and Hannah, the

wife of Garret Hawlenbeck. Signed Deborah van Boskerk. Wit: Daniel van Ryper and Andrew van Horne.

4 Dec 1800, Elizabeth Marselius, widow, of Bergen Twp., Bergen Co., New Jersey to Jacob Marselius, of Harrington Twp., Bergen Co., New Jersey, $3000.00, 120 acres...line of John Fleerboom...and 3 acres, adjoining...and 72 acres...line of Isaac Delemater, Abraham Blauvelt and Abram Ackerson. Signed Elizabeth (x) Marselius. Wit: John Dedrix and Sylvester van Bueren.

7 Oct 1800, Thomas McDowell, Stephen Johns jr. and James Schureman, executors of estate of David Williamson to Peter Ward, $15.00. Signed Thomas McDowell, Stephen Johns Jr. and James Schureman. Wit: John Schureman and Andrew Kirkpatrick.

28 Jun 1800, Peter Valentine, of Independence Twp., Sussex Co., New Jersey and Amacy & Margaret Landon, of Bergen Twp., Bergen Co., New Jersey to Charles Shoemaker, of Harrington Precinct, Bergen Co., New Jersey, £12, late in the procession of Margaret Valentine...Jacob Valentine, devised to his wife, and after his death to his three sons, equal shares, whereas Henry Valentine died intestate and Peter, Amacy and Margaret being heirs of two fourths of all Henry's share. Signed Peter Valentine, Amasa Landon and Margret (x) Landon. Wit: Petrus Haring and David Anderson.

13 Apr 1792, John Rattoone, of Middlesex Co., New Jersey to Francis and Simon van Winkle, of Bergen Co., New Jersey, £39.7, 56.7 acres... corner to John Degraw. Signed John Rattoone. Wit: Abraham Ryerson and Martin Ryerson.

14 Feb 1793, Francis van Winkle, of Saddle River Twp., Bergen Co., New Jersey to Simon van Winkle, of Essex Co., New Jersey, £0.25, 51.7 acres...purchased of John Rattoone. Signed Francis T. van Winkle. Wit: John H. (x)

Garretson and Thomas Wills.

28 Sep 1792, John Rattoone, of Perth Amboy, New Jersey to Simon van Winkle, of Saddle River Twp., Bergen Co., New Jersey, £34.25, 48.93 acres...line of heirs of William Gibson. Signed John Rattoone. Wit: Abraham Ryerson and Sarah Ryerson.

4 Feb 1800, Tunis van Bussen, of Slotterdam, Bergen Co., New Jersey to Herman van Bussen, yeoman, £162, 32 acres...line of Abraham Toers, heirs of Catlina Toers and Joost Cough... Herman van Bussen, father of said Tunis and Herman devised 21 Jan 1799 to his daughter Caty van Bussen and to his two sons 51 acres. Signed Tunis van Bussen. Wit: Doctor John Garretson and Richard van Horne.

24 Nov 1800, Doctor Ebenezer & Elizabeth Blachly Jr., of Paterson, Essex Co., New Jersey to Rev. John Phillips, of Bergen, Bergen Co., New Jersey, $373.72, 46 acres...in Saddle River Twp ...line of Abraham Willis,, Benjamin Vincent, Roelif Jacob van Houten, Derick van Houten, Jacob Ricker, John Jacobus, Alexander Richards and Cornelius van Winkle. Signed Ebenezer Blachly Jr. and Elizabeth Blachly. Wit: Bryant Sheys and Ebenezer S. Blachly.

6 Feb 1800, Tunis van Bussen, of Slotterdam, Bergen Co., New Jersey to Herman van Bussen, yeoman, of same, £162.5, 9.5 acres...Herman van Bussen, father of said Tunis and Herman devised 21 Jan 1799 to his daughter Caty van Bussen and to his two sons 51 acres. Signed Tunis van Bussen. Wit: Doctor John Garretson and Richard van Horne.

15 Dec 1800, Hendrick J. Zabriskie, of New Barbadoes Twp., Bergen Co., New Jersey of William & Margaret Williams, of New Barbadoes, Bergen Co., New Jersey, £130, 11 acres...line of heirs of Samuel Hillem. Signed William Williams and Margaret Williams. Wit: David Lozier and John van Houten.

1 Dec 1800, Albert J. Zabriskie, Henry J. Zabriskie and Abraham J. Zabriskie, all farmers, of New Barbadoes Twp, Bergen Co., New Jersey to Elshe Hopper, (widow of Garret Hopper), of Franklin Twp., Bergen Co., New Jersey, $100.00, 5 acres...line of John Christopher. Signed Henry Zabriskie, Albert Zabriskie and Abraham Zabriskie. Wit: William (x) Folly and Abraham Westervelt.

22 Feb 1800, Willimpie Rutan, (widow of Abraham J. Rutan) and Abraham J. Rutan, both of Harrington Twp., Bergen Co., New Jersey to Cornelius Zabriskie, blacksmith, of New Barbadoes Twp., Bergen Co., New Jersey, $1400.00, 3.7 acres...and 4.25 acres...line of John Zabriskie and Jacobus A. Bogart. Signed Willimpie Rutan and Abraham J. Rutan. Wit: Anne (x) Westervelt and Abraham Westervelt.

24 Nov 1800, John D. Demarest, of Hackensack Twp., Bergen Co., New Jersey to Isaac Nicoll, of same, £150, 18 acres...line of Roelif Bogart and Daniel Demarest. Signed John D. Demarest. Wit: William Williams and John Terhune.

10 Apr 1800, Joseph & Cattena Whitten, of Franklin Twp., Bergen Co., New Jersey to Adam van Norden, of same, $731.25, 45 acres...in Saddle River Precinct and Franklin Twp...corner to James Blauvelt, George Snyder and Jacob Ackerman. Signed Joseph Whitten and Cattena (x) Whitten. Wit: James Blauvelt and John David Haring.

23 Jan 1799, Stephen Rudd, of Hackensack Twp., Bergen Co., New Jersey to Dr. John Campbell, of New Barbadoes Twp., Bergen Co., New Jersey, £350, 5.43 acres...bounded by Wiert Banta, Thomas Howard and John Demarest. Signed Stephen Rudd. Wit: George Campbell and Alexander James.

23 Jan 1799, Stephen & Anne Rudd, release of dower rights of Anne Rudd in sale to John Campbell. Signed Stephen Rudd and Anne Rudd. Wit: George Campbell and Alexander James.

1 Jul 1800, Cornelius & Polly Smith, of New York City to John Stagg, of Franklin Twp., Bergen Co., New Jersey, 250.00, 5 acres...line of James Ackerman. Signed Cornelius Smith and Mary Smith. Wit: Albert Wilson and Abraham Hopper.

25 Nov 1800, William & Mary Ely and John & Ellenor Paulisen, all of Hackensack Precinct, Bergen Co., New Jersey to Elizabeth Demarest, wife of Jacobus Demarest Jr., of same, $5.00, 13 acres...line of Albert van Voorhees, Jacob van Boskerk, Garret Demarest and Peter Christie... 7 acres, adjoining. Signed William Ely, Mary Ely, John Paulisen and Ellenor Paulisen. Wit: Nicholas Degroot and Josiah Johnson.

10 Nov 1800, George & Rachel van Boskerk, of New Barbadoes Twp., Bergen Co., New Jersey to and Henry Traphagen Jr., of same, $182.50, 19 acres...heirs of Hendrick Brinkerhof, Peter Zabriskie and Garret van Giesen...purchased of Henry van Voorhees and Jacob van Voorhees, 2 Oct 1799. Signed George van Boskerk and Rachel van Boskerk. Wit: Jacob Zabriskie Jr. and Jarvis Pearsall.

6 Jan 1800, George & Charity Bogart, taylor, of Hackensack Precinct, Bergen Co., New Jersey to John C. Bogart, of same, $52.08, 15.62 acres... linen of Jacob Lozier, John Ackerman and Peter Christie. Signed Charity Bogart. Wit: Mary Bogart and John Haring.

16 Apr 1799, Daniel J. & Effie Demarest, yeoman, of Hackensack Twp., Bergen Co., New Jersey to James D. Demarest, cordwinder, of same, £350, 130 acres...line of William Westervelt, Daniel D. Demarest and Peter J. Demarest. Signed Daniel J. Demarest and Effie (x) Demarest. Wit: Bath Huspey and Roelif D. Demarest.

12 May 1798, Joost & Hendrica Cough, of Saddle River Twp., Bergen Co., New Jersey to Mary Cough, (daughter of Joost Cough Jr., and grand

daughter of said Joost Cough), of same, love and affection, 80 acres...line of Dr. John Garretson, Mocal Gillam, Mathus Newkerk, children of Aaron Cough and Phillip van Blerkum. Signed Joost Cough. Wit: Alexander James and John McCarty.

20 Sep 1800, Isaac J. Blauvelt, yeoman, of Franklin Twp., Bergen Co., New Jersey to Henry Spear, yeoman, of same, $0.75, 1 acres...line of Abraham D. Ackerman and Abraham J. Blauvelt. Signed Isaac J. (x) Blauvelt. Wit: Peter Haring and David P. Haring.

4 Aug 1800, Richard J. & Margaret van Horne, of New Barbadoes Twp., Bergen Co., New Jersey to Henry Spear, of Saddle River Twp., Bergen Co., New Jersey, $62.50, 5 acres...line of John D. Bardan, Jacob D. Bardan and John Archibald. Signed Richard J. van Horne and Margaret van Horne. wit: John S. Banta.

15 Apr 1799, Daniel Lines, of Pompton Twp., Bergen Co., New Jersey to Coerrat Lines, of same, £70, 24 acres...corner to tract formerly belonging to Anthony Beam, Abraham Lines and Conrad Lines...and 50 acres, adjoining. Signed Daniel (x) Lines. Wit: Abraham Lines and John Collins.

14 Oct 1800, Peter & Anne Hopper, of Saddle River Twp., Bergen Co., New Jersey to Cornelius U. Westervelt, of Paterson, Essex Co., New Jersey, $3000.00, 80 acres...between John Hopper and Henry Mead and between Garret van Ryper and James Jacobus...and 31 acres, adjoining...formerly sold by John Hopper to Andrew Bacoman and also 3 acres conveyed by said John Hopper to Henry Hopper. Signed Peter Hopper and Anne Hopper. Wit: Henry Dooremus, Abraham Willis, William Colfax and Michael Hopper.

12 Nov 1800, John D. & Nelly Demarest, of Bergen Co., New Jersey to John R. Bogart, of same, $2000.00, 15.25 acres...line of Benjamin D. Demarest, Jacob D. Demarest...and 20.75

acres...line of Peter Christie and Jacob D. Demarest...and 3.5 acres...line of Dower P. Westervelt and Peter Christie...and 5.75 acres, adjoining. Signed Johannes Demarest and Nelly (x) Demarest. Wit: Mathew Concklin and John Westervelt Jr.

15 Nov 1800, John R. & Elizabeth Bogart, of Hackensack Precinct, Bergen Co., New Jersey to James C. Demarest, of same, $825.00, 20.75 acres ...line of Dower P. Westervelt, Peter Christie, Jacob D. Demarest. Signed John Bogart and Elizabeth (x) Bogart. Wit: William Westervelt, Abraham Demarest and David Kip.

22 Mar 1800, James & Mary Jacobus, of Bergen Co., New Jersey to Garret vander Hoof, of same, $325.00, 34 acres...in Saddle River Twp...line of Henry Mead. Signed James (x) Jacobus and Mary (x) Jacobus. Wit: Alexander Ryerson and Andrew Bondman.

2 Dec 1899, James & Mary Jacobus, of Saddle River Twp., Bergen Co., New Jersey to Andries Bowman, of same, $162.00, 2 acres...corner to land said Bowman purchased of John Hopper... and 10 acres...line of Peter Hopper. Signed James (x) Jacobus and Mary (x) Jacobus. Wit: Alexander Ryerson and John J. Jacobus.

13 Nov 1800, Samuel & Elizabeth Banta, farmer, of Franklin Twp., Bergen Co., New Jersey to Abraham A. Quackinbush, taylor, of same, $1250.00, 61.33 acres...on a map made in 1767 by George Ryerson, Jonathan Hempton and Benjamin Morgan and returned to Robert Morris, who sold 10 Jan 1797 to Cornelius & Mary Demarest, who sold 8 Jul 1799 to said Samuel Banta. Signed Samuel (x) Banta and Elizabeth (x) Banta. Wit: David Ackerman and Abraham Westervelt.

15 Nov 1800, Abraham Banta, of Bergen Co., New Jersey to Abraham A. Quackinbush, $1.00, his interest in previous property. Signed Abraham (x) Banta. Wit: Anne Westervelt and Abraham Westervelt.

1 Feb 1800, Isaac & Hendrykie Kip, of Saddle
River Twp., Bergen Co., New Jersey to John Kip,
of same, £40, 4 acres...corner to Thomas Barker,
Quilliam and James Terhune and Stephen Terhune.
Signed Isaac Kip and Hendrykie (x) Kip. Wit:
Alexander James and Quilliam Terhune.

1 Feb 1800, Nicholas Kip, of New Barbadoes Twp.,
Bergen Co., New Jersey and Isaac Kip, of Saddle
River Twp., Bergen Co., New Jersey to John Kip,
of Saddle River Twp., Bergen Co., New Jersey,
£310, 20 acres...corner to lot sold by said
Nicholas and Isaac Kip to James Terhune. Signed
Nicause (x) Kip and Isaac Kip. Wit: Alexander
James and Jacob Terhune.

10 Feb 1797, Hessel & Caty Ryerson, of Saddle
River Twp., Bergen Co., New Jersey to Lawrence
van Boskerk, of Harrington Precinct, Bergen Co.,
New Jersey, £1620, 158 acres...line of John H.
Ryers and John C. Westervelt...and 19.05 acres
...line of Richard Stanton. Signed Hessel
Ryerson and Caty (x) Ryerson. Wit: Abraham
Willis and Richard Day.

6 May 1795, Cary & Hester Ludlow, gentleman, of
New York City to Abraham Rattan, yeoman, of
Franklin Twp., Bergen Co., New Jersey, £200.4,
68.75 acres...line of Lucas cooper, James
Mourison and John DeBaun. Signed Cary Ludlow and
Hester Ludlow. Wit: George Ludlow and Garret A.
Ackerman.

3 Nov 1800, Luke Kiersted, doctor, of Kingston,
Ulster Co., New York to John C. Stagg, of
Franklin Twp., Bergen Co., New Jersey, $100.00,
20 acres...line of Abraham Stagg and Adam van
Norden...part of 100 acres in Saddle River Twp.,
Jacob Roelif van Houten, deceased, of Saddle
River Twp., Bergen Co., New Jersey, sold to said
Kiersted, then of New York City, 16 May 1771.
Signed Luke Kiersted. Wit: Peter Star and
Abraham van Houten.

3 Nov 1800, Luke Kiersted, doctor, of Kingston,
Ulster Co., New York to John A. Rutan, of

Franklin Twp., Bergen Co., New Jersey, $140.00, 48.71 acres...in Franklin Twp...corner to Adam van Orden, John C. Stagg, Richard Degraw, John W. Pulis...part of 350 acres, Jacob Roelif van Houten, deceased, of Saddle River Twp., Bergen Co., New Jersey, sold to said Kiersted, then of New York City, 3 Nov 1748. Signed Luke Kiersted. Wit: Peter Star and Abraham van Houten.

3 Nov 1800, Luke Kiersted, doctor, of Kingston, Ulster Co., New York to John W. Pulis, of Franklin Twp., Bergen Co., New Jersey, $257.50, 41.5 acres...part in Franklin Twp...corner to John Rutan...and 10 acres...line of Richard Degraw...part of 100 acres in Saddle River Twp., Jacob Roelif van Houten, deceased, of Saddle River Twp., Bergen Co., New Jersey, sold to said Kiersted, then of New York City, 16 May 1771. Signed Luke Kiersted. Wit: Peter Star and Abraham van Houten.

3 Nov 1800, Luke Kiersted, doctor, of Kingston, Ulster Co., New York to Ralph J. Romine, of Saddle River Twp., Bergen Co., New Jersey, $50.00, 10 acres...line of John A Rutan and John C. Stagg. Signed Luke Kiersted. Wit: Peter Star and Abraham van Houten.

19 Nov 1793, Walter & Catharine Rutherford, now of New Jersey to Peter Francisco, farmer, Bergen Co., New Jersey, £30.35, 31.34 acres...where Peter Jacobusse formerly lived. Signed Walter Rutherford and Catharine Rutherford. Wit: Anty Laussat and Jeremiah Ballara.

18 Sep 1800, Abraham Ryerson, of Bergen Co., New Jersey to Charles Oldham, of same, $94.00, 50.39 acres...in Pompton Twp...corner to 29.55 acres returned to Walter Rutherford. Signed Abraham Ryerson. Wit: Benjamin Roome and Peter (x) Francisco.

18 Sep 1800, Abraham Ryerson, of Bergen Co., New Jersey to Jacob Jacobusse, of same, $98.00, 52.40 acres...in Pompton Twp. Signed Abraham Ryerson. Wit: Benjamin Roome and Charles Oldham.

18 Sep 1800, Abraham Ryerson, of Bergen Co., New Jersey to Peter Francisco, of same, $95.00, 81.51 acres...in Pompton Twp. Signed Abraham Ryerson. Wit: Benjamin Roome and Charles Oldham.

18 Sep 1800, Abraham Ryerson, of Bergen Co., New Jersey to Peter Francisco, of same, $102.00, 54.5 acres...in Pompton Twp. Signed Abraham Ryerson. Wit: Benjamin Roome and Charles Oldham.

14 Dec 1800, Albert & Mary Wilson, of Franklin Twp., Bergen Co., New Jersey to Morris Sharp, of same, $294,75, 56 acres. Signed Albert Wilson and Mary (x) Wilson. Wit: Abraham A. Terhune and Abraham Willis.

19 Jan 1800, Elizabeth van Houten, (widow of Crynus van Houten), of Franklin Twp., Bergen Co., New Jersey to Isaac Day, yeoman, of same, $187.50, 50 acres...line of William van Voorhees and Fredrick Storm. Signed Elizabeth van Houten. Wit: John Quackinbush and Peter J. van Blerkum.

4 Oct 1796, James Parker and Walter Rutherford, executors of estate of John Stevens to Isaac Day, of Franklin Twp., Bergen Co., New Jersey, £184.2, 105.27 acres...line of Michael Hawden. Signed James Parker and Walter Rutherford. Wit: Joseph Hankinson Jr. and John Haring.

5 Jan 1799, Samuel Cobb, of Hanover, Morris Co., New Jersey and Andrew Bell, of Perth Amboy, Middlesex Co., New Jersey to David Board, of Ringwood, Bergen Co., New Jersey, £15, 10.1 acres...corner to Cornelius Board's 5 acres assigned 4 May 1754. Signed Samuel Cobb and Andrew Bell. Wit: Lambert Barberie and Benjamin Jayce.

12 Dec 1798, Silas Condict, of Morris, Morris Co., New Jersey to Nathaniel Board, of Pampton, Bergen Co., New Jersey, $97.20, 60.75 acres... corner to 16.6 acres David Board returned to Peter van Crook Livingston. Signed Silas Condict. Wit: Eliza T. Cook, Lemuel Cobb and Theodotia Condict.

11 Nov 1800, John & Sarah Old, of Bergen Co., New Jersey to Nathaniel Board, of same, $250.00, 25.6 acres...at Ringwood...part of tract returned to Josiah Ogden, John Ogden, David Ogden Jr., David Ogden Sr. and Uzal Ogden 24 Apr 1740, who sold to Peter Hawenclever and then sold by sheriff 6 Jan 1796 to John Travis, merchant, of Philadelphia, Pennsylvania who sold 17 Jan 1798 to John Old. Signed John Old and Sarah Old. Wit: William Colfax and E. Stillwell.

2 Mar 1800, Henry J. & Leah Vreeland, of Bergen Co., New Jersey to John Anderson, merchant, of same, $275.00, 2 acres...in New Barbadoes Twp... line of George van Boskerk, deceased and estate of Abraham D. Brower. Signed Henry J. Vreeland and Leah Vreeland. Wit: Francis Wade and Archibald Wade.

1 Jan 1800, Jacob & Anne Stoltz, of Franklin Twp., Bergen Co., New Jersey to Lodwick Megheler, of same, £100, 15 acres. Signed Jacob Stoltz and Anne Stoltz. Wit: Abraham Westervelt and Peter Westervelt.

27 Feb 1801, Cornelius & Ann Cooper, of Bergen Co., New Jersey to John Anderson, of same, $500.00, 35 acres...corner to John vander Beck, Isaac vander Beck, Isaac Bardan. Signed Cornelius Cooper and Ann Cooper. Wit: Jacob Garretson and Nehemiah Wade.

14 Feb 1801, Jacob & Sarah Pryor, of Bergen Twp., Bergen Co., New Jersey to Herman van Zile, of Franklin Twp., Bergen Co., New Jersey, $312.50, 5.95 acres...line of John Diedericks. Signed Jacob Pryor and Sarah Pryor. Wit: John Havner and John Seely Jr.

30 Nov 1795, Cornelius & Sarah van Horne, Johannes & Maria Myer, of Franklin Twp., Bergen Co., New Jersey to Martin Myer, yeoman, of same, £180, 80 acres. Signed Cornelius van Horne, Sarah (x) van Horne, Johannis (x) Myer and Maria (x) Myer. Wit: Peter Ward and John Pulis.

11 Mar 1801, Peter Meysinger, of Franklin Twp., Bergen Co., New Jersey to Jonathan Traphagen, of same, $22.50, 1.5 acres...corner to land said Meysinger sold 8 Jul 1793 to James Christie. Signed Peter (x) Meysinger. Wit: Peter Traphagen and Henry Wammamaker.

19 Jun 1800, Samuel Cobb, of Hanover Twp., Morris Co., New Jersey to Fredrick Storm, of Franklin Twp., Bergen Co., New Jersey, $128.84, 64.42 acres. Signed Samuel Cobb. Wit: Abraham Ackerman and Abraham Verbryck.

5 Apr 1800 Trustees of County. Signed John A. Berry, Henry Berry, Henry P. Kip, Isaac E. Vreeland and Jacob G. Brinkerhof.

27 Oct 1800, Richard Edsall Jr., of Sussex Co., New Jersey to Joseph Bord and Joseph Tichiner, of Bergen Co., New Jersey, $303.20, 101.06 acres. Signed Richard Edsall Jr. Wit: Suly Edsall and James Suly.

10 Mar 1795, Abraham & Hetty van Boskerk, shopkeeper, of New York City to John van Boskerk, farmer, of Bergen Co., New Jersey, £1214, 180.9 acres...corner to Hendrick Cooper, Samuel Helm...and 2 acres, adjoining...and 19 acres, adjoining...and 10 acres, adjoining... line of Lucas van Boskerk. Signed Abraham van Boskerk and Hetty van Boskerk. Wit: A. Stagg and R. Therman.

22 Dec 1800, James & Mary Jacobusse, of Saddle River Twp., Bergen Co., New Jersey to Roelif Jacobusse, of same, $66.60, 2.75 acres...line of Hessel Hopper. Signed James (x) Jacobusse and Mary (x) Jacobusse. Wit: Abraham Ryerson and John Mead.

5 Aug 1800, James & Cathalina Laroe, of Pompton Twp., Bergen Co., New Jersey to Richard Francisco Jr., of Morris Co., New Jersey, $1800.00, 73 acres...line of Robert Gold... and 11.1 acres, adjoining. Signed James Laroe and Cathalina Laroe. Wit: John Lozier and John

Francisco.

5 Dec 1800, Merselius M. van Giesen, merchant, of New York City to Roelif van Houten, carpenter, of Saddle River Twp., Bergen Co., New Jersey, $130.00, 8 acres...corner to John van Giesen, Richard van Houten, Cornelius Low and Peter van Houten. Signed Merselius M. van Giesen. Wit: Abraham Godwin and Garret Stephens.

10 Jan 1801, Peter & Leah van Houten, of Saddle River Twp., Bergen Co., New Jersey to Robert van Houten, of same, $214.84, 13.75 acres...line of John Dooremus, Jacob Stagg. Signed Peter H. van Houten and Leah van Houten. Wit: Abraham Willis and O. Badiah.

## Chapter 13

### 1793 Tax List

### Ratables-Arranged by Neighbors

### Bergen County, New Jersey

### Bergen Township

Abraham Pryor, Garret van Oberhoof, Jacob Pryor, Levy Ross, Jacob Buice, William Britton, Peter Messelor, Cornelius van Vorst, John van Vorst, Vardine Elsworth, Cornelius Garrabrants, Cornelius Garrabrants, Mindert Garrabrants, John van Horne, Garret van Horne, Nicholas Vreeland, Michael N. Vreeland, Aaron vander Ditt, Peter Fountaine, Abram Perine, Henry Brinkerhof, Henry H. Brinkerhof, Joseph Waldron Jr., Jasper A. Pryor, John Collard, Maria Hammond, Joseph Waldron, Daniel Sickels, John Kelly, Antebe Earle, James Earle, Paul Sunyea, Robert Greenless, Robert R. Greenless, Frederick Devone, John Derge, John Williams, John S. Williams, Nathaniel Earle, Elias Earle, William Earle, John Lee, Henry Earle, William Danielsen, Robert Earle, Henry van Giesen, Andrew Bogart, Aaron Devone, Jemimz Umings, Cornelius Hoiler, Bernardos Disendors, Jacob Brower, Abram Dobuckerman, Joseph Brower, John F. Brower, Henry W. Earle, Mathias Ludlam, William Day, Thomas McDaniel, Anthony Ludlam, Jacob Degraw, Samuel Lyons, Elijah Gardner, Samuel Whited, James van Horne, Rodmen Veilds, John Bertholf, John Smith, Cerines Bertholf, James Bertholf, Johan Henry Raye, John Stephens, William Crum, Daniel D. Smith, John Lealy, Ganet van Giesen, Hack Giesen, Thomas van Giesen, Reynier Earle, John E. Earle, Andrew Engle, James Devaul, Abble Smith, Henry Ackerman, Job Smith, Daniel Smith, John D. Smith, Edmund Kingsland, James Outwater,

William Randle, Cornelius Dooremus, John Daily, Enoch Smith, Runa Ludlam, Garret Hornbeck, John Earle, Jesse Hide, William Day, David Hennion, Abram Sickels, John Heffener, John Everson, John S. Everson, Cornelius Smith, Hellernegh van Houten, John van Houten, Michael van Houten, Daniel Dedrix, Stephen Simeson, Jacob Collard, Henry van Winkle, John Winner, Martin S. Winner, John Cole, Henry Cole, Jacob van Boskerk, Abran Langden, James Earle, Richard Earle, Samuel van Giesen, William Day, David Anderson, Ganet Johnson, Joseph C. Houghland, Daniel S. Dedrix, Walter Clendenny Jr., John Mesire, James Welch, Jasper A. Pryor, Daniel van Winkle, Jury van Winkle, Jasper Pryor, Jacob Nudkook, Daniel van Ryper, Richard van Ryper, Michael Simmons, Stephen Simmons, John Sickels, Martin Winner, Peter Stuyversant, Nicholas Toers, Henry Jackson, Teodorus Jackson, Andrew Holter, William Holter, John Waine, Philip Billops, Adrian Post, Adam Rap, Peter Rap, Egbert Post, Abram Spear, George McDaniel, Jasper Zabriskie, Benjamin Zabriskie, John Zabriskie, Jacob van Horne, George Frasher, Thomas Dickson, William Brambush, Engle Brambush, David Brambush, Sarah van Suile, Peter Post, George McFire, John Devoe, Charity Stockholm, John Post, Peter Larosen, Benjamin Corvill, Edward Devaul, Andrew Quateer, Peter van Boskerk, Cornelius Vreeland, Israel Oakley, Jesse Oakley, John van Boskerk, James van Boskerk, John Mitchell, George Coomus, Barent van Horne, Peter Cole, Andrew van Horne, Cornelius van Boskerk, David van Boskerk, Richard Coomus, Jasper Cadmus, Michael Vreeland, George M. Vreeland, Cornelius van Boskerk, Aughye Vreeland, Mary Brown, Richard Vreeland, Thomas Cubberly, George Vreeland, John G. Vreeland, Ganet Vreeland, John Vreeland, Michael S. Vreeland, Peter Garrabrants, Ganet H. van Ryper, Ganet S. van Ryper, Juny van Ryper, George Shepherd, John Marselius, William Elsworth, Henry Newkerk, John van Houten, John S. van Houten, Seal Merectus, Josiah Hornblower, Daniel S. van Winkle, Jacob Everson, William Meadow, Joseph Quinby, Matthew Newkerk, Garret Newkerk, Aaron Newkerk, John Dicterison, Levines

Winner, Edo Winner, Zacharias Sickels, George D. Mott, Michael Demott, Abram Sickels, Joseph van Winkle, Peter Sip, Hartmin Sickels, Robert Sickels, Peter Sickels, Matthew S. Newkerk, Ganet van Ryper Jr., John van Wagener, Abram van Winkle, James Lapsly, Patrick Grimes, John G. Lake.

Franklin Township

Anthony Lines, John P. van Houten, Henry Brown, Abraham Lines, Abraham Lines Jr., Daniel Lines, Conrad D. Lines, Abraham C. Lines, Joseph Bartrim, Andrew An. Hopper, James Beam, Conrad Beam, Anthony C. Beam, Joost Beam, Abraham Beam, Anthony Beam, John A. Beam, John Beam, Anthony A. Beam, Bernardus Derbryk, James Earle, Peter Slott, John Brown, James Monks, John Springer, Jacob Waters, John Hogan, Joseph Stone, Charles Steward, Joseph Hogan, John Jaguish, George Ryerson, John Scott, Christopher Tomur, Henry Richer, John Allen, David Teachman, William McCann, John Marchet, Richard Cooper, Dedrick Tise, Joseph Boaro, John Bartow, James Board, James Board Jr., David Board, David Board Jr., John McMullin, Dennis Morris, Dennis Morris Jr., Widow Strock, James Ward, Thomas Caghill, Peter Moselee, Benjamin Cooly Jr., Angles Monrow, Andrew Miller, Joseph Morse, Zachariah White, Samuel Bailey, Elias Bailey, Peter Fisher, Isaac Fisher, Peter Stout, John Sandford, David Scoffold, Samuel Bruin, John Price, Hezikiah Scoffold, Benjamin Cooly, Robert Colm, Joseph Woodruff, Daniel Woodruff, Joseph Tithone, Thomas van Zile, Abraham van Zile Jr., Eber Harrington, Abraham van Zile, William Crawford, Reuben Shaw, William Wright, Zebulon Wright, Ephriam Wright, George Everitt, Isaac Mead, Abner Dooly, Benjamin Dooly, David Sandford, George Dean, Thomas Willing, John Austin, Nicholas Teachman, William Bennett, Alexander Morison, John Ryerson, John Homer, James Johnson, Bethuel Titchoner, Thomas Marygold, David Sealsbury, John Storm, Widow Beach, Charles Beach, Widow Robertson, Jenias Peltzer, Godpey Aorrigh, William Mullen, Samuel Titus, David Stone, Andrew Harpinding, David Dutches, Henry Afler, Robert Spear, Abraham J. Garretson, Helmegh Garretson, Abraham H. Garretson, Jacobus Demarest, Anthony Bartrim, William Colfax, Thomas Hammon, Stephen I. Bogart, James S.

Bogart, Hezekiah Springer, Stephen Springer, Abraham Manning, Harmanus Bross, Cornelius Allen, Gilis Mead, James Mahonnon, Henry Storm, Ganet van Allen, Fredrick Storm, John F. Storm, Peter Ackerman, John Neafie, Stephen Bertholf, David Bertholf, John Bertholf, Benjamin N. Romine, Peter D. Demarest, Abraham G. Garretson, Ganet Neafie, Aury Garretson, John van Orden, Jacob Storm, John A. Ackerman, Jacobus Laroe, John P. Post, Jacob Cough, James Cough, John Nelson, Conrad Pulis, Conrad Fisher, John W. Hopper, William Hopper, Guilliam Hopper, Isaac Post, Cornelius Post, Abraham J. Post, Abraham Post, Henry Miller, John Maby, Barent Weaver, Abraham Zabriskie, Benjamin Bertholf, Peter Lozier, Andrew Hopper, Jacob Haring, Jacobus Bertholf, John Haring, John Haring Jr., Garret W. Hopper, William Tephogen, William Hennion, Michael Post, Adolph Shurte, Garret Degraw, Samuel Man, Widow Bush, James Bush, Henry Ferderiks, Aldoph Wammamaker, David Fox, John Christie, Henry Fox, William Fox, Nicholas Himeon, James Christie, Joseph Wyatt, William Jenkins, Peter Tannery, William Ackhart, Joost Eckhert, David Christie, Nicholas Bavenhyse, George Lurante, Auson Myer, Samuel Bertholf, Cornelius Firshead, Barent Firshead, Andrew Hennion, Christian Pulis, Henry Pulis, Abraham Pulis, Abraham A. Hopper, John Ackerson, Peter D. Tise, Conrad D. Winter, Peter Bogart, States Bogart, James I. Bogart, Peter Ward, Daniel Healy, John Campbell, James Pulisfelt, John I. Pulisfelt, Henry Winter, Adolph Carlough, Christian A. Carlough, Jacob Hopper, John Myer, Christian Byerman, Martin Myer, Cornelius B. van Horne, Henry Bogart, Abraham Blauvelt, David Hopper, John D. Hopper, Henry D. Hopper, Jonathan van Gelder, John Fox, Cornelius Degraw, Henry Ridnae, Henry van Gelder, Racly I. Westervelt, John Masserse, Peter Hennion, Derick Tise, Henry D. Tise, Jacob Young, Jacobus van Gelder, Frederick Post, Jacob Billue, Harman Carlough, John Carlough, Peter Ramsey, Mary Ramsey, Jerry Carlough, Abraham J. Banta, Jacob Banta, Isaac Alyee, Jacob Alyee, John Rose, David Ackerman, Abraham Terhune, Albert

Zabriskie, Jacob Zabriskie, Garret A. Ackerman,
Andrew A. Hopper, John J. Zabriskie, Jacob J.
Zabriskie, Andrew J. Zabriskie, Allye Zabriskie,
Harmon Lutkins, Cornelius J. Bogart, John D.
Reynon, Peter van Houten, Casparus Schuyler,
Peter Schuyler, Philip Schuyler, Philip J.
Schuyler, John van Wagener, Arent Schuyler,
Peter M. Singer, Stephen Fishback, Derick
Wammamaker, John Meysinger, Derick C.
Wammamaker, Peter Wammamaker, Henry Wammamaker,
John van Horne, Jacob Hennion, David Hennion,
Michael Bavenhyse, Widow Bavenhyse, David Byand,
Christian Wammamaker, Conrad Wammamaker, Leonard
Tserman, Nicks Meysinger, Benjamin Wistwell,
John B. Wistwell, Henry Traphagen, Henry
Traphagen Jr., James Traphagen, John Peck, Henry
M. Terhune, Johannes Degraw, John Hennion,
Abraham Stagg, John Witty, Isaac Demilt, John
Bayard, Samuel Banta, Abraham S. Banta, Abraham
Jansen, Isaac Munerse, Peter Munerse, Jacobus
Munerse, Carl DeBaun, John DeBaun, John Moore,
Isaac Day, Joost Degroot Jr., Soloman Day, Jacob
Shoemaker, Michael Fisher, Michael Fisher Jr.,
David Fisher, Nathan Lane, Daniel Burges, James
Burges, Gabriel Spring, Phillip Rapman, John
Straak, Anthony Maig, William van Schyve, James
Dadbs, John Dooremus, Joseph van Horne, Joost
van Boskerk, John Apeamans, Conrad Fox, Rynhurt
Bush, Conrad Bush, Henry Bush, Thomas Banta,
David van Blisham, John D. van Blisham, Andrew
G. Hopper, Abraham J. Hopper, Nicarie Hopper,
Andrew DeBaun, Petrus DeBaun, Jacob DeBaun Jr.,
Jacobus DeBaun, Jacob DeBaun, Joost DeBaun,
Albert Terhune, John Terhune, Abraham D.
Terhune, Henry D. Terhune, Albert D. Terhune,
Andrew Terhune, Lousona Shirley, Paulis
Quackenhus, John A. Westervelt, James Ackerman,
David Ackerman, John D. Ackerman, Peter A.
Ackerman, Garret Hopper, John G. Hopper, Abraham
Hopper, Henry A. Hopper, Abraham Quackinbush,
Aury J. Ackerman, Abraham J. Ackerman, John
Ackerman, Jacobus Bogart, John S. Bogart,
Stephen Bogart, Abraham Rutan, Abraham
Westervelt, Archibald A. van Boskerk, Jonathan
A. Holcomb, Albert Ackerman, Thomas van Dien,
Derick van Dien, Andrus van Dien, Cornelius van

Dien, Cornelius G. van Dien, Harman van Dien, Albert van Dien, Jacob vander Beck, Cornelius vander Beck, Abraham vander Beck, Henry G. Hopper, Paulis vander Beck, Jacob P. vander Beck, Henry Hopper, John van Bussen, Garret D. Ackerman, David D. Ackerman, Thomas van Norden, Abraham D. Ackerman, John D. Ackerman, Abraham J. Blauvelt, John Archibald, Isaac Hopper, Garret A. Hopper, John van Emburgh, Henry van Emburgh, Peter P. van Emburgh, John Westervelt, Garret Ackerman, Albert Hopper, Peter Hopper, Abraham H. Hopper, Andrew H. Hopper, William Ackerman, Albert van Voorhees, Elshi Hopper, John G. Hopper, John J. Hopper, John A. Hopper, Rev. William P. Reypen, Henry Bertholf, William McBell, John Parleyman, John Dehuys, William Sutton, Albert Wilson, William Holly, Henry Oldis, John Fell, Peter Post, Henry Beselas, Jacob Valentine Jr., Morris Sharp, David Valentine, Conrad Knight, Wiert Valentine, Albert Smith, John Christopher, Henry Zabriskie, Widow Staker, Conrad Staker, Thomas Stagg, Joseph Johnson, William Nagush, Samuel Bush, Peter Debard, Jacob Valentine, Charles Degraw, Jacob Stubbs, John McCall, Peter Demarest, Charles Strills, Tudwiek Masher, John Powleson, Abraham Mark, Egbert van Zile, Edward Earle, James Cairns, Derick Masher, Cornelius Lozier, Joost van Cleave, Adam Snyder, Thomas Snyder, Andrew Snyder, David Cairns, Andrew D. Hopper, Adam van Norden, Garret Lydecker, Jesse Chapple, Carper H. Huere, David Haring, Henry Hisbee, Valentine Swin, Isaac Blauvelt, Isaac Blauvelt Jr., John Perry, Jacob Quackinbos, Barent Quackinbos, John Rutan, Cornelius Decker, William Decker, Abraham Wright, Simon van Winkle, John Cairns, John van Ryper, John Romine, John I. Rutan, James L. Ackerman, David H. van Vlishorn, Daniel I. Rutan, Thomas Rutan, Daniel Rutan, Henry W. Pulis, John W. Pulis, Cornelius J. Banta, John Banta, Abraham Hand, John Hicks, Jacob van Saun, Jacob van Ryper, John I. Ackerman, Jacobus I. Ackerman, John Harris, John B. van Horne, John I. Banta, John Mitchell, Abraham van Zile, Peter van Zile, Abraham van Ryper, John Potter, Aris Post, Genet

A. Post, Richard Dyckman, Samuel van Winkle, Simon van Winkle, Jacob Romine, Benjamin Romine, Daniel I. Blauvelt, Nicholas Romine, Albert van Zile, George Dooremus, Daniel Smith, Henry van Winkle, Henry Bertholf, Jerry Snyder, Roelif van Houten, Jacobus van Houten, James A. Ackerman, Peter P. Tise, Edo Marselius, Cornelius A. Post, John Post, Ryer Ryerson, Cornelius van Houten, Martin van Houten, John van Houten, James Kint, Henry Perine, Conrad Rarve, Garret J. Blauvelt, William Degruis, John Toers, Lawrence Ackerman, John J. Ackerman, John J. Storm, John Willis, Phillip Raive, Albert Romine, Samuel Romine, Albert R. Romine, Conrad Packer, John W. Packer, Nicholas Ackerson, Daniel Gerais, John Caerte, Avic Caerte, Benjamin Gerais, Lewis Winter, John D. Tise, John Hinselpecker, Peter Pulisfelt, Peter P. Pulisfelt, Henry Fredericksen, Conrad Stuss Jr., Conrad Stuss, William Pulis, Michael Stuss, William Winter Jr., William Winter, William Caerte, Abraham van Voorhees, Abraham J. van Voorhees, Daniel van Voorhees, Albert van Voorhees, John A. van Voorhees, Peter Stuss, Jacob Stuss, Abraham Lozier, Robert McCull, Samuel Ferguson, Henry McFicher, Martin Graaf, Henry van Zile, Isaac van Blerkum, John Lozier, John T. van Blerkum, Daniel Blauvelt, James Sickels, Isaac Storm, John I. Eckerson, Aury Ackerman, Garret Blauvelt, John Blauvelt, Garret G. Ackerman, Abraham G. Ackerman, John van Blerkum, John I. van Blerkum, John Michles, Todwick Michles, John C. Stagg, Dr. Merrit Smith, Honerist Carlough, John fedeback, Casparus Zabriskie, Andrew I. Hopper, John Collins, James Parker, Robert R. Livingston, Casparus Cough, William van Voorhees.

## Hackensack Township

Henry J. Brinkerhof, Simon Demarest, Ruthe van Wagon, Guilliam Outwater, Jacobus Brinkerhof, Garret J. Brinkerhof, Albert C. Zabriskie, John Crummil, David vander Linde, John vander Linde, Jacobus vander Linde, Guilliam vander Linde, Aury vander Linde, Henry F. Brinkerhof, John C. Zabriskie, Albert C. Westervelt, John C. Westervelt, Casparus Westervelt, Derick S. Brinkerhof, Seba Brinkerhof, Jacob S. Brinkerhof, Albert J. Brinkerhof, George J. Brinkerhof, John Powleson, Cornelius Bogart, Albert C. Bogart, Henry C. Bogart, Jacob C. Bogart, Nicanse Brinkerhof, Richard Westervelt, Cornelius Banta, Jacob C. Banta, Roelif P. Bogart, John P. Bogart, Albert Terhune, Albert A. Terhune, Daniel Christie, Joost Zabriskie, Richard Zabriskie, Joost Lozier, Wiert D. Banta, John D. Banta, Jacob D. Banta, Abraham D. Banta, Antul Banta, Giles Bertholf, John Bertholf, Margaret Bertholf, Jacob Lozier Jr., Niclas Degroot, John Merchirone, John Ackerman, John Ackerman Jr., John J. Bogart, John Bogart, Moses Ackerman, Thomas Kip, George van Boskerk, William Duncan, Peter D. Christie, Douglas Cairns, Lawrence van Horne, John Heathen, George Ryerson, Stephen Slutt, Caleb Wade, William Clark, Cornelius Houghland, Abraham Collins, John Zabriskie, William Williams, Mary Duffy, Richard Heathen, John van Suie, John Demarest, Jacobus J. Demarest, William Ely, Peter Heathen, John Degroot, Cata Gorden, John Snyder, Jacob Smith, Peter J. Demarest, Jacobus Demarest, Peter Jac Demarest, John J. Demarest, Berkhout Klasbaugh, David Demarest, Jane Demarest, Guilliam Demarest, Albert Demarest, John Devone, Abraham Devone, David Anderson, Jacobus Powleson, Powleson Powleson, George Wilson, Dr. Beckman van Bueren, Albert Waldron, Jacobus Waldron, Jacob Camble, William Camble, Casparus Demarest, Samuel Wood, Joost C. Zabriskie, Garret Zabriskie, David J. Anderson, Peter

Lozier, John J. Anderson, Peter Demarest, David
P. Demarest, Daniel Helm, Isaac Nicoll,
Cornelius Myer, William Demarest, David S.
Demarest, Simon D. Demarest, Cornelius Bogart,
Stephen Bogart, Hendrick Bogart, Jacob Lozier,
Jacob Bogart, Albert Bogart, John van Boskerk,
Peter van Boskerk, Jacob van Boskerk, John
Pillion, John Bogart, John R. Bogart, Roelif
Bogart, David R. Bogart, Derick Brinkerhof, John
Percell, James Westervelt, Daniel N. Demarest,
John B. Westervelt, Peter DeBaun, Dower P.
Westervelt, Cornelius P. Westervelt, David S.
Demarest, David D. Demarest, William Westervelt,
Rev. Solomon Freligh, Jacob D. Demarest, David
R. Demarest, Henry D. Brinkerhof, Benjamin
Demarest, John D. Demarest, Richard Banta, David
J. Demarest, Peter W. Christie, John van Dalson,
Maj. Isaac Kip, Eve Banta, Jacob Quackinbush,
John Quackinbush, David P. Demarest, William
Christie, Daniel D. Demarest, Grant D. Demarest,
Garret Demarest, Daniel J. Demarest, Jacobus D.
Demarest, Peter J. Demarest, James Christie,
Roelif D. Demarest, Henry Verdon, John J. Banta,
Samuel Demarest, Peter S. Demarest, Yury
Westervelt, Roelif Demarest, John G. Huyler,
David Archibald, Cornelia Banta, Peter
Westervelt, John P. Westervelt, Benjamin P.
Westervelt, John C. Westervelt, Jacobus D.
Westervelt, John West, John Huyler, Jacob
Percell, Josiah Johnston, Sin James Jay, Nancy
Erwin, Even Jones, John Blowfelt, Wilhelmus
Huyler, Peter Degraw, John Bofardus, Wiert
Banta, Roelif Westervelt, John R. Westervelt,
Dower R. Westervelt, Roelif Westervelt, Jacob
Demarest, Derick Banta, Abraham Ackerman, John
S. Banta, Jacob Demott, Daniel Romine, Charity
Roeliffe, Johannes Brinkerhof, Roelif
Brinkerhof, Henry R. Brinkerhof, Jonathan
Dickson, Niclas Westervelt, Elizabeth Banta,
Gidion Vorvalour, Aury Westervelt, Albert A.
Westervelt, Dower J. Westervelt, Maj. John
Westervelt, Benjamin Westervelt, Jacobus B.
Westervelt, Benjamin B. Westervelt, Peter B.
Westervelt, Richard Scott, Peter Baker, Peter
Demarest, David Lozier, Henry Carlough, Conradus
Carlough, Margaret Carlough, Barnadus Ryder,

Peter Demarest, Roelif Demarest, Abraham Lozier, Thomas Harris, Abraham Lozier Jr., Elias Day, Garret Lydecker, Cornelius Lydecker, Frederick van Wagener, Henry Norman, John G. Benson, Peter Stinberger, Jacobus Lydecker, John Benson, John Harris, Garret G. Lydecker, Henry Demott, Jeremiah Degroot, Eve Couenoven, Jacob Couenoven, John Demott, William Udell, Pelegh Richins, Derick Vreeland, Michael Vreeland, Simon Carlough, Samuel S. Moore, Jacob T. Moore, Jacob Nagel, Samuel T. Moore, Harriman Raton, Cornelius Degroot, John Johnston, Aldolphus Carlough, Andrus Anderson, Samuel J. Moore, John van Zile, John Joseph, Daniel Raton Jr., Giles Wooliot, John King, John Lyt, Stephen Bourdett, Christeen Bourdett, Abraham Moore, Peter Bourdett, Benjamin Bourdett, Samuel J. Moore, Daniel Saulter, John Decker, Cata Westervelt, Nathaniel Blundish, Samuel Ellis, John Conder, John Anthony, William Day, Michael J. Vreeland, John Becker, Luke Peterson, Joseph Peterson, James Thompson, Casparus B. Westervelt, John Edsall, Aaron Devone, Isaac Hammon, William vander Vorst, Rinehart Hoffman, Peter A. Degroot, Aury Degroot, Michael Tueser, John van Cleave, William Lozier, Phillip Durcell, Thomas Clark, Seba Banta, Entony Britain, John Verborn, Henry Banta, Jacob Degroot, Peter Degroot, Garret Banta, Cornelius G. Banta, Cornelius Vreeland, Michael Vreeland, Richard Vreeland, Cornelius Vreeland Jr., David Day, John Day, Niomy Lozier, Jacob Edsall, Robert Miller, Samuel Edsall, Hartman Brinkerhof, John Brinkerhof, Abraham Muntasa, Niclas Nagel, Peter Demarest, John Bourdett, John Smith, Able Smith, Michael Moore, Benjamin Westervelt, Christopher Harehart, Jacob Banta, Aury Banta, Peter Hasenfrax, Abraham Ogden, Jacob C. Zabriskie, William Cairns, Mary Westervelt, Ram Rappleye.

## Harrington Township

Sarah Bogart, Martin Hagen, Peter Bogart, Matthew Bogart, Aaron Gilbert, Mary Talman, Daniel Vervalen, Jacob Percell, Joseph Gorden, Martin Powleson, Aury Auryansen, Johannis Vervalen, Daniel Vervalen, Barent Nagel, Isaac Nagel, John Auryansen, Resalvert Auryansen, Daniel Dulark, David Nagel, Jonathan Martin, James Concklin, Jacob Ferdon, Benjamin Blacklidge, Jacob Cole, Barent Cole, Peter Cole, Samuel Demarest, Jacob Cole, James Westervelt, Daniel van Soyoen, Margaret Valentine, Cornelius Vervalen, David Campbell, Bernard Vervalen, Isaac Morris, John Walling, Thomas Kennedy, Johannes Westervelt, Jacob Powleson, Derick Haring, Abraham Vervalen, Thomas Blanch, John Ferdon, William H. Ferdon, Johannes Ferdon, Johannes Blauvelt, Johannes Nagel, John Maby, David Haring, Abraham Haring, Abraham Rycher, John Rycher, Peter Maby, Joseph Seaman, Jacob Concklin, Nicholas Gessamer, Mary Ludlow, Peter Buys, Daniel Haring, Henry Mentho, Abraham Haring, Thomas Eckerson, Abraham Haring, Peter A. Haring, Jacobus Blauvelt, Abraham Quackinbush, Abraham Delemater, John Hogencamp, Johannes T. Haring, Margaret Blauvelt, John Perry, Johannes Haring, Fred Haring, John F. Haring, Jacob Haring, Fred Haring, Cornelius Blanock, Isaac Delemater, Pronsy Haring, Abraham DeBaun, Cornelius Eckerson, Garret Eckerson, Herman Blan, Jacob Marselius, Jules Marselius, John Durie, Simon Durie, Peter Marselius, Abraham Blauvelt, Daniel Blauvelt, Anaatye Blauvelt, Isaac T. Blauvelt, Abraham Haring, Jacob Wortendyke, Jacob Blauvelt, Mary Westervelt, Leonard Degraw, David Haring, John Haring, D. Chandler, Abraham Blauvelt, Richard Blanch, William Degraw, Abraham Haring, Peter Haring, Hendrick Volk, Cornelius van Horne, Abraham Demarest, David Demarest, Christian van Horne, David Durie, Charles How, Jacob Haring, John Durie, John Durie, Hendrick Zabriskie,

Jacobus Demarest, Samuel Peck, Jacob Peck,
Johannes Peck, Samuel Peck, Hendrick Haring,
Hendrick Demarest, John Zabriskie, Thomas
Campbell, William Campbell, Peter Demarest, Luke
van Boskerk, Joseph Concklin, Andrew van Dun,
Cornelius Kuyper, Albert van Voorhees, Carel P.
DeBaun, Jacob van Wagener, Johannes van Wagener,
William van Wagener, David Demarest, Christian
Shuert, John Lozier, John Ackerman, Derick
Ackerman, Luke Cornell, Barent Waldron, Derick
Kuyper, Johannes Myer, John D. Ackerman, Jacob
Hopper, John vander Water, Jacobus Alyee,
Guilliam Bogart, Abraham G. Demarest, Garret
Demarest, Jacobus Demarest, Thomas Demarest,
Christian Blauvelt, Cornelius Haring, Abraham
Bogart, Edward Eckerson, Jaen Wortendyke,
William Anderson, John Valen, Peter Post, Fred
Wortendyke, Peter Wortendyke, Cornelius
Wortendyke, Rymir Wortendyke, John Eckerson,
David Forshear, John Perry, Cornelius Forshear,
Peter Portiss, Peter Haring, Abraham Post, Jacob
Wortendyke, John Forshear, John Campbell, Isaac
Maby, Nicholas Waldron, Abraham Waldron,
Nicholas Peterson, Barent Forshear, Welhelm
Graham, Ryer Ryers, John Ryers, Michael Ryers,
Jacob Stagg, George Haconbac, Aldolf Shurte,
Garret Vryper, Johannes Vryper, Herman Vryper,
Jacob Eckerson, Thomas Eckerson, Thomas Toers,
Abraham Daty, Andrew Hopper, Stephen Hopper,
Jacob Hopper, Hendrick Hopper, Abraham Hopper,
Albert Zabriskie, Lowrens van Boskerk, Thomas
van Boskerk, John van Boskerk, Jacob van Horne,
John van Horne, Garret Ackerman, Andrew Hopper,
Abraham van Boskerk, Thomas van Boskerk, Henry
Banta, Thomas van Boskerk, David Baldwin,
Abraham Terhune, Jacob Terhune, Jacobus Bogart,
Albert Terhune, Hendrick Terhune, David
Ackerman, Albert Ackerman, Cornelius Bogart,
Abraham Devaster, Andrew Zabriskie, John
Zabriskie, Benjamin Zabriskie, Johannes Waldron,
Fred Blauvelt, Samuel Durie, John Bogart, Albert
Bogart, John Westervelt, John Haring, Isaac
Bogart, Daniel Westervelt, Garret Durie, Peter
Westervelt, John Banta, Jacob Banta, John J.
Banta, Hendrick Banta, Conrad Storm, Hendrick
Storm, Jury vander Beck, Powles vander Beck,

Albert Bogart, Lowrans Toers, Cornelius Demarest, Casparus Westervelt, James Demarest, Samuel Demarest, James Bogart, Abraham Cadmus, Jacobus Wortendyke, Fred Wortendyke, Garret Valen, Hendrick Storm, Abraham Hopper, Peter DeBaun, Jacob DeBaun, David Demarest, John Demarest, William Pritan, Peter Demarest, Daniel Peck, Johannes van Horne, Daniel van Horne, Ephy van Shawn, Staats Storm, Peter Winter, Catharine Myer, John Myer, John Blauvelt, Fytye van Donk, William Peterson, Cornelius Peterson, John Fleerboom, John vander Beck, Jacob Fleerboom, Cornelius Blauvelt, Mindert Maby, Peter Maby, Isaac DeBaun, Daniel Perry, Jacobus Demarest, John Taylor, Jacobus Blauvelt, Johannes Perry, Ryndert Hopper, Jacobus Perry, Peter Perry, Jacobus Blauvelt, Isaac Waldron, John DeBaun, Cornelius Waldron, William Waldron, Mary Bogart, Peter Bogart, Cornelius Haring, Abraham Haring, Joseph Blauvelt, Cornelius Blauvelt, Christian Campbell.

## New Barbadoes Township

Peter Terhune, Jeremiah Everson, Caty Hopper, Richard N. Terhune, Richard Terhune, John Terhune, Albert Terhune, Jacobus Terhune, Michael van Winkle, Luke van Winkle, David van Bush, Tunus van Iderstine, Michael van Iderstine, John T. van Iderstine, Theodorus van Winkle, Martinus van Winkle, Jury van Winkle, Michael Bush, Jury Bush, Casparus Bush, John van Iderstine, Walling van Vorst, Casparus van Vorst, Toda van Iderstine, Peter van Iderstine, Francis van Iderstine, Casparus van Iderstine, George van Iderstine, Helmegh van Winkle, Augustus Jay, Walling van Winkle, John van Winkle, Jacob van Winkle, Isaac van Winkle, Robert Blair, Jacob van Norstrandt, Cornelius Degraw, Garrabrant Juriansen, Garrabrant Juriansen Jr., John Skidmore, Andrew Stewart, James Ernis, Casparus Degraw, Thomas Lockerman, Derick Bergen, Samuel Lewis, Jacob van Winkle, Lodewyke Metseker, John Jaroleman, John Kerrick, Francis Degraw, Hendrick Outwater, Tunes Brown, Henry H. Brown, James C. Jaroleman, Gilbert van Emburgh, Abraham Kingsland, Henry Kerrick, John Harrison, William Webb, James Butler, Sarah Spear, Johan Butler, John Rattan, Anne Kingsland, Thomas Hurley, Henry Ozben, Jane Kingsland, James Jaroleman, John Smith, Jane McPeek, Thomas Brown, David Kingsland, Aaron Bailey, Catherine Hurley, Charles Ozben, John Schuyler, James Furlo, Arent Schuyler, Phillip A. Schuyler, John Roosevelt, Fredrick Riseman, John Smith, Michael Glason, Harmen Hunt, Thomas Brown, Solomon Nicoll, Henry Edowson, Benjamin Sandford, Andrew Moore, William Toers, William Davis, Thomas Davis, Michael Sandford, William Sandford, Peter Sandford, Abraham Sandford, William D. Sandford, George Sandford, Durell Williams, Anne Still, Gilbert Howden, Enoch Sandford, Cornelius Toers, Abraham Toers, George Dooremus, William Ludlow Ogden, Reuben Carter, Jacob Ogden, Francis Toers, Peter Cadmus, Joseph Vites, Joseph Vites Jr., Margaret van Emburgh, John van Emburgh, Thomas Shepherd, Cornelius

Shepherd, Moures Mourison, John Shepherd, Richard Phillips, Culbert Featherstone, Benjamin Sparlow, John Walton, Thomas Dawson, Garrabrant Garrabrants, John Walker, Joseph Miller, Henry Kingsland, Peter Bross, John Dust, Edmund William Kingsland, Barent Richards, John Sullivan, Abraham Riker, Albert Riker, Garrabrant Horpse, Garret van Ryper, Jacob van Ryper, James Christie, John Juriansen, Garret van Vorst, Christopher Juriansen, Hessel Juriansen, Hendrick Kip, Peter Kip, Hermanus van Iderstine, Casparus van Iderstine, Henry Kip, Derick van Horne, Enoch Vreeland, Jacob Berry, John Berry, William Berry, John W. Berry, Phillip Berry, Phillip Berry Jr., Peter Allen, Abraham Allen, John Bush, John Outwater, Jacob Outwater, Nicholas Outwater, Justine Dumon, Jacob Hast, Abraham W. Depeyster, John van Boskerk, James Campbell, William Campbell, Jeremiah Pope, Christopher Pope, Andrew Donley, John A. Ackerman, John Bashtin, Abraham Ackerman, Abraham A. Ackerman, Nicholas Loby, Jacob Earle, John Wallace, Thomas Allen, John vander Beck, Thomas Chapple, William van Emburgh, Alexander Currie, Evert Rykeman, Tobias Rykerman, Daniel Rykerman, Patrick McFadden, Elijah Morrel, William Young, Matilda Dugan, William Warner, Evarardus Warner, John Cassady, William Fair, Lawrence D. Ackerman, Hendrick Barr, Selvester Morris, Richard Ackerman, Simon Simonson, John van Bueren, Lawrence A. Ackerman, George van Giesen, John van Giesen, Lawrence Ackerman, Michael Post, Cornelius Ackerman, Peter Ackerman, Lawrence P. Ackerman, Jacob Hopper, Henry Hopper, Jacobus Brinkerhof, Henry van Bayke, Elizabeth vander Linde, Margaret Houseman, Daniel Cully, Michael B. Terhune, Isaac Vreeland, Abraham Vreeland, Necandle Terhune, Powels Terhune, Aghye Fielding, Daniel Fielding, Enoch Vreeland, John Metseker, Isaac E. Vreeland, Thomas Vreeland, John Vreeland Jr., John Vreeland, Peter Vreeland, Benjamin Vreeland, George Brinkerhof, Henry Brinkerhof, Jacob Brinkerhof, Samuel Berry, Henry Berry, Caleb Williams, Jacob vander Pool, Elias Provoost, Peter Zabriskie, Morris Earle,

Archibald Campbell, Robert Campbell, John Earle, Thomas Gardner, Rev. Wolmudus Kuyprus, John Varick, Elenor Bogart, John Varick Jr., Andrew Stimson, George Finn, Isaac Ward, Jonathan Baldwin, Jacob van Houten, Adam Boyd, Cornelius Terhune, John Bertholf, John Chapple, Francis Dougery, Isaac Laubaugh, Isaac van Giesen, Jacobus Bertholf, Alexander Miller, Powels vander Bake, Nehemiah Wade, Cornelius Cooper, Isaac Bardan, Henry Bardan, Roland Hill, Alexander P. Waldron, Adolph Waldron, Thomas Rozell, Jeremiah Steeves, Isaac vander Bake Jr., John Terhune, John Joost Zabriskie, Elihu Airs, John Terhune, Peter J. Terhune, Jacob Terhune, Richard I. Terhune, Roelif Terhune, Nancy Terhune, William Hammel, Henry Rattan, Jacob vander Bake, Peter Degroot, Albert A. van Voorhees, Albert van Voorhees, John van Orden, David Brewer, Elizabeth Brewer, Abraham Devone, Peter Brewer, George Taylor, John Brewer, Uzal Meeker, Peter Christopher, John Robertson, John Zabriskie Jr., John Zabriskie, David Brewer, Jacob J. van Saun, Annanias Campbell, Jacob Bogart, John Bogart, Barent Cole, Israel Pearsall, George van Boskerk, John Bardan, Cornelius van Saun, Albert van Saun, Jacob Ja van Saun, David van Saun, David Anderson, Andrew Zabriskie, Wert Banta, John Bogart, Cornelius Bogart, Gabriel Hymer, Joost Zabriskie, John Demarest, Mary King, Joost Demarest, Helmus van Wagener, Art Kuyper, Jacob DeBaun, Jacob van Voorhees, Lucas van Voorhees, Peter Christie, Margaret Kuyper, Richard J. Kuyper, Hendrick van Voorhees, John van Voorhees, Jacob Tenike, Peter P. Demarest, John Magangie, John van Boskerk, Luke van Boskerk, Hendrick Kuyper, Richard H. Kuyper, Cornelius Kuyper, Garret C. Kuyper, Thomas Kuyper, Isaac van Voorhees, Necansie van Voorhees, Derick Demarest, Cornelius van Horne, John Bogart, David Ackerman, Cornelius Bogart, Joost Burr, Albert Romine, Jacobus Bogart, Stephen Terhune, Isaac van Saun, Jacob van Saun, Egbert van Saun, Henry Banta, Cornelius van Saun, Cornelius Banta, Jacob C. van Saun, Lucas van Saun, Isaac van Saun, Guilliam Terhune, Stephen Terhune, James Magriger, Jacobus

Terhune, Isaac van Giesen, Nicholas Demarest, Tunes Helm, Daniel Helm, Syntye Helm, Albert H. Zabriskie, Abraham A. Zabriskie, Garret A. Zabriskie, Hendrick J. Zabriskie, Jacob H. Zabriskie, Albert J. Zabriskie, Cornelius Bogart, Andrew J. Zabriskie, John A. Zabriskie, Jacob J. Zabriskie, John J. Zabriskie, Jacob Bogart, Herman Lutkins, Henry Lutkins, Stephen Lutkins, Albert J. Zabriskie, Jacob J. Zabriskie, Garret Hopper, Albert Hopper, Cornelius Bogart, Abraham Bogart, Ninian Holmes, Jacobus Bogart, Henry Laubaugh, Jacobus Rattan, Abraham Rattan, Abraham D. Rattan, John J. Zabriskie, Herman van Dien, William Wright, Abraham Wright, John Wright, Joost Bogart, Albert C. Zabriskie, Christian Zabriskie, Christian A. Zabriskie, John Anderson, Casparus Bogart, John D. Terhune, Stephen Terhune, David Terhune, Henry Terhune, Samuel Provoost, Casparus Cough, Albert Cough, Jacob C. Zabriskie, Garret C. Zabriskie, Samuel Thompson, Albert P. van Voorhees, Thomas Basker, Garret Oldis, John Lutkins, Isaac Kip, Guysbert Lake, Necansie Kip, John Kip, John D. Bardan, John N. Romine, Nicansie Romine, John Romine, Daniel Romine, John Tiller, Dr. William Burnet, Zebulon Jones, Garretson, Tunes Jaroleman, John Ogden, Isaac Natman, Jonathan Sayre, Harminus Spear, Abraham Spear, William King, Henry Jaroleman, Abraham H. King, William Clark, Josiah Hornblower, John Spear, Joseph Goings, Tuttle, William Dow, Phillip van Cortlandt, John Berry, John Sip, Helmegh Sip, Hermanus van Wagener, Derick van Ryper, Derick Vreeland, Hermanus Vreeland, John J. Sip, John E. Vreeland, Roelif van Bryke, Stephen Bourdett, John P. Westervelt, Jacobus Brinkerhof, Seba Brinkerhof, Albert Brinkerhof, John Powleson, George J. Brinkerhof, Wert D. Banta, Peter D. Christie, William Carber, Roelif Brinkerhof, Derick Brinkerhof, John Brinkerhof, Samuel Demarest, Benjamin Westervelt, Elisha Bourdett, Albert Terhune, John Gill, William Hornblower, Casparus Zabriskie, Peter Wilson, Jacobus Powleson, Guilliam Outwater.

Saddle River Township

Dr. Phillip Day, Richard Day, Peter McColm, William Fisher, William Read, Thomas Beakhorn, Edward Keelar, Jacob Ricker, Henry Jacobus, Roelif van Houten, David Spear, John Jac. van Houten, John van Houten, Elizabeth van Houten, Cornelius R. van Houten, John H. van Houten, John Benson, John Benson Jr., David Benson, Garret Benson, Daniel Benson, Cornelius van Houten, Roelif C. van Houten, Edo Marselius Jr., John W. van Winkle, Walling van Winkle, Martin van Blerkum, Adrian van Houten, Garrabrant van Houten, Richard van Houten, John van Giesen, Helmegh van Giesen, Peter Road, Adrian Cole, David Halsey, Peter van Houten, Isaac Cronk, John Bogart, Peter Porter, Jonathan Halsted, Joseph Waller, Benjamin Wensen, John Grathan, Richard Stanton, Christian Brower, Will Brower, Isaac vander Beck, Able McFerson, Herman van Blerkum, Widow Burham, Lawrence van Norden, John Rattan, Hessel Ryerson, John H. Ryerson, John C. Westervelt, Cornelius Westervelt, Garret van Ryper, John van Allen, Peter van Allen, John G. van Allen, John D. Ryerson, John Earle, Widow Ryerson, Jacob Ackerman, Thomas P. Wills, John E. Westervelt, Uriah Westervelt, Cornelius U. Westervelt, John G. van Wagener, Reynier Blanchard, John Bowers, John Bogart, John R. Bardan, Jacob D. Bardan, Reynier Bardan, Ephriam Backer, Garret van Wagener, Garret van Wagener Jr., Hessel Garretson, John P. Garretson, John J. Garretson, Garrabrant Garretson, Cornelius D. van Ryper, Cornelius J. van Ryper, Garret Garretson, Garret Garretson Jr., John van Horne, Thomas van Horne, Jacobus Post, Richard Ludlow, Albert Wright, Uriah van Ryper, Abraham Ho, Abraham Cadmus, Henry Dooremus, Peter Dooremus, Andrew Cadmus, Cornelius Cadmus, Girtya Cadmus, Cornelius J. van Houten, John C. van Houten, Thunis Bardan, Phillip van Bussen, Herman P. van Bussen, Peter P. van Bussen, Barent Spear, John B. Spear, Henry Laroe, Thomas van Bussen, John McCarty, Adrian Post, George Cadmus, Dr. John Garretson, Herman van Bussen Jr., Joost cough, Cornelius Helm, Cornelius Post, Herman C. Post, Mermke Ackerman, Robert Glass, Abraham Bush,

Thomas van Ryper, Isaac van Ryper, Samuel
Reading, John Bush, George Banta, Isaac van
Houten, Jury Bush, Meriner van Winkle, Richard
Terhune, Roelif van Bryck, Widow Hopper, James
Houseman, Garret Hopper, Jacob Hopper, John P.
Ackerman, Cornelius Myer, Joost Cough, Michael
Guilliam, Samuel Toers, Jacob Toers, Abraham
Post, Jacob van Winkle, Henry van Giesen, Garret
Turis, John Turis, Henry Ackerman, John
Christie, Lucas van Saun, Richard van Horne,
John A. Post, Albert Westervelt, John Bervort
George Dooremus, Garret Odle, John Kip, Isaac
Kip, Stephen Terhune, John Ackerman, Samuel
Bervort, John H. Garretson, John D. Bardan, John
Bardan Jr., John vander Beck, Henry Lutkins,
Herman vander Beck, Casparus Cough, Peter
Brower, John C. Post, John P. vander Beck, Peter
Hopper, Garret P. Hopper, Jacob Demarest, James
Demarest, Michael Ortley, George Ryerson, John
G. Ryerson, Henry Swain, John Bardan, Francis
Ryerson, John Degraw, John van Blerkum, Hessel
Dooremus, Henry Dooremus, Richard Degraw, John
Degraw, Lenah Degraw, John van Winkle, Francis
van Winkle, Jacob Synder, David van Horne, john
Ridgewar, Martin Helm, Roelif Romine, David
Romine, Isaac Stagg, John Romine, Jury H. Post,
John Riker, Paul van Devort, John Drummond,
Nathaniel Luker, John Hancock, John Stagg,
Joseph Edwards, John Helm, Obediah Foru, Richard
H. van Houten, Peter van Houten, Jonathan Dad,
John H. Dooremus, John Mattis, John Martin,
Jacob Beakhorn, John Laroe, John Laroe Jr., John
Ford, Nicholas Ford, Daniel Zelef, Seras Taylor,
Jacob B. Dooremus, Roelif van Houten, Garret
Neafie, Will Tearman, Roelif C. van Houten,
Abraham Spear, David Dooremus, Henry B. Spear,
Jacob Spear, Henry Fradries, Abraham T. Spear,
Thunis Spear, David D. Hennion, David Brower,
David Brower Jr., John R. van Houten, John I.
Hennion, Thunis J. Hennion, Edo Marselius, Jacob
Bardan, Albert Jac. Bardan, Nicholas Romine,
Uriah van Ryper, Cornelius Marselius, Abraham
Ackerman, James Ackerman, Cornelius Hennion,
Will Spear, David Hennion, John van Ryper, Elvan
Hoyet, Elias Hoyet, William Drummond, Peter
Knight, Joseph Fector, Robert Drummond, John

Drummond, John Lightpipe, David P. Hennion, Adam Short, Phillip J. Schuyler, Walter Nicoll, Peter Schuyler, Samuel Springer, Whale Springer, Pharis Doty, Will Colfax, Caspar Schuyler, John Pratt, Peter Schuyler, Nehemiah Odle, Charles Ogden, Jacob Veader, Cornelius Veader, Daniel Haycock, Thomas Haycock, John Richards, James McCawley, John McClain, Henry McClain, John J. van Houten, Aaron Houghland, Martin Ryerson, Jacobus Bertholf, John Beam, John A. Hennion, William Rogers, Adrian Post, John Dobs, Garret Post, Mary Ryerson, Will Adams, Jacob Bardan, John Guilliam, Henry van Wagener, Helmegh van Wagener, John van Wagener, Peter Line, John H. van Wagener, Anthony Line, Thunis G. Ryerson, Richard Ryerson, Widow Mary Ryerson, George G. Ryerson, John McKensey, John Damar, James Skitts, Israel Miller, Martin G. Ryerson, Abraham Decker, Barent van Devort, Thomas Sanders, Robert Murphy, Will Shippy, Reynier Bertholf, John Bertholf, Aaron Schuyler, Adonijah Schuyler, Phillip A. Schuyler, Aaron P. Schuyler, John Ryerson, Guilliam Ryerson, Thomas Murphy, Peter Row, Richard van Ryper, Garret van Ryper, Staats Storm, Abraham Storm, Galine Ackerman, John Ackerman, John Sunerland, Abraham Hennion, William Leary, Thomas Carman, James Gibney, Nicholas Lozier, Abraham Gould, John A. Gould, John Lozier, Henry Doyal, Daniel Guard, Michael Cook, Francis Cook, Winant Speaker, Jacob Speaker, John Sanders, Yellis Francisco, Nathaniel Francisco, Roelif Jacobusse, Hessel Peterson, Michael Freeland, Thomas Post, John E. Freeland, John D. Freeland, Richard D. Freeland, James Mullen, James Freeland, James Freeland, Benjamin Morris, Tobias Wagoner, Michael Wagoner, Merian Hopper, Henry van Norden, John Smith, John Kennar, Peter Francisco, Thomas Jacobus, John H. Smith, Henry Smith, Andrew van Norden, David van Norden, Martin Brown, Peter Snyder, John Wright, Abraham Shaigat, Widow Cole, Jacob Cole, Cornelius Davenport, Samuel Soward, David Merenis, Garret Merenis, John U. Davenport, John Davenport, Abraham vander Hoff, Will Kimble, Charles Oldham, John Pitts, John Wetherholt, William Helm, Michael Stagg, Ephriam

Cassamore, John L. Davenport, Mathias Massacar, James Stagg, Ebenezer Burnet, Ralph Burnet, John Welling, Isaac Ellison, James van Norden, Will Francisco, Labon Roberts, Peter H. Francisco, John McLoud, John McLoud Jr., John U. Knows, John Knows Jr., John Cannady, Peter Roma, Anthony Merian, George Smith, Martin Seckolster, Robert Gould, Abraham Freeland, Abraham Freeland Jr., Jacob Francisco, John A. Freeland, Isaac Hawlenbeck, Garret Hawlenbeck, John P. Mead, Simon Mead, Peter van Zile, Archibald Duffy, Richard Higgs, John McClennon, Abraham van Zile, James McCurdy, Jacob Bradwell, John Yeaty, John Brown Jr., John Brown Sr., Roelif Jacobus, Widow Jacobus, Samuel Jones, Nicholas Jones, Thomas Jones, George L. Ryerson, George Ryerson Jr., John van Winkle, Henry Cook, Garret van Ryper, Garret van Ryper Jr., John G. van Ryper, Daniel Worden, John Hopper, Henry Hopper, Guilliam Jacobus, Jacobus G. Jacobus, Henry Mead, Gilbert Francisco, Matthew Buck, Yellis Mead, John Y. Mead, William Ryerson, Widow William Ryerson, Widow van Blerkum, Andrew Boman, Abraham Ryerson, John D. Day, Thomas Day, Garret vander Hoff, Richard Ryerson, Widow T. Ryerson, Garret Jacobus, Jacob Dooremus, Cornelius Dooremus, George C. Dooremus, Cornelius Kip, Phillip Doyal, Nicholas Kip, Henry Kip, James Jacobus, Widow Hopper, Henry Dooremus, Vincent Chandler, William Youngman, Benjamin D. Lamart, Henry Massacar, Albert Bardan, Walter Knap, John Knap, Isaac Knap, David Day, Samuel van Saun, Isaac van Saun, Albert van Saun, Matthew Cronk, Roelif Dooremus, David Carr, Adolphus Waldron, John Moore, Jacob van Ryper, Thunis Hennion, Henry Hennion, Hessel Hennion, Simon van Ess, Simon van Ess Jr., Henry P. Berry, Robert Colfax, John Mead, Anthony Mandeville, William Mandeville, Henry Demott, James van Ess, Simon van Winkle, Jacob van Winkle.

# INDEX

Aber
  Jobiah 211
  Mary 211
Abrahamse
  Cornelius 46
  Jacob 44
Acker
  Cornelius 242, 271
Ackerman
  Abraham 13, 19, 22, 38, 53-55, 63, 75, 86, 88, 93, 106, 108, 120, 125, 156, 196, 283, 294, 300, 304
  Abraham A. 300
  Abraham D. 277, 291
  Abraham G. 292
  Abraham J. 123, 290
  Abraham Jr. 22, 29, 34, 55, 114
  Abraham L. 114
  Albert 121, 232, 259, 265, 266, 290, 297
  Aury 292
  Aury J. 182, 290
  Catherina 188
  Cornelius 300
  David 5, 16, 19, 36, 56, 69, 109, 123, 125, 150, 193, 204, 232, 256, 266, 278, 289, 290, 297, 301
  David D. 222, 291
  David Davidie 53
  David G. 186
  David Johannes 269
  David John 56
  David L. 29, 54
  David Lawrence 17, 18, 20, 38
  Davyed L. 30
  Deghea 268
  Derick 95, 297
  Egbert 19
  Elizabeth 109, 193, 222
  Galine 305
  Garret 20, 36, 69, 80, 186, 193, 248, 291, 297
  Garret A. 247, 248, 279, 290
  Garret D. 91, 183, 222, 291
  Garret G. 292
  Glybert 59
  Helena 55, 186
  Hendrikjo 22
  Henry 136, 285, 304
  Jacob 78, 110, 113, 129, 212, 213, 220, 231, 236, 262, 263, 268, 275, 303
  Jacob A. 268
  Jacob D. 222
  Jacob Lawrence 33
  Jacobus 19, 65, 108, 123, 163
  Jacobus I. 291
  Jacobus Lawrence 18

James 241, 276, 290, 304
James A. 292
James Jr. 241
James L. 291
James W. 265, 266
Johannes 212
Johannes D. 61
Johannes Davidie 158
Johannes Lawrence 18
Johannis 19, 65
Johannis David 34
Johannis Lawrence 33
John 74, 77, 109, 118, 121, 136, 193, 247, 255, 276, 290, 293, 297, 304, 305
John A. 92, 289, 300
John D. 186, 259, 266, 290, 291, 297
John G. 91, 109, 193
John I. 291
John J. 92, 204, 247, 292
John Jacobus 102
John Jr. 293
John P. 304
Lawrence 15, 32, 66, 108, 114, 164, 166, 186, 292, 300
Lawrence A. 107, 184, 186, 221, 300
Lawrence D. 300
Lawrence J. 108
Lawrence P. 259, 300
Ludwig 2, 15

Marmaduke 213
Mary 156
Mermke 303
Moses 293
Peter 158, 248, 256, 260, 265, 289, 300
Peter A. 188, 290
Rachel 186
Richard 215, 300
William 123, 265, 291
Ackers
  Garret 81, 146
Ackerson
  Abram 273
  Garret 158
  John 76, 122, 160, 289
  Nicholas 292
  Richard 242
  Thomas 240, 249
Ackhart
  Josiah 132
  William 132, 289
Adams
  Will 305
Adolph
  Peter 118
Afler
  Henry 288
Airs
  Elihu 301
Albertson
  Albert 1
  John 186, 197
  William 186, 197
Alex
  William 47
Alexander
  James 17, 30, 32, 44, 46, 53, 120, 148, 165, 197, 198
Allaies
  Alexander 14

Joane 14
Allen
　Abraham 66, 75,
　　76, 79, 85, 100,
　　137, 144, 154,
　　215, 223, 300
　Cornelius 289
　Hepel 79
　John 288
　Peter 100, 137,
　　223, 269, 300
　Sarah 100, 223
　Thomas 145, 300
Allison
　Hannah 81
　Henry 73, 80, 81
Alsop
　Thomas 27, 28
Alyee
　Albert 78, 98,
　　265
　Ann 110, 111
　Isaac 289
　Jacob 289
　Jacobus 110, 111,
　　297
　Jan 33
　John 47
　Leonard Huygode
　　32
　Maria 98
　Peter 47
Anderson
　Albert 192
　Andrus 295
　David 107, 168,
　　204, 220, 229,
　　238, 273, 286,
　　293, 301
　David J. 293
　Elbert 183
　James 211
　John 166, 173,
　　234, 236, 282,
　　302
　John J. 294

Nickole 14
　William 15, 297
Andries
　Claes 26
　Michael 46, 52
　Sarah 26
Anns
　William 36
Anthoneson
　Anthony 22
Anthony
　John 295
Aorrigh
　Godpey 288
Apeamans
　John 290
Applebee
　James 269
Applewhite
　Henry 8
　Hoesba 8
　Hoster 12
　Thomas 12, 42, 75
Archibald
　David 122, 148,
　　213, 294
　John 236, 277,
　　291
Arell
　Peter 166
Arents
　Jacob 38
Arnold
　John 8, 10
Arsmitt
　Cornelius 46
Ashfield
　Lewis M. 126, 171
　Lewis Morris 126,
　　171
　Patience 44, 48,
　　67
　Richard 41, 44,
　　46, 48, 49, 67,
　　72, 109, 126,
　　167, 171, 175,

221
Ashietas
  Richard 8, 49
Aster
  Elenah 254
  Ellen 262
  Henry 254, 262
Aukins
  Douwse 46
Auryansen
  Aury 296
  Daniel 240
  Garret 238, 240, 241
  John 240, 296
  Resalvert 296
  Yan 240
Austin
  John 288
Ayesagg
  Benjamin 243
  Susan 243
Backer
  Ephriam 303
  Hendrick D. 4
  Richard 18
Bacoman
  Andrew 277
Badiah
  O. 284
Bagley
  Elizabeth 27, 28
  Timothy 27, 28
Bailey
  Aaron 299
  Elias 288
  Samuel 288
Baird
  Francis 75
Baker
  Jonathan 111
  Peter 294
  Richard 44, 145
Baldwin
  Anamas 169, 187
  Ann 74

  Anne 140, 170
  Catharine 72
  Daniel 105, 126, 191
  David 120, 148, 238, 297
  Hannah 131
  Jonathan 301
  Jotham 158
  Nicholas 262
  Phebe 105
  Stephen 56, 76, 91, 92, 140
  Widow 74, 85
  William 87
Ball
  Edward J. 197
  Edward John 204, 205, 222
Ballara
  Jeremiah 280
Bamper
  Jacob 73, 88, 125
Bancker
  Abraham 188
  Catharine 243
  Evert 254, 255, 272
  Gerard 216, 230, 243
Banks
  Mary 50, 52
Banta
  Abraham 103, 278
  Abraham D. 293
  Abraham J. 289
  Abraham S. 290
  Albert 159
  Albert H. 122, 162
  Anna 112
  Annaetye 103
  Annatie 260
  Anne 112
  Annetie 36
  Antul 293

Aury 49, 251, 295
Boren Epkese 2
Cornelia 294
Cornelish 122
Cornelius 32,
  293, 301
Cornelius Epka 32
Cornelius Epken
  28
Cornelius G. 295
Cornelius J. 291
David 58, 160,
  161
Derick 112, 161,
  179, 195, 196,
  203, 204, 294
Derick Johannis
  53, 161
Elizabeth 208,
  278, 294
Epka 32
Eve 294
Garret 134, 215,
  217, 295
George 304
Hannah 168
Hendrick 50, 51,
  58, 114, 119,
  132, 152, 159,
  160, 214, 215,
  251, 266, 297
Hendrick H. 134
Hendrick
  Hendrickse 145,
  159
Hendrick Jr. 39,
  62
Hendrick Sebe 214
Hendrick Sieberie
  36
Hendrick Sieberie
  Jr. 36
Hendrick Siebesse
  52
Henry 44, 84,
  203, 214, 295,
  297, 301
Henry Epkon 6
Hila 160, 161
Jacob 7, 21, 48,
  53, 55, 160,
  161, 170, 289,
  295, 297
Jacob C. 259, 293
Jacob D. 293
Jacob Henrichson
  6
Jan 47
Jannetie 103
Jebe M. 151
Johannes 112,
  142, 161, 260
Johannis Derick
  53
Johannis Duchse
  161
John 31, 42, 90,
  100, 105, 142,
  190, 195, 208,
  223, 259, 260,
  291, 297
John A. 208
John C. 260
John d. 293
John H. 103
John Hendrickse
  122
John Hn. 76
John I. 291
John J. 57, 112,
  232, 233, 294,
  297
John S. 179, 204,
  244, 259, 277,
  294
Leah 119, 151
Lena 159
Lenah 215
Margaret 231
Margaret Stebena
  231
Mary 39, 100, 223

Nicholas 151
Paulus 87, 96
Peter 131
Rachel 179, 204, 232, 259
Richard 294
Samuel 208, 211, 278, 290
Seba 119, 295
Siebe 122, 131
Siebese 45
Thomas 290
Thomas P. 231
Weart H. 168
Wert 96, 107, 168, 247, 301
Wert D. 302
Wert Epkese 2
Weyntye 159
Widow 259
Wiert 39, 88, 89, 119, 160, 275, 294
Wiert D. 293
Bantow
  John 176
Barbene
  Andrew 168
Barberie
  Barberie 20
  John 14, 33, 36, 38, 70
  Lambert 197, 281
  Peter 33
  Potter 14
Barclay
  John 12, 26
  John Lord 26
Barcoff
  Henry 132
Bard
  Doctor 115
  John 188, 255
  John Sr. 188
  Samuel 188
Bardan

Albert 60, 68, 71, 306
Albert Jac. 304
Catrina 222
David 64, 71, 86, 123, 141
Derick 222
Elshe 229
Hendrick 68, 72, 117, 124, 125
Henry 229, 253, 301
Isaac 84, 173, 282, 301
Jacob 60, 71, 129, 261, 304, 305
Jacob D. 222, 268, 277, 303
Jacob J. 130
Jan 9, 16, 41, 68
John 5, 8, 16, 20, 23, 28, 41-43, 59, 60, 61, 64, 67-69, 71, 73, 82, 83, 131, 151, 183, 201, 221, 232, 256, 301, 304
John Albertse 272
John D. 59, 136, 222, 229, 268, 269, 277, 302, 304
John Jr. 35, 304
John R. 213, 222, 303
Maricha 68
Mary 82
Rebecca 261
Rebecka 261
Reynier 59, 222, 232, 303
Thunis 303
Tunis 227
Vroutie 41, 221

Barentsen
  Derick 13, 167,
    221, 222
  Elisabeth 13
Barhans
  Samuel 237
Barker
  Thomas 279
Barlton
  Neweri 185
Barquo
  Jacobus 141
  Mary 141
Barr
  Hendrick 230, 300
Barrow
  Carolina 9
  John 9
Bartow
  John 288
Bartrim
  Anthony 132, 134,
    186, 193, 194,
    261, 288
  Hendrick 11
  Henry 172
  Hester 193, 194
  Hettie 132
  Joseph 42, 156,
    198, 207, 221,
    288
Bashtin
  John 300
Basker
  Thomas 302
Basset
  Ann 140
Batholf
  John 230
Baudinot
  David 110
  Elias 80, 100,
    109, 110
  Elisha 80
  John 110
  Maria Catherine
    110
  Mary 110
  Mary Catharine
    109, 110
  Susannah 110
Bavenhyse
  Michael 290
  Nicholas 289
  Widow 290
Bayard
  Anna Maria 209
  Blandance 16
  Johannah 209,
    219, 220
  John 209, 219,
    220, 290
  Judith 7
  M. 191
  Nicholas 7, 26
  Samuel 11
  William 105, 106,
    124, 256
Bayeux
  Thomas 25
Beach
  Charles 288
  Jonathan 258
  Widow 288
Beaiver
  Abraham 75
Beakhorn
  Jacob 304
  Thomas 303
Beam
  Abraham 288
  Anthony 44, 72,
    175, 215, 217,
    277, 288
  Anthony A. 288
  Anthony C. 288
  Conrad 171, 193,
    288
  Jacob 175
  James 288
  John 288, 305
  John A. 288

Joost  72, 75, 77,
  79, 171, 187,
  193, 288
Bear (See Beer)
  Hendrick  114
  Henry  113
Becker
  John  198, 295
Beckman
  James J.  124
  Magnus  158
  R. S.  194
  Samuel  105, 158
  William  67
Beer
  Hendrick  16, 19,
    114
Belcher
  Adam  156
  J.  53
  Jonathan  53
Bell
  Andrew  197, 210,
    238, 258, 281
  Robert  82
  Susannah  210
  William  132, 199
  William B.  168
  William M.  131,
    170, 174, 187,
    198, 231, 242
Bennett
  Jacob  86
  John  77
  William  288
Benson
  Albert  88
  Caty  77
  Cornelia  154
  Cornelius  88
  Cristopher  62
  Daniel  303
  David  162, 303
  Elizabeth  88
  Garret  145, 160,
    162, 170, 303

  Genet  88
  Jacob  88
  Johanna  51
  Johannes  147, 157
  Johannis  44
  John  59, 74, 76,
    77, 84, 88,
    91-93, 96, 97,
    107, 119, 120,
    122, 142, 144,
    148, 157, 189,
    218, 219, 222,
    224, 234, 258,
    295, 303
  John G.  122, 198,
    224, 225, 237,
    295
  John Jr.  101,
    107, 142, 219,
    303
  Maria  122
  Marretye  157
  Mary  77, 142
  Mathew  35, 47,
    51, 88
  Oliver  88
  Rebecke  107
  Rebeke  107
  Richard  150, 270
Benthall
  Mercy  48, 49, 67
Bently
  Mary  8
Bergen
  Derick  299
  Elizabeth  216,
    243, 271, 272
  Richard  121, 152,
    153, 157, 174,
    189, 216, 243,
    268, 271, 272
  Tunis  121
Bergie
  Capt.  33
Bergs
  Jacobus  141

Berry
  Abraham 229
  Carolina 12
  Catharine 220
  Hendrick 80, 99, 125
  Henry 136, 173, 174, 190, 218, 246, 247, 260, 283, 300
  Henry P. 306
  Jacob 229, 300
  John 1, 2, 5, 6, 14-16, 19, 20, 22, 24, 27, 29-31, 33-36, 42, 44, 47, 48, 57, 62, 68, 100, 114, 145, 185, 193, 229, 233, 246, 259, 300, 302
  John A. 283
  John Jr. 12
  John W. 300
  Lawrence Richard 19
  Philip 99, 193, 218, 257
  Phillip 300
  Phillip Jr. 300
  Richard 48
  Samuel 7, 137, 169, 233, 259, 300
  William 185, 242, 300
Bertholf
  Benjamin 107, 113, 155, 156, 289
  Cerines 285
  Corynes 265
  Crynase 75, 97
  Crynes 265, 268
  David 289
  Garret 92, 100
  Geiles 92
  Giles 293
  Guilliam 54, 58, 63, 64, 66, 69, 86, 93, 104, 106-108, 113, 139, 149, 160, 161, 167, 170, 189, 239, 248
  Hendrick 113
  Henry 291, 292
  Jacobus 68, 92, 189, 289, 301, 305
  Jacobus C. 103, 104
  James 107, 113, 118, 133, 134, 189, 190, 285
  Johannes 192, 207
  John 106, 107, 113, 201, 207, 285, 289, 293, 301, 305
  Leah 93, 107, 189
  Luke 108
  Margaret 293
  Maritye 107
  Nesulty 107
  Nrose 87
  Oseltie 189
  Quilliam 85, 87, 104, 192, 196
  Rachel 108
  Ragel 108
  Reynier 305
  Samuel 70, 75, 97, 107, 289
  Stephen 108, 289
  Susan 265
  Wert Guilson 118
  Weybrough 134, 192, 207
  Yellis 95
Bervort

John 304
  Samuel 304
Beselas
  Henry 291
Best
  Cornelius 131,
    197
Beyerd
  Samuel 83
Bicklay
  William 49
Bileston
  Edward 194
  Elizabeth 194
  Ruth 194
Billops
  Philip 286
Billue
  Jacob 70, 289
  Johanna 70
Blachly
  Ebenezer Jr. 274
  Ebenezer S. 274
  Elizabeth 274
Blacklidge
  Benjamin 105,
    106, 124, 142,
    172, 179, 208,
    215, 229, 238,
    239, 245, 296
  Peter 245
Blagge
  Benjamin 35, 47
  Edward 35, 47
Blair
  Robert 167, 299
Blan
  Herman 296
Blanch
  Andrew 270
  Isaac 82, 88,
    115, 164, 216,
    239, 242
  Isaac Jr. 111
  Richard 164, 242,
    262, 296

Richard J. 112
Thomas 296
Thomas Jr. 239,
  242
Blanchard
  Reynier 303
Blank
  Catharine 212,
    228
  Jacob Jr. 212,
    228
  Jacob Sr. 212,
    228
  Mary 212
  William J. 202
Blanock
  Cornelius 296
Blaslin
  Abraham 11
Blauvelt
  Abraham 78, 162,
    227, 273, 289,
    296
  Abraham J. 277,
    291
  Abraham Y. 200
  Anaatye 296
  Christeen 77
  Christian 241,
    297
  Cornelia 241
  Cornelius 146,
    298
  Cornelius J. 226,
    235
  Daniel 230, 240,
    244, 292, 296
  Daniel I. 292
  Elizabeth 244
  Fred 297
  Garret 240, 241,
    292
  Garret H. 77, 78
  Garret J. 292
  Isaac 291
  Isaac J. 277

Isaac Jr. 291
Isaac T. 230, 296
Jacob 296
Jacob J. 227
Jacobus 296, 298
James 236, 237, 275
James T. 236
Johannes 159, 296
Johannes H. 228
Johannis H. 113
John 179, 292, 298
John A. 230, 240, 241
Joseph 158, 298
Margaret 296
Richard 252
Teunis 158
Thomas 241
Blowfelt
  John 294
Blundish
  Nathaniel 295
Board
  Cornelius 281
  David 281, 288
  David Jr. 288
  James 288
  James Jr. 288
  John 223
  Nathaniel 281, 282
Boaro
  Joseph 288
Bockenhoven
  Cornelius
    Christoff 3
Bofardus
  John 294
Bogart
  Abraham 236, 297, 302
  Albert 84, 100, 125, 244, 250, 262, 294, 297, 298
  Albert C. 293
  Albourt 7, 9
  Alida 82, 83, 141
  Andrew 285
  Anna 212, 213
  Blonina 1
  Casparus 227, 239, 302
  Cathyntie 243
  Cattyntie 258, 259
  Charity 276
  Cornelius 83, 90, 104, 109, 123, 124, 148, 150, 177, 183, 193, 216, 224, 227, 234, 237-239, 248, 293, 294, 297, 301, 302
  Cornelius J. 104, 124, 290
  Cornelius Ja 237
  Cornelius L. 107, 108
  David R. 294
  Elenor 301
  Elisabeth 9, 48
  Elizabeth 108, 235, 236, 248, 278
  Galem 77
  Garret 216
  Gasye 149
  Geashe 149
  George 48, 276
  Gilbert 7
  Giliam 166
  Gilyaem J. 204
  Guilliam 244, 247, 248, 250, 258, 259, 297
  Guilliam J. 243
  Guoline 62
  Gyllejaem 149

Helena 209
Hendrick 136,
 244, 248, 294
Hendrick R. 122
Henry 248, 250,
 289
Henry C. 293
Isaac 43, 50, 51,
 64, 72, 78, 81,
 103, 104, 149,
 189, 297
Jacob 9, 55, 81,
 125, 147, 196,
 203, 204, 216,
 235, 294, 301,
 302
Jacob C. 293
Jacobus 43, 72,
 93, 103, 106,
 110, 124, 128,
 149, 193, 268,
 290, 297, 301,
 302
Jacobus A. 235,
 275
Jacobus Cornelius
 64
Jacobus J. 92,
 106, 265
Jacobus S. 90,
 143
James 105, 212,
 298
James I. 289
James J. 191
James L. 108, 163
James S. 125,
 151, 289
Jan 33
Jane 248
Johannes 62, 149
Johannes G. 96
Johannis 50, 120
John 41-43, 95,
 107, 112, 133,
 151, 162, 222,
 235, 236, 244,
 248, 250, 278,
 293, 294, 297,
 301, 303
John C. 247, 276
John Cornelis 8
John J. 179, 247,
 293
John P. 179, 204,
 293
John R. 277, 278,
 294
John Roelif 53
John S. 290
John T. 179
Joost 302
Leya 149
Lucas 108, 239
Luches 90
Mary 276, 298
Matthew 296
Nicholas 10, 71,
 82, 83, 141, 253
Peter 1, 253,
 265, 289, 296,
 298
Quilliam 49
Rebecca 112
Roelif 2, 9, 48,
 112, 122, 133,
 162, 255, 275,
 294
Roelif P. 293
Rudolfus 6
Sarah 296
Seba 238
States 289
Stephen 183, 212,
 290, 294
Stephen I. 288
Stephen J. 213
Steven 43, 91
William 93, 161
Boggs
 Thomas 59, 73,
 74, 78

Bohe
  Abraham 39
Bohr
  Hendrick 29
Bollen
  Joannis 8
  Joannis Sr. 8
Boman
  Andrew 306
Bond
  John 93
Bondman
  Andrew 278
Bonnel
  Joseph 48
Bonney
  James 98
Bord
  Joseph 283
Bos
  Coeuradus 29
  Joserva 17
Bosch
  Annetye 85
  Hendrick 85
Bosh
  Johannes 2, 15
  Joshua 10
Boss
  Conradt 165
  Johannis 2
Boudinot
  Catharine 165
  Elias 1, 5, 9,
    11, 12, 25, 36,
    38, 193
  Elisha 165, 219,
    220
  Marie Catherine
    193
  Mary 11, 193
Bourd
  Cornelius 81,
    120, 121, 198
  Cornelius D. 126
  David 81, 86,
    102, 120, 121
  Elizabeth 121
  James 71, 73, 80,
    85-87, 89, 90,
    92, 93, 102,
    120, 121, 124,
    136, 137, 146,
    160
  Joseph 120, 121,
    198
  Mary 120
  Philip 111
Bourdett
  Benjamin 295
  Christeen 191,
    192, 295
  Christian 133,
    270
  Clashee 191, 192
  Eleanor 194
  Elenor 67
  Elisha 302
  Hannah 9, 34, 38
  John 295
  Nelly 67
  Peter 194, 295
  Stephen 9, 21,
    31, 34, 38, 67,
    68, 79, 99, 131,
    141, 158, 160,
    161, 192, 194,
    295, 302
  Stephen Jr. 58
  Stephen Sr. 58
  Steven 97
Bower
  Charity 9
  Jury 9
  William 9
Bowers
  Incroape 9
  John 303
  William 9
Bowman
  Andries 278
Boyd

Adam 83, 85, 89,
　92, 93, 99, 107,
　124, 144, 156,
　167, 168, 186,
　196, 203, 211,
　301
　Catharine 144,
　　168
　John A. 271
　Thomas 216, 242
Boyle
　Eglinton M. 209
Brackholst
　Anthony 7, 10,
　　108, 195
　Henry 13, 54, 108
　Mary 54, 108
Bradwell
　Jacob 306
Brambush
　David 286
　Engle 286
　William 286
Brass
　Adolph 26
　Anna 175
　Catharine 158
　Harman 158
　Harmanus 145,
　　158, 175
　Hendrick 19, 28,
　　36
　Henry 18, 22, 36,
　　86
　Herman 5
　Lucas 86
Brawn
　Daniel J. 86
　David 112
　Henry 265
Breste
　Christoff 3
　Cornelius 3
Brewer
　David 301
　Elizabeth 301

Jacob 119, 173
John 147, 301
Marytie 147
Peter 135, 301
Samuel 174
Bricker
　Hannes 167
　Susanna 19
　Thomas 19, 21
Briges
　Edward 199
Briggs
　Thomas 72
　Walter 62, 145,
　　159
Briksman
　Henry 196
Brinkerhof
　Abby 84
　Adrian 99
　Adriana 99
　Albert 133, 203,
　　267, 302
　Albert J. 293
　Angenietie 43
　Annatye 84, 93
　Antie 66
　Antie H. 66
　Anton 6
　Bailtic 203
　Balsha 203
　Carl Jorten 2
　Catharine 66
　Clasoh Jorisen 2
　Cornelia 203, 204
　Cornelius 3, 38,
　　41, 46, 48, 51,
　　52, 57, 170, 246
　Cornelius
　　Hindriksen 26
　Cornelius Jorten
　　2
　Derick 6, 123,
　　204, 224, 294,
　　302
　Derick S. 293

Elizabeth 84, 93, 94
Garret J. 293
George 76, 93, 203, 233, 246, 259, 267, 300
George G. 242
George H. 66
George J. 293, 302
George Jr. 133
Hartman 57, 80, 99, 114, 125, 173, 191, 192, 295
Hendrick 66, 84, 133, 141, 149, 160, 161, 162, 225, 226, 276
Hendrick C. 80
Hendrick Cornelius 57
Hendrick George 66
Hendrick H. 66
Hendrick Jorisen 2
Henry 84, 93, 94, 133, 142, 209, 285, 300
Henry D. 294
Henry F. 293
Henry H. 285
Henry J. 246, 293
Henry Joris 22
Henry Joseph 6
Henry R. 294
Jacob 6, 18, 66, 84, 224, 246, 300
Jacob G. 283
Jacob S. 293
Jacobus 21, 38, 41, 43, 48, 58, 66, 76, 84, 93, 123, 133, 293, 300, 302
Jacobus H. 66
Jacobus Hendrickse 160
James 133, 203, 246
Johannah 84
Johannes 294
John 133, 179, 224, 225, 295, 302
Joris 84, 161, 223
Lena 84, 223
Mardalena 84, 93, 94, 223
Margritye 66, 76
Nicanse 293
Nicause 223, 254
Nicholas H. 66
Nicolic 84
Nicose 84, 94, 125
Nieucoe 93
Roelif 179, 294, 302
Sarah 93
Seba 66, 84, 223, 267, 293, 302
Sebe 203
Siba 204
Sike 100
Thomas 153
Yannetye 141
Britain
  Entony 295
Britton
  William 285
Brodrick
  Anthony 67
Brooks
  Abraham 35
  Cornelius 189
Brookschank
  Alexander 146
Bross

Harmanus 289
Peter 300
Brower
  Abraham 14, 49,
    164, 176, 269
  Abraham D. 257,
    282
  Adolf 16
  Adolph 54
  Aldrih 32
  Christian 303
  David 49, 183,
    185, 304
  David Jr. 304
  Dina 49
  Eldrick 15
  Elenner 183
  Ellener 183
  Jacbo Ja 251
  Jacob 62, 168,
    232, 285
  Jacob Jr. 135
  Jannetie 49
  John 195, 204,
    232
  John F. 285
  Joseph 285
  Lawrence 242
  Lea 49
  Peter 183, 232,
    304
  Petrus 49
  Theodorus 183
  Will 303
Brown
  Abraham 157, 165
  Caty 201
  Daniel Isaac 59,
    64, 123
  David 54, 169
  Henry 137, 288
  Henry H. 299
  Isaac 57
  Jacob 155
  James 153, 210,
    261

John 169, 288
John Jr. 151,
  165, 306
John Sr. 306
Joseph 170
Lawrence 202
Mariah 165
Martin 305
Mary 286
Thomas 171, 177,
  202, 213, 299
Tunes 299
Widow 179
Brucker
  Susanna 4
  Thomas 4
Bruin
  Samuel 288
Brush
  Peter 260
Bryant
  Cornelius 2
  Pieter Cornelis
    22
Bryne
  John 247
Buck
  Matthew 306
Buckbee
  Benjamin 247
Budd
  Joanna 211
  William 169, 211
Buice
  Jacob 285
Buirtis
  William 56
BulsTelt
  Hendrick 132
Bureaux
  John Harvey 252,
    253
Burgan
  Gill 66
Burger
  John 43

Margaretha 17
Warner 4, 17, 18,
  20, 28, 29
Burges
  Daniel 290
  James 290
Burham
  Margaret 268
  Samuel 120
  Widow 241, 249,
    266, 303
Burk
  Annatye 86
  Cusparus 177
  Garret 177
  Hendrick 86
Burnet
  Ebenezer 306
  John 56, 69
  Justus 192
  Ralph 229, 306
  William 56,
    165-167, 245,
    302
Burr
  Aaron 170
  Joost 301
Burton
  William 159
Buryan
  Indian 46
Bush
  Abraham 303
  Casparus 299
  Conrad 290
  Hendrick 69, 214
  Henry 290
  James 289
  Johann 80
  John 300, 304
  Joshua 215
  Jury 299, 304
  Ludwig 260
  Michael 299
  Rynhurt 290
  Samuel 78, 149,
    291
  Staats 127
  Widow 289
Butler
  Daniel 251
  James 299
  Johan 299
  John 165, 251
  Judith 251
Buys
  Peter 296
Byand
  David 290
Bye
  David 145
Byerman
  Christian 289
Cadignan
  Lewis 201
Cadmus
  Abraham 58, 146,
    189, 207, 298,
    303
  Abram 58
  Anderies F. 58
  Andrew 303
  Blandena 189
  Cattalya 207
  Cornelius 303
  Dedrick 46
  Effy 221
  George 97, 210,
    221, 303
  Girtya 303
  Hartman 58, 127
  Isaac 58
  Jasper 220, 221,
    286
  Johannis 58
  John 119
  Peter 133, 134,
    189, 299
  Richard 220, 221
  Thomas 144
  Thomas F. 58
Cadwalader

Thomas 199
Caenroot
  Octavo 39
Caerte
  Avic 292
  John 292
  William 292
Caghill
  Thomas 288
Cairns
  David 291
  Douglas 88, 293
  Gesse 88
  Hub. 61
  James 291
  John 88, 124, 291
  Will 88
  William 147, 295
Caldwell
  Esther F. 207
Camble
  Jacob 293
  John 16
  Martin 1
  Maryon 16
  William 293
Cammazaar
  Daniel 76
  Jasie 76
Camp
  Phebe 129
  Stephen 67
Campbell
  Alleda 157
  Alltie 156, 157
  Ann 66
  Annanias 301
  Annatye 238
  Archibald 71, 85, 87, 92, 118, 133, 134, 136, 144, 145, 156, 158, 166, 182, 202, 224, 301
  Catharine 85, 156
  Christian 102, 240, 241, 298
  David 178, 194, 238, 296
  George 66, 154, 164, 187
  Hannah 85, 154
  Jacob 156, 157
  James 230, 300
  John 96, 275, 289, 297
  Robert 104, 145, 156, 159, 163, 164, 166, 168, 173, 174, 176, 203, 205, 259, 301
  Samuel 77
  Sarah 194
  Simon 198
  Thomas 297
  William 297, 300
Cample
  Abraham 39
Cane
  James 271
Cannady
  John 306
Canness
  James 145
Cannon
  James S. 213
Carber
  William 302
Cark
  Abraham 157
Carl
  John 101, 104
Carle
  Md 18
Carlough
  Adolph 289
  Aldolphus 295
  Christian A. 289
  Conradus 294
  Harman 289
  Henry 294

Honerist 292
Jerry 289
John 289
Margaret 294
Simon 295
Carman
  Richard 238
  Thomas 305
Carnes
  John 237
  P. 91
  William 91
Carols
  Samuel 70
Carpenter
  Hannah 73
  Moses 73
Carr
  Cornelius 244
  David 226, 306
Carre
  Louis 25
Carson
  Mary 80, 81
Carter
  Catharine 169, 258
  Geurt 41
  Reuben 126, 169, 202, 257, 258, 299
Carting
  George L. 42
Cartwright
  Phillip 24, 26
  Thomas 54
Case
  Stephen 74
Casey
  Michael 228
Cassady
  Hannah 163, 164
  John 82, 85, 92, 107, 156, 163, 164, 186, 202, 300

Cassamore
  Ephriam 306
Cavelier
  John 26, 46
Cayler
  Henry Jr. 198
Ceard
  James 138
Challen
  William 220
Chambers
  Davis William 12
  J. 24
  John 24, 49, 68
  Widow 76
  William 11
Chandler
  D. 296
  Vincent 306
Chapman
  George Warren 243
Chapple
  James 74, 85, 100, 209
  Jeso 123
  Jesse 291
  John 69, 100, 223, 301
  Mannon 236
  Thomas 92, 100, 203, 223, 300
Charrett
  Philip 8
Chetwood
  John 173
Chidlaw
  Mary 272
Christeen
  John 16, 22, 23, 30, 31, 34, 35, 38, 43, 47, 48, 50-52, 55, 165, 170
  Naomi 35, 55
  Sarah 55
Christian

Cornelius 2, 9
Johann 6
John 5
Lovorane Cornelius 9
Christie
  Charles 198
  Daniel 76, 100, 162, 293
  David 49, 131, 289
  Elizabeth 247
  Helena 213
  James 70, 88, 90, 105, 125, 132, 283, 289, 294, 300
  James D. 149
  John 89, 243, 289, 304
  John W. 141
  Peter 166, 176, 217, 220, 247, 276, 278, 301
  Peter D. 293, 302
  Peter W. 294
  William 171, 213, 294
Christopher
  John 275, 291
  Peter 301
Claesen
  Annetje 30
  Bartole 7
  Cornelius 33
  Derick 65
  Hartman 30
Clark
  Elizabeth 117
  John M. 169, 193, 218, 219, 246, 254
  Rachel 169, 193, 218, 219, 246, 254
  Robert 139

  Thomas 295
  William 87, 117, 176, 217, 293, 302
Clarkson
  Mary R. 272
Clausant
  Derick 210
Clem
  Elizabeth 234
  John 184, 234
Clemmes
  Alexander 253
Clendenny
  Jannekie 226
  Walter 226
  Walter Jr. 286
Cobb
  Lemuel 281
  Samuel 240, 241, 281, 283
Cochran
  James 54
Cocoro
  Nicholas 179
Codweis
  Benjamin 36
  John Conrad 2, 3, 5, 6, 8, 10, 12, 14, 20, 22, 28, 41
Coe
  John 83
  Martha 202
  Mathew D. 212
  Matthew D. 202
Coff
  Jacob 158
Cogh
  Johann Caspar 39
Cole
  Adrian 303
  Barent 147, 151, 296, 301
  Barnet 248, 269
  Benjamin 252

David 270
Henry 177, 191, 216, 286
Jacob 296, 305
Jacob J. 230
John 286
Peter 77, 125, 160, 221, 230, 231, 286, 296
Samuel 183, 230
Sarah 230
Widow 305
Willet 193
Colfax
  Hester 195
  Robert 306
  Will 305
  William 91, 95, 156, 159, 179, 195, 219, 221, 224, 261, 277, 282, 288
Collard
  Charity 185
  Jacob 286
  James 142
  John 157, 185, 285
Collins
  Abraham 147, 164, 220, 293
  Catharine 164
  John 132, 175, 194, 215, 217, 277, 292
Collogh
  Eva 71
  James M. 71
Colm
  Robert 288
Comfort
  Gerard 31
Concklin
  Elizabeth 200
  Hester 199
  Isaac 53, 54, 70, 81
  Jacob 199, 200, 296
  Jacob Jr. 199
  James 296
  John 1
  Joseph 297
  Lewis 121
  Lewis S. 256
  Mathew 278
  Williaim 264
  William 254
  William Jr. 254
Conder
  John 295
Condict
  John 250
  Silas 281
  Theodotia 281
Conselyea
  John 257
Cooder
  John 270
  Rachel 270
Cook
  Eliza T. 281
  Francis 135, 305
  Henry 306
  Michael 80, 305
Cooly
  Barent 27
  Benjamin 288
  Benjamin Jr. 288
  Margarita 27
Coomus
  George 286
  Richard 286
Cooper
  Ann 168, 173, 255, 282
  Anne 146
  Clyde Johnston 1
  Cornelius 15, 68, 69, 146, 149, 168, 173, 269, 282, 301

Derick　270
　　Gilbert　153
　　Hendrick　66, 283
　　Henry　267
　　John　220, 235
　　Lucas　279
　　Margretye　66
　　Peter　255
　　Richard　90, 204,
　　　236, 255, 258,
　　　259, 265, 288
　　Richard J.　220,
　　　255
　　Richard P.　269
Cornelius
　　John　9, 76, 210,
　　　212
　　Lawrence　136
Cornell
　　Luke　297
Corsen
　　Cort　40
　　Mary　80
Corson
　　Daniel　247
　　Elizabeth　247
Corteen
　　Albert　11
　　Garret　3, 4, 11
　　John　10
　　Potter　10
Cortlandt
　　Jacobus　24
　　Jaque　40
　　John　16
　　Philip　210
Corvill
　　Benjamin　286
CoSaart
　　David　39
Couenoven
　　Eve　295
　　Jacob　295
Cough
　　Albert　302
　　Casparus　201,
　　　292, 302, 304
　　Caty　201
　　Cough　277
　　Elias　201
　　Hendrica　276
　　Jacob　97, 106,
　　　134, 207, 289
　　Jacobus　75, 136
　　James　289
　　Joost　200, 231,
　　　274, 276, 277,
　　　303, 304
　　Joost Jr.　276
　　Maria　97
　　Mary　75, 134,
　　　192, 200, 207,
　　　276
Coulter
　　William　216
Courter
　　Peter　192
　　William　197
Covashausen
　　Jacob　59
Cowerover
　　Johanna　132
　　Samuel　132
Crain
　　John　229
Cranck (See
　　Cronkhite)
　　Gentry　126
　　Mathew　126
Crane
　　Abigail　198, 202
　　John　229
　　Joseph Jr.　254
　　Sally　254
　　Sayer　105
Crannell
　　Robert Jr.　26
Crawford
　　Patrick　242
　　William　288
Creyan
　　Patrick　221

Crins
　Frederick 104
　Nartman 186
Crofts
　Charles 242
　Mary 242
　Richard 242
Crolius
　Mary 193
　William 193
Cromline
　Charles 12
　Daniel 11
　Daniole 12
Cronk
　Isaac 303
　Matthew 306
Cronkhite
　Gentry 83, 181
　Mathew 83, 135, 181
Crookshank
　Alexander 71
Crum
　William 211, 285
Crummil
　John 293
Cubberly
　Jacob 268
　Thomas 177, 268, 286
Cully
　Daniel 300
Cumming
　John G. 219, 220
　John N. 253, 258
　John Noble 252
　Sally 252
　William J. 254
Currie
　Alexander 300
Curtis
　Joseph 206
Cutting
　William 170
Cuyler

　Barnt R. 197
　Henry 196, 197, 205, 242
Dad
　Jonathan 304
Dadbs
　James 290
Daily
　John 132, 133, 286
Daly
　John 133
Damar
　John 305
Dampin
　Thomas 242
Daniel
　Thomas M. Jr. 272
Danielsen
　Ann 7, 13
　David 7, 13, 19, 24, 35, 47
　William 177, 285
Darcy
　Augustine 123, 151
Daty
　Abraham 297
Davenport
　Amfrid 102
　Cornelius 182, 183, 202, 305
　Humphry 182, 183
　Jacob 183
　John 182, 183, 305
　John L. 306
　John M. 182
　John U. 305
　Leonard 182, 183
　Nathaniel 182
　Peter 202
Davey
　Cujuthine 132
　William 210
David

James 60
Davis
  Elizabeth 254,
    257, 264
  James 35, 227
  Joannis 1
  Jonathan 198
  Samuel 70
  Thomas 299
  Timothy 227, 228
  Widow 228
  William 144, 153,
    154, 185, 299
Daviss
  John 4
Dawesa
  Paul 45
Dawson
  Thomas 300
Day
  Abigail 257
  Abraham 68
  Ann 11
  Benjamin 149,
    163, 171, 184,
    186, 187, 255,
    258
  Daniel 216
  David 65, 67,
    171, 186, 255,
    258, 295, 306
  Derick 35, 49,
    126, 256
  Elias 91, 140,
    179, 198, 295
  Hannah 181, 184
  Hendrick 50
  Henry 44, 76, 257
  Isaac 51, 281,
    290
  Jacob 44, 216,
    226
  Jane 226, 227
  John 25, 45,
    50-52, 55, 59,
    63-67, 76, 83,
    89, 111, 115,
    119, 120, 134,
    135, 137-139,
    146, 147, 149,
    151, 152, 155,
    157, 163, 171,
    177, 179, 180,
    184, 186, 191,
    192, 195, 213,
    214, 216, 227,
    234, 237,
    255-260, 295
  John D. 306
  John Jr. 57, 214
  John W. 67
  Mary 198
  Michael 234
  Naomi 55, 66, 191
  Nathaniel 226,
    227
  Peter 129, 155,
    171, 186, 255,
    258
  Phebe 137, 155
  Philip 171, 184,
    186, 255, 258
  Phillip 133, 134,
    303
  Richard 84, 99,
    107, 118, 137,
    138, 140, 142,
    170, 171, 176,
    179, 181, 184,
    186, 255, 258,
    266, 267, 279,
    303
  Soloman 290
  Teunis 126
  Thomas 234, 255,
    256, 306
  Thunis 255
  William 11, 12,
    50-52, 216, 226,
    285, 286, 295
  William Ancha 67
  William W. 67

Daykins
  Robert 12
Dayling
  William 14
Dayton
  Elias 83, 88
de Mumorus
  Peter Samuel 251
Dean
  George 288
Debane
  Carrol 16, 21,
    49, 57
  Isaac 51
  Jacob 48, 110,
    150, 163
  James 163
  Peter 110
Debard
  Peter 291
DeBaun
  Abraham 205, 208,
    212, 296
  Andrew 290
  Ann 212
  Carel P. 297
  Carl 114, 249,
    290
  Charles Prendhomme
    251-253, 268
  Isaac 265, 298
  Jacob 259, 290,
    298, 301
  Jacob Jr. 290
  Jacob P. 270
  Jacob T. 255
  Jacobus 290
  John 240, 249,
    270, 279, 290,
    298
  Joost 33, 290
  Myntie 210, 250
  Peter 204, 210,
    250, 294, 298
  Petrus 255, 258,
    290

  Yan 212
DeBorre
  Charles Henry
    Lambert Mary
    Trierdhommel
    201
Decker
  Abraham 194, 305
  Cornelius 291
  John 295
  William 237, 291
DeCrimsheir
  John 56
Dedrix
  Abraham 132
  Cornelius 178
  Daniel 177, 212,
    251, 286
  Daniel S. 286
  Garret 178
  Hester 177
  Johannis 177
  John 210, 212,
    232, 273
Degraw
  Ann 256
  Casparus 122,
    150, 174, 184,
    216, 230, 299
  Charles 291
  Cornelius 289,
    299
  Elenor 230
  Elizabeth 75
  Francis 299
  Garret 289
  Jacob 249, 285
  Johannes 290
  John 75, 249,
    256, 273, 304
  Leander 247
  Lenah 304
  Leonard 230, 249,
    256, 296
  Lundert 75
  Peter 122, 294

Richard 75, 83,
    148, 175, 238,
    249, 256, 280,
    304
William 20, 296
Degroot
  Aaeto 68
  Aates 68
  Ary 51
  Arya 52
  Aury 50, 295
  Belloman 251
  Celena 132
  Cornelius 295
  Halamar 214
  Hester 119
  Jacob 132, 133,
    152, 166, 191,
    214, 234, 237,
    257, 295
  Jacobus 249
  Jeremiah 295
  Johannah 237
  John 132, 133,
    157, 191, 234,
    293
  Joost Jr. 290
  Nicholas 271, 276
  Niclas 293
  Peter 50-52, 55,
    119, 152, 177,
    214, 295, 301
  Peter A. 119,
    257, 295
  Peter Sr. 132
  Statts 141
Degruis
  William 292
DeHensck
  John 174
Dehuys
  John 291
Dekey
  Christian 46
  Thomas 35, 47,
    48, 51

Delaney
  Oliver 196, 198,
    205, 212
Delemater
  Abraham 229, 235,
    247, 296
  Isaac 145, 146,
    273, 296
  Isack 68
  John 203
Demarest
  Aaron 89
  Abraham 100, 111,
    125, 172, 180,
    203, 230, 262,
    278, 296
  Abraham D. 262
  Abraham G. 297
  Albert 293
  Anne 168
  Antye 168
  Aria 40
  Benjamin 49, 294
  Benjamin D. 277
  Benjamin P. 81
  Casparus 293
  Catharine 166
  Cornelius 112,
    191, 278, 298
  Daniel 68, 162,
    172, 191, 211,
    236, 269, 275
  Daniel D. 105,
    276, 294
  Daniel J. 276,
    294
  Daniel N. 294
  Daniel S. 89
  David 8, 10, 16,
    20, 21, 31, 33,
    34, 40, 41, 48,
    49, 53, 54, 59,
    66, 75, 125,
    130, 137, 150,
    166, 184, 190,
    195, 203, 204,

221, 232, 238,
247, 293,
296-298
David A. 267
David Au. 265
David D. 90, 294
David J. 294
David Jacobus 77
David Jr. 9, 40,
49
David P. 81, 166,
168, 204, 205,
294
David R. 294
David S. 90, 207,
294
David Samuel 40,
203, 205
David Samuel Jr.
40
David Sr. 40
Davis S. 294
Derick 301
Effie 276
Elizabeth 270,
271, 276
Garret 262, 276,
294, 297
Grant D. 294
Guilliam 70, 151,
211, 220, 247,
293
Hendrick 105, 297
Hester 166
Jacob 16, 17, 51,
57, 89, 119,
222, 231, 236,
294, 304
Jacob D. 243,
277, 278, 294
Jacob P. 81, 203
Jacobus 209, 262,
271, 288, 293,
297, 298
Jacobus D. 262,
294

Jacobus J. 247,
270, 271, 293
Jacobus Jr. 276
Jacobus P. 149,
205
James 138, 163,
180, 188, 190,
202, 212, 234,
235, 240, 241,
247, 266, 298,
304
James C. 278
James D. 231,
240, 276
Jane 293
Jasper 163, 194,
202
Johannes 57, 278
Johannis 53, 54,
57
Johanny 71
John 7, 14, 49,
137, 145, 168,
190, 194, 195,
203, 204, 236,
255, 262, 271,
275, 293, 298,
301
John D. 262, 275,
277, 294
John J. 90, 133,
293
John Johan 168
John Jr. 33
John P. 81, 203
John Peter 205
John Sr. 32, 33
Joost 70, 117,
157, 207, 301
Lea 49, 67, 97
Magdalena 243
Maria 208
Mary 10, 20, 67,
240, 241, 278
Matye 208
Nelly 277, 278

Nicholas 302
Peter 40, 102,
 106, 112, 166,
 174, 184,
 203-205, 208,
 211, 231, 262,
 269, 291, 294,
 295, 297, 298
Peter D. 97, 262,
 289
Peter Day 114
Peter J. 105,
 106, 236, 276,
 293, 294
Peter Jac 293
Peter John 203
Peter P. 81, 215,
 271, 301
Peter S. 124, 294
Pieter 106
Pieter Y. 57
Potter 14
Rachel 163, 202
Roelif 105, 142,
 174, 294, 295
Roelif D. 276,
 294
Samuel 8, 10,
 100, 130, 160,
 162, 190, 195,
 203, 204, 294,
 296, 298, 302
Samuel B. 135
Samuel C. 142
Samuel Jr. 40
Samuel P. 137,
 248
Samuel Sr. 10,
 20, 39, 168
Samuel Symese 162
Sarah 66, 236
Simon 10, 20, 31,
 40, 78, 125, 293
Simon D. 294
Simon David 40
Simson 96

Susannah 70
Thomas 297
Widow 211
Wilhelmina 137
William 294
William D. 90
Demeray
 Johannis 57
Demeyer
 H. 34, 49
Demilt
 Isaac 290
Demisten
 Dominic 103
Demoldt
 Jores 116
Demoot
 Jacob 82
 Mattis 62
 Peter Ja 134
Demoresque
 Jacob 23
 John 23
 Nicholas 23
 Sarah 23
DeMott
 Clasen Matty 38
 Franseynlie 260
 George 72, 139,
  253
 Hendrick 68
 Henry 295, 306
 Jacob 68, 159,
  259, 294
 John 100, 125,
  215, 234, 259,
  295
 Jorie 68
 Mathias 4, 11, 68
 Matire 61
 Matthias 11
 Mattys 145, 159
 Michael 68, 212,
  287
 Sinety 259
Demsey

Elizabeth 69
Dennis
  Anthony 126, 172
Dennison
  Daniel 193
Denny
  Hendrick 117
  Henry 85, 93, 95, 163
  Mary 85, 163
DeNoyillas
  John 55
Depeyster
  Abraham W. 267, 300
Der Vorst
  Peter Samuel 251
Derbryk
  Bernardus 288
Derge
  John 285
Derick
  Daniel 150, 212
Deriemer
  Johannis 49
Derpey
  Nicholas 96
Desbrosses
  Ralleau Andre 20
Devaster
  Abraham 297
Devaul
  Edward 286
  James 285
Devaux
  Nicholas 42
Dever
  William 42
DeVime
  Ann 81
  Peter 81
Devisme
  Ann 231
Devoe
  John 286
Devone

  Aaron 226, 285, 295
  Abraham 253, 293, 301
  C. Greudhornme 231
  Frederick 285
  John 293
DeWitte
  Jan 39
Deylog
  Richard 83
DeYoung
  Joan Los Marsl
  Jandos Marosl 7
Dick 103
Dickson
  Jonathan 294
  Thomas 286
Dicterison
  John 286
Dideson
  David 147
Diedericks
  Abraham 178, 210
  Anna 207
  Cornelius 178
  Daniel 178
  Garret 160, 178
  Hannes 146
  Johannes 96, 178
  John 207, 253, 282
  Wander 38, 178
  Wendel 1
Dierei
  Jan 105
Dillon
  Patrick 107
Dinah 103
Disendors
  Bernardos 285
Dobbs
  Catherine 193
  Joseph 193
  William 74, 193

Dobs
  John 305
Dobuckerman
  Abram 285
Docary
  William 10
Dodd
  John 257
  Jonathan 159
Donetson
  Daniel 171
Donewise
  Poulus 3
Donley
  Andrew 300
Dooly
  Abner 288
  Benjamin 288
Dooremus
  Aagye 131
  Affey 126
  Cornelius 32, 61,
    171, 206, 215,
    286, 306
  Cornelius H. 206
  David 304
  Effie 131
  George 35, 58,
    126, 130, 136,
    140, 171, 222,
    258, 292, 299,
    304
  George C. 306
  George G. 190
  George H. 126
  George J. 258
  Gorlyme 62
  Hendrick 61, 124,
    131, 171
  Henry 219, 277,
    303, 304, 306
  Hessel 79, 189,
    304
  Jacob 101, 270,
    306
  Jacob B. 304
  Jan 61
  John 101, 126,
    130, 181, 284,
    290
  John H. 304
  Nancy 101
  Nelly 270
  Peter 303
  Roelif 306
  Simon 169, 257
  Stynlia 206
  Styntia 206
  Thomas 35
Doty
  Ferres 219
  Pharis 305
Dougery
  Francis 301
Douglas
  George 107
  William 7, 61,
    188
Dow
  William 122, 140,
    227, 228, 302
Dowese
  Paul 61
Dowsen
  Herman 58
  Tunis 58
Doyal
  Henry 305
  Phillip 306
Doyle
  Henry 176
Drake
  Cornelius 32
  Marytie 32
Drummond
  Elshe 172
  James 152, 165,
    233
  John 120, 139,
    172, 304, 305
  Rachel 152, 165
  Robert 172, 174,

336

304
William 116, 136,
  241, 304
Duane
  James 52
Dubois
  Benjamin 187
  Peter 56, 170,
    185
Dudley
  John 195, 236
Duffield
  John 153, 189
  Samuel 153, 189
Duffy
  Archibald 306
  Mary 203, 293
Dugan
  Matilda 300
  Thomas 194
  widow 163
Dulark
  Daniel 296
Dumon
  Justine 300
Duncan
  Elisabeth 44
  George 24, 45, 46
  James 18, 24, 35,
    44-46, 62, 145,
    159
  Martha 46
  Mary 46
  Michael 45, 46
  Thomas 46, 263
  William 293
Dunham
  Azariah 75, 144
  James 144, 159
Dunlap
  John 86, 158
Dunnom
  Azariah 270
Dunscomb
  Edward 209
Dupont

E. J. 251
Durcell
  Philip 257
  Phillip 295
Durie
  Anatta 242
  Daniel 78, 79,
    119
  David 106, 120,
    125, 172, 296
  Elizabeth 242
  Garret 106, 297
  Jan 34, 106, 120
  Jan Sr. 51, 120
  John 10, 20, 21,
    34, 40, 49, 54,
    70, 95, 105,
    106, 158, 227,
    259, 296
  John J. 227
  John P. 106, 158,
    179
  John Sr. 106
  Mary 227
  Paul 241, 242
  Peter 114, 269
  Potter 2
  Samuel 78, 97,
    159, 297
  Simon 81, 241,
    242, 296
  Vannetye 78, 79
  Weyntye 78
Dusell
  Phillip 152
Dust
  John 300
Dutches
  David 288
Duval
  John 242
Duzan
  Martha 86
Dyckman
  Rebecca 107
  Richard 292

Sampson 107
William 97
Dyke
    William 193
Earle 199
    Abigil 21
    Alice 42
    Andrew 70
    Antebe 285
    Antelbee 57
    Anthony 57
    Antilby 80
    Byneon 172
    Clausia 172
    Edward 1, 2, 5,
        15, 26-28, 31,
        53, 123, 151,
        172, 173, 291
    Edward Jr. 1, 19,
        22, 25, 26, 31,
        42
    Edward Sr. 5, 42
    Elias 285
    Elisabeth 5
    Eliza 57
    Elizabeth 57, 80,
        259
    Elsey 172, 272
    Enoch 31
    Francytie 42
    Hannah 15, 31
    Henry 111, 285
    Henry W. 285
    Jacob 300
    James 285, 286,
        288
    John 21, 31, 130,
        136, 138,
        149-151, 153,
        154, 172, 173,
        221, 223, 249,
        254, 259, 272,
        286, 301, 303
    John E. 285
    John S. 149
    Joost 59

M. D. 48
Marmaduke 31, 48
Mary 63, 64, 172,
    199, 203
Morris 208, 300
Nathaniel 42,
    226, 285
Peter 70
Philip 31, 56,
    57, 80, 173
Phillip 151
Rebecca 31, 48
Rebekah 48
Reynier 144, 192,
    285
Richard 130, 150,
    151, 153, 154,
    173, 199, 286
Robert 63, 64,
    191, 199, 285
Silvester 31, 34,
    54, 58
Veautye 80
William 31, 34,
    38, 54, 55, 69,
    116, 159, 203,
    285
William Jr. 55
Eaton
    Catharine 226
    Richard 176, 216,
        217
Ebbets
    Daniel J. 251
Eckerson
    Abraham 227
    Anganietye 208
    Annatie 208
    Catharine 156
    Cornelia 208
    Cornelius 227,
        296
    Daniel 76
    David 156, 208,
        211
    David Jacob Thomas

208
Edward 156, 208, 297
Garret 271, 296
Hannah 208
Hendrick 208
Jacob 208, 297
John 208, 297
John I. 292
Lenah 208
Maria 208
Peter 208
Sarah 208
Thomas 200, 208, 245, 296, 297
Thomas Sr. 208
Yanitye 208
Eckhert
  Joost 289
Edowson
  Henry 299
Edsall
  Adolph Phillip 45
  Hila 44
  Jacob 191, 237, 295
  James 53
  John 14, 15, 24, 25, 50-52, 57, 295
  Mary 45, 50-52
  Philip 44
  Richard 19, 21-24, 27-29, 31, 35, 39, 44, 47, 49
  Richard Jr. 283
  Richard Sr. 103
  Ruth 44
  Samuel 24, 30, 35, 41, 45, 47, 48, 51, 52, 59, 67, 133, 157, 295
  Suly 283
Edtsler

  Ellen 261
  Henry 261
Edwards
  Herman 11
  Joseph 304
Egbert
  Casparus 189
  Peter 189
  Walling Jr. 189
Elbertse
  Elbert 40
Eleves
  John 242
Eley
  Benjamin 74
Ellis
  James 135
  Samuel 191, 192, 270, 295
  William 216, 234
Ellison
  Henry 75, 241, 242
  Isaac 306
Elsworth
  Ahasucrus 110
  George 110
  Nicholas 24
  Sarah 23, 24
  Theophilus 23, 24
  Vardine 285
  William 286
Ely
  Mary 271, 276
  William 247, 270, 271, 276, 293
Emott
  James 9
  John 110
  Mary 110
Engle
  A. 251
  Andrew 195, 199, 285
  Janet 195
Epkoy

Cornelius 9
Derick 9
Hendrick 9
Ernis
  James 122, 174, 230, 299
  John 216
  William 39, 40, 75, 111, 121, 122
Erwin
  Nancy 294
  Walter 198
Ester
  Johannes 59
Esterlin
  Johannes 59
Ettis
  William 227
Everitt
  George 288
Everson
  Jacob 132, 286
  Jeremiah 299
  John 135, 286
  John S. 286
Faboucough
  John 152
Fair
  William 300
Fairbarin
  John 134
Farcle
  Rachel 251
Farmar
  Jasper 50, 52
  Maria 50, 52
Farmer
  Thomas 39
Farrand
  Ebenezer 240
Fashun
  Abraham 242
Fauconnier
  Peter 20, 25, 33, 36, 38, 47, 50, 51, 60, 70
  Potter 14
  Theodore 14
Featherstone
  Culbert 300
Fector
  Joseph 304
Fedeback
  John 292
Fell
  John 60, 63, 70, 242, 291
  Peter 185
  Susannah 185
Fellis 103
Felter
  John 244, 250, 251
Ferd
  John 89
Ferderiks
  Henry 289
Ferdon
  Abraham 62, 172
  Jacob 296
  Johannes 244, 296
  Johannis 52
  John 73, 183, 241, 296
  Wilhelm 72, 113
  Wilhelmus 229, 244, 245
  William 73
  William H. 245, 296
Ferguson
  Samuel 292
Feurt
  Bartholomew 1, 12, 25, 35, 110
  Breishetome 5
  Hans Balho 5
  Magdalena 1, 12, 35
Field
  Joseph 114

Rodman 111
Fielding
  Aghye 300
  Akeyea 178
  Daniel 300
  Echie 243
Fielts
  John 189
  Joseph 189
Fine
  John 250
Finn
  Elizabeth 67
  George 301
  Robert 67
  Soloman 67
Firk
  Nicholas 111
Firm
  Elizabeth 172
Firshead
  Barent 289
  Cornelius 289
Fish
  John 270
  Nicholas 111
  Rachel 270
Fishback
  Stephen 290
Fisher
  Catherine 63
  David 290
  Isaac 288
  John 69, 124
  Michael 165, 290
  Michael Jr. 290
  Peter 63, 102, 288
  William 303
Fitch
  Joseph 55, 56
  Mary 55, 56
Fleerboom
  Elizabeth 253
  Jacob 205, 298
  Jacobus 158

  John 158, 253, 273, 298
Fleming
  James 82
  John 73
Folch
  Abraham 36
  Hendrick 39
Folks
  Henry 111
Folly
  William 275
Forbie
  Joseph 68
Ford
  David 246
  John 304
  Nicholas 304
Forger
  Samuel 208
Forman
  Affey 103
  Cuphemia 103
  Lewis 103
Forshear
  Abraham 233, 239, 249, 250, 264
  Barent 297
  Cornelius 297
  David 264, 297
  Elizabeth 239, 249, 250
  John 264, 297
  Mary 264
  Polly 264
  William 240, 249
Forster
  Mille 21
  Rebeca 21
Foru
  Obediah 304
Foster
  Ebenezer 57
Fountaine
  Peter 285
Foust

Arthur 242
Fox
  Conrad 290
  Coomack 88
  David 289
  Henry 289
  Jacobus 137
  John 131, 289
  William 289
Fradries
  Henry 304
Francis
  Mathias 21
  Thomas 5, 6, 20, 22, 34
Francisco
  Gilbert 306
  Jacob 306
  John 284
  Nathaniel 305
  Peter 280, 281, 305
  Peter H. 306
  Richard Jr. 283
  Will 306
  Yellis 305
Franks
  Thomas 31
Frasher
  George 286
Fredericksen
  Andris 17
  Hendrick Jr. 106
  Henry 292
  Robert 231
  Thomas 11, 17, 20, 109, 153
Freeland
  Abraham 306
  Abraham Jr. 306
  James 305
  John A. 306
  John D. 305
  John E. 305
  Michael 270, 305
  Richard D. 305

Freligh
  Solomon 125, 146, 168, 171-173, 205, 294
Fresch
  John Jacob 242
Fresnean
  Andrew 14, 20, 33, 36, 38, 70
Fritch
  John 224
  Petertie 224
Fuerk
  John Jacob 87
Fullwood
  Charles Hade 145
  Charles Slade 152, 270
Furlo
  James 299
Gach
  Thomas 57
Gale
  Anthony R. 221
  Samuel 131, 251
Gardner
  Elijah 285
  Genioh 89
  John 26
  Thomas 104, 163, 301
Garrabrants
  Abraham 146
  Cornelius 3, 52, 146, 160, 179, 251, 285
  Garrabrant 146, 184, 195, 300
  Garrabrants 52
  Garrebrant 193
  Harp 39, 121
  Harper 193
  Harport 25
  Harps 111
  Jacob 226
  Jacob Jr. 228

Mindert 285
Peter 286
Garretson 302
  Abraham 14, 15,
    41, 54, 58, 81,
    167, 221, 232
  Abraham G. 289
  Abraham H. 288
  Abraham J. 288
  Ann 13
  Aury 289
  Cornelius 148
  Elisabeth 13
  Garrabrant 62,
    175, 303
  Garret 4, 7, 8,
    13-15, 40, 41,
    62, 65, 81, 167,
    178, 221, 232,
    261, 262, 303
  Garret Ivers 7
  Garret Jr. 8, 13,
    303
  Gartia 219
  Helmegh 288
  Henry 213
  Herman 18
  Hessel 303
  Jacob 15, 213,
    282
  Jacobus 13, 14
  Johann 11
  Johannes 7, 58,
    167
  Johannis 13, 15,
    38
  John 41, 109,
    200, 213, 219,
    231, 241, 274,
    277, 303
  John C. 180
  John G. 241, 249
  John H. 120, 206,
    222, 241, 250,
    274, 304
  John J. 303
  John P. 175, 303
  Jursoa 178
  Margaret 206
  Mary 261
  Nelly 241
  Neshe 221
  Netie 232
  Nise 7, 13-15
  Peter 41, 167,
    221, 232
  Potter 7, 14, 15
  Rachel 221, 232
  Samuel 127
Gaugy
  John M. 202
Gault
  Robert 158
Gautier
  Andrew 173, 202,
    209, 252
  Elisa 268
  Eliza 202, 268
  Elizabeth 202
  Hannah 202, 209,
    252
  Thomas 202, 225,
    268
Geiner
  John 200
  John Sr. 200
Genchen
  John 95
Genst
  John Jr. 42
Gerais
  Benjamin 292
  Daniel 292
Gessamer
  Nicholas 296
Gibney
  James 305
Gibson
  William 274
Giese
  Reynier N. 57-59,
    62

Gilbert
  Aaron 142, 296
  Ann 142
  Hannah 155
Gill
  John 152, 189, 216, 302
Gillam
  Mocal 277
Gillenland
  Thomas 237
  Thomas J. 221
Gisner
  John 200
Glason
  Michael 299
Glass
  Robert 303
Goble
  Luther 257
Godwin
  Abraham 87, 109, 147, 284
  David 122, 234, 250
  Henry 63, 65, 69
  Phebe 87
Goelet
  Catharine 110
  Catherine 143
  Mary 110
Goings
  Joseph 302
Gold
  Robert 283
Gorden
  Cata 293
  Joseph 296
Gotrius
  Nathan 244
Gould
  Abraham 80, 305
  Encreas 227
  Encuas 270
  John A. 305
  Robert 192, 306

Gouverneur 33
  Abraham 16, 23, 25, 29, 39, 46, 49, 51, 52, 53, 164, 189
  Abraham N. 53
  Elisabeth 52
  Isaac 187
  Jacoba 50, 52
  Margret 121
  Maria 52
  Mary 50
  Nicholas 50, 52, 120, 121, 198
  Samuel 120, 121, 198
Graaf
  Martin 292
Graham
  Welhelm 297
Gramm
  David 242
  Hanna 151
Grant
  Ann 76
  Hermanus 10
  William 76, 78
  Zephaniah 155
Grathan
  John 303
Graves
  Boonen 201
Greenless
  Robert 285
  Robert R. 285
Gremow
  Jacob D. 191
Griffith
  John 63
Grigg
  John 154, 155
Grimes
  Patrick 287
Griswold
  Joseph 88, 97
  Sarah 97

Groff
  Morter 271
Grumman
  Hannah 113
  Ichabod 113, 173
Guard
  Daniel 305
Guest
  John 29
Guilliam
  John 305
  Michael 304
Gunter
  John 255
Gutchens
  Peyathes 210
Hackert
  F. 54
Hackinback
  George 104, 169
Haconbac
  George 297
Hageman
  Peter 96
Hagen
  Martin 296
Haigs
  Mary 21
  Obadiah 21
Haily
  Jacob 20
Hall
  Ann 24
  Antia 219
  Hannah 48
  Richard 24
  Thomas 219
Hallen
  Theodore 58
  William 147
Hallet
  Jacob 204
  Jacob W. 204
  James 199
  Phebe 199
  Robert 199

  Susanna 204
Halsey
  David 153, 303
  Phebe 153
Halsted
  Jonathan 303
  Joseph 202
  Matthias 126, 144
Hamilton
  John 42, 69, 77
Hamman
  Isaac 203, 214
Hammel
  Elizabeth 186
  William 89, 96,
    138, 186, 301
Hammon
  Isaac 295
  Thomas 288
Hammond
  Elisha 107
  Maria 285
Hampton
  Jonathan 61, 191
Hancock
  John 304
Hand
  Abraham 260, 291
Hankinson
  Joseph Jr. 281
Hanly
  Patrick 159
Hannebal 54
Hanson
  Holkosh 14
Harding
  Henry 8, 12
  Isabella 12
Hardwick
  Nicholas 29, 95
Harehart
  Christopher 295
Haring
  Abraham 11, 73,
    102, 146, 230,
    232, 236, 240,

245, 252, 296, 298
Abraham A. 236
Abraham Abr. 73
Abraham David 248, 250
Abraham J. 227, 247
Angenike 100
Cornelius 16, 20, 75, 77, 82, 84, 89, 92, 93, 96-98, 101-107, 111, 118, 120, 122, 124, 128, 129, 131, 144, 146, 148, 159, 163, 164, 169, 174, 195, 216, 249, 297, 298
Cornelius D. 120, 244, 249
Daniel 70, 83, 105, 199, 201, 235, 247, 296
Daniel D. 88, 100
Daniel J. 247
Daniel Sr. 120
David 81, 90, 112, 113, 143, 150, 236, 291, 296
David A. 228, 229, 244
David P. 159, 271, 277
Derick 241, 296
Doruko 11
Elbert J. 204
Elizabeth 199, 226, 232, 235
Fred 296
Fredrick 247
Fredrick G. 227
Garret F. 240, 241

Hendrick 120, 297
Jacob 100, 194, 205, 262, 289, 296
Jacob C. 120
Johannes 296
Johannes T. 296
Johannis 16
John 72, 84, 96, 97, 104, 120, 132, 144, 148, 158, 169, 170, 182, 183, 195, 197, 203, 204, 210, 212, 243, 245, 251, 264, 268, 276, 281, 289, 296, 297
John C. 146, 253
John D. 235
John D. Sr. 182
John David 227, 230, 236-238, 240, 241, 243, 244, 248, 250, 258, 259, 262, 275
John F. 229, 296
John J. 229
John Jr. 289
Mary 158, 228, 229
Peter 40, 73, 81, 82, 84, 89, 103, 187, 226, 277, 296, 297
Peter A. 229, 296
Petrus 72, 75, 78, 93, 102, 129, 148, 159, 174, 180, 182, 200, 229, 230, 232, 234, 235, 240, 241, 243, 244, 247
Peturs 240, 273

Pronsy 296
Saley 194
Samuel 226
Sarah 205, 240
Harkone
  Patience 44
Harmansen
  Annetye 30
  Dauwe 41
  Dofew 4
  Dow 11
  Dowg 4
  Hans 30
  Tryntie 30
Harpinding
  Andrew 288
Harrah
  Ezekiel 116
Harriman
  John 24
Harrington
  Eber 288
Harris
  Ann 76
  Anna 91
  Anne 101, 140
  Anny 91
  Caty 77
  Ezekiel 67
  Henry 40, 129,
    138, 201, 222
  Jan 16
  John 76, 77, 79,
    291, 295
  Joseph 79
  Nashie 222
  Thomas 91, 133,
    134, 295
  Zukano 9
Harrison
  Elizabeth 183
  John 299
  Thomas 180
Harsmander
  Daniel 41
Hart
  Bernard 164, 166
  Patience 49, 67
  Thomas 49, 67
Hartmann
  Elias 3
  Enoch 3
  Fytis 210
  Luke 2
  Vitio 3
Hartone
  Thomas 44
Hartwick
  Johanis 21
Harty
  Johanes 21
Harwell
  Edmund 82
Hasenclever
  Peter 198
Hasenfrax
  Peter 295
Haspending
  Andrew 157
  Maria 157
Hast
  Jacob 300
Haswell
  Edward 150
Havner
  John 282
Hawden
  Michael 62, 166,
    281
Hawenclever
  Peter 242, 282
Hawlenbeck
  Garret 49, 62-64,
    103, 139, 273,
    306
  Hannah 64, 273
  Isaac 116, 139,
    141, 176, 306
  Isaac Jr. 134
  Jacob 113
Haycock
  Daniel 305

Thomas 305
Hayes
  Samuel 220
Hazard
  Mary 220
  Thomas 220, 221
Healy
  Daniel 289
  Joseph 48, 49, 67
Hearny
  James 168
Heart
  Michael 91
Heathen
  John 147, 293
  Peter 293
  Richard 100, 125, 205, 293
Heavner
  John 214, 215
Hebberd
  John 271
Hedden
  James 258
  Job 111
  Phebe 111
Heffener
  John 286
Helm
  Benjamin 98, 218
  Cornelius 303
  Daniel 294, 302
  Elizabeth 218
  John 304
  Martin 304
  Samuel 215, 255, 269, 283
  Syntye 302
  Tunes 302
  William 305
Hempton
  Jonathan 278
Hendricksen
  Hendrick 103
  John 111
Hendrix

Francis 35, 36, 38
Hennion
  Abraham 305
  Andres 58
  Andrew 264, 289
  Annetyo 8
  Catharine 59
  Catrena 190
  Caty 264
  Cornelius 140, 159, 166, 167, 172, 181, 185, 304
  Daniole 8
  David 59-61, 67, 71, 190, 241, 286, 290, 304
  David D. 145, 304
  David Daniolson 8
  David J. 145, 185
  David P. 305
  Garret 140, 141, 145, 170
  Henry 136, 200, 306
  Hessel 306
  Jacob 290
  Johannis 8, 60
  John 60, 101, 116, 155, 199, 290
  John A. 305
  John I. 304
  Mary 140, 141
  Peter 105, 264, 289
  Tennes 60
  Teunis 145
  Theumis 131
  Thumis 97
  Thunis 306
  Thunis J. 304
  Tunis 60
  William 289
Herde

Robert 195
Hernt
  John 95
Herrnig
  Daniel 51, 54
Heyden
  S. 71
Hibbard
  John 205, 220
  John D. 210
Hicks
  John 291
Hide
  Jesse 286
Higgs
  Richard 306
Hilbrant 91
Hilcocks
  George 60
Hill
  Andrew 56
  Anthony 56, 74
  Robert 63, 92
  Roland 141, 301
  Rowland 64, 71, 172
  Uriah 56, 74
  William 56
Hillem
  Samuel 274
Himeon
  Nicholas 289
Hinselpecker
  John 292
Hisbee
  Henry 291
Hock
  Jacobus 134
Hodge
  James 168, 173, 223
  Sarah 223
Hoeghoost
  Gerard 146
Hoffman
  Josiah Ogden 163

Martin 163, 166
Nicholas 164
Rinehart 295
Hogan
  John 187, 288
  Joseph 288
Hogelandt
  Francis 119
Hogencamp
  Altia 235, 247
  Altye 235
  John 296
  John M. 190
  Martin 226, 229
  Martin J. 235, 247
  Martynes 235
Hoiler
  Cornelius 285
Holcomb
  Jonathan A. 290
Holder
  Jan 215
Holdipp
  Hillcord 12
  Mary 12
Holdrum
  William 265
Holly
  William 291
Holmes
  Benjamin 56
  Martin 175
  Ninian 302
Holter
  Andrew 286
  William 286
Homer
  John 288
Hooper
  Robert Lettice 23, 24, 29, 49
Hopper
  Abraham 111, 124, 149, 276, 290, 297, 298

Abraham A. 289
Abraham H. 291
Abraham J. 290
Albert 87, 291, 302
Andrea 152
Andres 97
Andrew 107, 183, 248, 289, 297
Andrew A. 123, 247, 290
Andrew An. 288
Andrew D. 291
Andrew G. 290
Andrew H. 188, 291
Andrew I. 292
Andrew W. 72
Andrie 36
Andrus 104
Anne 277
Catharine 109
Caty 299
Cornelius 127, 128
David 289
Elshe 212, 275
Elshi 291
Garret 19, 77, 92, 240, 264, 275, 290, 302, 304
Garret A. 152, 291
Garret J. 91, 129, 256
Garret P. 263, 304
Garret W. 72, 78, 264, 289
Guilliam 289
Hendrick 6, 19, 56, 104, 109, 149, 297
Henry 81, 170, 277, 291, 300, 306
Henry A. 290
Henry D. 289
Henry G. 291
Hessel 255, 256, 283
Hester 77
Isaac 291
Jacob 127, 130, 158, 204, 255, 264, 289, 297, 300, 304
Janet 76
John 96, 101, 102, 104, 120, 170, 174, 181, 182, 187, 195, 197, 213, 257, 277, 278, 306
John A. 89, 146, 291
John D. 289
John G. 290, 291
John J. 291
John W. 73, 97, 107, 182, 187, 289
Margaret 78
Mary 72, 123, 247, 248
Mathias 22
Merian 305
Michael 277
Nicarie 290
Peter 77, 213, 231, 263, 277, 278, 291, 304
Peter A. 211
Ryndert 298
Stephen 297
Widow 304, 306
William 189, 289
Hordie
  James 140
Hornbeck
  Garret 286

Hornblower
  Elizabeth 116
  Josiah 75, 116,
    117, 153, 210,
    215, 270, 286,
    302
  Margaret 152,
    188, 189, 216
  Margareth 153
  Margaretta 153
  William 152, 153,
    188, 189, 216,
    302
Horpse
  Garrabrant 300
Houghland
  Aaron 305
  Adrian 51
  Catharine 40
  Cornelius 137,
    147, 196, 293
  Joseph C. 286
Houseman
  Abraham 27, 30,
    75, 249, 256
  Charles 14, 42
  Garrabrant 27
  James 304
  John 35
  Margaret 300
Houtenburgh
  Margrieta 30
  Peter 22, 23
How
  Charles 296
Howard
  Thomas 164, 190,
    194, 210, 275
Howden
  Gilbert 299
Howell
  Mat. W. 166
  Nehemiah 69
Hoyer
  Cattrine 31
  Eriens Christians
    30, 31
Hoyet
  Elias 304
  Elvan 304
Hricos
  Charles A. 202
Huddolstow
  William 11, 12
Hudson
  John T. 251
Huere
  Carper H. 291
Hughes
  Thomas 122
  widow 107
Hulf
  Paul 88
Hulms
  Henry 89
  William 89
Hun
  Jacob 186
  Peter 185
Hunman
  John 76
Hunt
  Harmen 299
  John 22, 23, 34
Hunter
  Robert 61
Hurbbut
  Joseph 218, 219
Hurley
  Catherine 299
  Peter 76
  Thomas 299
Huspey
  Bath 276
Hutchins
  John 58
Huyler
  Cornelius 226
  John 215, 294
  John G. 294
  John Jo. 142
  Sarah 177

W. Helmus 142
widow 164
Wilhelmus 294
Huysman
  Albert 114
  Isack 83
  Jacobus 125
  James 127, 128
Hymer
  Gabriel 301
Isaac
  William 73
Jackson
  George 242
  Henry 286
  L. 195
  Teodorus 286
  William 93, 210
  William Jr. 124
Jacobus
  Bartell 3
  Elenor 3
  Garret 306
  Guilliam 306
  Henry 303
  Jacobus G. 306
  James 277, 278, 306
  John 274
  John J. 278
  Mary 278
  Roelif 255, 256, 258, 306
  Rudolph 244
  Thomas 305
  Walling 48
  Widow 306
Jacobusse
  Garret 112, 148, 149, 186
  Gertruy 141
  Jacob 112, 113, 280
  Jacobus 69, 141
  Jacobus G. 166
  Jacobus Gust 166

James 101, 283
John 141
Margaret 171
Mary 186, 283
Peter 280
Rachel 154
Roelif 141, 283, 305
Jaguish
  John 288
James
  Alexander 225, 231-233, 244, 251, 275, 277, 279
  Josiah 264
Jansen
  Abraham 290
  David 11
  Jan Anderso 77
  Johann 26
Jaroleman
  Edward 23
  Elizabeth 219
  Henry 302
  James 75, 299
  James C. 299
  John 32, 39, 75, 219, 299
  Mary 75
  Teunis 126, 172
  Tunes 302
Jarvis
  James C. 191
Jay
  Augustus 299
  John 156
  Sin James 294
Jayce
  Benjamin 281
Jenkins
  John 228
  Lambertas 70
  Lambertes 75
  William 289
Jessup

Daniel 71, 93
Jo 48
Johns
  Henry S. 261
  Stephen Jr. 273
Johnson
  Andrew 151, 187
  Deborah 220
  Dob. 212
  Doctor 196, 205
  Elizabeth 211
  Ganet 286
  James 23, 288
  Johannes 27, 30
  John 132, 174,
    187, 211, 267,
    270
  Joseph 90, 101,
    291
  Josiah 220, 247,
    257, 271, 276
  L. 26
  Margaret 241, 242
  Mary 270
  Robert 75, 131
  Samuel 270
  Simon 50
  Thomas 241, 242
  Tunis 20
Johnston
  Andrew 18, 26,
    33, 41-43, 60,
    65, 69, 166,
    167, 182, 195,
    204, 261
  Catharine 33, 60
  James 36
  Johannis 61
  John 62, 73, 147,
    165-167, 204,
    268, 295
  Joseph 101
  Josiah 294
  Katherin 18
  Lewis 26
  Margaretta 206

  Mary 261
  S. 44
Jones
  David 36
  Even 294
  Nicholas 306
  Phineas 147
  Samuel 147, 306
  Thomas 148, 306
  William 127
  William George
    127, 128
  Zebulon 302
Jonsen
  Abraham 31
Joosten
  Rut 40
Jorden
  Joseph 238
Joseph
  John 295
Juglis
  Thomas 57
Juriansen
  Aury 150
  Christopher 157,
    184, 185, 214,
    300
  Garrabrant 149,
    150, 157, 184,
    299
  Garrabrant Jr.
    299
  Garret 7, 110,
    178
  Hendrick 5, 6, 9
  Hessel 300
  Jacob 4
  Jan 25
  Johannes 178
  John 100, 110,
    149, 150, 157,
    184, 193, 300
  Jurie 184
  Margaret 178
  Margaritie 178

Nassel 174
Neallie 157
Thomas 10, 20, 141
Kahawan 23
Kamaka
  Daniel 76
Kane
  James 238
Kanous
  Jacob 237
  John George 237
Kark
  Henry 183
Kaugh
  Casparus Jr. 201
Kearney
  Michael 24
Keating
  John 238
Kedney
  John 146
Keelar
  Edward 303
Kells
  James 209
Kelly
  John 179, 214, 285
Kennar
  John 305
Kennedy
  Jane 261
  John 261
  Robert 257, 261
  Thomas 296
Kenney
  Daniel 73, 82
Kenny
  Daniel 82
Kent
  James 141
Kerbride
  Joseph 44, 72, 137
Kerrick

  Henry 299
  John 299
Kersout
  John 126
Kiersted
  Jannottye 30
  Lucas 30, 36, 54
  Luke 279, 280
Kill
  Bellemans 119
Kimble
  Will 305
King
  Abraham H. 302
  Adam 7, 29
  Anthony 146
  Aury 140
  Henry 122
  John 10, 295
  Mary 7, 301
  Rachel 10
  William 144, 153, 302
Kingsland
  Aaron 79
  Abraham 79, 299
  Anne 299
  Burnel R. 189
  Burnett N. 153
  Carolina 12
  David 299
  Edmond 11, 25, 35, 36, 116, 152, 153
  Edmond William 99, 115, 116, 152
  Edmund 1, 9, 12-15, 27, 28, 197, 285
  Edmund William 74, 188, 189, 216, 272, 300
  Edward 15, 43
  Edward William 154, 269

Gustavus 122
Gustavus Jr. 35
Henry 75, 81,
  272, 300
Hoster 12
Isaac 2, 12, 43,
  48, 53, 58, 59,
  62, 79, 87, 167,
  180
Isabella 12
Jane 299
Johanna 59
John 12, 111
Joseph 79, 183
Major 77
Mary 12, 15, 35,
  74, 115, 152,
  153, 188, 189
Nathaniel 2, 5,
  8, 9, 11, 12,
  22, 25, 35, 100,
  110
Nathaniel Jr. 12
Roger 195
William 27, 29,
  53, 57, 62, 81,
  87, 115, 153,
  189, 270, 272
Kingston
  John 202
Kint
  James 292
Kip
  Abraham 244
  Caty 126, 223
  Cornelius 35,
    126, 171, 306
  David 278
  Elizabeth 66
  Hendrick 19, 20,
    27, 29, 30, 66,
    76, 100, 114,
    123, 127, 152,
    165, 184, 270,
    300
  Hendrykie 279
  Henry 101, 126,
    138, 300, 306
  Henry P. 259, 283
  Hester 244
  Isaac 66, 172,
    174, 223, 236,
    263, 268, 279,
    294, 302, 304
  Isaack Jr. 32
  Jacob 114, 127
  Jacobus 18, 33
  James 76
  Jane 268
  Joan 117
  John 66, 268,
    279, 302, 304
  Margaret 116
  Maryrite 71
  Necansie 302
  Niasey 57
  Nicanse 248
  Nicasie 124, 156
  Nicasius 20
  Nicause 279
  Nicaway 76
  Nicholas 5, 20,
    99, 104, 116,
    126, 131, 268,
    279, 306
  Nicolas 131
  Nicose J. 116
  Nikasie 22
  Peter 66, 100,
    109, 123, 152,
    300
  Richard 104
  Thomas 293
Kirkpatrick
  Andrew 273
  Jane 209
Klasbaugh
  Berklout 293
Knact
  Conrad 231
Knap
  Isaac 306

John 306
Walter 306
Knight
  Conrad 211, 291
  George Carott 12
  Peter 304
Knott
  Peter 267
Knows
  John Jr. 306
  John U. 306
Kock
  Jacobus 70
Kuyler
  Catharine 253
  Hendrick 252, 253
Kuyper
  Art 301
  Catharina 213
  Catharine 159, 160, 179, 201
  Cornelius 50, 79, 98, 297, 301
  David 50
  Derick 49, 297
  Elias D. 153
  Garret 213
  Garret C. 301
  Hendericus 201
  Henderius 71, 73, 85-89, 91-93, 95, 111, 117, 124, 136, 137, 146
  Hendrick 19, 57, 179, 210, 219, 301
  Hendrickus 160
  Hendrius 138
  Henricus 171
  Margaret 301
  Peter 140
  Richard 98
  Richard H. 301
  Richard J. 301
  Thomas 301

Kuyprus
  Wolmudus 301
Labagh
  Hendrick 23
  Henry 272
  William 191, 199
Lacolamb
  Lewis 201
LaFeurt
  Bartholomew 5
Lake
  Gilbert 202
  Guysbert 302
  John G. 287
Lamart
  Benjamin D. 306
Lambecker
  Johannis Philip 45
Lambert
  John 213
Lance
  Johannes 186
  Margaret 186
Landon
  Amacy 273
  Amasa 273
  Margaret 273
  Margret 273
Lane
  Nathan 290
Langden
  Abran 286
Langevelt 39
Lapsly
  James 287
Laroe
  Abraham 47, 48
  Cathalina 283
  Conrad 74
  Elizabeth 59
  Hannah 70
  Hendrick 46, 72, 103, 104, 189
  Henry 303
  Jacobus 70, 84,

104, 106, 134,
 136, 192, 207,
 289
Jacobus S. 70, 75
James 47, 283
Joannis 9
Johannes 72, 103,
 104, 189
John 69, 103,
 104, 304
John Jr. 304
Lambartus 190
Lambert 59
Margaret 103, 104
Mary 103
Nicholas 13
Rebecca 104
Samuel 46, 134,
 136, 192, 207
Thomas 6, 8, 10
William 1, 9
Wybregh 47
Larosen
 Peter 286
Lasy
 Nelly 102
Laubaugh
 Henry 302
 Isaac 301
Lauries
 Gawen 47
Laussat
 Anty 280
Law
 Lawrence 81
 Robert 77
Lawrence
 Ann 124
 Arnet 41
 Caty 263, 264
 Francina 24
 Francis 51
 George 233, 263,
  264
 I. Jr. 176
 Isaac 15

James 124
John 150
John Jr. 150
Sarah 176
Thomas 1, 9, 14,
 19, 20, 22, 24,
 27, 31, 42, 51,
 150, 176, 195
William 14, 22,
 35, 47, 48, 51
Lawton
 Isaac 154
 Thomas 154
Le Roux
 245
 Abraham 95
 John 24
Leake
 John 172, 184
 John George 116,
  151, 172, 173,
  195, 226, 228,
  251
 Robert 151, 173
 Robert William
  116, 151
Lealy
 John 285
Leary
 William 305
Ledsend
 Isaac 95
Lee
 James 34, 38, 192
 John 285
 Mary 67
 William 67, 160
Lefferts 124
 Derick 123, 124
 Nancy 124
Lehrman
 Garret 81
Leishear
 Fenety 101
 Hellabrant 101
 Peter 101

Leonard
  David 89
  William 89
Leslie
  George 26, 41,
    42, 61, 65, 99,
    116
  Mr. 151
Levy
  Hayman 56
Lewis
  Abraham 215
  Cornelius 215
  Daniel Jr. 215
  Daniel Sr. 215
  Morgan 262
  Samuel 216, 299
  Timothy 60
Lien
  Abraham 72
  Conrad 72
  Daniel 72
  John 72
  Mary 72
Light
  Peter 132
Lightpipe
  John 305
Linbe
  Jurrianse 14
Line
  Anthony 305
  Peter 146, 305
Lines
  Abbraham C. 132
  Abraham 217, 277,
    288
  Abraham C. 288
  Abraham Jr. 288
  Anthony 288
  Catherine 217
  Clorche 175
  Coerrat 277
  Conrad 217, 219,
    277
  Conrad D. 288

Coonrat 175
Cornelius 217
Daniel 175, 277,
  288
Daniel Jr. 217
Henry 108
Jacobus 132
James 194
Jury 217
Richard 215, 217
Little
  Mathias 267
  Matthias 246
Livesey
  Paulus 239
  Robert 21, 44,
    46, 51, 70, 76
Livingston
  Gilbert 74
  Materoin 262
  Robert R. 292
Loby
  Nicholas 300
Lockerman
  Thomas 299
Lodge
  Abraham 34,
    36-38, 45, 46,
    50-52
Loofbourrow
  Catharine 57
Loots
  Paulus 48
Lotes
  Johannis 112
Lott
  Abraham 174
  John 9
Love
  Robert 2, 26
Loverance
  Peter 6
Loverence
  Andreas 4
  Derick Epkoy 9
  Jonathan Jr. 81

Loverencesen
  Loverence 9
Lovers
  Brefant Androsen 7
Lovervance
  Andris 6
Low
  Cornelius 284
Lowry
  Gawin 21, 32
Lozier
  Abraham 62, 65, 140, 149, 237, 271, 292, 295
  Abraham Jr. 295
  Abram 62, 123, 140
  Ann 82
  Anne 140
  Arene 101
  Christian Claas 33
  Cornelius 69, 106, 119, 123, 124, 136, 236, 291
  David 97, 130, 136, 145, 224, 225, 274, 294
  Derick 70, 149
  Hellabrant 53, 122, 140
  Jacob 62, 133, 136, 149, 237, 276, 294
  Jacob Jr. 293
  Jan 77
  Jane 69, 106
  Jannetie 69
  Jaocb 247
  John 76, 82, 140, 179, 194, 255, 258, 259, 265, 267, 269, 283, 292, 297, 305
  Joost 293
  Leah 224, 225
  Lucas 65
  Mary 62, 149, 194
  Neome 97
  Nicholas 3, 47, 74, 97, 269, 305
  Nicolas 130
  Niomy 295
  Peter 91, 101, 105, 140, 165, 236, 255, 289, 294
  Polly 62, 65
  William 77, 119, 177, 257, 295
Lubbertson
  Lubbert 6
Ludlam
  Anthony 285
  Mathias 285
  Runa 286
Ludlow
  Abraham 263
  Cary 263, 279
  Francis 46
  Gabiel 46
  Gabriel H. 113
  Gabriel W. 166
  George 263, 279
  Henry 73, 113, 199, 200, 229
  Hester 263, 279
  James 148
  John R. 205
  Mary 36, 37, 46, 296
  Richard 303
  William 46
  William C. 263
  William H. 113
Luke
  Abraham 193, 194, 196
  Anna 193, 194
Luker

Nathaniel 304
Lurante
  George 289
Lutkins
  Aybijah 74
  Harmon 28, 108, 290
  Henry 82, 302, 304
  Herman 82, 235, 302
  John 93, 302
  Lybetje 58
  Peter 73, 82, 108
  Stephen 302
Lydecker
  Abraham 49, 67, 97, 161, 180, 234
  Abraham A. 180
  Albert G. 180
  Anna 234
  Annie 180, 234
  Annye 180
  Catharine 59, 124
  Cornelius 49, 147, 154, 180, 217, 234, 295
  Cornelius A. 180
  Cornelius Alb. 234
  Cornelius Garret 234
  Elizabeth 147
  Garnet 72
  Garott 19
  Garret 4, 20, 22, 27, 59, 85-87, 89, 90, 91-93, 95, 96, 111, 117, 122, 124, 132, 140, 147, 162, 166, 180, 291, 295
  Garret A. 180, 234
  Garret Alb. 234
  Garret G. 122, 157, 180, 295
  Gerard 20
  Gorrot 19
  Guryda 145
  Jacobus 295
  John 180, 234
  John A. 180
  John Alb. 234
  Ledey 162
  Margaret 180, 234
  Maria 145
  Martyntye 180, 234
  Neeltie 19, 20, 22
  Rachael 147
  Rebecca 180, 234
  Rebeckah 234
  Rebekah 180
  Ryck 19, 22, 44
  Ryithe 157
  Samuel 124
  Samuel Benson 59
Lynson
  Catharine 145
Lyons
  David 210
  Rhoda 210
  Samuel 285
Lyt
  John 295
Maby
  Abraham 65, 199
  Isaac 264, 265, 297
  Jasper 200
  John 246, 253, 289, 296
  Minden 265
  Mindert 298
  Peter 200, 296, 298
  Peter J. 265
  Sally 200, 265

Sarah 200
Macashorter
  Ahp B. 151
MacFerren
  Patrick 163
Machett
  John 228
Mackaness
  Thomas 209
Mackelsen
  Enoch 3
  Janmetre 3
  Johann Cornelius
    3
Mackelson
  Andrew 10, 20
  Catharine 4
  Charles 4
  Elias 4, 9
  Enoch 4, 14
  Johannis 4
  William 10, 20
Macklane
  Catharine 61
  Solomon 61
  William 61
Mackleen
  Daniel 36
Mackness
  Jacob 138
Mackrel
  John 229
Maclesand
  Charles 16
Macphidvis
  Helena 50
Magangie
  John 301
Magriger
  James 301
Mahonnon
  James 289
Maig
  Anthony 290
Major
  Henry 18, 56
Malhu
  Benjamin 118
Mamerise 23
Mammen
  Abraham 90
Man
  Samuel 289
Mandeville
  Anthony 95, 137,
    306
  David 7, 39
  Garret 9
  Hendrick 7
  William 306
  Williamphey 137
Manes 23
Manning
  Abraham 76, 79,
    80, 101, 112,
    121, 151, 289
March
  Peter Barbarsen
    46
  Robert Watch 42
Marchet
  John 288
Marinus
  Anna 108
  David 108, 109,
    183, 187, 231
  Jacob 18
  John 268
  Peter Jacob 40
  Selvester 113
Mark
  Abraham 291
  Jacob 153, 154,
    265
  Lewis 265
Marker
  John 202
Marsan
  Michael 265
Marschalik
  Andrew 36
Marselius

Allia 171
Cornelius 253,
  304
Edo 60, 66, 145,
  292, 304
Edo Jr. 147, 303
Edward 116
Elizabeth 273
Jacob 226, 227,
  242, 273, 296
Johannis 178
John 85, 171,
  214-216, 253,
  286
Jules 296
Lois 170
Marsel 253
Marseles 216
Meseslies 102
Peter 38, 93,
  118, 178, 296
Seil 155, 216
Marsh
  Henry 90
  John Heyser 39
Marshallen
  Thomas 147
Martese
  Roelif 114
Martin
  Ann 24, 31
  James 24, 31
  John 304
  Jonathan 296
Marygold
  Thomas 288
Masaer
  Abraham 12, 14
Masher
  Derick 291
  Tudwiek 291
Massacar
  Henry 271, 306
  Mathias 306
Masserse
  John 289

Mativeson
  Catharine 1
Matlack
  White 154
Mattack
  White 154
Mattis
  John 304
Mattyse
  Cornelius 34
Mattysien
  Hendrick 40
May
  Alexander 60
Mayer
  Elsie 31
  Henry 5, 6, 31,
    42, 48, 61
Mayes
  Cornelius 227
  Matteyntye 227
McBell
  William 291
McCall
  John 210, 291
McCann
  William 288
McCarty
  John 200, 277,
    303
McCawley
  James 305
McClain
  Henry 305
  John 305
McClennon
  John 306
McCohen
  Solomon 56
McColly
  James 186
  Rachel 186
McColm
  Peter 303
McCull
  Robert 292

McCullen
  Robert 85, 86
McCurdy
  James 217, 218, 250, 306
  Jane 217, 218
McDaniel
  George 286
  Thomas 285
McDongall
  Agnes 262
McDowell
  Alexander 18, 41, 42, 65, 212
  Andrew 48
  John 48
  Thomas 273
  William 48
McElse
  W. 129
McEwen
  Martha 158
  William 158
McFadden
  Patrick 156, 163, 300
McFerson
  Able 303
McFicher
  Henry 292
McFire
  George 286
McIntire
  Dorcas 268
  George 173, 268
McKensey
  John 305
McKinley
  James 44, 50, 51, 57
McKnight
  Charles 187, 269
  Doctor 154
  Mary 187, 269
  Mary Scott 269
McLoud
  John 306
  John Jr. 306
McMullin
  John 288
McPeek
  Jane 299
McWhorter
  Alexander 258
  Alexander C. 170, 243
Mead
  G. 117
  Giles 126, 130, 216, 217
  Gilis 289
  Henry 95, 101, 102, 112, 147, 148, 171, 184, 192, 277, 278, 306
  Henry J. 113
  Isaac 173, 288
  Jacob 54, 112, 113, 139, 148, 166, 198, 213
  John 101, 112, 148, 283, 306
  John J. 101
  John Ja. 120, 148
  John P. 306
  John Y. 306
  Margareth 101
  Mary 101
  Peter J. 116
  Rachael 171
  Simon 306
  Yelles 198
  Yellis 306
Meadow
  William 286
Meason
  Gilbert 242
Meeker
  Uzal 301
Megheler
  Lodwick 282

Mehelm
  John 158
Meidebarger
  Lewis 143
Mellows
  David H. 166
Mentho
  Henry 296
Merchirone
  John 293
Merectus
  Seal 286
Merenis
  David 305
  Garret 305
Merian
  Anthony 240, 306
Merurau
  John 133
Mesire
  John 286
Messeher
  Hendrick 81
Messelor
  Peter 285
Mestayer
  Ceasar 166
  Mary Magdalena 166
Mestell
  Christian 226
Metseker
  John 300
  Lodewyke 299
Meyer
  Andrus 105
  Cornelius 176, 200, 201, 203, 208
  Franiytie 42
  Henry 5, 42
  Jacob 135
  Jacob J. 208
  Janitie 42
  Janotne 12
  Johannes 22
  Johannis 12
  Johannis M. 208
  John 72, 86, 105, 136, 208, 267
  John J. 208
  Lidia 208
  Manemanus 120
  Maria 208
  Mary 208
  Marya 136
  Rachel 208
  Sarah 208
  Thomas 208, 210
Meysinger
  Conrad 89
  Cornelius 90
  John 290
  Margareth 89
  Margried 89, 90
  Nicholas 90, 97, 98, 264
  Nicks 290
  Peter 88, 90, 283
  Susanna 90
Michiels
  Cornelius 26
  Tadoas 30
Michles
  John 292
  Todwick 292
Milbourne
  Jacob 45, 52
  William 52
Miller
  Alexander 301
  Andrew 288
  Henry 289
  Israel 305
  Joseph 300
  Robert 295
Millinberry
  Lewis 75
Mills
  Thomas C. 180
Minaer
  Johannes 58

Minfarl
  Johann 23
Mitchell
  Edward 184
  John 286, 291
Mo
  Abraham 303
Moenaghe 48
Moffat
  John 205
Mollemott
  Elenor 5, 31, 34
Mompeson
  Ann 27, 29
  Martha 27, 28
  Roger 3, 4, 11, 12
Monks
  James 288
Monrow
  Angles 288
Montanye
  Abraham 55, 62, 166, 170
  John J. 166
  Sarah 55
Montgomery
  Robert 245
Moore
  Abraham 295
  Andrew 299
  Anne 217
  Edward 16
  Elizabeth 206
  Hester 170
  Jacob 217
  Jacob T. 295
  James 55
  Janne 267
  John 55, 59, 62, 68, 77, 79, 82, 170, 185, 267, 290, 306
  John Jr. 33, 142
  Lewis 206
  Mary 115
  Michael 50, 62, 68, 295
  Richard 38
  Samuel 24, 25, 31, 44, 53, 55, 58, 59, 62, 67, 68, 141, 145, 211, 234
  Samuel J. 295
  Samuel James 180
  Samuel Jr. 50, 170
  Samuel S. 295
  Samuel Sr. 55, 68, 170
  Samuel T. 295
  Sarah 55, 170
  Thomas 55, 59, 62, 68, 170
  William A. 115
Moott
  John 7
Morant
  Adam D. 193
Morgan
  Benjamin 191, 278
Morinscott
  John 270
Morison
  Alexander 288
Morland
  Rhoda 46
Morrel
  Elijah 300
Morris
  Benjamin 305
  Dennis 288
  Dennis Jr. 288
  Elenor 35, 47, 48
  Fraina 21
  Gouverneur 246
  Isaac 142, 146, 296
  Jacob 6, 17
  James 245, 246, 262

Joseph 35, 47, 48, 51
Juris 21
Lewis 32, 245
Richard 113, 169
Robert 142, 160, 163, 191, 249, 278
Robert Hunter 148, 165, 169
Samuel Jr. 48
Selvester 300
Theophilis 42
Morse
  Joseph 288
Moselee
  Peter 288
Moses
  Isaac 56, 205
  Reyne 205
Mott
  George D. 287
Motter
  George 110
Mourison
  Abraham 53
  James 249, 250, 267, 279
  Moures 300
Mullen
  James 305
  William 288
Mumo
  Peter Jay 269
Munerse
  Isaac 290
  Jacobus 290
  Peter 290
Muntasa
  Abraham 295
Murden
  Joseph Robert 206
Murphy
  James 70
  Robert 305
Muse

Hutchinson 242
  Robert 242, 243
Myer
  Auson 289
  Catharine 298
  Cornelius 294, 304
  Garret 229
  Johannes 237, 282, 297
  Johannis 268
  John 289, 298
  Maria 268, 282
  Martin 268, 282, 289
  Mary 268
Nagel
  Abraham 240
  Alana 150
  Anna 73
  Barent 16, 73, 296
  Barney 77
  David 150, 172, 296
  Guesslocert 150
  Isaac 172
  Jacob 217, 295
  Johannes 296
  John 72, 73
  Mary 77
  Nagel 296
  Niclas 295
  Resolurt 73
  Sarah 73
  William 73, 150
Nagush
  William 291
Nash
  Jacob Mae 129
Natman
  Isaac 302
Neafie
  Ann 13
  Catharine 106, 170, 187

Caty 169
Cornelius 141, 163
Ganet 289
Garret 304
Hans 221, 232
Johann 41
Johannis 13, 32
John 79, 89, 96, 97, 104, 106, 120, 129, 168-170, 179, 187, 195, 289
Lena 257
Lenah 256
Neart
  John 149
Necker
  Matthew 214
Neil
  Robert 105, 191
Neilson
  John 31
Nelene
  Cornelius 191
Nelson
  John 289
Nevill
  John 29
Nevins
  Peter 39
Newkerk
  Aaron 286
  Caty 213
  Garret 32, 210, 213, 286
  Hendrick 132, 151, 213
  Henry 213, 286
  Jacob 115, 137, 151, 155, 226
  Jane 213
  Mathew 132, 138
  Mathew P. 137
  Mathius 96
  Mathus 277

  Matthew 210, 213, 252, 286
  Matthew G. 213
  Matthew P. 214, 215
  Matthew S. 287
  Matthias 151
  Matthias P. 119, 151
  Matthus 252
  Roelif 244
Nice
  Robert 79, 110
Nicoll
  Deborah 176
  Edward 251
  Eleanor 251
  Isaac 72, 102, 159, 176, 185, 207, 217, 275, 294
  Margret 176
  Ronsolacer 24
  Sarah 176, 255
  Solomon 299
  Wallace D. 168
  Walter 305
  Walter D. 176, 255
  William 32, 40, 217
Nix
  Harmana 64
Noble
  Abel 190
Noell
  Thomas 19
Norg
  John 13
Norman
  Henry 295
North
  William 29
Norton
  Thomas 30
Nowell

Elizabeth 24
Monseth 24
Samuel 54
Thomas 24, 31
Nudkook
  Jacob 286
O'Hare
  Alexander 8
Oakley
  Elizabeth 188
  Israel 165, 188, 286
  Jesse 286
  John 188
Obrign
  Charles A. 137
Odell
  Garret 136
Odle
  Benjamin 170
  Garret 304
  Nehemiah 305
Ogden
  Abraham 139, 164, 197, 229, 242, 295
  Ann 206
  Charles 102, 206, 305
  Charles S. 176
  David 121, 155, 156, 164
  David A. 242
  David B. 229, 242, 251, 258
  David Jr. 120, 121, 198, 282
  David Sr. 120, 198, 282
  Elizabeth 103
  Elizabeth G. 207
  Gabriel 102, 103, 168, 206
  Jacob 257, 258, 299
  John 80, 81, 155, 198, 282, 302
  Jonah 198
  Joseph 30
  Josiah 282
  Lewis 131
  Mary 206
  Marytie 270
  Matthias 126
  Moses 155, 206
  Robert 61
  Samuel 219, 220, 257, 258, 264
  Thomas S. 205
  Uzal 155, 198, 206, 216, 243, 270, 282
  William 205
  William Ludlow 299
Ogilvie
  Ann 150
  Anne 151
  George 130, 150, 151
  John 150
  Margaret 150
  Margareth 151
  Mary 150
Old
  John 198, 282
  Sarah 282
Oldham
  Charles 280, 305
Oldis
  Garret 108, 302
  Henry 291
Ortley
  Michael 241, 249, 304
Osborne
  Anna 202
  Bridget 252
  Charles 114
  John 266
Oster
  John 68

Outwater
  Ann 209
  Anne 209
  Antie 224, 225
  Attia 209
  Catalina 209
  Doctor 226
  Elizabeth 246
  Gilian 100
  Gilm 185
  Guilliam 209,
    223, 225, 302
  Gulliam 293
  Hannah 154
  Henderichia 137
  Henderikia 137
  Hendrick 299
  Jacob 41, 66,
    103, 114, 137,
    157, 200, 209,
    221, 227, 232,
    246, 254, 300
  Jacobus 123
  James 77, 269,
    285
  John 70, 74, 78,
    85, 87, 91, 103,
    105, 113, 119,
    123, 133, 136,
    137, 146, 153,
    154, 157, 169,
    173, 174, 181,
    184, 185, 190,
    192, 193, 199,
    209, 216, 219,
    223, 224, 229,
    232, 237, 241,
    243, 246, 247,
    254, 258, 260,
    269, 272, 300
  Maritie 209
  Martintie 232
  Martyntie 41
  Nicholas 216,
    246, 300
  Quilliam 224
  Rachel 246
  Thomas 32, 103,
    163, 235, 241,
    247
  Thomas Francis
    154
Ozben
  Charles 299
  Henry 299
Packer
  Conrad 292
  James 131
  John W. 292
Pake
  John D. 262
  Uschelshe 262
Palmer
  Henry 109
Pane
  John 231
Pantgiband
  Charles 201
Parcel
  Jacob 135, 142
  Nicolas 21
  Walter 57
  William 105
Parker
  Eliza 222
  Elizabeth 246
  Gertrude 222
  Gerturde 246
  James 82, 97,
    144, 150, 182,
    196, 197, 222,
    241, 242, 246,
    281, 292
  John 30, 244
Parleyman
  John 291
Parmylor
  Par 34
  Par. 62
Parrlesse
  Gerettie 66
  John 66

Patterson
  Christian 11
  Elizabeth 1, 24
  Euphonica 219, 220
  John 53
  William 24, 219, 220
Paul
  Thomas 197
Paulisen
  Craltye 270
  Ellenor 271, 276
  Jacobus 82
  Johannes 109
  John 39, 199, 271, 276
  John J. 270
  Martin 9, 13, 22, 142
  Paulus 247
  Petrus 109
Peak
  John 236
Pearsall
  Israel 301
  Jarvis 276
Peck
  Daniel 298
  David 56, 111
  Jacob 56, 297
  Jacobus 49-51, 54, 55
  Johannes 105, 297
  Johannis 162
  John 146, 290
  Samuel 297
Peers
  John 33, 34
  John C. 141
Peggy 187
Peltzer
  Jenias 288
Pennington
  Aaron 228, 258
  Mary 228, 257, 258
  Phebe 169, 187, 198, 202, 257, 258
  Samuel 228
  William S. 169, 187, 198, 202, 257, 258
Perce
  Jane 151
Percell
  Jacob 294, 296
  John 294
Perhamus
  Theodous 271
Perine
  Abram 285
  Henry 292
Perry
  Daniel 298
  Jacobus 298
  James 188
  Johannes 298
  John 72, 129, 291, 296, 297
  Peter 235, 247, 298
Peterson
  Cornelius 298
  Hessel 32, 119, 136, 167, 206, 305
  Joseph 295
  Luke 214, 295
  Nicholas 297
  Peter H. 119
  William 298
  Yurrie 206, 263
Petterson
  Clas 2
Peyoter
  Abraham W. D. 116
Phillip 23
Phillips
  Fredrick 4
  John 274

Richard 87, 300
Phillis 209
Pike
  William 57
Pillion
  John 294
Pinhorne 199
  Elizabeth 27, 28
  John 11, 14, 28, 35
  Martha 27, 28
  Mary 27, 28
  Mount 27, 28
  William 1, 6, 9, 27, 28, 53
Pitts
  John 305
Pollet
  Richard 17
Pope
  Christopher 158, 300
  Jeremiah 145, 163, 300
  Jermiah 224
  Mary 224
  Richard 32
Porter
  Peter 303
Portiss
  Peter 297
Post
  Abraham 118, 140, 252, 289, 297, 304
  Abraham J. 289
  Adrian 11, 41, 271, 286, 303, 305
  Adrian P. 138, 271
  App 65
  Aris 291
  Caspar 200
  Catherine 227, 228
  Cornelius 127, 201, 202, 289, 303
  Cornelius A. 292
  David 227
  Egbert 96, 178, 179, 215, 286
  Elbert 178
  Elizabeth 140, 186
  Frederick 289
  Garret 139, 305
  Garret C. 201
  Genet A. 292
  Helmegh 118
  Henry 137
  Herman C. 303
  Isaac 289
  Jacobus 65, 116, 167, 191, 219, 303
  Johannes 127
  John 75, 111, 185, 191, 286, 292
  John A. 304
  John C. 304
  John F. 153
  John J. 176, 177
  John P. 92, 289
  Jury H. 304
  Michael 289, 300
  Nashie 271
  Peter 41, 62, 69, 116, 177, 186, 209, 251, 286, 291, 297
  Peter P. 271
  Ralph 189
  Roelif 190
  Sarah 215, 251
  Thomas 305
Potter
  Arian 11
  John 236, 291
  Paulus 11

Powleson
　Elizabeth 228, 229
　Henry 141, 145, 260
　Jacob 296
　Jacobus 293, 302
　James 228, 229
　John 237, 291, 293, 302
　Martin 296
　Mary 145
　Nieltya 157
　Paul 157
　Powles 157
　Powleson 293
Pratt
　John 305
Price
　Elizabeth 206
　Helena 206
　John 288
　Michael 190, 206
　Philip 62
　Stephen 206
Prine
　Abraham 157
Pritan
　William 298
Provoost
　Catherine 28
　Cornelius 88
　David 1-3, 5-8, 11-16, 20, 26, 28, 33, 34-36, 38, 40, 41, 43-45, 47, 48, 49, 50, 57, 68
　David M. 104
　David Sr. 28
　Effe 60
　Elias 100, 125, 202, 214, 221, 223, 243, 300
　Henry 210
　J. B. 231
　J. Fred 231
　James Marcus 170
　John Bartow 170
　Samuel 57, 155, 156, 302
　William 12, 15, 21-23, 25-35, 38-42, 44-48, 51, 55, 57, 60, 62, 64, 70, 71, 83, 86, 123, 124, 248
Pryor
　Abraham 155, 210, 214, 232, 285
　Capt. 149
　Caspar 12
　Casparus 115, 140, 214, 215, 226
　Hannah 12
　Hartman 214
　Jacob 12, 226, 282, 285
　Jacob Jr. 140
　Jasper 115, 123, 215, 226, 286
　Jasper A. 285, 286
　Joan 12
　Johannis 12
　Loohyle 12
　Sarah 282
Puffering
　John 163
Pular
　William 245
Pulis
　Abraham 289
　Christian 289
　Conrad 289
　Henry 289
　Henry W. 291
　John 237, 249, 282
　John D. 268

John W. 280, 291
William 292
Pulisfelt
  Aavies 132
  Abraham 264
  Christian 63, 64, 128
  Christoyaum 64
  Henry 204
  Jacob 78
  Jacobus 63, 64, 128, 265
  Jacobus Paulus 78
  James 289
  Joannis 64
  Johannes 63
  Johannis 51
  John 123, 124
  John I. 289
  Johnann 267
  Lectye 78
  Peter 292
  Peter P. 292
Quackenhus
  Beatus 88
  Catharine 88
  John 220
  John M. 87, 130
  John Manntius 81, 90, 119
  Lryntye 90
  Paulis 290
Quackinbos
  Barent 291
  Jacob 291
Quackinbush
  Abraham 111, 212, 228, 256, 290, 296
  Abraham A. 96, 256, 278
  Catharine 256
  Cornelius 230, 235, 240
  Jacob 67, 86, 142, 156, 176,
    262, 294
  James 134
  John 231, 281, 294
  Tunis 262
Quateer
  Andrew 286
Querau
  Philip 154
Quillem
  James M. 89
  Sarah 89
Quinby
  Joseph 213, 286
Raive
  Phillip 292
Raling
  Edward 15
Ramsey
  Jane 261
  Mary 289
  Peter 254, 261, 289
  Rachel 208
Randle
  William 286
Ranger
  Martin 40
Rap
  Adam 214, 215, 286
  Arionca 214, 215
  Peter 286
Rapman
  Phillip 290
Rappleye
  Ram 295
Rarve
  Conrad 292
Raton
  Daniel Jr. 295
  Harriman 295
Rattan
  Abraham 279, 302
  Abraham D. 302
  Henry 301

Jacobus 302
John 299, 303
Rattoone
  John 197, 210,
    273, 274
  Robert 238
Raye
  Abraham 249
  Johan Henry 285
  Nicholas 249
Read
  Joseph 39
  William 303
Reading
  James 127, 128
  Samuel 84, 177,
    215, 304
  Sarah 215
Reaxing
  William 122
Redner
  Hendrick 69
Reed
  Bower 197
  John 262, 272
  William 184
Reid
  Augustine 245
  John 24
Remmey
  Catherine 193
  John 193
Remsen
  John H. 201
Remsy
  Wilyam 30
Researrick
  George 39
Reynon
  John D. 290
Reypen
  William P. 291
Rhodes
  Benjamin 242
Richards
  Alexander 274

Barent 300
Burnel 189
Burnet 195, 216,
  270, 271
Burnett 152
Elephalet 112
John 39, 40, 66,
  75, 111, 121,
  123, 195, 243,
  269, 270, 305
Mary 39, 40, 111,
  121
Paul 52
Samuel 39
Warner 39, 40,
  111, 121, 122
William 74
Richer
  Henry 288
Richins
  Pelegh 295
Ricker
  Jacob 274, 303
Rickman
  Thubias 57
Riddie
  Charles 201
Ridgewar
  John 304
Ridgway
  John 237, 263
  Margaret 237
Ridnae
  Henry 289
Ridonzase
  Able 1
Riker
  Abraham 300
  Albert 300
  Gerardus 150
  John 200, 304
  Margaret 150
Riseman
  Fredrick 299
Roach
  Anne 120

Nicholas 120
Road
  Peter 303
Roberts
  Labon 306
Robertson
  Elizabeth 228
  John 301
  John Stark 262,
    272
  Robert 131
  Susannah 262, 272
  Widow 288
Robinson
  William 242
  William H. 118
Rodman
  John 67
Roebuck
  Peter John 250
Roeliffe
  Charity 294
  Helmegh 16, 109
  Margaret 259, 260
  Morta 100, 259,
    260
  Sinety 259, 260
Rogers
  William 305
Roma
  John 44
  Peter 306
Rome
  Cornelius 98
Romine
  Albert 292, 301
  Albert R. 292
  Benjamin 292
  Benjamin N. 289
  Carhina 5
  Claas 44
  Claes 16, 56, 57,
    104
  Clase 5
  D. 85
  Daniel 59, 179,
    259, 294, 302
  Daniel J. 259,
    260
  David 304
  Derick 74, 213
  Durie D. 87
  Francis 74
  Frans 181
  J. 205
  Jacob 202, 208,
    238, 292
  Jacob P. 152
  Jan 19, 74, 99
  John 5, 18, 26,
    35, 43, 44, 65,
    74, 85, 86, 88,
    94, 124, 148,
    156, 159, 187,
    191, 212, 248,
    291, 302, 304
  John Claes 56
  John Jr. 43, 213
  John N. 302
  John R. 213
  Julia 86
  Juliana 248
  Lamitye 124
  Margaret 259
  Margretye 259
  Marregretie 259
  Nicansie 302
  Nicholas 268,
    292, 304
  Ralph J. 280
  Robert 61
  Roelif 43, 212,
    213, 304
  Roeloff 65
  Sametie 44
  Samotie 35
  Samuel 292
Rommel
  John Christian
    Frederick 189
Roney
  Claas Janse 34

Ronkling
  Isaac 187
Roome
  Benjamin 280, 281
  Elizabeth 64, 69, 123, 154
  Jacob 64, 69, 71, 123, 154
  Peter S. 176
Roorbach
  Barent 130, 150, 151
  Mary 150
  Mary M. 151
Roosevelt
  Cornelius C. 158
  Isaac 158, 159, 168
  Jacobus 168
  James 168
  John 44, 299
  John J. 114
  Nicholas 100, 153, 154, 218
  Nicholas J. 265
Rose
  Catharine 212
  Isaac 264
  John 132, 212, 289
  Jonathan 58, 73, 192
  Timothy 73, 190
Ross
  John 110
  Levy 285
  Robert 187
Rossel
  Mary 165
Rouset
  David 26
Row
  Peter 305
Rozell
  John 89
  Thomas 165, 227, 301
Rudd
  Anne 275
  Stephen 194, 210, 275
Rudyard
  Thomas 39
Rulisson
  Martin 76
Russell
  Caleb 229
  Catel 89
  Sylvester D. 229
Rutan 175
  Abraham 5, 91, 108, 152, 167, 183, 193, 240, 249, 250, 270, 290
  Abraham J. 235, 275
  Abraham W. 91
  Daniel 25, 33, 176, 291
  Daniel I. 291
  Danioll 5
  Derick 211
  Eldert Jacobus 77
  Jacobus 235
  Johannes 124
  John 74, 189, 211, 280, 291
  John A. 237, 279, 280
  John I. 291
  John J. 77
  Mary 249
  Paulus 145
  Sarah 167
  Thomas 291
  Willeinfrie 235
  William 145
  Willimpie 275
Rutherford
  Catharine 152, 280

Catherine 198
John 262, 272
Walter 82, 97,
    131, 144, 150,
    152, 165,
    196-198, 233,
    245, 262, 272,
    280, 281
Rycher
    Abraham 296
    John 296
Ryckman
    Evert 59, 85-87
    Sarah 86
Ryder
    Barnadus 294
Ryenon
    Derick 96
    George 87
    John F. 96
    John Frane 96
    John J. 78
    Linah 78
    Martin 87, 100
Ryers
    John 121, 124,
       297
    John H. 279
    Michael 121, 297
    Ryer 297
Ryerse
    Abraham 112, 120,
       148
    Anna 69
    Anne 112
    Annice 69
    Arvn 121
    Elizabeth 166
    George 51, 52,
       59-62, 69, 71,
       72, 106, 109,
       112, 126, 147,
       149, 166, 191,
       195
    George S. 148
    Isaac 231

John 147, 220
Jorst 16
Luke 195
Martin 69
Martin Jr. 69
Mary 109
Theunis Jr. 166
Tunis 112
William 69
Ryerson
    Abigail 193, 219
    Abraham 131, 171,
       181, 193, 200,
       207, 255, 256,
       258, 273, 274,
       280, 281, 283,
       306
    Agnes 194
    Alana 193
    Alexander 278
    Catharine 148
    Catherine 217
    Caty 279
    Derick 263
    Elenor 193, 213
    Francis 1, 171,
       194, 197, 256,
       304
    Francis D. 249,
       256
    Francis G. 193,
       194
    George 1, 3, 5-7,
       9, 10, 13-15,
       23, 50, 54, 67,
       82, 89, 90, 102,
       103, 134, 148,
       171, 173, 174,
       176, 180, 191,
       192, 194, 197,
       213, 219, 256,
       278, 288, 293,
       304
    George F. 193,
       196
    George G. 193,

219, 305
George Jr. 306
George L. 306
Grela 193, 194
Guilliam 305
Hassel 148, 205
Hessel 176, 213,
  219, 237, 279,
  303
Jacob 261
Jane 218
John 99, 148,
  176, 219, 261,
  288, 305
John D. 303
John F. 62, 148,
  213, 238
John G. 137, 176,
  193, 196, 219,
  268, 304
John H. 303
John J. 102, 180,
  220, 262
John Ja 261
John Jr. 263
John L. 91, 102
Lenah 219
Luke 54
Luke Jr. 54
M. 213
Margaret 261
Marie 194
Martin 10, 109,
  139, 171, 194,
  218, 229, 273,
  305
Martin F. 250,
  266
Martin G. 137,
  193, 305
Martin J. 127,
  168, 206
Martin John 139
Mary 180, 181,
  189, 190, 193,
  266, 267, 305

Nanthe 193
Nassel 175
Nelly 194
Peter 217
Rebecca 1
Richard 102, 129,
  171, 181, 194,
  219, 305, 306
Richard G. 193
Ryer 18, 71, 261,
  292
Ryon 1, 15
Sarah 274
T. 306
Theunis 194, 266,
  267
Theunis G. 193
Thunis G. 305
Thurnis 181
Tunis 129, 135
Widow 91, 303,
  306
William 184, 192,
  255, 256, 306
Rykeman
  Evert 300
Ryker
  John 200
  John J. 244
Rykerman
  Daniel 300
  Tobias 300
Sackett
  Augustus 135
  James 111
  Joseph 135
  Joseph Jr. 122
  Samuel 111, 122,
    135
  William 111
Salter
  Catime 145
  Daniel 145
Sanders
  Egbert 184, 192
  John 305

Peter 184, 192
Thomas 305
Sandford
 Abraham 228, 299
 Benjamin 189,
  202, 228, 258,
  299
 Catharine 1
 David 288
 Elijah 228, 257
 Enoch 169, 257,
  299
 George 299
 Jacob 14
 John 187, 198,
  254, 288
 John P. 228
 Mary 228
 Michael 257, 299
 Peregrine 257
 Peter 169, 227,
  228, 258, 299
 Peter P. 228, 254
 Rachel 228
 Sarah 1, 169,
  211, 227, 254,
  257
 Thomas 228
 William 1, 7, 10,
  12, 20, 257, 299
 William D. 299
Sargent
 Jonathan 39
Sarrell
 William 66, 68,
  69, 86
Saulter
 Daniel 295
Saunier
 Gauen 155
 Margaret 226
 Paul 135, 226
Sayre
 David 198
 Jonathan 302
 Samuel 96, 102

Schenck
 P. 103
Schink
 Peter T. 81
Scholtzen
 Martin 87
Schott
 John Harris 269
Schureman
 James 273
 John 273
Schuyler
 Aaron 305
 Aaron P. 305
 Abraham 246
 Adomial 261
 Adonijah 305
 Arent 7, 10, 25,
  35, 54, 117,
  139, 153, 189,
  215, 290, 299
 Arent F. 153, 154
 Arent J. 114,
  261, 265
 Caspar 91, 305
 Casparous 139
 Casparus 71, 91,
  167, 206, 290
 Clasparius 41
 Isaac 139, 155
 Jan 10
 Johannis 52, 114
 John 57, 113,
  114, 153, 261,
  299
 Mary 206, 261
 Peter 108, 114,
  135, 139, 155,
  195, 206, 290,
  305
 Peter J. 261
 Philip 102, 139,
  290
 Philip A. 114,
  153, 154, 189
 Philip J. 195,

290
  Phillip 38, 108,
    139, 155
  Phillip A. 299,
    305
  Phillip J. 305
  Sevantio 10
  Swan 261
Scoffold
  David 288
  Hezikiah 288
Scott
  John 288
  John M. 75
  John Morin 66
  John Morris 123,
    187
  Lewis A. 269
  Mary 269
  Richard 198, 294
  William 159
Seahulfter
  John T. 240
Sealsbury
  David 288
Seaman
  Benjamin 175
  Edmund 175, 248
  Edmund Jr. 164,
    173
  Edward Jr. 164
  Elizabeth 147,
    164, 173, 174,
    195, 203
  John 137
  John E. 164
  Joseph 296
Sebring
  Johannis 39
Seckolster
  Martin 306
Seely
  John 172, 173
  John Jr. 282
Sendorf
  Mary 151

Seton
  Andrew 242
Sevin
  Felter 264
Seward
  Samuel 183
Seymmes
  John Cleves 74,
    81, 170
Shackerly
  Mary 135
Shaigat
  Abraham 305
Shaorts
  Adolpus 59
Sharp
  Anthony 139
  Elizabeth 246,
    267
  Isaac 139, 182
  Joseph 139, 246,
    267
  Morris 211, 281,
    291
Shaw
  Charles 113
  John 118
  Martin 131
  Mary 69, 133, 134
  Reuben 288
  William 184
Shepherd
  Cornelius 300
  George 286
  James 114
  John 300
  Thomas 300
Sherer
  Gilbert 97, 131,
    197
Sherwood
  Anna 232
  Anny 232
  Isaac 256, 266
  Isaac Jr. 232,
    248

Sheys
  Bryant 274
Shinnsman
  Herman 17, 20,
    43, 45
Shipboy
  Thomas 56
Shippy
  Will 305
Shirley
  Lousona 290
Shoemaker
  Charles 273
  Jacob 290
Short
  Adam 305
Shotwell
  Banjamin 98
  Benjamin 96
Shuert
  Christian 297
Shults
  John 245, 246,
    272
Shumaker
  Henry 240
Shurte
  Adolph 289
  Aldolf 297
Shut
  Dolf 190
Sickels
  Abraham 68, 138
  Abram 286, 287
  Daniel 142, 151,
    185, 210, 212,
    285
  Hartmen 155
  Hartmin 287
  James 292
  Johannes 139
  John 119, 210,
    251, 286
  Peter 226, 287
  Robert 1, 11, 41,
    118, 287

Zacharias 52,
  116, 118, 138,
  139, 155, 171,
  179, 209, 210,
  214, 226, 228,
  257, 258, 264,
  287
Sillcock
  Valentine 245
Silva
  Joize Roiz 203
  Jose Roir 205
Simeson
  Stephen 286
Simmons
  David 55, 63, 131
  Edmund 216
  Elizabeth 63
  Michael 140, 212,
    253, 286
  Peter 10
  Simon 85, 86, 94,
    154, 186
  Simon Jr. 113
  Stephen 286
Simonson
  Simon 223, 224,
    300
Simson
  Simon 149
Singer
  Peter M. 290
Sip
  Abraham 44
  Caenraot 44
  Garret 213
  Helena 60
  Helmegh 302
  Helmehg 270
  Helmogh 191
  Jacob 60
  Johannes 3
  Johannis 270
  John 38, 45, 157,
    302
  John J. 302

Peter 212, 253,
  272, 287
Sitors
  Andrew 242
Skidmore
  John 299
Skinner
  William 41-43, 65
Skitts
  James 305
Slade
  Charles 77, 167
Slator
  Catharine 4
  L. 4
Sleack
  Lucy 242
  Mary 242
Slott
  Peter 288
Slutt
  Leah 155, 156
  Stephen 293
Slynmott
  Caspar 11
Smith 55
  Abble 285
  Abel 53, 54, 129,
    180, 192
  Abel J. 192
  Able 295
  Abraham 77, 182
  Albert 211, 291
  Cornelia 10, 165,
    172
  Cornelius 121,
    276, 286
  Daniel 53, 54,
    57, 80, 105,
    154, 172, 173,
    179, 191, 192,
    199, 201, 213,
    253, 285, 292
  Daniel D. 285
  Daniel Jr. 191
  Daniel Sr. 190
  Ebenezer 155, 254
  Elias 10
  Elizabeth 192
  Enoch 111, 129,
    192, 286
  George 39, 306
  Henry 305
  Isack 122
  Jacob 77, 142,
    244, 293
  James 16
  James R. 258
  Job 53, 54, 57,
    111, 116, 126,
    129, 154, 165,
    172, 192, 199,
    285
  Job Jr. 154
  John 10, 24, 50,
    68, 82, 105,
    127, 165, 166,
    172, 180, 197,
    199, 285, 295,
    299, 305
  John D. 285
  John Felter 237
  John H. 305
  John J. 180
  Joseph 172, 191,
    192
  Joseph Jr. 129
  Mary 276
  Mary Scott 269
  Merrit 292
  Michael 24, 47,
    170
  Michael Jr. 35
  Michael Sr. 35
  Morris 129, 192
  Nancy 192
  Nathan 90, 105
  Phebe 192
  Philip 54, 192,
    272
  Phillip Sr. 129
  Polly 276

Potten 78
Samuel 269
Sarah 135
Thomas 18, 141
William Hooker 56
William P. 165,
    198, 202, 219
William Ross 149,
    217
William Smith 223
Snyder
    Adam 124, 156,
        291
    Andreas 236
    Andrew 175, 236,
        262, 263, 291
    George 236, 237,
        262, 275
    Jacob 134, 135,
        175, 180
    Jerry 292
    John 293
    Margaret 134,
        135, 175, 180
    Margret 175
    Mary 262, 263
    Peter 305
    Rachel 262, 263
    Thomas 175, 236,
        262, 263, 291
Soarner
    William 145
Sodwill
    John Conrad 110
Soloman
    Hannah 267
Sonmans
    Peter 20, 23, 25,
        26, 29, 32, 34,
        38, 47, 49, 56,
        95
Sously
    Michael 56
Soward
    Samuel 305
Sparlow

Benjamin 300
Speaker
    Jacob 305
    Winant 305
Spear
    Abraham 106, 113,
        119, 172, 241,
        252, 302, 304
    Abraham T. 304
    Abram 286
    Amos 106, 119
    Barent 106, 119,
        303
    Barent Hendrick 7
    Benjamin 58, 106,
        119, 185
    Catharine 146
    David 177, 303
    Francis 146
    Hans 25, 29, 95
    Hans Hendrich 7
    Harminus 302
    Hendrick 7, 39,
        226, 229, 235
    Hendrick Janson 7
    Henry 226, 235,
        236, 247, 277
    Henry B. 140, 304
    Hermanes 103
    Jacob 185, 304
    John 70, 71, 89,
        95, 144, 302
    John B. 303
    Magdalina 7
    Marettye 235
    Maria 71
    Marrettye 229
    Martie 226
    Martiye 70
    Naomi 252
    Robert 288
    Sarah 299
    Thunis 304
    Will 304
Sperling
    John 40

Spring
  Bernard 221
  Gabriel 290
Springer
  Hezekiah 289
  John 70, 211, 288
  Samuel 305
  Stephen 289
  Whale 305
Squire
  Elijah 99
  Nathan 92
  Nicholas 180
Stagg
  A. 283
  Abraham 47, 48,
    173, 174, 279,
    290
  Albert 131
  Antie 47, 48
  Benjamin 51
  Christopher 205
  Cornelius 36
  Elenor 5, 13
  Elizabeth 205
  George 47
  Hendrickie 47, 48
  Isaac 304
  Jacob 47, 173,
    174, 284, 297
  James 306
  Johannes 36
  Johannis 47, 48,
    61
  John 1, 2, 13,
    25, 36, 47, 100,
    159, 276, 304
  John C. 237, 279,
    280, 292
  John T. 205
  Josiah 229
  Margarite 47
  Marretie 48
  Marritie 47
  Michael 305
  Thomas 291
  William 5, 13,
    30, 47, 70
Staker
  Conrad 83, 88,
    291
  Widow 291
Stanton
  Jane 130, 131
  Richard 113, 130,
    131, 279, 303
Star
  Peter 279, 280
Stator
  Catharine 4
  L. 4
Statwell
  Benjamin 96
Steenhuys
  Englebert 178
Steeves
  Jeremiah 301
Steinmott
  Caspar 4
Steinway
  Cornelius 41
  Cortland 56
Stephens
  Garret 189, 284
  John 148, 285
  Rachel 148
Steuben
  Frederick William
    Baron De 196,
    203
Stevens
  Gideon 70
  John 24, 62, 82,
    97, 131, 137,
    144, 150, 172,
    196, 281
  John Jr. 93
  Sarah 123
Stevenson
  Albert 6
Steward
  Charles 288

Stewart
  Andrew 299
Still
  Anne 299
Stillwell
  Daniel 17
  E. 282
  Richard 40
Stimson
  Andrew 107, 301
  Hendrickie 107
Stimus
  Doctor 159
Stinberger
  Peter 295
Stockholm
  Charity 231, 251, 286
Stockton
  Samuel W. 121
Stoltz
  Anne 282
  Jacob 282
Stone
  David 288
  John 41
  Joseph 288
Stoothof
  Garret 16, 32
Storm
  Abraham 305
  Conrad 297
  Frederick 111
  Frederik 90
  Fredrick 281, 283, 289
  Hendrick 208, 297, 298
  Henry 271, 289
  Isaac 292
  Jacob 63, 289
  John 288
  John F. 289
  John J. 292
  Staats 212, 298, 305

Stants 188
States 196, 205
Stout
  Peter 288
Stoutenburgh
  Mergreta 27
  Peter 18, 22, 23, 27-30, 32, 34
Straak
  John 290
Strills
  Charles 291
Strock
  Widow 288
Stubbs
  Jacob 291
Stuss
  Conrad 292
  Conrad Jr. 292
  Jacob 292
  Michael 292
  Peter 292
Stuyversant
  John 214, 215
  Peter 115, 116, 151, 155, 185, 286
Styles
  Doctor 220
Stymather
  Ezekiel 159
Stymott
  Isaac 99
Stynmott
  Ann 12
  Garott 14
  Hannah 12
  Johannis 12, 14
Sullivan
  John 300
Suly
  James 283
Sunerland
  John 305
Sunyea
  Paul 285

385

Sutton
  William 291
Swain
  Henry 304
Swin
  Valentine 291
Synder
  Jacob 304
Talman
  Bregho 11
  Bregho Dowson 11
  Cornelius 142
  Dow 11
  Mary 296
  Tunis Dowson 11
Tannery
  Peter 289
Taylor
  David 53
  George 201, 301
  John 298
  Seras 304
Tea
  Johannes 100
Teachman
  David 288
  Nicholas 288
Tearman
  Annake 55
  George 51, 54, 55, 57
  John 60
  Nancy 55
  Will 304
Tebow
  Peter 129, 135
Teed
  Andrew 173
  Rachel 173
Ten Eyck
  Andrew 207
Tenike
  Jacob 301
Tenill
  Ephraim 61
Tennet
  John Peter 240
Tephogen
  William 289
Terhune
  Abraham 91, 193, 289
  Abraham A. 281
  Abraham D. 248, 290
  Aghy 239
  Albert 6, 22, 27, 30, 66, 104, 127, 163, 236, 267, 290, 293, 297, 299, 302
  Albert A. 97, 102, 293
  Albert D. 290
  Albert J. 210
  Allebert 77
  Anche 9
  Andrew 250, 290
  Ann 186
  Barent 77
  Catharine 168, 177
  Catherine 204
  Cornelius 301
  David 74, 157, 239, 245, 297, 302
  Derick 104, 185, 248, 254
  Derrick 57
  Eleanor 244
  Guilliam 268, 301
  Hendrick 297
  Henry 302
  Henry D. 290
  Henry M. 290
  Jacob 66, 90, 125, 127, 154, 155, 157, 168, 174, 182, 184, 187, 204, 209, 215, 216, 218,

219, 234, 253,
254, 267, 279,
297, 301
Jacobus 103, 299,
302
James 244, 267,
268, 279
Jane 254
Johannes 177, 248
Johannis 66, 160
John 71, 77, 99,
122, 128, 164,
175, 210, 230,
275, 290, 299,
301
John D. 239, 302
Lambertus 84
Michael B. 136,
300
Michase 125
Nancy 186, 301
Necandle 300
Necaus 66
Nicamic 99
Nicanse 244
Nicause 256
Nicawsey 137
Nichase 99
Nicholas 75, 116
Peter 244, 299
Peter J. 301
Polly 267
Powels 300
Quilliam 279
Richard 127, 128,
216, 267, 299,
304
Richard I. 301
Richard J. 266,
267
Richard N. 299
Roelif 99, 125,
301
Stephen 78, 155,
156, 239, 279,
301, 302, 304

Terrill
John 77, 79, 169,
193, 218, 219,
246
Sarah 169, 193,
218, 219
Teusbury
Elizabeth 244-246
William 244-246
Then
Margareth 265
Therman
R. 283
Thibow
Garret 172
Thin
James 244
Thomas
Frederick 178
John 3, 62
Thompson
Alexander 228
Hasakiak 126
Hezekial 83, 88
James 111, 121,
134, 295
James Jr. 134
Johann 11
John 60, 82, 150,
165-167, 197,
238
John H. 185
Mary 11, 148
Samuel 302
Sarah 121
Thurman
Nicholas 78
Ralph 132, 168,
209
Richard 132, 168
Tice
Dederick 138
Tichiner
Daniel 221
James 221
Joseph 283

Tiller
  John 302
Tise
  Abraham 264
  Christian 141
  Dederick 50, 193, 194
  Derick 106, 288, 289
  Henry 263
  Henry D. 289
  Jenny 193, 194
  Johannis 50
  John D. 292
  Peter D. 289
  Peter P. 292
Titchoner
  Bethuel 288
Tithone
  Joseph 288
Titsort
  Jacob 49, 53-57, 59, 69, 123
Titus
  Samuel 288
Toers
  Aaron 244
  Abraham 274, 299
  Catlina 274
  Cornelius 254, 299
  Francis 299
  Franke 254
  Jacob 96, 304
  John 292
  John Arents 11
  Lawrence 96
  Lawrence Arent 32
  Lowrans 298
  Marytie Lawrence 32
  Nicholas 286
  Samuel 202, 304
  Thomas 297
  William 299
Tomur

  Christopher 288
Tongretaw
  Jane 100
Toor
  Abraham 200
  Cloes Arentson 178
  John Arentson 178
  Lawrence 17
  Lawrence Arentson 178
Toris
  Nicholas 210
Tourse
  Nicholas 116, 140, 151
Towiskbeing 23
Townly
  Richard 40, 58, 222
Traphagen
  Hendrick 132
  Henry 201, 209, 290
  Henry H. 201
  Henry Jr. 221, 276, 290
  James 290
  Jonathan 47, 283
  Margaret 201
  Peter 283
Travis
  Elizabeth 198
  John 198, 242, 282
Trelease
  Charles 258
  Jane 258
Treson
  William 170
Troy
  Francis 110
Tserman
  Leonard 290
Tuers
  Abraham 227, 228,

        257
    Anne   89
    Cornelius   257
    Frances   211
    Francis   169, 202,
        210, 257
    Janetie   171
    Johannes   108
    Nicholas   171, 212
    Widow   228
Tueser
    Michael   295
Tunison
    Derick   4, 41
    Derick Jr.   11
Turis
    Garret   304
    John   304
Turnbull
    George   165
Turner
    John   252
    Thomas   257
Turse
    Abraham   201
    Jacob   201
Tuttle   302
    David   169
    James   107
Tysen
    Elisabeth   39
Udell
    William   295
Umings
    Jemimz   285
Ureance
    Christopher   122
Ustick
    Peter   135
Valen
    Garret   298
    John   297
Valentine
    David   291
    Henry   273
    Jacob   273, 291

    Jacob Jr.   291
    Margaret   239,
        273, 296
    Peter   273
    Wiert   291
Valleau
    Abraham   58
    Elizabeth   79
    Jesias   56
    Magdalena   63, 157
    Magdaline   51
    Magdelen   51, 245
    Magelen   50
    Peter   38, 50, 149
    Theodore   50, 51,
        53, 61, 68, 158
    Theodorus   50
van Aerlandt
    Cornelius   65, 149
van Aertene
    Peter   88
van Alah
    Gane   190
    William   190
van Ale
    Garret   43
    Hendrik   90
    Henry   43
    Peter   43, 90
van Allen
    Andreas   79
    Charity   139
    Ganet   289
    Garret   79, 90
    Hendrick   54, 90,
        108
    Henry   135, 175,
        264, 265
    Hepel   80
    Jane   59
    John   72, 78, 79,
        90, 91, 135,
        189, 196, 220,
        303
    John G.   303
    John H.   79

Myntie 220
Nieshe 196
Peter 74, 91,
  135, 139, 151,
  196, 303
Peter J. 108
Rundrick 79
Sally 148
William 59, 196,
  205, 212
van Ame
  Moses 113
van Bayke
  Henry 300
van Bechteen
  Derick 3
  Michael 3
van Blerkum
  Ann 60
  Catharine 243
  Caty 243
  Elenor 6
  Fredmanus 56
  Gilbert 6, 151
  Gisbert 31, 34,
    41-43, 48, 61
  Gynbert 56
  Gysbert 1, 27, 30
  Haramanus 61, 250
  Harremanus 60
  Herman 303
  Isaac 271, 292
  Jan 60
  Jane 222, 223
  Johannis 33, 38
  John 43, 60, 63,
    83, 134, 135,
    141, 239, 243,
    256, 292, 304
  John I. 292
  John T. 292
  Loria 1
  Martin 303
  Nicholas 222, 223
  Peter 56, 60, 87,
    92, 141, 143,
    184
  Peter J. 281
  Peter Jan 60
  Peter Johnse 60
  Peter P. 76, 92,
    138
  Phillip 277
  Pitt Jan 14
  Sarah 135
  Susanna 56
  Widow 306
van Blisham
  David 290
  John D. 290
van Boskerk
  Abraham 54, 64,
    91, 104, 111,
    148, 168, 188,
    194, 195, 202,
    204, 220, 221,
    283, 297
  Abraham J. 87
  Andreas 14, 188,
    197
  Andres 3, 26, 188
  Andrew 15, 36,
    149
  Andrew Jr. 36
  Andries 220
  Andris 34
  Anna 231
  Annatie 250
  Archibald A. 290
  Casparus Danole
    11
  Cornelius 97,
    104, 148, 178,
    221, 238, 272,
    286
  David 53, 78, 286
  Deborah 272
  Doctor 176, 216,
    217
  Freytie 45
  Gatia 255, 267,
    270

George 220, 221,
   229, 257, 276,
   282, 293, 301
Hannah 269
Hester 194
Hetty 283
Htye 64
Jacob 98, 276,
   286, 294
Jacobus 49, 62,
   105, 188, 220,
   235
James 213, 286
Jane 194, 195
Jeremiah 231
John 87, 106,
   111, 119, 123,
   136, 158, 169,
   171, 188, 215,
   230, 255, 265,
   267, 269, 283,
   286, 294, 297,
   300, 301
John A. 250
John J. 70, 270
Joost 31, 290
Lauren L. 78
Laurens L. 57
Laurins 104
Lawrence 30, 33,
   45, 46, 52, 54,
   64, 67, 104,
   158, 203, 250,
   251, 266, 279
Lawrence J. 133
Lawrence L. 54,
   56, 62, 73
Lawrens 69
Lourens L. 58,
   59, 70, 71
Loverance 3
Lowiers L. 53
Lowrens 297
Lucas 176, 220,
   269, 283
Luke 203, 297,
   301
Margaret 188, 220
Mary 250
Paulus 15, 16
Peter 30, 110,
   171, 211, 221,
   248, 286, 294
Rachel 221, 276
Silvester 210
Thomas 2, 3, 5-7,
   10, 15-23, 27,
   31, 36, 104,
   120, 148, 188,
   194, 195, 248,
   297
Thomas A. 250
Thomas L. 238
Treyutie 31
Tryntie 30
William 204
Yannetie 148
Yarmerbey 238
van Brunt
   Aeltie 40
   Claas 40
   Cornelius 40
   Fryntie 40
   Joost 40
   Maria 40
   Nicholas 40
   Roelif 126
van Bryck
   Bernard 84
   Roelif 304
van Bryke
   Roelif 302
van Bueren
   Beckman 89, 90,
      156, 157, 165,
      293
   Blandenah 219
   Catharine 174
   Doctor 154
   James 54, 65, 93,
      219
   John 144, 156,

173, 174, 180,
205, 272, 300
Sylvester 273
van Burgh
  Johannes 22
van Bush
  David 299
van Bussen
  Caty 274
  David 232
  Herman 200, 274
  Herman Jr. 303
  Herman P. 303
  John 291
  Peter P. 303
  Phillip 136, 303
  Thomas 303
  Tunis 274
  Wybregh 47
van Cleave
  Caty 177
  John 177, 252,
    257, 295
  Joost 291
van Cobleiune
  Elee 60
van Cortlandt
  Hackensack 39
  Jacobus 23, 24,
    45
  Phillip 146, 302
van Crook Livingston
  Peter 281
van Dalsen
  John 179
van Dalson
  Helena 171
  Henry 79, 97,
    244, 252
  Jan 213
  John 171, 213,
    244, 252, 294
  William 97, 244,
    252
van Dam
  Kip 49, 171

  Rip 67, 126
van Deen
  Andries 265
  Sarah 265
van Devort
  Barent 305
  Paul 304
van Dien
  Albert 291
  Andrew 92
  Andrus 290
  Cornelius 55, 77,
    114, 291
  Cornelius G. 291
  Derick 93, 290
  Garret 6, 14-16,
    19, 29, 56, 114
  Harman 291
  Hendrick 55, 93,
    114
  Herman 302
  Thomas 92, 290
  Viont 16
  Vroutie 29
  Vroutine 15
van Donk
  Fytye 298
van Dun
  Albert 231
  Andrew 297
  Andries 269
  Garret 60
van Dussen
  John Bernard 95
van Emburgh 71
  Abraham 113, 114,
    117, 158, 183,
    185
  Catharine 1, 10,
    32, 35
  Cornelius 58
  Elizabeth 158,
    183
  Gedion 54
  Gilbert 35, 71,
    114, 140, 144,

153, 183, 299
Henry 291
Jacobus 114
James 69, 140
Johann 1, 10
Johannes 4, 19,
  28, 77
Johannis 6, 16,
  21, 32, 35
John 60, 79, 87,
  103, 146, 211,
  291, 299
Margaret 299
P. V. 163
Peter P. 291
Rachel 10, 113,
  114
Simon 113, 114,
  117, 139, 189
William 86, 87,
  92, 114, 139,
  140, 224, 300
William Ja 141
William S. 71
William Sandford
  23, 29, 32, 71,
  82
van Ess
  James 306
  Simon 306
  Simon Jr. 306
van Gallen
  Catharine 2, 3
  Catriantia 4
  Loverance 2-4
van Gelder
  Abraham 47, 70,
    104, 205
  Henry 103, 289
  Jacobus 289
  James 63, 204
  Jonathan 132, 289
  Weynett 63
van Giesen
  Antiea 6
  Bartham 108

Bashan 108
Cornelia 27
Cornelius 189
Derick 141, 163,
  195
Elizabeth 183,
  184
Ganet 285
Garret 184, 186,
  276
George 99, 125,
  151, 153, 183,
  184, 259, 300
Giesen 186
Hack 285
Helmegh 153, 303
Hendrick 13, 27,
  30, 85, 199, 248
Hendrick Claes 50
Henry 285, 304
Hester 114
Isaac 5, 6, 16,
  22, 23, 27, 30,
  44, 72, 74, 78,
  85, 86, 151,
  160, 184, 186,
  189, 190, 199,
  301, 302
Jane 108
John 73, 78, 80,
  82, 108, 116,
  141, 163, 171,
  184, 190, 284,
  300, 303
Jores 57
Joris 27, 30, 248
Klaefye 30
Maltye 190
Marcelius 163
Marcelius M. 141,
  171, 189
Merselius M. 284
Mettie 45
Reynier 27, 30,
  45, 49-53, 57,
  58, 63, 64-66,

    70, 76, 114,
    186, 195
  Richard 163
  Samuel 286
  Thomas 285
van Hask
  Arendt 120
van Horne
  Aeltie 40
  Andres 220, 221
  Andrew 220, 252,
    268, 273, 286
  Anna 156
  Antye 222
  Baffie 221
  Barent 64, 286
  Bovert Bovertson
    7
  Brian 171
  Catrina 222
  Cattrin 252
  Christain 100
  Christian 230,
    296
  Cornelius 40, 92,
    96, 100, 190,
    220, 221, 262,
    268, 282, 296,
    301
  Cornelius B. 289
  Cornelius Jr. 92
  Cucas 49
  Daniel 258, 259,
    298
  Daniel J. 243
  David 304
  Derick 50, 58,
    300
  Derick B. 191
  Elizabeth 188,
    222, 245, 265,
    266
  Garret 285
  Jacob 120, 169,
    251, 252, 286,
    297

  Jacob Berentse 46
  James 144, 245,
    285
  Johannes 230, 298
  Johannis 57
  John 2, 39, 51,
    57, 65, 96, 116,
    157, 169, 171,
    185, 187, 188,
    190, 191, 210,
    212, 215, 222,
    224, 225, 232,
    265, 266, 285,
    290, 297, 303
  John B. 188, 291
  John J. 111
  Joseph 290
  Kitty 252
  Lawrence 59, 77,
    293
  Lucas 8, 162
  Lukus 40
  Lybetje 58
  Margaret 222,
    260, 277
  Margarity 232,
    233
  Marrilys 58
  Nashie 222
  Rachel 190
  Richard 152, 260,
    263, 274, 304
  Richard J. 222,
    232, 233, 277
  Rut 26
  Rutgert 3, 26, 46
  Ruth 39, 46
  Rutt 22
  Sarah 282
  Thomas 222, 258,
    260, 263, 303
van Houten
  Cornelius 130
  Abraham 75, 108,
    218, 279, 280
  Achie 45

Adriaen 109
Adrian 243, 244, 303
Adrian A. 241
Anantie 200
Annetye 73
Brian 145
Catharine 109, 126
Catrena 126
Catrientye 83
Corenlius R. 155
Cornelius 43, 107, 129, 146, 147, 213, 244, 258, 292, 303
Cornelius A. 140
Cornelius H. 119
Cornelius J. 136, 303
Cornelius Jo 119
Cornelius Kol. 119
Cornelius R. 154, 303
Crynus 281
Derick 142, 195, 274
Derick G. 241
Elizabeth 241, 281, 303
Fehr 83
Fythe 126
Garrabrant 69, 87, 142, 155, 179, 218, 303
Garret 108, 109, 153, 163, 171, 181, 184
Hallimign 115
Haun 178
Hellemige 132
Hellernegh 286
Helmegh 83, 109, 116, 126, 138, 140, 142, 155, 170, 179, 200, 218
Helmegh Cor. 119
Helmegh I. 58
Helmegh Jo. 119
Hendrick 109
Henry Jo 119
Isaac 304
Jacob 112, 168, 195, 267, 301
Jacob J. 241
Jacob Roelif 279, 280
Jacobus 292
James 72
Johannes 109, 269
Johannes A. 109, 147
Johannis 109, 170
Johannis J. 113
John 102, 109, 116, 125, 129-131, 138, 139, 160, 168, 190, 191, 206, 244, 274, 286, 292, 303
John C. 303
John Cor. 119
John H. 137, 138, 303
John J. 305
John Jac. 303
John Jr. 113
John P. 288
John R. 304
John S. 286
Leah 205, 206, 284
Marretie 51, 52
Martin 292
Mary 139, 168
Matie 154, 155
Mattye 146, 147
Michael 286
Peter 109, 139,

153, 206, 284,
290, 303, 304
Peter H. 206, 284
Peter Helmag 205
Peter Helmegh 109
Peyntie 126
Printkey 126
Pruntie 83
Rachel 139
Richard 142, 284,
303
Richard G. 142,
258, 266, 267
Richard H. 130,
135, 304
Robert 244, 284
Roelif 32, 43,
45, 51, 72, 80,
97, 113, 124,
131, 195, 213,
284, 292, 303,
304
Roelif C. 303,
304
Roelif H. 200
Roelif Jacob 274
Rudolph 244
Turnis 73
Yammetye 83
Yannaty 126
van Huysen
Harman 79
Harmanus 79
Harmonus 93
Hermanus 84
Rachel 79
van Iderstine
Casparus 214,
299, 300
Franics 299
George 299
Hermansu 300
Jannes J. 77
John 299
John T. 77, 299
Michael 299

Peter 299
Taddus 232
Tade 243
Toda 299
Tunis 218
Tunus 299
van Kalle
Theodore 74
van Kull
Kile 160, 173,
188, 201, 209,
213, 219, 251,
252
van Lambecker
Johannis Phillip
45
van Lieton
Jacob 40
van Loverence
Rettman 4
van Meets
Tulman 210
van Ness
Jacob 207
Mary 207
Simon 10, 176
van Norden
Adam 124, 236,
275, 279, 291
Andreas 39
Andrew 305
Benjamin 229
David 305
Gabriel 71
Harmanus 137, 138
Henry 305
James 306
John 183
Lawrence 266,
268, 303
Thomas 291
van Norder
David 107
van Norshandt
Jacob 5
van Norstrandt

Christopher 184,
  213, 214, 270
Hannah 184, 185
Jacob 25, 103,
  109, 213, 299
Jacob Jr. 109
van Oberhoof
  Garret 285
van Oostrum
  Henry Johnson 3
van Orden
  Adam 280
  Andreas 2
  Andris 40
  Antie 53
  David 51, 53
  John 95, 289, 301
  Lawrence 249
  Peter 57
van Orstrant
  Hendrick 11
  Christopher 75
van Rath
  Eleanor 268
van Reypen
  Adrian 227
  Andries 118
  Antye 206
  Catharine 132
  Cornelius 169,
    187, 212
  Daniel 66, 80,
    119, 123, 136,
    139, 155, 169,
    177, 179, 185,
    202, 212, 227,
    252, 253
  Derick 91
  Elisabeth 123
  Elizabeth 66, 123
  Fredrick 121, 238
  Garret 72, 101,
    119, 137-139,
    157
  Garret J. 115,
    136, 212

  Garret Jr. 132
  Harman 14, 77
  Harp 122
  Isaac 152, 191
  Jane 227
  John 116, 191
  Jurie S. 206
  Leah 206
  Margaret 206
  Mathias 92
  Richard 200, 209,
    253
  Simon J. 206
  Styntia 206
  Thomas 96, 102,
    127, 128, 130,
    191
  Tunia Thomas 191
van Roden
  Abraham 227
  Abraham M. 201
  Minetye 227
van Rottenburgh
  Ely B. 129
  Ernst Baron 129
  William Earnest
    Baron 125
  William Ernst
    Baron 129
van Ryper
  Abraham 291
  Cornelius 232
  Cornelius D. 303
  Cornelius J. 303
  Daniel 171, 232,
    233, 272, 286
  Derick 302
  Ganet H. 286
  Ganet Jr. 287
  Ganet S. 286
  Garret 171, 232,
    251, 277, 300,
    303, 305, 306
  Garret J. 232
  Garret Jr. 306
  Isaac 214, 215,

    304  
Jacob 193, 200,  
  291, 300, 306  
Jacob C. 260  
Jane 214  
John 172, 291,  
  304  
John G. 306  
Juny 286  
Lenah 232  
Manacha 200  
Margaret 178  
Peter 190  
Richard 232, 286,  
  305  
Simon 263  
Thomas 177, 215,  
  218, 219, 223,  
  304  
Uriah 262, 272,  
  303, 304  
van Saen  
  Isaac 125, 147,  
    151, 203, 206  
  Jacob 173  
  John 54, 70  
  Leah 181  
  Lenah 191  
  Lucas 83, 136,  
    165, 191, 203  
  Luke 173  
  Samuel 61, 83,  
    126, 181  
van Saun  
  Albert 301, 306  
  Cornelius 301  
  David 301  
  Egbert 301  
  Isaac 196, 204,  
    254, 301, 306  
  Jacob 249, 263,  
    291, 301  
  Jacob C. 301  
  Jacob J. 301  
  Jacob Ja 301  
  Lucas 268, 301,  

    304  
  Luke 196, 204  
  Samuel 306  
van Schiven  
  Geerchen 21  
  John 21  
van Schyve  
  William 6, 290  
  Wooten Williamson  
    6  
van Seil  
  Abraham 107  
  Andrew 107  
  Catharina 20  
  Derick 18, 20  
  Johannis 33, 38  
  Michael 107  
van Seoik  
  Hendrick 56  
van Shawn  
  Ephy 298  
van Sice  
  John 108  
van Soyoen  
  Daniel 296  
van Storlant  
  Jacob 39  
van Suie  
  John 293  
van Suile  
  Sarah 286  
van Thustien  
  Hermanus 152  
van Vlishorn  
  David H. 291  
van Voorhees  
  Abraham 196, 197,  
    292  
  Abraham J. 292  
  Adam 186  
  Albe 69  
  Albert 86, 106,  
    108, 155, 156,  
    186, 196, 245,  
    254, 271, 276,  
    291, 292, 297,

301
Albert A. 301
Albert J. 173
Albert N. 271
Albert P. 302
Alche 166, 167
Daniel 164, 176, 292
Elizabeth 186, 267
Helena 186
Hendrick 66, 207, 215, 254, 265, 301
Henry 276
Isaac 66, 125, 190, 254, 301
Issac 125
Jacob 66, 254, 255, 267, 269, 270, 276, 301
Jacobus 36, 42, 92, 183, 196
James 267, 270
John 69, 77, 186, 194, 196, 301
John A. 185, 186, 292
John R. 177
Lucas 301
Margaret 186
Necansie 301
Nicause 254
Nicouse 66
Peter 164, 176, 269
Rachel 186
William 69, 77, 196, 281, 292
Yan 196
van Vorst
 Casparus 156, 266, 299
 Cornelius 67, 100, 113, 152, 160, 173, 212,
285
Garret 13, 36, 152, 223, 233, 259, 300
Henry 266
John 270, 285
Maling 100
Margaret 266
Vorst 226
Walling 152, 299
van Wagener
 Altia 157
 Altie 224
 Antie 224
 Attia 157
 Catharine 146
 Catrina 187
 Frederick 295
 Garret 59, 160, 187, 213, 222, 231, 303
 Garret G. 127
 Garret Garretson 58
 Garret Jr. 303
 Heliningar 46
 Helmegh 146, 265, 305
 Helmeh 207
 Helmus 301
 Hendrich 146
 Hennes 146
 Henry 305
 Hermanus 302
 Jacob 66, 78, 115, 116, 129, 160, 165, 177, 210, 212, 297
 Jacob Garret 52
 Johannes 146, 178, 210, 297
 Johannis 43, 59
 John 97, 99, 116, 130, 136, 157, 207, 224, 225, 231, 265, 287,

    290, 305  
  John G. 303  
  John H. 207, 305  
  Leah 224  
  Peter Garretse 59  
  Rolof 157  
  Sarah 157  
  William 297  
van Wagon  
  Ruthe 293  
van Winkle  
  Abraham 72  
  Abram 287  
  Ane 243  
  Arya 43  
  Cornelius 274  
  Daniel 45, 72, 286  
  Daniel Jr. 212  
  Daniel S. 286  
  Elizabeth 75, 181  
  Francis 175, 180, 273, 304  
  Francis T. 273  
  Helmegh 238, 299  
  Hendrick 178  
  Henry 95, 213, 219, 237, 253, 286, 292  
  Isaac 299  
  Jacob 1, 72, 116, 238, 244, 299, 304, 306  
  Jacob Mallings 109  
  Jacob Wallings 35  
  James 233  
  Johanna 61  
  Johannis 167  
  Johannis S. 167  
  John 107, 147, 152, 167, 181, 200, 213, 214, 223, 233, 259, 270, 299, 304, 306  
  John S. 270  
  John W. 303  
  Joost 76  
  Joseph 68, 210, 212, 226, 253, 287  
  Jury 210, 212, 286, 299  
  Luke 77, 299  
  Margaret 1, 72  
  Marines 177  
  Marinus 127, 128, 215, 223  
  Martinus 299  
  Marynes 177  
  Meriner 304  
  Merynes 201  
  Michael 79, 81, 299  
  Peter 61  
  Pryntie 260  
  Samuel 292  
  Simeon 167  
  Simeon J. 167  
  Simon 75, 76, 102, 174, 237, 249, 256, 268, 273, 274, 291, 292, 306  
  Simon Jn. 270  
  Simon Jr. 116, 141  
  Theodore 218  
  Theodorus 230, 232, 233, 244, 299  
  Walling 152, 266, 270, 299, 303  
  Walling Jacob 2  
van Woerdt  
  Tennes 68  
van Wyck  
  Abraham 25  
van Zandt  
  Jacobus 81  
van Zane

    Isaac 164, 175
    Jacob 107
van Zile
    Abraham 175, 288,
        291, 306
    Abraham Jr. 288
    Albert 74, 166,
        175, 190, 292
    Egbert 123, 199,
        291
    Evert 30
    Harmanus 199, 271
    Henry 292
    Herman 282
    Johannes 173
    John 81, 295
    Patte 271
    Paty 271
    Peter 61, 63, 81,
        118, 165, 174,
        175, 190, 291,
        306
    Rachel 74, 175,
        190
    Sarah 123, 199
    Thomas 288
vander Bake
    Isaac Jr. 301
    Jacob 301
    Powels 301
vander Beck
    Abraham 87, 104,
        211, 291
    Anne P. 172
    Chatrian 10
    Cornelius 291
    Harm 264
    Henry 206
    Herman 250, 304
    Isaac 43, 68, 97,
        99, 104, 172,
        181, 184, 186,
        205, 229, 232,
        243, 250, 282,
        303
    Isaac Jr. 104,

        141, 164, 165,
        184, 189, 205,
        227, 234, 253
    Isaac P. 203
    Jacob 32, 70, 71,
        77, 177, 250,
        264, 291
    Jacob P. 291
    Jacobus 33
    Jan 87
    Johanna 202
    John 83, 202,
        222, 223, 282,
        298, 300, 304
    John P. 304
    Jury 297
    Paulis 291
    Paulus 2, 6, 13,
        16, 28, 33, 36,
        43, 61, 68, 87,
        185, 189, 197
    Peter P. 263
    Poules 146
    Poulus 15, 16,
        19, 20, 31
    Poutus 17
    Powles 206, 297
    Powlus 10
    Rachel 104, 165,
        172, 184, 227,
        250
    Sally 250
    Solomon 84
    Yan 239
vander Bilt
    Aronlson 7
    Jan Aronlson 7
    John Aevtle 45
    John Antje 61
    Magdalina Hans 7
vander Burgh
    Peter 53
vander Cook
    Chattrian 10
    Mickole 10
    Sarah 10

vander Ditt
  Aaron 285
vander Heul
  Hendrick 30
vander Hoff
  Abraham 305
  Garret 306
vander Hoof
  Cornelius 79, 151
  Egbert 103
  Elizabeth 79
  Garret 155, 278
  Hendrick 51
  Hoof 46
  Jacob 103
  Johannes 103
  Johannis 44
  John 55
  Lidia 208
  Sarah 155
vander Linde
  Adriana 99
  Ariaentie 49, 51
  Aury 293
  Benjamin 99, 121
  Bm. 77
  David 293
  Dominic Benjamin 83
  Elizabeth 99, 121, 300
  Guilliam 293
  Hendrick 16, 19, 21, 48-51, 83
  Henry 29, 50, 51, 95
  Jacobus 156, 293
  Joas 46
  John 293
  Peter 2
  Roelif 49, 83, 103, 122
  Rollos 9
  Rouluf 21
  Rudolphus 8
vander Nan
  John 34
vander Pool
  Catharine 69, 70
  David 69, 70, 217
  David Jr. 217
  Deborah 217
  Jacob 172, 300
  John 258
vander Voch
  James 131
vander Vope
  John 110
vander Vorst
  Cornelius 105, 127
  Jonas 145, 149
  Paul 133
  Paulus 52
  William 295
vander Water
  John 297
  William 248, 255
Varick
  Abraham 17-21, 83
  Jacob 6
  Jacobus 34
  Jan 4, 30
  John 16, 28, 105, 107, 158, 164, 166, 301
  John Jr. 187, 301
  Richard 159, 168
  Sarah 28
Varlott
  Nicholas 24, 26, 45
Vaughan
  Edward 41, 42
Veader
  Cornelius 305
  Jacob 305
Veal
  Joseph 56
Veale
  Joseph 8, 55
Veilds

Rodmen 285
Venese
Evert H. 243
ver Bruyck
  Dominic 83
  Samuel 83
Verbergh
  William 107
Verborn
  John 295
Verbrick
  Ann 254
  Antye 253
  Barnardus 127, 129
  Henry 253, 254
  Roelif 131, 203, 254
  Samuel 49, 131
Verbryck
  Abraham 283
Verdon
  Henry 294
Vergeseau
  Peter 109
  Susannah 109
Vervalen
  Abraham 77, 296
  Bannadus 238, 239
  Bernard 296
  Cornelius 296
  Daniel 296
  Daniel A. 142
  Derick 113
  Elizabeth 77
  Fredrie 228
  Johannis 296
  Marrety 238, 239
  Mary 245
  Samuel 244, 245
Verway
  Jan 16
  John 20, 150
Vincent
  Benjamin 159, 274
  Elizabeth 159

Visme
  Ann D. 231
Vites
  Joseph 299
  Joseph Jr. 299
Volk
  Abby 230
  Abraham 15
  Hendrick 111, 121, 296
  Henry 96, 230
  John 15
  Thomas 230
Vorvalour
  Gidion 294
Vreeland
  Aatie 178
  Abraham 61, 80, 243, 300
  Achie 45
  Aefie 39
  Aghtie 26
  Anna 66
  Anntye 178
  Ante 96
  Aughye 286
  Benjamin 26, 300
  Catharine 66
  Claas 32
  Claes 65, 96, 98
  Cornelius 3, 45, 286, 295
  Cornelius Jr. 295
  Cornelius Machielle 45
  Cornelius Michaelse 61
  Derick 32, 55, 66, 234, 295, 302
  Echtie 26
  Eden 188
  Elias 26, 127, 142
  Elias E. 47
  Elias S. 142

Elizabeth 98
Enoch 3, 26, 39, 66, 152, 187, 193, 243, 272, 300
Enoch G. 169
Enoch George 233, 259
Ganet 286
Garret 95, 98, 160, 177
Genetye 98
George 18, 26, 48, 58, 65, 66, 126, 167, 177, 215, 249, 256, 286
George E. 47
George M. 286
Hartman 256
Hartman M. 98
Helmagh 142
Helmegh 60, 188
Henry J. 257, 282
Hermanus 302
Isaac 30, 31, 34, 185, 243, 300
Isaac E. 283, 300
Isack 29
Jacob 26, 66, 67
Jacob C. 268
Jacob E. 271, 272
Jacob En 272
Jane 219
Janetye 60
Janito Mackelson 3
Jannica 142
Johanna 61
Johannes 96, 178
Johannis 65, 178
John 65, 79-81, 96, 126, 130, 142, 171, 177, 210, 215, 225, 243, 286, 300

John E. 302
John G. 142, 286
John Jr. 300
Klaas 209
Leah 282
Maritie 272
Mary 3, 272
Michael 26, 44, 45, 50-52, 59, 61, 63, 65, 98, 160, 177, 178, 200, 209, 214, 216, 227, 234, 259, 260, 286, 295
Michael Cornelius 57, 177
Michael G. 142
Michael H. 98
Michael Hartman 98
Michael Hartmanse 98
Michael J. 295
Michael N. 285
Michael S. 286
Mycal 219
Nicholas 114, 115, 157, 177, 209, 215, 225, 285
Peter 300
Randy Hartman 98
Richard 209, 222, 286, 295
Simon 185, 243
Stephen 213
Thomas 300
Wilhelmus 188
Vreoll
  Isaac 88
Vryper
  Garret 297
  Herman 297
  Johannes 297
  John 169

vvan Houten
  John 80
Wachtauj 23
Wade
  Archibald 157,
    282
  Caleb 176, 293
  Caleb Jr. 217
  Francis 205, 227,
    243, 271, 282
  Jane 122, 205,
    211
  Jonas 126, 144,
    176, 217
  N. 184
  Nehemiah 116,
    122, 127, 128,
    134, 144, 154,
    155, 164, 168,
    173, 174, 180,
    184, 189, 190,
    194, 196, 201,
    205, 209, 211,
    215, 217, 225,
    227, 229, 234,
    243, 267, 271,
    282, 301
  Nick 149
  Patience 176
  Phebe 176
  Zane 201
Wagener
  George 260
Wagoner
  Michael 305
  Tobias 305
Waine
  John 286
Waldron
  Abraham 297
  Adolph 53, 123,
    141, 184, 301
  Adolphus 124,
    131, 253, 306
  Adoph 234
  Adophus 269

Albert 293
Alex B. 131
Alexander P. 154,
  301
Alexander Phenix
  154
Andrias 204
Barent 297
Cornelius 298
Isaac 298
Jacobus 293
Johannes 62, 146,
  297
Johannis 62
John 190
Joseph 185, 226,
  285
Joseph Jr. 285
Nicholas 297
William 298
Walker
  John 300
Wallace
  John 300
Waller
  Joseph 303
Walley
  Mary 8
Walling
  John 296
Walton
  John 300
Wammamaker
  Adolpus 78
  Aldoph 289
  Christian 73, 78,
    290
  Conrad 73, 290
  Dederick 73
  Derick 3, 88, 290
  Derick A. 97
  Derick C. 290
  Derik C. 78
  Henry 72, 93, 98,
    182, 187, 258,
    283, 290

Ludwig 73
Maritye 73
Marytie 78
Peddter 73
Peidder 78
Peter 73, 78, 97, 98, 290
Richard 89
Thomas 265
Wandle
  Daniel 131
Waolsey
  Zephaniah 74
Ward
  Chloe 92
  Isaac 158, 186, 301
  James 288
  Jonas 92
  Nancy 244
  Neal 242
  Nehemiah 126
  Peter 96, 104, 106, 126, 128, 159, 170, 174, 187, 195, 244-246, 273, 282, 289
  Smith 264
Warman
  Martha 27, 28, 36, 37, 44, 54
  Richard 27, 28, 32, 35, 37
Warner
  Evarardus 300
  William 300
Waters
  Jacob 288
Watkins
  John W. 81
Watson
  Joseph 59
  Potter 12
  Thomas 49
Watts

Robert 261
Weaver
  Barent 289
Webb
  William 299
Weggersen
  Wessel 46
Welch
  James 286
Welling
  John 183, 306
Wells
  John 170
Wels
  Willimina Maria 69
Wenman
  Martin 1
  Thomas 46
Wensen
  Benjamin 303
Wentworth
  William 141, 145
Wessels
  Edward 36
  Lucas 268, 272
  Luke 268, 271, 272
  Margaret 268
  Wessel T. 83
West
  John 294
  Samuel 220, 221
Westervelt
  Aaron J. 207
  Abraham 57, 72, 76-79, 88, 90, 92, 98, 104, 107, 108, 123, 124, 135, 152, 156, 157, 160, 169, 170, 181, 182, 187, 197, 199, 201, 211, 212, 219, 224, 228, 235, 238,

239, 240,
248-250, 253,
256, 258, 260,
263-265, 267,
275, 278, 282,
290
Abraham. 102
Abram 56, 57
Albert 217, 235,
249, 304
Albert A. 237,
248, 294
Albert C. 293
Ann 229, 263
Anne 206, 235,
253, 263, 264,
275, 278
Annie 250
Antye 205
Area 101
Aury 101, 294
Benjamin 82, 97,
101, 106, 133,
149, 166, 170,
180, 198, 203,
212, 213, 264,
294, 295, 302
Benjamin B. 294
Benjamin Johannis
53
Benjamin P. 294
Benjamin R. 194
Casparus 66, 99,
159, 293, 298
Casparus B. 295
Cata 295
Cathalintye 105
Cathelinty 248,
249
Cornelius 91,
111, 213, 220,
222, 231, 237,
268, 303
Cornelius P. 294
Cornelius U. 277,
303

Daniel 297
Darvis 91
Dawer 96, 101,
125
Derick 224
Douwe 112
Dower 112, 140
Dower J. 294
Dower P. 278, 294
Dower R. 179, 294
Eliza 263
Elizabeth 112,
134, 213
Hannah 213, 214
Jacob 140
Jacobus B. 294
Jacobus D. 294
James 294, 296
Johanes 134
Johannes 146, 296
Johannes P. 142
Johannis 53
Johannis C. 213
John 56, 62, 76,
91, 96, 99, 101,
112, 140, 157,
163, 173, 174,
184, 213, 214,
222, 227, 230,
232, 237, 249,
256, 260, 261,
263, 266, 291,
294, 297
John A. 190, 247,
248, 290
John B. 134, 135,
294
John C. 205, 206,
243, 268, 279,
293, 294, 303
John E. 303
John J. 84, 86,
179, 196
John Ja 91
John Jr. 278
John P. 294, 302

John R. 294
John U. 231
Juriaen 1
Jurian 1, 197
Jurie 35
Jurion 5, 8
Juris 36, 37, 44
Jury 62
Juryan 29
Luke 214
Maria 249
Mary 227, 230, 231, 249, 295, 296
Nicholas 209
Niclas 294
Peter 105, 267, 282, 294, 297
Peter A. 197, 248, 249
Peter B. 133, 134, 294
Pieter 20
Racly I. 289
Ralph 199
Ralph A. 235
Rebecca 112
Richard 293
Roelif 9, 39, 56, 57, 60, 72, 74, 75, 82, 83, 90, 92, 99, 159, 168, 170, 196, 294
Roelif Benjamin 64
Ruloph 57
Sarah 194
Stephen 146, 222, 231
Stephen A. 248
Urey 213
Uriah 268, 303
William 229, 231, 276, 278, 294
Winetye 227, 230

Wyntie 32, 66
Yury 294
Westfield
  Moses 126
Wetherholt
  John 305
Wheeler
  Sally 257
White
  Anthony 160, 201, 251, 252
  John 36
  Zachariah 288
Whited
  Samuel 285
Whitfield
  William 228
Whitten
  Abraham 226, 229, 235, 236, 247
  Catlyntie 236, 237
  Cattena 275
  Caty 229, 235, 236
  Joseph 236, 237, 275
Wickoff
  Hendrick 17
Wilcox
  Joseph 198
  Phebe 198
Williams
  Caleb 202, 229, 300
  Durell 299
  Elias 29, 163
  Hugh 216, 243
  John 285
  John S. 285
  Margaret 216, 274
  William 173, 205, 216, 271, 274, 275, 293
Williamson
  David 273

Doctor 272
Hue 272
Lawrence 39
William 24
Willing
  John 103
  Thomas 288
Willis
  Abraham 98, 147,
    165, 169, 170,
    175, 176, 190,
    231, 239, 241,
    268, 272, 274,
    277, 279, 281,
    284
  Alexander 271
  Caty 147
  John 79, 167,
    175, 292
  John Jr. 175, 190
  Richard 242
  T. 250
Willock
  George 18, 26,
    33, 42, 43, 62,
    65, 166, 195,
    261
  William 110
Wills
  Thomas 220, 222,
    263, 268, 274
  Thomas P. 303
  W. 264
Wilson
  Abraham 163, 209
  Albert 75, 109,
    129, 132, 149,
    150, 231, 276,
    281, 291
  Catharine 269
  George 293
  James 149
  Mary 150, 281
  Peter 72, 74,
    84-86, 89, 92,
    99, 107, 127,
    140, 146, 173,
    183, 214, 223,
    229, 253, 269,
    302
  Peter A. 209
  Philip 209
Winne
  Johannis 213
  John 155
  Levines 115
  Levinnes 213
  Martin 41
Winner
  Eden 212
  Edo 287
  Hannah 60
  John 286
  Levines 287
  Lorinese 60
  Martin 286
  Martin S. 286
Winter
  Conrad D. 289
  Henry 289
  Lewis 292
  Peter 298
  Peter W. 197
  William 197, 292
  William Jr. 292
Wisner
  Henry 146
Wistwell
  Benjamin 290
  John B. 290
Wittsee
  Catharine 238
  Henry 238
Witty
  John 290
Wood
  Israel 129, 255
  Samuel 203, 293
  Vroutye 203
Woodhull
  Jesse 207
Woodruff

Benjamin 156
Daniel 288
Isaac 193
Joseph 288
Woodward
  Jesse 194
Woolcox
  Joseph 121
Wooliot
  Giles 295
Worden
  Daniel 306
Wormold
  Henry 141
Wortendyke
  Cornelius 199,
    262, 271, 297
  Fred 297, 298
  Frederick 208
  Jacob 227, 296,
    297
  Jacobus 298
  Jaen 297
  Peter 297
  Rymir 297
Wright
  Abraham 291, 302
  Aertine 15
  Aertje 18
  Albert 206, 245,
    303
  Ephriam 288
  Hannah 245
  James 30
  Johannis 16
  John 2, 5, 13,
    15, 18, 28, 54,
    129, 159, 302,
    305
  William 56, 288,
    302
  Zebulon 288
Wyatt
  Joseph 289
  Ralso 12
Wyhoff

Albert 258
Wynants
  Mathias 229
Wynkoop
  Cornelius 54
  Martin 40
Yales
  Robert 134
Yates
  Richard 263
Yeaty
  John 306
Yeomans
  Jeremiah 195
  Johannaton 226
  Johnnaten 228
  William 163
Yertes
  John 169
Yorkes
  Eldrick 243
Yorks
  Poulus 36
Young
  Jacob 204, 289
  John 121
  William 300
Youngman
  William 306
Yurianse
  Garrabrant 230,
    270
  Yerrye 270
Zabriskie
  Abraham 265, 275,
    289
  Abraham A. 302
  Abraham J. 275
  Albert 2, 9, 33,
    60, 72, 96, 98,
    120, 125, 130,
    147, 159, 160,
    162, 169, 188,
    224, 225, 235,
    250, 254, 275,
    290, 297

Albert C.   82, 85,
   96, 180, 199,
   229, 239, 246,
   254, 258, 293,
   302
Albert H.   82, 302
Albert J.   98,
   275, 302
Albertus   8
Allye   290
Andreas   77, 98,
   130, 239
Andreas G.   239
Andreas J.   98
Andreis   74
Andrew   239, 297,
   301
Andrew J.   290,
   302
Andries   150
Ann   174, 264
Anna   66, 214
Barent Christian
   Bekenne   33
Benjamin   193,
   252, 286, 297
Casparus   154,
   193, 292, 302
Catharine   164
Catrina   187
Christian   33, 74,
   76, 108, 130,
   160, 161, 162,
   239, 302
Christian A.   219,
   239, 247, 248,
   261, 302
Christian J.   239
Christina   187
Cornelia   157
Cornelius   239,
   275
Elizabeth   164,
   175
Frances   177
Garret   156, 191,
   245, 293
Garret A.   302
Garret C.   302
Hendrick   74, 224,
   296
Hendrick C.   239
Hendrick J.   274,
   302
Henry   265, 275,
   291
Henry A.   235
Henry J.   265, 275
Henry O.   235
Jacob   2, 27, 29,
   30, 33, 34, 95,
   98, 108, 124,
   130, 136, 141,
   144, 155, 156,
   160-162, 215,
   235, 239, 290
Jacob C.   245,
   295, 302
Jacob H.   82, 264,
   302
Jacob J.   235,
   290, 302
Jacob Jr.   243,
   276
Jasper   202, 251,
   252, 286
Jenny   252
John   2, 10, 20,
   49, 76, 82, 98,
   101, 117, 135,
   149, 160-162,
   175, 196, 207,
   265, 275, 286,
   293, 297, 301
John A.   302
John C.   82, 85,
   293
John J.   77, 98,
   290, 302
John Joost   301
John Jr.   118,
   137, 147, 151,

161, 162, 164,
 175, 195, 203,
 204, 301
Joost 3, 40, 53,
 66, 71, 72, 82,
 112, 119,
 160-162, 177,
 187, 239, 248,
 253, 293, 301
Joost A. 167
Joost Alb. 168
Joost C. 168, 293
Leah 239
Maria 74, 248
Marikotois 8
Martina 127
Mary 239, 248,
 265
Meihoth 2
Michael 252
Nicholas 160
Peter 61, 63, 65,
 66, 68, 70, 71,
 76, 85, 86, 93,
 99, 125, 127,
 128, 131, 136,
 144, 151, 158,
 160, 161, 186,
 208, 209, 214,
 276, 300
Richard 180, 185,
 293
Sarah 187
Seintie 180
Yoost B. 132
Zelef
 Daniel 304

www.ingramcontent.com/pod-product-compliance
Lightning Source LLC
Chambersburg PA
CBHW050831230426
**43667CB00012B/1957**